A

HATTON GARDEN

GRAY'S-INN LANE

QUEEN SQ.

BLOOMS-BURT SQUARE

RED LION SQUARE

Gray's Inn

British Museum

HIGH HOLBORN

HOLBORN

HOLBORN HILL

St. Andrew's Church

CHANCERY LANE

FETTER LANE

GOUGH SQ.

LINCOLN'S INN FIELDS

Lincoln's Inn

DRURY LANE

GT. QUEEN ST.

Rolls

BOLT CT.

FLEET STREET

B

LONGACRE

BOW ST.

RUSSELL ST.

Covent Garden Theatre

Piazza Coffee-house

Drury Lane Theatre

Rose Tavern

Clifton's Chop-house

Temple Bar

St. Dunstan's Church

St. Clement's Church

Mitre Tavern

Temple Ch

St. Bride's Church

Anne's church

Slaughter's Coffee-house

Shakespeare Tavern

COVENT GARDEN MARKET

Davies' Shop

New Church

(Dr. Johnson's Chambers)

Black Lion Inn

ster LA.

Bedford Coffee-house

HENRIETTA ST.

TAVISTOCK ST.

SOUTH-

Turk's Head Coffee-house

Somerset Coffee-house

The Temple

LEICESTER FIELDS

(Sheridan's House)

THE STRAND

(Garrick's House)

Somerset House

arlane's se)

Savoy

Temple Stairs

Whitefriars Stairs

St. Martin's in-the-Fields

Savoy Stairs

Somerset Water Gate

CHARING CROSS

C

ra use

Spring Gardens

Northumberland House

Cupers Garden

THE BROAD WALL

WHITEHALL

Scotland Yard

Whitehall Stairs

HORSE GUARDS PARADE

Privy Garden

N

NARROW WALL

VINE STREET

Plantation Office

Cockpit

DOWNING ST.

Privy Garden Stairs

W

E

ANGEL ST.

(Boswell's Lodgings)

S

D

GT. GEORGE ST.

(Wilkes's House)

Manchester Buildings

WESTMINSTER BRIDGE

ST GEORGE'S FIELDS

St. Margaret's Church

Westminster Bridge Stairs

THE NEW ROAD

House of Lords

H. of Commons

Westminster Abbey

Westminster Hall

Westminster School

0   1/4   1/2 Mile

4

5

THE YALE EDITIONS OF

The Private Papers of James Boswell

Boswell's
LONDON JOURNAL
1762-1763

NOW FIRST PUBLISHED FROM THE ORIGINAL MANUSCRIPT

PREPARED FOR THE PRESS, WITH INTRODUCTION AND NOTES

BY FREDERICK A. POTTLE

STERLING PROFESSOR OF ENGLISH, YALE UNIVERSITY

WITH A PREFACE BY CHRISTOPHER MORLEY

McGRAW-HILL BOOK COMPANY, INC.

NEW YORK   LONDON   TORONTO

FIRST EDITION

V

EDITORIAL COMMITTEE

50055

CONTENTS

LIST OF ILLUSTRATIONS

PREFACE

*And now, O my journal! . . . Shalt thou not
flourish tenfold?*

BOSWELL, 16 July 1763

As the express trains between London and Liverpool go racing
across the Midlands, the passenger can see, for a minute or so, the
noble bulk of Lichfield Cathedral. It rises above the green fields
of Staffordshire, a couple of miles west of the line, landmark
of the town where Samuel Johnson was born. I'm afraid many
travellers miss that glimpse, and I know I have caused puzzled
looks by nudging attention to it; but there must also be others who,
when they see the spire, think momentarily of the extraordinary
life, and the endless fountain of ink, that began below it. When I
last saw it (autumn, 1949), on account of some weakness in the
great flèche, it was "reticulated and decussated" in steel scaffold,
fine as cobweb, hardly less spectacular than the cathedral itself.

I remember that glimpse as an emblem of the work, patient
these many years, of scholars and collectors who, before they are
done, will have given us exciting new perspectives not only on
Johnson, but, more to the present purpose, on his friend and
biographer, James Boswell. With equal craft and judgment the
scholars and collectors have clustered about a famous edifice,
mending, supporting, renewing the tall spire. The parable is not
exact: there was certainly no instability in the great Cathedral of
Biography, *The Life of Samuel Johnson:* but that masterpiece begins to emerge, from devoted masonry and restoration, taller and
more decorative than ever. Of that intricate scaffolding this book
is a small but critical platform. These notes, or well-meant
nudges, are not for the architects and experts; only for riders in
the train.

ix

Perennially, fact reasserts prevalence over fiction. It would be impossible to invent any detective story so fantastic as the history of the Boswell Papers, running through five generations from Scotland to Ireland, and from their initial suppression and neglect by those most intimately concerned, to their discovery, a century and a half later, their purchase by an American, and then their eventual transfer to a safe new haven in the vaults of the Yale University Library. To understand what happened we must go back to Boswell's strict Presbyterian family.

From the first, Boswell's family had disapproved of his association with Johnson, and even more of his profligate way of life. At twenty-one he had fathered an illegitimate child; afterwards his amorous escapades had been both numerous and notorious; still later, though devoted to his wife ("that valuable woman"), he had been incapable of remaining faithful to her. Small wonder, then, that by the time he died he was already a legend of impropriety, which death transmuted to the skeleton in the family closet. The papers he left—and especially the uninhibited journals, of which this volume is one—served only to confirm this impression of him within the home circle at Auchinleck; and later events, as we shall see, reinforced it further. So it would appear that the family legend of Boswell as an ancestor to be on the defensive about, and therefore to be kept under cover, took firm hold and was passed on from generation to generation.

But "his chosen lifework," as Professor Chauncey B. Tinker has said of Boswell, was "defeating the forces of oblivion." Even Tinker, at that moment (1922), did not know how decisively Boswell had defeated them. The process took a long time, but at his death, in 1795, it was already well begun. Being both a canny Scot and a lawyer with an eye to the future, Boswell left a will in which he named three of his friends as trustees of his unpublished manuscripts: Sir William Forbes, the Reverend W. J. Temple, and Edmond Malone. The fact that he took this precaution is proof enough that Boswell attached considerable importance to his papers, no matter what his immediate heirs may have thought.

Temple died in 1796, only a year after Boswell, without having seen the papers. Forbes was evidently alarmed by the nature of the manuscripts. He considered them unpublishable, but equally undestroyable. He died ten years later, in 1806. So far as we know, his only editorial contribution to the problem was to insert at various places in the journals markers bearing the note: "Exceptionable Passage" or "Reprehensible Passage."

The third executor, the Irishman Malone, was of a different sort. Distinguished scholar and analyst of Shakespeare, he had recently (1790) published his famous edition of the plays; perhaps he yearned, as a born editor would, for another job equally severe. It was Malone who with kindness and wisdom had kept poor split-minded Boswell to the great task he had to finish before he died. The deuce with the law, Malone must have said; the deuce with standing for Parliament; and the deuce also (in moderation) with wine and women. Get on with the *Life*. Night after night, in his "elegant library," Malone corked the decanter and uncorked Boswell's portfolio of scrawl-handed memos.

It had taken Boswell more than twenty years to assemble these multifarious and multitudinous jottings about Johnson, and now the exhausting compilation had to be carried through by a breaking man, ridiculed by paragraphers and cartoonists, half-crazed by melancholia, dissipation, disappointment in law and politics, the death of his wife, and perplexities of money and his children's education. But he had Malone to keep him at it. Together, they went over the collected material. What a story-telling painting it would make, a fit partner for the famous engraving of Johnson reading the manuscript of Goldsmith's *Vicar of Wakefield*. Boswell was the curator of Johnson's memory, but Malone, in those last bewildered years, was curator of Boswell. As Geoffrey Scott wrote: "Malone worked day after day beside Boswell because he discerned his genius, his human need, the treasure of his cargo, and the imminence of his shipwreck."

So, even after death, Boswell had his usual luck. Of his chosen executors, Forbes was a busy banker in Edinburgh and probably as easily shocked as bankers have to be. Temple was a parson in remote Cornwall, less shockable than a banker, but urn-buried in family pains of his own. But the third was the exceptional Malone, acute and experienced editor. So far as we can guess at this distance, he did all that friend and critic can. Though he did not advise publication of the papers (resistance by Boswell's family would have been too strong to permit it anyhow), he saw to it that they were preserved.

The reproach used to be that Boswell's executors never met to discute their problem. If not, so much the better: none felt free to destroy anything. We know that Forbes and Malone corresponded and sent boxes of the papers to and fro by wagon. The upshot was that they decided (since the papers had been willed for the benefit of Boswell's younger children; the heir, Sir Alexander, had the estate) to wait until the younger son, James Boswell, Jr., who had more of his father's tastes than Alexander, would be old enough to offer mature opinion. Malone was left with the belief that most of the manuscripts had been returned to Auchinleck.

But at this point Malone's handwriting becomes an element in the story. It has been ingeniously suggested: Did Malone write of a certain manuscript that it "had been *burned* in a mass of papers," or "*buried* in a mass of papers"? That is one of the small red herrings that have slipped through the seines of scholarship. We know the answer now, or at least the major answer; but for years it was assumed, on the authority of Malone's possibly misread word, that at least a part and probably all of Boswell's papers had been destroyed. What seems likely is that whoever found himself in possession of any of the notes and journals took one horrified and fascinated look, and shoved them into the nearest closet.

Malone died in 1812. Both the Boswell sons, Sir Alexander (familiarly known as Sandy) and Jamie the Younger, died in 1822. James, Jr., died of illness, and Sandy was killed in a duel shortly afterwards.[1]

[1] Alexander Boswell, "a high-spirited, clever, and amiable gentleman, of frank and social disposition" (Croker's characterization) was, like his father,

The mansion at Auchinleck was left to a group of semi-noble dames who were naturally timorous of anything associated with their great-grandfather. The portrait of Johnson by Sir Joshua Reynolds, so Sir Walter Scott said, was moved from the drawing room to the attic, face to the wall. The papers, if any, were presumed destroyed. This attitude need not surprise us. There are still plenty of well-bred people who prefer life to turn its face to the wall.

But even in the dampest closets the bony pattern of Old Mortality is durable. Never did any skeleton resume so much mortal flesh so many years later.

---

a passionate Tory. He contributed to a rather disreputable Tory newspaper bitter anonymous attacks on one James Stuart of Dunearn, a lawyer in Edinburgh, a man with whom he was outwardly on good terms. These attacks were witty but outrageous, and especially charged Stuart with cowardice. (Stuart, who was a man of family, was treated with contempt for having embraced the lucrative profession of solicitor rather than the gentlemanly one of barrister. Alexander Boswell, among other things, called him a "fat coward" and said he would draw "bills, wills, and petitions" or "*aught* but a trigger.") Stuart got hold of the office papers of the newspaper and found from the manuscripts of the articles that Alexander Boswell was the author. When Sir Alexander returned from London after James's funeral, he found a card waiting for him, and two days later received a challenge. He refused to apologize, and met Stuart in a duel at the farm of Balbarton, an ancient Boswell property. Sir Alexander, a good shot, fired into the air; Stuart, who had never fired a pistol before, fired without taking aim and wounded Sir Alexander mortally. The spinal cord was severed just below the neck. He was carried to the near-by house of his elderly cousin Claud Boswell, Lord Balmuto. The family was in the midst of a house-cleaning, and a portrait of Sir Alexander's grandfather, Lord Auchinleck, was lying on the bed where Sir Alexander was to be placed. The men who removed the picture from the bed had Sir Alexander's blood on their hands, and it is said that the back of the picture still shows the stains. Sir Alexander, who was of course completely paralyzed, died next day. When Stuart was tried for murder, Lord Jeffrey, his chief counsel, read to the Court those passages of Boswell's *Life of Johnson* in which Johnson defends duelling as a form of self-defence, and Boswell admits that if he himself were affronted, he would think it necessary to fight. The jury acquitted the accused without leaving the room.

To ramify the history of the papers and the Boswell family tree, through its failure of heirs male and marriages in the distaff, is a pleasure for specialists. Abridgement for the amateur need mention only the great turn-points in the century and a half after Boswell's death.

First, there was Macaulay's extraordinary essay and the condensed version of its characterization of Boswell included in his "Life of Johnson" in the *Encyclopædia Britannica*, a work spread in millions as a class room text. It was impressed on every schoolboy, in Macaulay's gorgeous rhetoric, that the greatest of all biographies outside Holy Writ was the work of a clown, zany, screwball, and buffoon. As *soutenance de thèse*, Macaulay's essay can never be surpassed; and never, by Boswellians, quite forgiven. No wonder the Boswell family, hypersensitive as only Scottish heirs can be, encouraged the notion that the reliques of their freakish ancestor had perished. Perhaps the wish was father to the thought: by now they may even have believed it.

Then happened a strange adventure. About 1840—no one has ever been able to tell me the precise date and circumstance—an English traveller, one Major Stone of the East India Company, was making purchases in the shop of Madame Noël in Boulogne. Major Stone found his supplies, whatever they were, wrapped in pages of manuscript signed with the large and legible name, *James Boswell*. All Madame Noël knew was that they were part of a bale of scrap she had bought from a junk-pedlar. Major Stone was smart enough to buy all that remained. They proved to be near one hundred letters written to the Reverend William Temple.

How did they happen to turn up in this unlikely place and fashion? For answer we go back to Boswell.

Of the many friendships in Boswell's life, two were critical. A man of temperament has friendships reaching many ways. There was the great one, world-known, reaching upward to Johnson; and another, candid and laxative—and in the long run no less significant—downward to his lifelong confidant, the parson Temple. To Temple he always told all. How comforting it is to have a confessor of one's own age. To Temple he confessed what he would never have mentioned to Johnson. This being the basis of their friendship, Temple cherished Boswell's letters and preserved them. But Temple had a daughter who married a too-lavish parson, Mr. Powlett, whom Boswell had once invited to breakfast and found congenial. Perhaps it was Powlett's memory of Boswell's charm that caused him, when he shot the moon and moved to France to escape creditors, to take with him his father-in-law's papers. And in due course, all unknowing, Madame Noël came into possession of the letters, presumably dispersed on Powlett's death, which occurred in 1834.

After Major Stone acquired them they circulated among various hands and were eventually published (sharply "castrated," as scholars say) in 1857. Eventually they came to safe-deposit in the Pierpont Morgan Library in New York, and were first published in full by Professor Tinker in 1924. I imagine the ghost of Boswell, relaxing into the Doric accent: "Heave awa', lads, I'm no deid yet."

Another cusp in the graph was drawn when great-granddaughter Emily Boswell, in 1873, married one of the ancient and noble family of Talbot, seated at Malahide Castle outside Dublin. Emily's sister and co-heir Julia, Mrs. Mounsey, had married a mayor of Carlisle, of which Border stronghold Boswell himself had once been Recorder. Mrs. Mounsey may seem unimportant to the Common Reader (as Johnson called us), but the fact of her existence was to prove of great cost and circumstance some seventy years later.

The Common Reader, privileged and otiose person, looks with most uncommon calm on the toils of scholars. Even this casual summary of better men's devotions must, however, mention the great and still laureate edition of the *Life* by George Birkbeck Hill (Oxford, 1887). This, and his succeeding collections of ana, were the primer and cornerstone of all modern reference. Dr. Hill, who relished most his honorary fellowship at Pembroke College, Oxford, Johnson's own "nest of singing birds," was refused entrance to Auchinleck, and harpooned the family in an essay in *The Atlantic Monthly*; this did not make access any easier for later pilgrims.

In 1905, ob. old Mrs. Mounsey, and the Auchinleck property and archives passed to the Hon. James Boswell Talbot, great-great-grandson, and heir of Malahide. Just when the papers were moved to Ireland I don't know. It must have been some forty years ago. Except for a sheaf of chance-choice items in an Ebony Cabinet (an heirloom to Boswell from a great-grandmother), they simply passed from one attic to another. They were shoved away anywhere convenient—some in a croquet box which afterwards became famous.

In 1921, the heir, James Boswell Talbot, succeeded to the title and castle of Malahide: a kindly man, interested in sports and horses and the estate; not much curious about papers, dimly rumoured disreputable, that had come down through his mother's family. He married, in middle life, a highly intelligent and sprightly lady of a theatrical background and with the keen sense of actuality and box-office that the stage implants. Soon after Lord Talbot's marriage, Professor Tinker's *Letters of James Boswell* (1924) was being widely reviewed in the press, and the remote observer begins to see the diagram of destiny taking shape.

Professor Tinker was one of the earliest of scholars to estimate Boswell, with magical Powder of Sympathy, as a phenomenon in himself even if he had never known Johnson. The eventual publication of all the Boswell Papers, of which this *London Journal* is the first, will provide overwhelming corroborative evidence to prove it.

On July 29, 1920, Tinker had written to the great Tom Tiddler's Ground of bibliography, the London *Times Literary Supplement*, asking if anyone knew of any letters of Boswell in private custody. *The Times* of London is not only the best printed newspaper in the world, it is the only one in which anything whatever printed causes eventual ricochet. One issue, regardless of date, is as good as another; it is printed on paper too asbestic for good kindling, so it is rarely destroyed. And it is read, not in a hurry, by the kind of elderly dons, parsons, eccentrics, to whom reading is dram and drug. In this instance, reply was prompt and explicit: Professor Tinker got an anonymous communication: "Try Malahide Castle." He looked up *Burke's Peerage* and noted the Boswell connection.

By felicitous coincidence the United States Consul General in Dublin at the time was a college classmate, Yale '99, and intimate friend of Tinker's, Mr. Charles Hathaway. With his aid and that of others, including the Ven. the Archdeacon of Dublin, discreet *pourparlers* were arranged. After some delay, the Consul and the Professor were invited to tea at Malahide. One loves to conceive the kind of letter Boswell himself would have written if he had wanted to crash the castle. Those who know his immortal brass in gaining access to Rousseau and Voltaire can well imagine it. (It is really odd that only in the case of Johnson did Boswell ever show some reticence.) In a memorandum tenderly Boswellian in tone, Professor Tinker has recorded his visit, which took place June 30, 1925.

"I was accompanied by the Consul General on the fateful Tuesday . . . I took with me, as a propitiatory offering, a copy of my edition of *Boswell's Letters*, published the year before. The gift was accepted, but without enthusiasm. It served only to increase the natural suspicions of my intentions."

One doubts whether Professor Tinker, *molto agitato*, really did justice to his tea and cucumber-and-cress sandwiches and caraway cake. It was finally Lord Talbot, puzzled and bored, who suggested the guests be taken to the next room to see the Ebony Cabinet. "I recall," says Tinker, "a magnificent escritoire of black oak, but of course one must make allowance for the tendency to heighten and colour memories now twenty-five years old." He saw, and was allowed to handle, "papers in a drawer stuffed full of manuscripts. There were letters of Boswell to his son Sandy—some manuscript sheets of the *Life*—a number of volumes of a diary—Lady Talbot told me that parts of it were not suitable for print."

There were also, the Talbots told the stricken scholar, at least two boxes of papers from Auchinleck that had never been opened. When was student ever so tortured? But Tinker pays honourable tribute to Lady Talbot's understandable coolness. "There was no reason why she should be well-disposed to an American who arrived wishing to know the nature and extent of the family papers. As the state of affairs was slowly disclosed to me, my dismay mounted with my fascinated attention. The mere existence of such treasures made my edition of the *Letters* seem *passée*. I saw that all that had been said and written about Boswell must now be revised. My state of mind was not happy.

"When we left, Lord Talbot descended the castle stairway with us, and held the door of the taxi for me to enter. He suggested that perhaps we might be inclined to visit Dublin again in the autumn, for the races . . . I told my friend that I had seen the Valley of Rubies."

That one glimpse was all that Tinker was to be granted as long as the papers remained at Malahide. But he came away with precious knowledge which others before him had sought in vain. He knew that the Boswell Papers—or at least a part of them—still survived; and he knew where they were. The news was revealed to few people, but of course spread. A famous American collector of rare manuscripts made a courageous effort. He sent a cable to Lord Talbot offering £50,000 for the papers. This was approximately a quarter of a million dollars at the then rate of exchange. Lord Talbot took umbrage that such an offer had been made for the family papers by a stranger, and he did not answer the cable. That was the end of that chapter.

Tinker also told his friend A. Edward Newton, and Newton next had a go at the papers. Again the stone wall. So when Newton saw that he, too, could get nowhere, he encouraged a friend of his to try his luck. There was nothing to lose by trying, and Newton told his friend that if anyone could succeed where others had failed and given up, he was the man.

Now enters the remarkable character of Lieutenant-Colonel Ralph Heyward Isham, who possessed precisely those qualities that our history requires. Not in any sense an academic person, he had nevertheless long been a student of the eighteenth century, and he was already a well-known Johnson collector. He had also, desirable for collectors, considerable funds. Though an American, he had lived much abroad, and had served a notable career in the British Army, rising to staff officer in the First World War. Courageous, gay, and reckless of wit, he had done champion service in humouring and restoring order among disaffected troops growling to be demobbed in 1919. Above all, perhaps, he knew that a straight line is not always the shortest distance between two points.

Through proper channels, Colonel Isham made his identity known to Lord Talbot, and expressed a wish to visit Malahide to see the Boswell Papers. No word or hint of wanting to buy them, you understand; he just wanted to look at them. And in due course, again through channels, Lord Talbot sent his answer: he would be glad to receive Colonel Isham at the castle if he chanced to be in the neighbourhood. Well, it just so happened that he chanced to be in the neighbourhood with reasonable but not unseemly haste. This was in 1926. He was received, he saw some of the papers, and the sequel proves that he got on well with Lord and Lady Talbot. He was invited to return, and later he spent several days as houseguest at the castle.

Only Colonel Isham, in the right time and place, can tell the complete details of what happened from this point on. For present purposes all we need to know is that, as Chaucer said somewhere in the glorious *Troilus:* "to fisshen then he leyde out hooke and line." And who has more fun: the fisherman in planning his lures, or the fish in being caught by the perfect angler? Here there is legitimate question as to who was fish, who fisherman. For, after cordial relationship had been won, it was Lady Talbot who made the first cast. Did Colonel Isham think the papers had real value? Oh yes, said he; no doubt of it.

That was the right answer. Lady Talbot could not have helped hearing of occasional auction sales at Sotheby's or elsewhere, and of casual Boswell holographs that had brought considerable guineas. As the Prayer Book says, she marked and inwardly digested. Then, too, there was that other American who had cabled his offer of £50,000 for the papers, sight unseen. Perhaps that meant they were worth even more.

So, the Colonel having given the right answer, a basis for fair dealing was established. It took many months of negotiation, but in the end, as Colonel Isham tells it, Lady Talbot persuaded him that they ought to sell the papers. In 1928, then, he was able to take title to the biggest single catch in literary angling. It included many treasures: some leaves of the manuscript of the *Life*, some letters to and from Boswell, and the journals—not, however, including the present one, which had never been at Malahide and was not then known to have survived.

In a story so replete with the incredible, one learns not to be surprised by anything—which is just as well, for the unexpected went on happening to the very end. An old box, supposed to contain a set of croquet implements, was found stuffed with manuscripts in 1930. Again, in 1937, Isham made personal search of the castle and turned up some remarkable things, including a pathetically intimate diary of Dr. Johnson's private anxieties. Then, in 1940, when the Government was looking for places to store food in wartime, the loft of a disused stable or outhouse at Malahide was cleared for this purpose—and what should turn up but two chests containing Boswell archives.

To a relic-destroying and apartment-living generation these repeated discoveries may seem beyond belief. Yet they happened. Malahide is an ancient moated castle with stone turrets and battlements; and in such a sprawling structure there are always innumerable garrets, cellars, cupboards, ancient chests, and similar depositories for any kind of plunder that one wants to put out of sight and yet cannot bear to part with. So it is perhaps not so fantastic after all that the papers, once their value was established, continued to turn up. At any rate, Colonel Isham, having started on the trail, had no choice but to follow the spoor to the very bottom of his bank account.

In the mean time, no less astounding was the adventure of Professor Claude Colleer Abbott, then Lecturer in English at the University of Aberdeen. Perhaps he is the best example in our time of Walpole's serendipity, characteristic of one who finds something he wasn't looking for. What Professor Abbott was actually looking for was material for a new life of James Beattie, an eighteenth-century Scottish philosopher, a friend of both Boswell and Johnson, but quite forgettable now. Abbott found it necessary to examine papers preserved at Fettercairn House, not far from Aberdeen, an estate of Lord Clinton. Lord Clinton is the direct descendant of Sir William Forbes, one of Boswell's literary executors. To his amazement, going through a capharnaum of miscellany (this was October, 1930, to January, 1931), Professor Abbott found what completely side-tracked him from Beattie. In bags, bundles, bean sacks, and helter-skelter through the closets and attics of an ancient house, he found some sixteen hundred letters and manuscripts and documents to, from, and by Johnson, Boswell, and their friends. Among them was the journal here printed. Presumably Forbes had examined these papers during his executorship and had not got around to returning them to Auchinleck before he died.

Professor Abbott's catalogue of the Fettercairn papers took time to prepare. Announcement of his discovery was not published until 1936 and immediately precipitated a legal battle.

Boswell, as a Scottish advocate, would have been professionally excited by the great lawsuit to determine the ownership of these Fettercairn papers. I can see him, with fresh-powdered wig, listening ghostlike to the argument. The cause was throng with claimants, eventually reduced to four: among them Colonel Isham, who had secured an assignment of the claim of Lord Talbot. Another was the residuary legatee of Mrs. Mounsey, the Cumberland Infirmary.

Experts have often told us that there is nothing so traditionally special as Scottish law. The cause, which fell into the ancient classification of multiplepoinding ("poinding" is pronounced "pinding"), was pleaded before the Court of Session in Edinburgh, which awarded the property in equal shares to Colonel Isham and to the Cumberland Infirmary as claimants deriving their interests from the sisters Emily and Julia, Boswell's great-granddaughters.

Legally, this settlement was quite correct. Practically, it presented a dilemma. For how are equal shares to be apportioned when the thing to be divided is, not money, but 1,607 items of literary material, the value of which still remains to be determined? The Cumberland Infirmary was for having the papers sold at auction and dividing the proceeds. But Colonel Isham wanted the papers themselves. In the end, after much negotiation, he succeeded in persuading the Cumberland Infirmary to sell its half interest to him; the price was agreed upon and the money paid. What with lawyers' fees, court expenses, and all the rest of it, old Mrs. Mounsey had cost the Colonel dear.

Colonel Isham had to wait until the Second World War was over to take possession of his new treasure. But at last came October 23, 1948, when a few friends assembled in his apartment in New York to celebrate the opening of the boxes from Fettercairn (which one of the Colonel's sons had super-cargoed across the Atlantic). With a keen sense of chronology, the evening was linked with October 23, 1773, when Johnson and Boswell, after passing sea-dangers, sat down in the inn at Inverary; and the usually abstemious Doctor called for "some of that stuff that makes Scotchmen happy." Colonel Isham, looking taller and more lean than ever, was certainly happy on this occasion; but afterwards, realizing that his successful quest had sapped his fortune, he began groping for a possible and seemly redemption. You will find his solution in a headline on the front page of *The New York Times* for August 1, 1949: "Yale Gets Boswell Papers."

The news account told how Boswell's archives had found permanent sanctuary at Yale through a gift from the Old Dominion Foundation of Washington, established by Paul W. Mellon, and through purchase of all the publishing rights by the McGraw-Hill Book Company.

Here the story seemed to end. But wonders never cease, and there is always room for a postscript. Recently, Lord Talbot died without issue. His title and the castle at Malahide passed to a relative who had no Boswell blood in his veins. The widowed Lady Talbot had to choose another residence; and the new Lord Talbot, in house-cleaning, found—what else but more Boswell papers? Not having any claim on them, he sent them to Lady Talbot; and, even as these lines are written, negotiations have been concluded for their acquisition by Colonel Isham and for their transfer to Yale.

So endeth the fantastic history of the Private Papers of James Boswell; and now beginneth their general publication.

One phase of Boswell that has not often been curiously discussed is that he was a Scot. A Scotchman with *brio* is a very queer fish. I have known a number of eccentric Scots (they are the New Englanders of Britain) and they all have that peculiar blend of farce and freak, high jinks and black bile, philosophy and folk-song, which are so likely to cancel out. They are equally tortured by ambition and low comedy. If a reckoning could be made of First Honours and Sent-Downs at Oxford, the Scottish students would show, in proportion to numbers, a high percentage of both.

Strange mixtures of pride and shyness are still characters of the talented Scot. Pious devotions and carnal frolic, wild generosity and granite retreat into budget, soft heart and hard head: these bewilder himself and others, too. His character, like his tongue, is proficient in two languages. Nothing of Boswell is more in vein than his ecstasy, in this journal, when after stinting himself (for romance!) on cheese and buns, he gets his allowance and parades the golden guineas on the table.

We can imagine how many times, returning half-happy and half-reluctant to the family estate at Auchinleck, Boswell may have brooded on the irony of the Horatian motto his father had inscribed over the door of the then-new mansion: *Quod petis hic est . . . animus si te non deficit aequus.* "Here is what thou seekest . . . if thou lackest not a steady soul." Alas, and also huzza, that is exactly what Boswell did lack. If he had lived by Roman motto, or by his own delicious "Inviolable Plan" (resolutions he drew up soon after this journal), we would never have heard of him.

Much of this journal was written in Downing Street, and Boswell is certainly not least in the list of remarkable men (and writers) who have lived in that by-way. The actual house in which he lodged no longer exists. It is somehow in tune with his canny side that his landlord, apparently a supply clerk in the near-by Plantations Office (Colonial Office, we would say later) was able to furnish him with "materials for writing in great abundance," and also with newspapers. Perhaps no one else in Downing Street, until Mr. Winston Churchill, had such faith in the perpetuity of paper, or such genius to justify that faith.

One smiles to notice that in the very first sentence of the scintillated *Lives of the Poets*, Johnson spoke of "the penury of English biography." Even as he poured that down the quill there was already gathering round his thunderstorm character the incomputable wealth of Boswell's memoranda: a drift of paper which later took the biographer himself six years to dig through. "Sorted till I was stupified," he says somewhere in a later journal. He emerged from it the greatest biographer who ever lived, and re-emerges now as the greatest of all self-biographers.

No figure of speech can outsay the greatness of Boswell's achievement. He became a force of nature, a tropical cyclone in two wheels: the clockwise centered on Johnson, the counterclockwise on Himself. In regard to Johnson he was rather like our modern rain-makers: he seeded every likely cloud with his dry ice to see what precipitation he could deduct. And the other wheel of the storm? What is lovelier than his note herein (28 July) when, after conversation with the Doctor about Swift and Addison, Boswell says: "We then talked of Me."

Maybe there never was anyone so young as Boswell was in the spring of 1763. We have always had trouble in visualizing him: George Dance's portraits are delightful, but all his subjects—whether Bozzy, or Mrs. Thrale, or whoever—have exactly the same profile. (Try them with tracing paper; you'll be astonished.) Even Sir Joshua didn't really catch him. Perhaps the young Thomas Lawrence came nearest. He showed the flat tip of the inquisitive trowel-nose—a comedian's nose—the pursed lips with their exquisite sense of relish, of savouring and tasting; and the ears a little flanged, for sharp listening. The intellectual arched brows, the luxurious double chin, the juridical crossed arms; and in the joy of tavern-talk all stewing and steaming horror within well and truly forgotten—that is our Boswell. You will find that portrait in Tinker's *Young Boswell*.

There was always something quite special (see Thackeray's ballad, for instance) about the age twenty-two. Its greatest excitement is the assurance that what you feel, or guess, or experience, is pure novelty; no one ever knew it before. Here you see the glory, the pathos, and the farce of youth. There are glimpses of London streets, the jostling chairmen, the taverns, playhouses (when Garrick was playing, the pit was full hours ahead of curtain-time), the midnight watch, public executions, shops, and routs or drums. If you are of books book-minded, you'll enjoy his sentimental visit to the printer who published the fairy-tales he had loved as a child, "where all my old darlings were printed." We like him for being disappointed in Oxford at his first visit. He made his usual gesture, drank the water of Isis and found it tepid. But see how instinctively he tried to find reality of his own, inviting Mr. Shepherd, the poet of Corpus Christi, to supper. Oxford depressed him almost as much as the hangings.

The drama of this particular journal is that it shows us a masterpiece trembling in the balance of to-be or not-to-be. It is a clinic on the prenatal care of biography. We see a young man blindly struggling against his weird. I don't think we had known before how hard Boswell really tried to get a commission in the Guards. Observe, too, that after the first rather infelicitous meeting it was Johnson, not Boswell, who made the advances. Note this little progression:

MAY 16. The first meeting, with Boswell setting down his impressions of Johnson as "a man of most dreadful appearance" whose "dogmatical roughness of manner is disagreeable."

MAY 24. Boswell's first call on Johnson: Johnson twice urges him to stay.

JUNE 13. Johnson asks why Boswell doesn't call oftener.

JUNE 25. Johnson says, "I have taken a liking to you."

JULY 14. "My dear Boswell," says Johnson, "I do love you very much." (One admits the bottle of port apiece as stimulus.)

JULY 30. Johnson says he will go to Harwich with Boswell to see him off for Holland.

Let it never be said that Boswell forced himself on Johnson.

The reader will see that young Boswell, at the time he met Johnson, was nearly crazed with internal tensions and anxieties; but so also was the Great Dictator. They were a generation apart (some thirty-one years), and the Doctor had outlived, perhaps even forgot, the carnal cravings of youth; but it was a friendship between two natural "hypochondriacks." To prowl the town from 4 P.M. until 2 A.M., seeking the drug of conversation, was Johnson's habit. To prowl the town, also in agony for stupor, was Boswell's despair. They met in the nick of time for both. Each became, for the other, the son or father he had never had.

Probably Boswell waked with a headache more often than any

human being on record. In his journals we read with terror his
innumerable resolutions to be more *"retenu,"* to build a more
"solid" character, to quit "rattling" (talking like a fool), because
we know it will immediately be followed by some grotesque excess.
Most singular of all, except to experienced observers of human misbehaviour, you will see how, when exalted by an evening of pious
conversation with Dr. Johnson, he at once rushes for the nearest
trull in the darkest alley. I doubt if anywhere in literature there is
such bodily confession of *le diable au corps*, the grotesque inter-
mixture of human agony and absurdity. With equal enthusiasm
(as said of Lord Byron) "he fell like a thunderbolt on the chamber-
maid," or in Italy, just after the present record, "opened fire on
three countesses at once."

Boswell was always a theatre-lover; but his best theatricals were
himself. He sat in the pit for a lifelong performance of that tragi-
comedy, *James Boswell*, and had his fluxes of glory and despair.
This journal is a curtain-raiser to the long melodrama that followed, the Thirty Years War among his different selves. He tells
Lady Mirabel (14 January) that he is running up and down the
town like a wild colt; but the colt was a race-horse getting ready for
the grandest of Grand Nationals. It is a fumbling but intuitive exercise for blue ribbons to come. He puts himself at practice jumps,
for instance the enchanting episode of testing his genteel address
by getting a sword on trust. This is perfect prelude to the later
comedy when he forces himself on Rousseau without bothering to
present his letter of introduction. He wished to reassure himself
that he could leap any barrier.

How much of any man's recorded life is, *in ultima ratione*,
irrelevant? The total of days in which Boswell could have seen
Johnson adds to only about two years and two months, but that
matters little in the calculus of the arts. Poor Traubel saw Whitman
thousands of times and could make nothing of it. Max Beerbohm
described just one luncheon with Swinburne so that we read it with
wet eyes. Art contradicts everything. Boswell would have been,
and was, an extraordinary man if he had never met Johnson. But

he did, and the *Life*, once written—and how nearly we never had it—became their mutual exponent and multiplier.

Both were writers of dictionaries. Johnson had written the lexicography of a language. Boswell wrote the Dictionary of a Man.

Doctor Johnson, in the last days, wondered where he would be buried. His friends assured him, in the Poets' Corner of the Abbey. There he lies, in the sunward transept, and the stone is cut in the Baskerville letter he admired. It carries also the hard-earned LL.D. He lies, as every pilgrim has noticed, side-by-side with David Garrick, as they had come to London together long before. That quadrangle of flat stones is more Theatre Corner than Poets' Corner, for his three neighbours are Garrick, Sheridan, and the forgotten John Henderson, who died young (less than a year after the Doctor), but an actor well-bespoken in his time. I used to wish that the fourth slab had been allotted to Boswell. No one has ever described to me his grave or inscription at Auchinleck. My curiosity is only the curiosity of a reliquarian; but in a way I'm glad that he rests on his own.

Professor Abbott, who made the discoveries at Fettercairn, tells how, on a night of cold snow in January, 1931, he was working alone, checking manuscripts and indexing letters:

"Frost had brought that dead silence in which the only living thing seemed to be the great log fire. I was startled by music coming from the far corner of the room, behind me. It was clear, thin, and stately, like a tune by Rameau, and it kept on and on. If a ghost approached, he was entering in style. But the explanation was more simple. A French musical box had chosen to come alive at that moment."

Perhaps it was the spirit of James Boswell, playing on his flute (as he did for the brave Corsicans) his old Scottish and skittish airs, perhaps *Corn Rigs Are Bonny*.

"May we not hope," says Professor Abbott, "that his ghost begins to be content?"

DIALOGUE WITH DR. JOHNSON

I doubt if this would be a book for Dr. Johnson. I shudder to think what he might have said. Perhaps:

"Sir, he has scandalized himself into immortality."

"Do you not think, Sir, that if there be a purgatory he is the liveliest ember in it?"

"The only purgatory for Bozzy would be not to be noticed."

"He rose above that long ago, Doctor. In the past thirty years the re-discovery of Mr. Boswell has been the most exciting adventure in English letters."

"Sir, that may be so. The assiduity of amanuenses may still elevate the scholar to grace. But I hope I have lost by now my most personal irascibilities. I am content to be, not the one whose *Life* Boswell wrote, but the one, otherwise little perused, whose *Life* was written by Boswell."

"And a Scotchman!"

"Let us not acuminate a point already too sharp. Pray remember I hired five Scotsmen as copyists for my *Dictionary*. You should have heard them burring together when they thought I was beyond earshot. Sir, the Scotch character is as irregular as their landscape. Here is a young laird, the disgrace of his respectable house, who in a century and a half has turned biography upside down. He has even become, I hear, the renown of a North American university."

"It does seem, if I may say so, Doctor, a trifle immoral."

"Alas, my dear Sir, I fear that in the long course literature has no morals whatever."

CHRISTOPHER MORLEY

Roslyn Heights, New York
May 16, 1950

EDITOR'S INTRODUCTION

§I

James Boswell was born at Edinburgh on 29 October 1740, the eldest son of Alexander Boswell, eighth Laird of Auchinleck[1] in Ayrshire. The Boswell family was an old one with excellent connections, and the estate was more than respectable: Boswell used to remark that the Laird of Auchinleck could ride ten miles on his own land. Thomas Boswell, the founder, had stood high in the favour of James IV of Scotland, had received from him the barony of Auchinleck in 1504, and had died with him at Flodden in 1513. Thomas's son David adhered to the cause of Queen Mary, as did a later David (the fifth Laird) to the cause of King Charles. Latterly the Boswells had become staunch Whigs. Though none of the lairds had attained to a title of nobility, they had connected themselves by marriage with many of the noble houses of Scotland. Alexander Boswell's mother was a Bruce, daughter of the Earl of Kincardine. His wife, Euphemia Erskine, came of even superior lineage: she traced her ancestry back through the Earls of Mar to that Earl of Lennox who was the grandfather of Lord Darnley. Boswell therefor could (and did) claim that the blood of the Bruce flowed in his veins, and on one occasion felt free to remind George III that he was his cousin.

Alexander Boswell, like his father before him, had followed the law and was a member of the Faculty of Advocates in Edinburgh. In 1754 he received the highest honour open to a member of his profession when he was elevated to the bench as one of the fifteen judges of the Court of Session, the supreme court in Scotland for civil cases. A year later he "took the double gown," that is, became in addition one of the five judges of the High Court of

[1] In the eighteenth century generally pronounced Affléck, which one may still hear locally. The prevailing pronunciation now follows the spelling, with open Scots ch (as in German) and the stress on the last syllable.

1

Justiciary, the supreme court for criminal cases. He assumed the style of Lord Auchinleck.[2]

The line of Auchinleck resembled the line of Hanover in that the reigning laird tended to be jealous of the heir and suspicious of his motives. During the lifetime of his grandfather, it is not likely that Boswell saw much of Auchinleck. Rather, he was born and, up to his ninth year, bred a city boy, living mainly in his father's house in Blair's Land, Parliament Close, Edinburgh. But after 1749, when his father came into the estate, though he was in the city at least during the winter term of the Court of Session, he must have spent half the year in the romantic groves of his ancestral domain. "Romantic groves" is Boswell's own phrase, but is judiciously chosen.

He had two brothers: John and David. At the time the present journal opens, Boswell is a little past twenty-two, John is about nineteen, and David is about fourteen.

Most Edinburgh boys went to the City's High School. Boswell received his elementary education in a select private school conducted by a Mr. James Mundell. At the age of thirteen—not unusual for those days—he entered the University of Edinburgh. This did not mean leaving home. There was only one undergraduate college in the University, and it did not provide living quarters or meals for its students. Boys from outside Edinburgh rented lodgings in private houses, and Edinburgh boys lived with their parents. Lord Auchinleck's household was of the strictest. He provided for his children a succession of domestic tutors or coaches —all young men preparing themselves for the ministry of the Church of Scotland—who lived in the family and drilled the boys in their lessons. The Reverend John Dun came when Boswell was

[2] This was not a peerage dignity. It entitled him to be addressed as "My Lord," but he remained in every sense a commoner. His proper signature, even in official acts, was "Alexander Boswell," and his son's name received no prefix of "Honourable." Indeed, making allowance for the greater ceremoniousness of the older country, the Scottish "Lord" as applied to judges is about the equivalent of the American "Mr. Justice."

eight and departed when he was twelve, having been rewarded
with the parish of Auchinleck. Then came the Reverend Joseph
Fergusson, and then (best liked of the lot) the Reverend William
McQuhae. McQuhae, who was not much older than his eldest
charge, became in fact a confidential friend, and by 1762 is one of
the three persons to whom Boswell is willing to show his journal.

McQuhae drops completely out of Boswell's life after this year,
but the other two confidants do not. Boswell met them both—boys
of fifteen or sixteen—in Robert Hunter's Greek class in 1755, and
formed with them friendships which began by being tender and
unreserved and grew only closer with the years. Both of these boys,
as it happened, were borderers: William Johnson Temple, an
Englishman from Berwick-on-Tweed, and John Johnston, a Scot
from a clan of Border marauders and Laird of Grange, a small
property in Dumfriesshire.

In Mundell's school Boswell was taught to admire Addison's
prose and to write English fluently and correctly, with surprisingly
few Scotticisms; at Mundell's, too, and at the College of Edinburgh
he received a solid training in Latin, and read closely and with understanding a good part of the poetry of Virgil, Horace, Ovid, and
Juvenal. He also got a respectable grounding in logic, theory of
poetry, and history of criticism. His teachers considered him
promising, and encouraged him to think that he had powers as an
author.

As a boy, he was timid—scared of the dark and terribly afraid
of ghosts; bashful in company, priggish, and puritanical. He had
some kind of "scorbutic" complaint when he was twelve for which
it was thought wise to send him to drink the waters at Moffat. He
was subject to fits of depression, and in his seventeenth year suffered a protracted illness that sounds like a nervous collapse. When
he emerged from it, he seemed to have undergone a physical and
mental transformation. He grew suddenly robust and almost
phrenetically active: a young man of average height (which then
meant five feet six or less), tending to plumpness, with very black
hair and eyes and a swarthy complexion. He now became vain,

amorous, gregarious. He began to frequent the theatre and to dangle after actresses; to scribble verses and to publish them. Before very long, besides being a wit, he emerged as a sceptic and a tireless, if somewhat grubby, man of pleasure. He wanted to be an officer in the Army; or, rather, he wanted to live the year round in London, and thought a commission in the Footguards the most eligible way of securing perpetual London residence.

He would have turned out something like this in any case, but the forms of his ambition were probably largely set by his intense admiration of his first patron, James Lord Somerville, a Scotsman whose romantic story may have furnished Scott with the plot of *The Fortunes of Nigel*. Born heir to a peerage which had been allowed to lie dormant for more than a century because of the poverty of the family, left an orphan at the age of twelve with several brothers and sisters dependent on him, Somerville set out in 1721, aged twenty-three, to make his fortune at Court. One old confidential servant accompanied him. Living in obscure lodgings in London, he contrived in public to make a show befitting his rank, obtained a commission in the Dragoons, married a wealthy widow, and when she died, married a second even wealthier. He was the friend of Pope and Allan Ramsay, and his house near Edinburgh was the resort of authors and actors, he having taken the illegal but tolerated theatre at Edinburgh under his protection. "He was the first person of high rank," remarked Boswell, "that took particular notice of me in the way most flattering to a young man fondly ambitious of being distinguished for his literary talents; and by the honour of his encouragement made me think well of myself and aspire to deserve it better." We need look no further than Lord Somerville for the source of Boswell's addiction to the society of actors during this period; nor for his "almost enthusiastic notion of the felicity of London" before he had ever been there; nor for his wish to hold a commission in the Army; nor even for his determination to marry an heiress.

Lord Auchinleck had other views. He had planned from the first that Boswell should be a lawyer, like his father and grandfather. Lord Auchinleck despised people who made a living by writing, and could not have been pleased by his son's verses in *The Scots Magazine*. Like any father at any time he thought actors and actresses bad company for a young man. And before he was nineteen Boswell had plunged deep. Lady Houston, a distant cousin, put in his care a comedy in manuscript "with a strict injunction that its author should be concealed." Boswell got it brought on the stage, saw it through rehearsals, and wrote a prologue for it. The play was damned—"and not injustly," as he candidly admits. But he kept his promise to Lady Houston and "consequently had the laugh and sneer of his country against him," it being generally believed that he had written the piece himself. And he fell "madly in love" with Mrs. Cowper, an actress in the Edinburgh company, and even wanted to marry her.

In the autumn of 1759 he matriculated at the University of Glasgow to continue his study of civil law, though he seems to have been more interested in Adam Smith's lectures in philosophy and *belles lettres*. If Lord Auchinleck had counted on a change of scene to reclaim him, Glasgow was a failure. There was no theatre there, but he made—or continued—a friendship with an Irish actor inappropriately named Gentleman, who dedicated a printed play to him, no doubt for a consideration. He was extremely unhappy, and in the spring of 1760 ran away to London with the intention of making his submission to the Roman Catholic Church. How he was persuaded to such a momentous decision will probably never be known, for it was one of the few episodes of his life that he was close-mouthed about. It seems pretty clear that the decision was made in Scotland; less clear (though probable) that until he got to London he had never attended Roman Catholic worship. Contemporary scandal says that he eloped with an actress who was a Papist and "reputed virtuous among *them*" (the actors), but the journal now published proves there was nothing in that charge. Mrs. Cowper may have been a "Papist" (almost nothing is known about her), but she was certainly not Boswell's mistress in 1759, she could hardly have accompanied him to London, and there is nothing whatever to show that they met there. It is possible that she did direct his attention to Roman Catholicism, and not at all unlikely that, as his *bête noire* Gibbon had done a few years earlier, he simply read himself into a conversion. What can be stated with certainty is that Boswell made the journey from Carlisle to London on horseback in two days and a half, riding night and day; that he took lodgings in the house of a Roman Catholic wig-maker; that he went promptly to the Bavarian Chapel and saw mass celebrated; that he was immediately received into the communion of the Church of Rome; that for a very brief time he played with the notion of going to France and entering a monastery.

If this submission to the Roman Church had been known, the consequences would have been very serious. As a professed Roman Catholic, Boswell could not have been an officer in the Army or Navy, could not have been a barrister or advocate, could not have been elected to Parliament or even have voted for a member, could not have held any place under Government; finally, could not have inherited the estate of Auchinleck, and could have enjoyed its revenues only by the connivance of his Protestant heir. Since the secret did not come out until long after Boswell's death, it is obvious that very few of his contemporaries had it. One who did, one who will receive a considerable amount of mention in the following journal, was Sir David Dalrymple, an advocate, midway in age between Boswell and his father, and a confidential friend to both. He tried to help out by sending Boswell a letter of introduction to Dr. Jortin, a well-known Anglican divine in London, hoping, one supposes, that Jortin could at least get the young man to conform to the doctrines of the Church of England. But more persuasive missionaries had already gone to work.

On arriving in London, Boswell had informed his father where he was, and his father had written to the Earl of Eglinton, an Ayrshire neighbour then residing in London, begging him to look the young man up. Eglinton's emissary found that in a disconcertingly short space of time Boswell had teamed up with Samuel Derrick, countryman and friend of Gentleman; that Derrick, as Boswell's "governor," was showing him the shabbier aspects of London "in all its variety of departments, both literary and sportive"; and that the young ascetic was proving a fumbling but eager pupil. Eglinton took him into his own apartment in Mayfair and salvaged him from what remained of his religious error by making him a more complete libertine, in all the senses of that word. The first thing was to arrange his sexual initiation (Derrick may already have attended to this); then Eglinton dazzled him and swept away the last of his strict and gloomy notions by introducing him "into the circles of the great, the gay, and the ingenious."

It was the real thing and no imitation. For a few delirious weeks Boswell hobnobbed with the scapegrace young Duke of York; he went up to the spring meeting at Newmarket and was given the privileges of the Jockey Club; he met and was flattered by Laurence Sterne, whose first two volumes of *Tristram Shandy* had made him the literary lion of the moment. He celebrated his connection with the Duke of York and the Jockey Club by a doggerel poem, *The Cub at Newmarket*, dedicated to the Prince; he indited a long verse epistle (unpublished) to Tristram Shandy. In almost no time at all he was clamouring for a commission in the Guards, sure proof that he had renounced Romanism. Lord Auchinleck temporized, let him stay some weeks longer with Eglinton, but finally made him come home "and take some time to consider of it." Boswell had been in London about three months. We are now at June, 1760.

The next three years were an almost continuous battle of wills between Boswell and his father. He went back into Lord Auchinleck's strict family, where he was always put to the question if he stayed out late at night, and studied law listlessly under his father's personal instruction. Lord Auchinleck did not quite veto the plan of a military life, though he disliked it. He grudgingly offered to procure Boswell a commission in a marching regiment, but declined absolutely to put any money into the Guards scheme. And he kept Boswell headed towards the law by telling him that once he had his way about the Guards, he would tire of the whole thing; hence he had better wait a year or two and meantime get some law.

Boswell was at times very doleful, but he devised compensations. With several of his "rattling" companions he founded a society for giggling and making giggle called the Soaping Club; "let every man soap his own beard" being (at least on Boswell's testimony) the current slang equivalent of *Fay ce que vouldras*. And he scribbled and published: poems in a miscellany by Scots gentlemen; a prose pamphlet (imitating Sterne's style) on Samuel Foote's scandalous play *The Minor*; poems printed anonymously in quarto pamphlets, one pamphlet with burlesque recommendatory letters by himself and two of his friends, one genially dedicated to himself. His father was trying to get him married, and he was willing to imagine himself madly in love with three or four eligible young ladies, so long as he ran no risk of committing himself. His behaviour from the time of his London trip had been licentious, his amours being chiefly of the venal or servant-girl variety, but he refers complacently to affairs with women of fashion, and did certainly have more than one such intrigue.

Because Temple had long since left the University of Edinburgh for Cambridge, Boswell's closest companion during this period was John Johnston, who was also preparing to practice law, though in the status of "writer" or solicitor rather than in that of advocate or barrister. But Johnston never scribbled, and was of little use to Boswell in his publishing schemes. His chief literary crony was a young officer whom he met at Fort George in May, 1761, when he was accompanying his father on a tour of the Northern Circuit. The Honourable Andrew Erskine, younger son of the Earl of Kellie, was a poetaster with shivers of genius. Burns greatly admired some of his lyrics. He was a prominent contributor to the miscellany of poems by Scots gentlemen. Boswell threw himself eagerly into this enterprise, and he and Erskine started a self-conscious literary correspondence. The other member of this triumvirate of wit was George Dempster, able and genial Scots politician, an older man who found pleasure in nonsense.

In that same summer of 1761, Thomas Sheridan, father of the more famous Richard Brinsley, came to Edinburgh to give a series of lectures on English elocution. Many Scots in public life were becoming ashamed of their native Doric, and Sheridan, a fanatical believer in the powers of elocution, promised to teach a correct English pronunciation. Boswell, who had already taken lessons from an English actor named Love, attended the lectures. He and Sheridan took to each other, and in no time at all he had made Sheridan his guide, philosopher, and friend. ("My dear Sir, keep me in the right path. My Mentor! My Socrates! direct my heedless steps!") Sheridan, who never was affluent, lent him money to pay some gambling debts he did not dare to tell his father about, and agreed to correspond with him. And he proposed a compromise solution to the battle of wills that was making both Boswell and his father so unhappy. Since the desire of Boswell's heart was London rather than the Army, and the desire of Lord Auchinleck's (as was presumed) was the law rather than Edinburgh, why should not Boswell enter one of the Inns of Court and prepare for the English bar? Boswell gratefully acceded and Sheridan actually caused him to be entered in the Inner Temple in November, 1761. Boswell seems to have acted in a sincere belief that his father had agreed to the arrangement, and was angry and shocked when Lord Auchinleck forbade his going to London. Before long he returned to his Guards scheme.

Boswell had come of age on 29 October 1761, and could no longer be treated as a child. Though Lord Auchinleck talked of disinheriting him, it was really not in his power to do so, for his marriage contract had settled his estate on his eldest son. In the spring of 1762, after having failed to cure Boswell of scribbling, extravagance, general flightiness, and stubborn persistence in his plan to live in London as an officer of the Guards, he decided that Boswell was probably irresponsible and took steps to protect the estate. He wrote out, and persuaded Boswell to copy and sign, a deed by which Boswell consented to be put under trustees of his father's choosing in case he succeeded to Auchinleck. The bait was another document by which Lord Auchinleck formally and unconditionally granted him an allowance of £100 a year, so that he could live out of the family if he chose. It was further agreed that if Boswell would pass his trials in civil law (the one really difficult hurdle in the way to the bar) he might go to London with an introduction to the Duke of Queensberry and try his best to obtain a commission through influence. On 30 July 1762 he passed the examination.

Throughout this trying period he was treated with great kindness by Lord Kames, one of his father's colleagues on the bench. Kames was better able to sympathize with the young man's unhappiness and perplexity than his estimable but unimaginative father, both because he wrote books himself and because in his own unhappy youth he had played with the idea of joining the King of Prussia's tall guards. In the autumn of 1762 Boswell accompanied Lord and Lady Kames in a tour of visits through the southern counties of Scotland. When Lord Auchinleck came to Edinburgh for the opening of the Winter Session, the final arrangements for Boswell's departure were made: Lord Auchinleck paid his debts and allowed him £200 a year. On Sunday 14 November Boswell went to a Church-of-England chapel (he had pointedly absented himself from Presbyterian worship the week before, it being Sacrament Sunday), dined with Lord Somerville, sat with West Digges, leading man of the Edinburgh Theatre, and supped with Lord Kames.

§II

Boswell kept a journal or diary by fits and starts from at least as early as the autumn of 1758, but with one possible exception his records up to the autumn of 1762 appear to have been unambitious. From 14 September 1762 (the beginning of his tour with Lord Kames) until at least 30 January 1765 he kept an elaborate continuous record on unbound quarto leaves. The portion covering the period from 14 September to 14 November 1762 ("Journal of My Jaunt, Harvest, 1762") was among the manuscripts in the original Isham purchase of 1927–1928, and was included in the first volume of Colonel Isham's privately printed edition. It was written for Mr. McQuhae, and (as we now learn) was undertaken as an exercise in preparation for the journal to be written in London. The long portion covering the London visit, from 15 November 1762 to 4 August 1763, was in 1928 given up as lost. It was discovered in 1930 by Professor Abbott at Fettercairn House, and is now printed for the first time. Letters since recovered from Malahide Castle show that it was written for John Johnston and sent to him in weekly parcels.

The London journal of 1762–1763, at least in its earlier portion, is the most carefully and elaborately written of all Boswell's journals. In his later journals he sometimes has more interesting matter, and as he grew older he became himself a more interesting man, but it is doubtful whether he ever displayed greater literary skill than he does here. What usually limits him is lack of time: he simply cannot find in the interstices of his work or his play the number of hours of uninterrupted calm necessary for the full recall and vivid expression which distinguish his best journalizing. But on this London jaunt he had almost literally nothing to do except to write. His main purpose—the soliciting of the Duke of Queensberry and the Countess of Northumberland—could at most occupy only an occasional hour. He knew few people in London, and his allowance was too narrow for much entertainment. Consequently he could, and did, spend many solitary hours in his rooms elaborating his journal with painstaking care.

One evidence of his feeling of unlimited time is the amount of dramatically cast dialogue which this journal contains. It is this— especially when accompanied by vivid stage directions—that makes *The Life of Johnson* so much superior to other biographies:

JOHNSON. . . . . "I am afraid I may be one of those who shall be damned" (looking dismally). DR. ADAMS. "What do you mean by damned?" JOHNSON (passionately and loudly). "Sent to Hell, Sir, and punished everlastingly."

In the journal generally, this sort of dramatic dialogue is relatively rare, the more usual style being statement in the third person or direct speech with narrative tags: "Dr. Johnson said," or "Replied he." Excepting the journal here printed, dramatic dialogue hardly occurs before the London journal of 1772. But here we have pages and pages of it: conversations between Boswell and Lady North-umberland, conversations between Boswell and Lord Eglinton, conversations between Boswell and the fair Louisa, conversations overheard in Child's Coffee-house:

1 CITIZEN. Pray, Doctor, what became of that patient of yours? Was not her skull fractured?
PHYSICIAN. Yes. To pieces. However, I got her cured.
1 CITIZEN. Good Lord.

No point in it: Boswell knows neither the speakers nor the patient. But there it is, an authentic bit of the genuine conversation of nearly two hundred years ago, caught in an eternal sunbeam.

It is important to remember that Boswell did not write his journal in daily installments as the events occurred. He would sometimes fall days behind and then catch up at a sitting. Since he was not writing in a hurry but was posting his journal at leisure-ly intervals, he could even plan it. Chance gave this journal what most of his journals lack, a beginning and an end, but he gave it a very artful middle. The reader will be likely to forget that Boswell generally knows his story something as a novelist does: he does not, of course, know everything that is going to happen to the end of the book, but he does know some chapters beyond the point where he is writing. An inferior artist would reveal this by anticipating, and so would give us a journal of the ordinary unliterary sort. In par-ticular, such a journalist, since he knows how things came out, would eliminate many of the significant steps by which the action advanced, and would take away the excitement of the present by making it always past. Boswell never anticipates: he writes every entry as though he were living it and were, like us, looking forward to see what is to happen next.[3] But it would be naïve to suppose that his knowledge of subsequent events is not affecting his writing. It helps him to select his details meaningfully, to create a significant forward-straining tension. The best illustration is the Louisa saga.

[3] An exception that proves the rule: the last sentence of the entry for 24 February 1763.

No comedy in any language shows more delightful suspense or a more unexpected reversal of situation at the end. Any one who thinks that Boswell did not know exactly what he was up to in every stage of that half-delighted, half-rueful exposure of himself is assuming something almost as enormous as the old nonsense about the hundred monkeys with typewriters hitting out at random the books in the British Museum. Not even Boswell could have given the matter the organization that he has given it if he had not had the perspective of a week on the events.[4]

Boswell's journal stands between the poles of Pepys and Rousseau. Of course to occupy that position it has to forego some of the virtues of either extreme. It does not have the cool, assured, masculine tact of Pepys, nor does it provide so lavish and accurate a recording of historical detail. Those qualities are signs of an almost complete lack of introspection. It does not have the piercing eloquence and continuous forensic warmth of Rousseau. Those qualities reflect a habit of introspection so complete as almost to lose touch with history. Boswell is as frank and trustworthy as Pepys, but he gives self-analysis like Rousseau: self-analysis which shows a skill comparable to Rousseau's in the dissection of motives, and which has a superior degree of detachment.

To the modern age with its insatiable interest in psychology, the confessional element of Boswell's journal may well be its most interesting feature. His kind of confession is almost unique. He is writing, as he himself frequently said, a history of his own mind. Not an apologia but a history: the difference is enormous. The recurring theme of Rousseau's Confessions is, "See how weak and vile I was, but yet how much better I was and am than other people." Boswell approaches the secret places of his own heart and mind with the detachment, the candour, and the responsibility of a historian. Not a mere chronicler, but a historian of the older school, a

[4] Boswell's covering letter to Johnston shows that the entries for 6 to 12 January were sent off on 18 January. This means (probably) that the paradisial climax of the Louisa story was written on the day on which Boswell "began to feel an unaccountable alarm of unexpected evil" (below, p. 149).

historian who considers history a branch of literature. That is to say, though he remains scrupulously within the bounds of historical circumstance, he seizes all his material imaginatively, he *creates* it.

The reason that the world has been so slow to grant Boswell unusual powers of imagination is that he was so completely successful in achieving historical solidity. In criticism generally, imagination has meant invention: no invention, no imagination. Actually, the two faculties have no necessary connection. Boswell in his journal is creating, but as he creates he remembers; that is, he is able to refer every stage of his construction to a whole active mass of organized past reactions or experience. His picture must not merely be lifelike and dramatic; it must also be "true." It must keep within the bounds of historical circumstance.

But if it is lifelike and dramatic, it did not get that way by a mere mechanical process of rote memory. It got that way because Boswell was a great imaginative artist—the peer in imagination of Scott and Dickens. Not in invention; in the creation of fictions he is not at all remarkable. And of course a lack of invention is a limitation. When a man creates a memorable fiction, a fiction in which the characters say wise and witty things, we properly give him credit not only for the power of expression that makes the whole vivid and absorbing but also for personal power of wit and wisdom. When a man by similar exercise of the imagination presents us with dramatic dialogues filled with wit and wisdom which we know he was constructing with the aid of memory, wit and wisdom which we know he could not have invented, we feel that he deserves a lower kind of praise. Other things being equal, he does. But in practice other things never are equal. Great power of imaginative realization can make up for lack of invention. By purely literary standards Boswell's journal deserves to rank very high.

I have been writing of it in general, and hope I shall not be thought to unsay what I have just said if I add a word of qualification concerning the journal here printed. The qualification does not detract from its literary merit (rather the contrary); it does affect somewhat its status as autobiography. Not until Boswell's journal becomes completely private can the biographer accept it as in all respects his standard of reference. In this case, so far as tone and attitude (not statements of fact) are concerned, the standard will rather be found in the strictly private memoranda which he was writing every day. Boswell was consciously writing the whole of this journal for his friend Johnston to read; and he gave it—not by misstatement of fact but by selection—a prevailing tone of zest and confidence which, during most of the time, he was far from feeling. Except for a few brief periods of his life—all later than this—Boswell suffered from a radical sense of insecurity and a basic lack of confidence. It was so during this London jaunt. When he surveyed himself each morning, he knew that most of the time instead of being what he wished to be—a brilliant, high-bred man of pleasure, poised, courtly, imperturbable, holding scoffers in awe by the rapier of his wit—he was really a raw, loud, romping, over-eager boy: greedy, stingy, and with brutal tastes.

And scared. Here he was, granted without reservation the chance he had begged, prayed, and fought for through three bitter years. To him in November, 1762, that chance seemed to contain every hope of happiness that life held for him. Could he make a go of the scheme that in Scotland had seemed so plausible? Or was he after all the weakling his father thought him? Would he have to go crawling back to Edinburgh defeated and ridiculous? It is pathetic to see him, freed for the first time in his life from his father's incessant scrupulous admonition, hedging himself round with substitutes. System: what else could be the secret of his father's worldly success? Consequently, a plan for his finances; a letter and twenty-four pages of journal to Johnston every Tuesday; memoranda to himself every morning: "Prepare like father. . . . Mark this and keep in pocket. You are not to consider yourself alone. You have a worthy father whose happiness depends on your behaving so as at least to give no offence; and there is a prudent way to save appearances. Be reserved and calm and sustain a consistent character. It will please you when high, and when low it will be a sure comfort,

though all things seem trifling; and when high again, 'twill delight. So when you return to Auchinleck, you'll have dignity."

Externally it all seemed to work out just as Lord Auchinleck
wanted it to. The journal shows Boswell slipping from hopefulness
into uncertainty, from uncertainty into doubt, from doubt into
despair, from despair into subjection. He gave up consciously and
for ever his darling scheme of the Guards and consented to dwindle
into a lawyer. What a pity, one thinks, that he could not have had
the consolation of knowing that these struggles with his father were
mere skirmishes, and that the real question of his vocation had been
settled. Before ever he left Scotland, bond unknown to him had been
given, and he had embarked on his life work. It was his journal,
that unrecognized, nameless work of art which an irresistible im-
pulse was forcing him to create.

§III

A young Scot setting out to conquer London could hardly have
chosen a more unpropitious month than November,1762. From
medieval times, when Scotland had been leagued with France in a
traditional alliance against England, Scots had been unpopular
south of the Tweed; and the immemorial mistrust between the two
nations had not been much diminished by the accession of the King
of Scots to the throne of England, nor even by the Act of Union
which, a century later, brought both countries under a single Parliament. The Act of Union had admitted the Scots to all the com-
mercial privileges of the Empire, a fact much resented by English
merchants. Three times since the Hanoverian succession, the Highlands had risen in armed rebellion: only seventeen years before,
Prince Charles Edward had led a Jacobite army almost to London.
(Any dweller or sojourner in London had a grim reminder of *that*
foray whenever he glanced above Temple Bar, where the heads of
two officers of Prince Charles's army still mouldered on pikes.)
Pitt's introduction of Highland regiments into the British Army,
though it helped to allay the suspicion of Scottish loyalty, provoked
English jealousy of Scottish officers competing for commissions.

Above all, the Prime Minister when Boswell came to London was intensely hated and was a Scotsman. John Stuart, Earl of Bute, had been the young King's instructor in the art of government and was now his favourite; he was also much esteemed by the King's mother, the Dowager Princess of Wales, whom scandal (no doubt falsely) reported to be his mistress.

In November, 1762, the country stood at the end of the most successful war in its history, the one which British historians call the Seven Years' War and Americans the French and Indian. The war had begun as an attempt to break the growing line of fortifications by which the French hoped to unite Quebec and Louisiana, and so to halt at the Alleghenies the westward expansion of the British colonies. It had ended, under the inspired dictatorship of William Pitt "the Great Commoner," with Great Britain in possession, not merely of the French forts in the Ohio valley, but also of the whole of Canada, of the West Indies, of the Philippines, and of India.

Bute represented an "end-the-war" movement, and to end the war it was necessary to get rid of the immensely popular Pitt. Pitt was humiliated in the Cabinet and resigned; and in May, 1762, Bute was appointed Prime Minister. His elevation, though strictly constitutional, had naturally roused the hatred of the politicians whom he displaced, and they concentrated their attacks on something he could not mend—his Scottishness. In addition, he had been given the impossible task of concluding a negotiated peace in such a way as to please everyone. The bulk of the people thought that he had made pusillanimous concessions: the return to France of the French West Indies and of the French fishing rights off Newfoundland; the return to Spain of Cuba and the Philippines.

Bute was not merely attacked for being a Scotsman; he was also charged with honouring and employing none but North Britons. One of the Opposition papers of the day maintained that out of sixteen names in one list of promotions eleven were Stuarts and four were Mackenzies. It is not easy to decide whether the charge of partiality was well-founded or not. Considering the population of the two kingdoms, it certainly does appear as though Scotsmen had secured a disproportionate share of awards in all the departments of British public life, but one would have been inclined to attribute this merely to the fact that the Scots are traditionally lean, hungry, ambitious, and able. However that may be, the Earl of Bute, like others of the favourites of George III, was certainly a fumbler. When he was appointed Prime Minister, he commissioned Tobias Smollett, the novelist, to undertake the publication of a party periodical in defence of his Government. Smollett, unluckily, was a Scot; and he chose for his paper a title which perhaps only a Scot or an American would have chosen: *The Briton*. John Wilkes, an English M.P., an adroit and unscrupulous demagogue, retorted with *The North Briton*. Wilkes roused the anger of the mob by ironical assurances that Bute and the Princess of Wales did *not* resemble that queen of England and her paramour who murdered Edward II and ruled the country in the name of a boy-king; and he played upon the fears of the mob by repeated warnings that an innumerable host of greedy Scotsmen was warping down the northern wind to eat up all the green fields of Old England. Charles Churchill, Wilkes's partner in *The North Briton*, a brilliant and savage satirist, was to write a Scots pastoral in which Scotland was characterized as the land where half-starved spiders preyed on half-starved flies.

The preliminaries of the Peace had been signed in France on 3 November, before Boswell left Scotland, and Henry Fox, an unpopular political opportunist, had been hired by the promise of a peerage to break the power of Bute's political enemies in the House of Commons through extensive distribution of patronage. Soon after Boswell's arrival in London, Parliament approved the preliminaries despite bitter opposition, the peers who opposed the Peace were stripped of their appointments, and a general expulsion of their placemen began. Resentment against Scotland and Scotsmen was general, unreasonable, and violent. No better illustration could be cited than Boswell's account of that scene at Covent Garden Theatre in which two officers of a Highland regiment, just landed in England after a victorious campaign in the West Indies, were pelted with apples by the gallery mob to the cry, "No Scots! No Scots!"[5] All this needs to be kept in mind in reading Boswell's first stumbling speech to Johnson: "Indeed, I come from Scotland, but I cannot help it."

Since the War was obviously all but over when Boswell set out for London, it must seem odd that he was so bent on securing a commission. And there are other things about the business that are puzzling to readers whose knowledge of military matters is confined to the procedures of the British Empire and the United States in our recent great wars. What help, for example, could Boswell have hoped to get from the Countess of Northumberland in a matter that appears to have concerned the Army and only the Army? The answers can be given, but need some space if they are to be intelligible. In the first place (to use the modern equivalents), Boswell was not offering to do his bit of war service as a reserve officer: he was electing a lifetime profession as an officer of the regular Army. Secondly, he was not by any means prepared to be satisfied with any kind of commission: he wished a commission in the Footguards. It was not at all his wish to be an active soldier. He was quite frank in admitting that he had no stomach for fighting in Germany or America or anywhere else. True, he was fascinated by the pomp and circumstance of military dress and martial parade, and found the social status of an officer attractive. But fundamentally what he wanted was London. The Footguards were household troops, the personal bodyguard of the Sovereign. In time of peace they would be stationed in London or Windsor, and even in wartime there was a fair chance that a Guardsman would remain through all vicissitudes, drilling and parading at St. James's. By securing a commission in the Guards, Boswell would have fitted himself with a gentlemanly profession that held the promise of keeping him in London with plenty of time to enjoy himself in the modes that he found most delightful.

At the end of 1762 the Army was not looking for officers. On the

[5] 8 December 1762: below, p. 71.

contrary, with the Peace at hand, it had far more officers than it needed, and was about to "break" (disband) more than fifty regiments and put their officers on inactive status. But even if this had not been the case, Boswell would still have needed either money or influence to get a commission. It was possible to be promoted from the ranks, but such promotion was rare. The normal way was to buy one's commission of the colonel of the regiment in which one wished to serve. Such transactions, to be sure, had to be approved by the King, so that even in the case of purchase, influence at Court was highly desirable. But without too much qualification it may be said that colonels were proprietors of their regiments; and as such, they were expected to make a good part of their income by selling commissions. (Also by pocketing part of the money they stopped from their men's pay, for clothes.) General officers, it may be added, received no additional pay as generals, but had to hold on to their perquisites as colonels of regiments if they were not to lose money by their promotions. The Footguards in 1762 consisted of three regiments, the colonels of which held the ranks respectively of Field Marshal, General, and Lieutenant-General in the Army.

Boswell could not follow the usual procedure and buy a commission in the Footguards, because his father refused to give him the money. It would not have been impossible for him to have got one through the influence of a Great Person like the Duke of Queensberry or the Countess of Northumberland. But the colonel in the case (Lord Ligonier or Lord Tyrawley or Lord Rothes) would certainly have expected a *quid pro quo:* the kind of favour, present or future, that a Great Person could bestow. If Boswell had been willing to take a commission in a marching regiment, the Duke or Lady Northumberland could have fixed him up and have put the matter out of mind as a trifle. But as practical politicians, they could not commit themselves to the extravagant outlay of patronage necessary for procuring a commission in the Guards unless they were sure that they could get some favours in return from Lord Auchinleck or from Lord Auchinleck's influential friends. And Lord Auchinleck had let it be known that any one who helped his son into the Guards was no friend of his. Boswell was defeated before he started.

Though wide knowledge of the literary, political, social, and economic history of England in the latter half of the eighteenth century does enhance the pleasure of reading Boswell's journal, the general reader may be assured that he can get on in it very well without being at all learned. It is almost true to say that one can read this book as one reads an historical novel like Tolstoy's *War and Peace*. If a reader merely dips into that great work here and there, he will find allusions which he does not understand, casual references to manners, customs, and events of the past concerning which he is partially or wholly ignorant. But if he reads the book continuously and attentively from beginning to end, he will find that all the obscurities that really matter get explained—explained, that is, sufficiently for the purpose at hand. It would be possible by extensive annotation of the right sort to make the journal here printed an introduction to the social life of London in the Age of Johnson, but to handle it in that way at its first printing would be a great mistake. It is primarily and essentially an essay in auto-biography; and the reader should repress the tendency to make it "old-fashioned," "quaint"—in short, a fancy-costume piece. If one had to take an extreme course, it would be much better to read this journal as though it were a completely contemporary book, with no apparatus at all.

But it is not necessary to take either the extreme course of thorough-going antiquarianism or the extreme course of "letting the document speak for itself." In the paragraphs that follow, I at-tempt to provide a general description of certain features of the life of London in the middle of the eighteenth century that appear prominently in Boswell's journal and are significantly different from present-day modes. In the annotation of the journal itself, I have assumed on the part of the reader a general knowledge of the eighteenth century, and have provided antiquarian notes only for those matters that I consider interesting in themselves and that seem to me likely to be obscure to any but the special student. Generally speaking, my object has been not to provide an education in the eighteenth century, but to illuminate Boswell's text: to make explicit its tacit assumptions and the connection of one part with another; to elucidate the significance *within Boswell's story* of this or that casually recorded event or encounter. The most useful portion of the notes has been drawn from unpublished parallel documents by Boswell himself, especially from his letters to John Johnston and his daily private memoranda. I have not thought it necessary to gloss unfamiliar words that can be found in a good small dictionary. Here and there I have called attention to a Scotticism, but with no intention of providing a complete list of Boswell's divergences from standard English. My object in such notes is merely to prevent misunderstanding or to guarantee the integrity of the text in places where an English or American reader might suspect a corruption. The index, which is more elaborate than is usual in books intended for the general reader, should be used to locate information given in other parts of the volume. And, finally, I am well aware that though I am editing for Great Britain as well as for America, I have sometimes given the apparatus a specifically American cast. The reason is simply that American readers will need more help than British readers.

To reach London from Edinburgh in 1762, if one did not wish to make the trip by sea or on horseback, one had the choice of stage-coach or post-chaise. In either case, one went all the way in the same vehicle, but changed horses every few miles. There was perhaps not much difference in the time required, but the post-chaise was more gentlemanly. The stage-coach, a heavy, jolting vehicle, carried six inside passengers of every social status who got on and off at different places along the road; like a modern bus, it arrived at inns at inconvenient hours and allowed insufficient time out for eating and sleeping. In a chaise you travelled all the way with only one other person, picked your own inns, and were sure of spending the nights in bed. On this trip Boswell came up in a chaise. His time by the east road (with nights spent at Berwick, Durham, Doncaster, and Biggleswade) was four days; his milage roughly one

hundred miles a day. The trip cost him £11. In London you travelled on foot, by hackney-coach, and by sedan-chair. The sedan-
chair, a vehicle like a little single-seated coach without wheels, was
carried on poles by two men, one walking before and one behind.

There were few or no hotels in London in 1762. Visitors who did
not have friends or relatives to put them up went temporarily to an
inn and then looked about for lodgings in a private house. Boswell
secured very comfortable rooms at the fashionable end of town for
£22 a year, he paying for his own coal and candles. He had breakfast (toast or rolls and tea) in his own lodgings, served by his landlord's maid but using supplies which he himself furnished. Before
breakfast, which was at ten, he had usually been out for a constitutional in the Park. Dinner, either with his landlord or abroad at a
chop-house, came at three, but four was coming to be the more
fashionable hour. Dinner was usually followed by tea at six o'clock.
Of supper, a meal served late in the evening, Boswell seldom partook. His journal and estimate of expenses show that he considered
from a shilling to one and sixpence enough to spend ordinarily for
dinner, but it must be remembered that he was on short allowance.
His tavern dinners with Johnson certainly cost much more.[6]

A young man loose on the town passed a good deal of his time in
coffee-houses, chop-houses, and taverns. Boswell went to a coffee-
house not so much for coffee or tea as to read the newspapers, of
which the better coffee-houses furnished several copies, to talk
politics, and to listen to other people's conversation. A coffee-house
did service as a cheap club. According to Johnson (a great authority
in such matters) a man might be in one for some hours every day
in very good company by spending no more than threepence. The
room was cheerful; there was a good fire; patrons sat by twos and
threes at small tables and spoke low so as not to disturb the others.
Different professions and groups had their favourite coffee-houses.

[6] Bills of two of Boswell's tavern dinners at meetings of The Club in 1785
have been preserved. For one of these he spent 14s., for the other £1-4-0. A
good deal of this would have been for wine. In 1762 he drank little, and
took such wine as he did drink mainly in the diluted form of negus.

Child's, in St. Paul's Church-yard, was Boswell's choice; he was probably directed to it by *The Spectator* of Addison and Steele, who mention it in their first number. It was frequented, not, as one might have expected, by booksellers, authors, and wits, but by physicians and solid citizens.

Chop-houses were places where a man went to be fed cheaply, expeditiously, and (generally) silently. If he wanted fuller service, wanted to talk and to linger over his meal, he went to a tavern, where he could get a private room. Taverns ranged all the way from highly respectable places like the Mitre in Fleet Street, where (again on Johnson's authority) if a young fellow led in a wench both parties at least had to be well dressed, to others that were not so particular; where, in fact, the waiters were in league with the wenches.

Besides the Royal Opera House in the Haymarket, there were only two licensed winter theatres in London, Drury Lane and Covent Garden. David Garrick was manager and chief actor at Drury Lane; John Beard, a great singer, managed Covent Garden. These houses (both of moderate size) presented mainly "legitimate" drama, both new and old, but supplemented it with musical plays, pantomimes, and spectacles. The run even of successful pieces was short, twenty performances of one play in a season being most unusual. At the Little Theatre in the Haymarket (a summer theatre) that extraordinary mimic Samuel Foote held forth, usually in entertainments of his own composition.

The doors of the theatres opened at four, and the plays began at six. One could not secure a seat anywhere in the pit or galleries except by occupying it when the doors opened or by sending a servant to occupy it. In 1762 nobody could be made to stand in queues; consequently there was always a dreadful jam at the entrances and people were often seriously hurt trying to get in. The waiting crowd inside was kept from too great restiveness by the First, Second, and Third Music. All the seats were backless benches. The most expensive were in the boxes, the next in the pit. The old "apron" of the stage (a projection in front of the proscenium, coming out past the boxes) was still retained, and most of the play was acted there. The scene (painted flats, as now) was lighted by two or three hundred tallow candles in large ring-shaped chandeliers over the stage. The right of theatre-goers to make an uproar if they disliked a piece was legally established and freely exercised. Malicious groups often got together in advance to "damn" a new play: that is, so to intimidate the actors and manager as to prevent the announcement from the stage that the play would be repeated. If a play could be damned on the first or second night, the author lost his benefit (the third night), which meant that he got nothing whatever. It had long been customary to reduce the price of seats one half at the end of the third act of the main piece, with the consequence that many people came then. Principally for the benefit of this second audience, the managers had long followed the practice of presenting a one-act farce or a pantomime as an afterpiece. An attempt to abolish the custom of second price in January, 1763 (not reported by Boswell because he was confined at the time), resulted in serious riots in which the audience tore up the benches and broke the chandeliers. To give the actors some protection from theatre mobs, a row of sharp iron spikes was set along the front of the stage. "Sitting at the spikes" was the eighteenth-century way of saying that one had a front-row seat in the orchestra (stalls).

Downing Street, where Boswell lodged during the greater part of his stay in London, is near St. James's Park, and in the Park Boswell obtained much of his amusement. There he could see the Footguards being drilled and paraded; and there, in the Mall, he could stroll back and forth in the company of ladies of the Court. After sundown the Park was given over to ladies of another kind, and being unlighted and unguarded except for an occasional raid from the police office in Bow Street, it was the scene of a good deal of business in a wicked way. (The gates were locked at ten at night, but sixty-five hundred people had keys issued by authority, and nobody knows how many unauthorized keys were in use.) The twentieth-century reader will perhaps not be too much surprised by the record of Boswell's traffic *al fresco* with ladies of the town in the Park, since he may have heard that such things occasionally happen today, but he may well be astonished by what appears to be extreme recklessness on Boswell's part in conducting such transactions in the streets and on the bridges of the city. If so, he must be reminded that in 1762 few of the streets of London were lighted at all, and that most of the side-streets and alleys were dark as the pit. The police force was of the slenderest. A single watchman, often old and decrepit, made the rounds with a lantern, crying the hour and giving evil-doers plenty of warning of his approach. If you *wanted* light, you hired a link-boy (boy with a flaring torch of pitch and tow) to precede you.

When spring came, you would wish to use the river as a thoroughfare. All along the bank were "stairs" or landing-places, where you could hire a rowboat with a uniformed waterman to take you up or down. You would probably wish to go out to Kensington Gardens, a beautiful pleasure ground attached to Kensington Palace, or to the gardens of Ranelagh in Chelsea, or of Vauxhall, across the Thames on the Surrey side. At Ranelagh and Vauxhall were dark walks and bright lights, music and supper parties. The great Rotunda at Ranelagh—a vaulted room nearly two hundred feet in diameter—was one of the wonders of the metropolis.

Period-pieces in the cinema and on the stage have made every one familiar with the general appearance of the costume of men and women in 1762. It may merely be mentioned that though Boswell wore his own hair and was very short of funds, he thought it necessary to have his hair powdered and dressed by a professional "every day, or pretty often"; that he felt he must have his shoes "wiped" daily; and that he insisted on "a suit of clean linens every day." It is a great mistake to suppose that people of fashion in the eighteenth century were generally dirty. In the matter of personal cleanliness, they were quite as fussy as people of the present day, perhaps even more fastidious.[7]

[7] Readers who wish fuller information about the eighteenth-century scene may be referred to the books from which the above paragraphs have been compiled: Peter Cunningham and H. B. Wheatley, *London Past and Present*,

§IV

Since Boswell's circle of acquaintance in London in 1762–1763 was a narrow one, the same persons come in over and over again in his journal. It has seemed to the editor that for some of the persons most frequently encountered, biographical sketches preceding the text will be more helpful than brief and disjointed identification by footnotes. A backward reference is given at the first occurrence of the name in the text; thereafter if one wishes to refer to these sketches, one can find them by using the index.

AUCHINLECK (Alexander Boswell), LORD. Fifty-five years old. A Scots lawyer, educated in Scotland and Holland; for the last eight years a judge. A classical scholar with a special fondness for Horace and Anacreon. Passionately devoted to the improvement of his estate, where he has just completed a fine new house with a motto from Horace prominently displayed across the front: it may be paraphrased as follows: "All you seek is here, here in the remoteness and quiet of Auchinleck—if you have fitted yourself with a good steady mind." Is decidedly impatient with those who have failed to acquire a good steady mind. Has the reputation of being a laborious and dispassionate judge, and is generally esteemed for manliness, frankness, candour, and dignity. The character he displays at home is less attractive. Towards his children he is stern, undemonstrative, suspicious, and overbearing. All three of his sons feel strong affection for him but are treated with chilling disapproval. Lady Auchinleck is gentle, pious, mystical, and completely dominated by her husband.

CHURCHILL, CHARLES. Thirty-one years old. A clergyman's son, educated at Westminster School, where he was contemporary with George Colman the dramatist, William Cowper the poet, and Warren Hastings. Made a reckless Fleet marriage while still

3 vols., 1891; W. S. Lewis, *Three Tours Through London*, 1941; A. S. Turberville (ed.), *Johnson's England*, 2 vols., 1933. The two latter are illustrated and contain extensive bibliographies. Roger Ingpen's edition of Boswell's *Life of Samuel Johnson* (various printings, 1907 and 1925) contains hundreds of cuts and plates illustrating persons and places mentioned in Boswell's book.

very young; took holy orders, served in a country parish, and then succeeded to his father's curacy in Westminster. His stipend there so small that he was forced to eke it out by teaching in a school for young ladies. Early in 1761 arranged a formal separation from his wife and appeared as an author with *The Rosciad*, a slashing attack on most of the actors and actresses of the day and the most successful satire to appear between Pope and Byron. Thereupon paid his debts, made an allowance to his wife, doffed his clerical black coat for a blue one, and began openly to live like a buck, though he will not resign his curacy till January, 1763. Became an admirer and intimate friend of Wilkes and a collaborator with him in *The North Briton*; about to publish *The Prophecy of Famine*, an extravagant but brilliant attack on Scotland and the Scots. A burly, heavy-faced man whom Hogarth will caricature as a bear in clerical bands with a club and a pot of porter. Truculent, independent, feared for his powers of satire. A brutal but honest poet, with occasional flashes of delicacy and charm.

DALRYMPLE, SIR DAVID. Thirty-six years old. Scotsman, lawyer, and man of letters. His father a viscount's grandson, his mother an earl's daughter. Because the family is Whig and Hanoverian with English leanings, had his early education at Eton; then went on (in the fashion normal for Scots lawyers) to the University of Utrecht in Holland. Succeeded to the family baronetcy and a moderate fortune at the age of twenty-four, but has continued to labour assiduously in his profession; will be elevated to the bench in 1766 as Lord Hailes. A learned, accurate, and hardworking lawyer who manages to carry on extensive antiquarian and literary pursuits and to publish a book or two every year. Has written familiar essays for English periodicals; is in correspondence with Horace Walpole and Thomas Percy, editor of the famous *Reliques*; will become (through Boswell's introduction) a respected correspondent of Dr. Johnson. One of Boswell's most admired models because of his learning, his English breeding and style, his successful excursions into the fields of history and *belles lettres*, and his firm Christianity. Dalrymple has great respect for

Boswell's father; is fond of Boswell and thinks him promising; and is labouring tactfully to smooth out their differences.

DEMPSTER, GEORGE. Thirty years old. A Scots lawyer with a small fortune who has abandoned the law for politics. Elected Member of Parliament in 1761 for the Forfar and Fife burghs, he will remain in Parliament for nearly thirty years. A Whig but not a "Patriot." Genial, imperturbable, a solid man, though fond of a jest. A decided sceptic in religion. At this time a bachelor; his sister Jeanie keeps house for him.

EGLINTON (Alexander Montgomerie), Tenth EARL OF. Scotsman. Thirty-nine years old. Succeeded to the peerage at the age of six; educated in Scotland and at Winchester; learned dancing, fencing, and riding at Paris. A sportsman and a rake; loves singing, and is prominent in the Catch Club. Distinctly able but very indolent; at one time seriously considered resigning his peerage so as to have a career in the House of Commons. A Lord of the Bedchamber and a Representative Peer; close friend of the Duke of York (the King's brother), and intimate with Lord Bute. A bachelor.

ERSKINE, THE HONOURABLE ANDREW. Scotsman. Twenty-two years old. Younger son of the fifth Earl of Kellie, who joined the Rebellion of 1745 as a colonel in the Jacobite army and was detained three years in the Castle of Edinburgh after its collapse. Because of his father's eclipse and the family poverty, spent what he himself calls a "blackguard" childhood; was first sent to sea and then entered the Army. Lieutenant in the Seventy-first Foot, but took no active part in the Seven Years' War; his regiment is about to be disbanded following the Peace, when he will go on half-pay. A tall, dark, indolent young man, painfully bashful in the company of strangers, but capable of gay and easy impudence in letters or intimate conversation. Has considerable ability as a versifier, and has published a good deal. Generally out of funds. Subject, like Boswell, to fits of depression.

GARRICK, DAVID. Forty-five years old. Son of a captain in the Army, his mother a native of Dr. Johnson's birthplace, Lichfield.

A pupil of Johnson's in an unsuccessful school for boys which was one of Johnson's early ventures; came up with Johnson to London in 1737, both hoping to make their fortunes. Both have, but in very different ways. While Johnson toiled for years in obscurity as a bookseller's hack, Garrick, having flirted briefly with the law and a wine business, leaped almost at once into highest fame as an actor. For twenty years now he has been the undisputed monarch of the British stage; is probably in fact the greatest actor who has ever lived. A clever playwright, occasional poet, and adapter; manager of Drury Lane Theatre. Has accumulated a fortune; owns a splendid house with a fine library. A small man whose behaviour on the stage is so natural that one forgets that he is acting, off-stage he seems all posture, calculation, and art. A genuinely kind-hearted man whose kindness, though obscured by his self-importance and bustle, still manages to show through.

GOLDSMITH, OLIVER. Thirty-two years old. Irishman, son of a poor clergyman in the established Church of Ireland. Educated at Trinity College, Dublin; studied medicine briefly at the University of Edinburgh; travelled the Continent, mainly on foot, and came back claiming a medical degree for which documentary evidence has never been produced. Has tried two or three times with no success to set up as a physician; has taught in a boys' school; and since 1757 has been a prolific literary hack, making translations, writing book reviews and biographies, and compiling all sorts of pleasant compendia. Has managed besides to bring out a few things of his own, especially a series of "Chinese letters" (*The Citizen of the World*), which discerning critics like Johnson think highly of. An ugly little man with a face like a pock-marked monkey's; a fumbling and ineffective talker because of his transparent eagerness to shine; absurd, warm-hearted, and lovable. He is in many ways the greatest literary figure of the era, certainly the most versatile genius, and will do work of high distinction in poetry, the essay, the novel, and the drama. At the end of 1762 he is only just coming to be known.

JOHNSON, SAMUEL. Englishman. Fifty-four years old. A large,

ugly, slovenly, near-sighted man, his face scarred by scrofula, his body distorted by compulsive tics, his speech interspersed with ab-sent-minded clucks and mutterings. For the last eleven years he has been a widower. A man of enormous learning, who has finally fought his way to eminence and the independence of a modest pension by the unlikely profession of bookseller's hack. Author of two fine gloomy poems and a tragedy which he now candidly admits he once thought too highly of. Compiler of the best English dictionary. Author of *Rasselas*, a short Oriental novel written to expound his favourite text that human life is everywhere a state in which much is to be endured and little to be enjoyed, and two series of essays, *The Rambler* and *The Idler:* forthright lay-sermons, mournful, eloquent, ironically humorous, in a ponderous but precise style which no one else has ever handled without making it ridiculous. Though he is frequently given to huge hilarity, his temperament is naturally gloomy to the point of despair. He has won his way to orthodox Christian faith but not to serenity of mind. A profound moralist and an heroically good man, he is slothful, dilatory, splenetic, and greedy. He has had to fight hard to make his way, and he still remains a gladiator. Talk has become his real profession, and when he talks for victory, he subscribes to no rules whatever. A very formidable man.

JOHNSTON, JOHN, OF GRANGE. Scotsman. Probably about Boswell's age (twenty-two). Boswell made his acquaintance in Robert Hunter's Greek class in 1755; Johnston was then wearing a coat with a straw-coloured lining which Boswell thought extremely elegant. Laird of a small property in Dumfriesshire. Though Boswell always calls Temple his most intimate friend, he has actually seen much more of Johnston and leans more heavily on him. An obscure "writer" (i.e., solicitor or attorney) in Edinburgh, Johnston is distinguished by neither wit nor great learning, but he possesses the virtues of unfailing loyalty and affection. Boswell's only complaint is that he is a very poor correspondent. Like Boswell he suffers from recurring fits of depression; like Boswell he entertains a passionate regard for the history of Scotland and so much of its scenery as can be connected with great historic events. Like Boswell he is a sentimental Jacobite and is strongly attracted to Episcopal devotions. In his bland and affectionate company Boswell feels more at peace than in that of any other mortal.

MACPHERSON, JAMES. Twenty-six years old. Creator of the English Ossian. A Highland Scot, educated for the ministry of the Church of Scotland. While taking on odd jobs of school-teaching and private tutoring, like other young clergymen waiting to be placed, stirred up great excitement with a handful of alleged translations from ancient Gaelic poetry. Sent by a subscription into the Highlands and Western Isles to recover the long poem of which he represented these pieces to be fragments, published at London at the end of 1761, under the patronage of Lord Bute, a work in rhythmical English prose called *Fingal*. *Fingal*, an epic poem in six books describing the invasion of Ireland by the king of Denmark in the third century A.D., professes to be the work of Ossian, son of Fingal, the king of Morven. It is having an enormous success, especially on the Continent, where serious critics will rate it superior to anything ever written except Homer and the Bible. In England, where there is strong political prejudice against the Gaelic language and those who speak it, the question of authenticity has been raised, and will be put more and more sharply until Johnson in his *Journey to the Western Islands of Scotland* (1775) will denounce *Fingal* as an imposture and Macpherson as an insolent and stubborn liar. Johnson will be much too sceptical in maintaining that there are no old manuscripts and no really ancient Gaelic poetry, but nearly everyone will come to agree that though Macpherson (who was actually not a good Gaelic scholar) had access to a wealth of heroic poetry from which he drew names, episodes, and general inspiration, the epic in six books was his own invention. Macpherson will publish another Ossianic epic, will become a Government hack, and will die rich. He will never make any really serious attempt to refute the charge of forgery. A large, handsome man with thick legs; morose, sceptical, licentious, and unamiable.

NORTHUMBERLAND (Elizabeth Seymour Percy), COUNTESS OF. Forty-six years old. Daughter of Algernon Seymour, Duke of Somerset, who, as heir through his mother of the vast Percy estates, was created Earl of Northumberland, with the unusual arrangement that if his own male line failed, this title should descend to his son-in-law, Lady Elizabeth's husband. The son-in-law, Hugh Smithson, a handsome Yorkshire baronet with a considerable fortune, accordingly has become Earl of Northumberland, and has assumed the name of Percy. He will be made Duke of Northumberland in 1766. Lady Northumberland is Baroness Percy in her own right. Walpole calls her "junketaceous" and credits her with an excess of patrician pride and ostentation. In view of the fact that the Earl is not a Percy at all and that the Countess had no male Percy ancestor nearer than her great-grandfather, Walpole considers their constant flaunting of the Percy name and fame somewhat ridiculous. Her entertainments at Northumberland House are famous and attended by all the great. Percy will dedicate his *Reliques* to her; Goldsmith will write a ballad for her amusement; and even as late as the publication of *The Life of Johnson* Boswell will brag of having "the honour of her Grace's correspondence, specimens of which adorn my archives." It is my impression that Lord Auchinleck had won Lady Northumberland's esteem by some piece of legal business he had done for her. At any rate, she had visited him at Auchinleck.

QUEENSBERRY (Charles Douglas), DUKE OF. Scotsman. Sixty-four years old. Succeeded to the dukedom at the age of thirteen. His wife, Lady Catherine Hyde, cousin to Queen Anne, is one of the most celebrated women of her day: Prior had written a flattering poem about her as a girl, and Walpole will add an equally flattering stanza when she is seventy-two. She was also the friend of Congreve, Thomson, Pope, and Gay; Gay was her special protégé, and lived in Queensberry House all the latter part of his life. The Duke was appointed Privy Councillor and Lord of the Bedchamber by George I and Vice-Admiral of Scotland by George II, but made the refusal of a license to Gay's *Polly* the occasion of a quarrel with

George II, threw up his appointments, and attached himself to the
Prince of Wales. He is accordingly *persona grata* to George III,
who has made him Privy Councillor and Keeper of the Great Seal
of Scotland, and during Boswell's stay in London will appoint him
Lord Justice General (nominal President of the High Court of
Justiciary, of which Lord Auchinleck is a judge). Distinguished
for his name and his rank; believed to be a person of influence because of his friendship with both the King and the Prime Minister.

SHERIDAN, THOMAS. Irishman. Forty-three years old. Educated
at Westminster School and Trinity College, Dublin. Went on the
stage as an undergraduate; acted in theatres in Dublin and London, managed the Theatre Royal in the former city. Though he has
received some high praise for his acting (Charles Churchill ranked
him as a tragedian next to Garrick), he thinks much more highly
of his work as a teacher of elocution and author of books on the
subject. His home in Henrietta Street, Covent Garden, is the resort
of eminent men; he has acquired enough influence with Alexander
Wedderburn, one of his Scots pupils, to persuade him to persuade
Lord Bute to give Dr. Johnson a pension. His special connection
with Boswell has been mentioned earlier in this Introduction. Husband of the clever Mrs. Frances Sheridan, who writes plays and
novels, and father of the famous Richard Brinsley Sheridan, at
this time a boy of eleven. A warm-hearted but opinionated man;
quick to take offence and bitterly unforgiving.

TEMPLE, WILLIAM JOHNSON. Englishman. Twenty-three years
old. Son of a Customs officer and Mayor of Berwick-on-Tweed; educated at the University of Edinburgh and at Cambridge. Like John
Johnston, met Boswell in Robert Hunter's Greek class in the autumn of 1755. Became Boswell's most intimate friend, Boswell at
that time being a bashful, priggish boy absorbed in poetry and
religion. Went on in 1758 to Cambridge to study law, and has
seen very little of Boswell since. Left Cambridge in 1761 and took
chambers in the Inner Temple; left London some time before Boswell's arrival to assist his father, who has become bankrupt and
has lost his post in the Customs. Has decided to abandon law for

the less brilliant but more certain provision of the Church, and at the end of the journal here printed has returned to Cambridge to qualify for holy orders. A man of spotless purity of morals, with the tastes of a scholar: regular, high-minded, timid, and complaining.

WILKES, JOHN. Englishman. Thirty-five years old. Son of a well-to-do London distiller, his mother a dissenter. Educated at a private school at Hertford and at the University of Leyden. Like Lord Auchinleck a lover of the classics. Separated from his wife, an heiress ten years his senior. Became High Sheriff of Buckinghamshire, then M.P. for Aylesbury. Believing that because of the malign influence of Lord Bute he has failed to secure the political rewards due him, he has set himself to harass Bute's government. He is now bringing out, in collaboration with the poet Charles Churchill, an anti-administration periodical called *The North Briton*. A man of learning and wit, of easy fine manners and imperturbable urbanity, he is in his political capacity capable of a degree of abuse for which "licentious" seems too mild a word. A profligate, a sceptic, a cynic, an opportunist, but never a hypocrite. Cross-eyed, very ugly.

§V

The manuscript of Boswell's London Journal of 1762–1763 is written throughout neatly and almost as legibly as a printed book on halves of sheets of uniform size, each folded to make two quarto leaves measuring $7\frac{1}{4}$ by $8\frac{3}{4}$ inches. These half-sheets are not "gathered" one inside another, but are used as units, the writing going straight through the four pages of each half-sheet. The manuscript runs to 736 pages (734 in Boswell's numbering). There are a few slight stains, but generally speaking the manuscript is in an excellent state of preservation. Unlike most of Boswell's journals, it has never suffered mutilation of any sort. In the present edition, which has been prepared for wide general reading, the spelling, capitalization, and punctuation have been reduced to accepted modern norms, and certain abbreviations and contractions have been expanded.[8] In a few cases where the spelling of a proper name in the manuscript appears to be eccentric but the "real" spelling remains doubtful, Boswell's spelling has been retained, with a footnote. All quotations in the Introduction and notes, whether from Boswell or other sources, have been standardized in the same fashion. Boswell's text has been broken up into paragraphs, following his own practice when (as in *The Journal of a Tour to the Hebrides*) he printed from his journal. A very few letters or short words inadvertently omitted by Boswell have been supplied silently, and one or two other clear inadvertencies (for example, mistakes in the date-lines) have been put right without notice. Where real perplexity exists, the reader is told so in a note. Notations which Boswell made in the margins of the manuscript at the time he was writing *The Life of Johnson* have been ignored when they added nothing of real interest to the original journal, or when it would have required a too-complicated note to explain them. Otherwise nothing has been omitted, nothing has been added, and nothing has been changed.

In numbering the footnotes, I have ventured to adopt a system rather common in eighteenth-century books, the system, in fact, which Boswell's printer employed in *The Life of Johnson*. Instead of numbering them in series starting over again with each page or each day of the journal, I have numbered them in recurring series of nine, disregarding pages and dates. The advantages of this system for editor and printer are considerable. It avoids the unattractive typography which results from the use of double reference figures in the text, and it eliminates the extensive resetting both of text and notes that is required in linotype composition if the notes

[8] The standard of spelling for all but proper names is the *Concise Oxford Dictionary*. For place-names the forms chosen are those of J. G. Bartholomew's *Survey Gazetteer of the British Isles* and *London Past and Present* by Peter Cunningham and H. B. Wheatley. Family names have been brought into conformity with the usage of *The Dictionary of National Biography*, Mrs. Margaret Stuart's *Scottish Family History*, G. E. Cokayne's *Complete Baronetage* and *Complete Peerage*, Sir James Balfour Paul's *Scots Peerage*, and various other special books of reference.

must begin a fresh series with each page. Such resetting is expensive and always introduces errors. The reader may be assured that he will find the system completely unambiguous and easy to follow.

I have received much assistance in preparing the edition from Miss Florence G. Marsh and Mr. Rufus Reiberg, students in the Department of English in the Yale Graduate School; and from Mr. Robert Burlin, Yale '50, holder of a bursary in Branford College.

The other members of the Editorial Committee have helped to define the editorial policy, have been in close touch with the work in all its stages, and have made many useful suggestions concerning the Introduction and the notes. Mr. T. B. Simpson has generously answered queries of all sorts, and has read the proofs. I wish also to acknowledge valuable assistance of one kind or another from Dr. Charles H. Bennett, Dr. R. W. Chapman, Professor Lewis P. Curtis, Mr. M. R. Dobie, Professor Archibald S. Foord, Mr. C. Beecher Hogan, Professor Helge Kökeritz, Dr. W. S. Lewis, Dr. C. A. Malcolm, Professor Henri Peyre, Mrs. Marion S. Pottle, Dr. L. F. Powell, and Professor Konstantin Reichardt.

F. A. P.

Yale University, New Haven
25 July 1950

He advised me to keep a journal of my life, fair and undisguised. He said it would be a very good exercise, and would yield me infinite satisfaction when the ideas were faded from my remembrance. I told him that I had done so ever since I left Scotland. He said he was very happy that I pursued so good a plan. And now, O my journal! art thou not highly dignified? Shalt thou not flourish tenfold? No former solicitations or censures could tempt me to lay thee aside; and now is there any argument which can outweigh the sanction of Mr. Samuel Johnson? He said indeed that I should keep it private, and that I might surely have a friend who would burn it in case of my death. For my own part, I have at present such an affection for this my journal that it shocks me to think of burning it. I rather encourage the idea of having it carefully laid up among the archives of Auchinleck. However, I cannot judge fairly of it now. Some years hence I may. I told Mr. Johnson that I put down all sorts of little incidents in it. "Sir," said he, "there is nothing too little for so little a creature as man. It is by studying little things that we attain the great knowledge of having as little misery and as much happiness as possible." [16 JULY 1763]

Journal from the time of my
leaving Scotland 15 Nov.r 1762.
Introduction

The ancient Philosopher certainly
gave a wise counsel when he said
"Know thyself". For surely this know
:ledge is of all the most impor:
:tant. I might enlarge upon this.
But grave & serious declamation
is not what I intend at present
A Man cannot know himself better
than by attending to the feelings
of his heart and to his external
Actions from which he may with
tollerable certainty judge what
manner of person he is. I have
therefore determined to keep a
dayly journal in which I shall
set down my various sentiments
and my various conduct which
will be not only usefull but very
agreable. It will give me a habit

Opening page of the manuscript.

Journal from the time of my
leaving Scotland 15 November 1762.

INTRODUCTION. The ancient philosopher certainly gave a wise counsel when he said, "Know thyself." For surely this knowledge is of all the most important. I might enlarge upon this. But grave and serious declamation is not what I intend at present. A man cannot know himself better than by attending to the feelings of his heart and to his external actions, from which he may with tolerable certainty judge "what manner of person he is."[1] I have therefore determined to keep a daily journal in which I shall set down my various sentiments and my various conduct, which will be not only useful but very agreeable. It will give me a habit of application and improve me in expression; and knowing that I am to record my transactions will make me more careful to do well. Or if I should go wrong, it will assist me in resolutions of doing better. I shall here put down my thoughts on different subjects at different times, the whims that may seize me and the sallies of my luxuriant imagination. I shall mark the anecdotes and the stories that I hear, the instructive or amusing conversations that I am present at, and the various adventures that I may have.

I was observing to my friend Erskine[2] that a plan of this kind was dangerous, as a man might in the openness of his heart say many things and discover many facts that might do him great harm if the journal should fall into the hands of my[3] enemies.

[1] James 1.24.　[2] See above, pp. 8, 29.
[3] Read "his." Boswell shifts his construction in the middle of a sentence, probably because he began a new page with "should."

Against which there is no perfect security. "Indeed," said he, "I hope there is no danger at all; for I fancy you will not set down your robberies on the highway, or the murders that you commit. As to other things there can be no harm." I laughed heartily at my friend's observation, which was so far true. I shall be upon my guard to mention nothing that can do harm. Truth shall ever be observed, and these things (if there should be any such) that require the gloss of falsehood shall be passed by in silence. At the same time I may relate things under borrowed names with safety that would do much mischief if particularly known.

In this way I shall preserve many things that would otherwise be lost in oblivion. I shall find daily employment for myself, which will save me from indolence and help to keep off the spleen, and I shall lay up a store of entertainment for my after life. Very often we have more pleasure in reflecting on agreeable scenes that we have been in than we had from the scenes themselves. I shall regularly record the business or rather the pleasure of every day. I shall not study much correctness, lest the labour of it should make me lay it aside altogether. I hope it will be of use to my worthy friend Johnston, and that while he laments my personal absence, this journal may in some measure supply that defect and make him happy.[4]

MONDAY 15 NOVEMBER. Elated with the thoughts of my journey to London, I got up. I called upon my friend Johnston, but found he was not come from the country, which vexed me a little, as I wished to bid him cordially adieu. However, I excused him to myself, and as Cairnie told me that people never took leave in France, I made the thing sit pretty easy.[5] I had a long serious con-

[4] See above, pp. 3, 8, 31. This entire journal was written with Johnston in mind, and was sent to him through the post in weekly parcels, each accompanied by a letter.

[5] Dr. John Cairnie, Edinburgh physician, as an active supporter of the exiled Stuarts had spent many years abroad. (When he died in 1791, Sir William Forbes reported to Boswell that he was dressed for burial in a shirt of Prince Charles Edward's, which he had carefully preserved for that purpose since

versation with my father[6] and mother. They were very kind to me. I felt parental affection was very strong towards me; and I felt a very warm filial regard for them. The scene of being a son setting out from home for the wide world and the idea of being my own master, pleased me much. I parted with my brother Davy, leaving him my best advices to be diligent at his business as a banker and to make rich[7] and be happy.

At ten I got into my chaise, and away I went. As I passed the Cross, the cadies and the chairmen bowed and seemed to say, "GOD prosper long our noble Boswell." I rattled down the High Street in high elevation of spirits, bowed and smiled to acquaintances, and took up my partner at Boyd's Close. He was a Mr. Stewart, eldest son to Ardsheal, who was forfeited in the year 1746.[8] He had made four voyages to the East Indies, and was now going out first mate. I made the chaise stop at the foot of the Canongate; asked pardon of Mr. Stewart for a minute; walked to the Abbey of Holyroodhouse, went round the Piazzas, bowed thrice: once to the Palace itself, once to the crown of Scotland above the gate in front, and once to the venerable old Chapel.[9] I next stood in the court before the Palace, and bowed thrice to Arthur Seat, that lofty romantic mountain

---

1745.) He also made something of a business of accompanying Scots patients to the Continent. Boswell had retained his services in a private matter later to be divulged.

[6] See above, p. 27, AUCHINLECK, LORD.

[7] A Scotticism. See above, p. 22, for explanation of the editorial policy followed in this volume with regard to Boswell's deviations from standard English.

[8] Whose estate was forfeited by the Government because of his active participation in the Rebellion of 1745.

[9] "The Palace of Holyroodhouse bears a resemblance to that of Hampton Court. It is of a quadrangular form, with a court in the centre, surrounded with piazzas. . . . Over the door, in the front of the Palace, is a small cupola for a clock, the roof of which is an imperial crown in stone-work" (Hugo Arnot, *The History of Edinburgh*, 1788, pp. 305–6). This passage, with what follows, shows that Boswell's nationalism and sense of locality, though gen-

on which I have so often strayed in my days of youth, indulged meditation and felt the raptures of a soul filled with ideas of the magnificence of God and his creation. Having thus gratified my agreeable whim and superstitious humour, I felt a warm glow of satisfaction. Indeed, I have a strong turn to what the cool part of mankind have named superstition. But this proceeds from my genius for poetry, which ascribes many fanciful properties to everything. This I have great pleasure from; as I have now by experience and reflection gained the command of it so far that I can keep it within just bounds by the power of reason, without losing the agreeable feeling and play to the imagination which it bestows. I am surely much happier in this way than if I just considered Holyroodhouse as so much stone and lime which has been put together in a certain way, and Arthur Seat as so much earth and rock raised above the neighbouring plains.

We then pursued our journey. I found my companion a jolly honest plain fellow. I set out with a determined resolution against *shaving*, that is to say, playing upon people;[1] and therefore I talked sensibly and roughly. We did very well till we passed Old Camus, when one of the wheels of our chaise was so much broke that it was of no use. The driver proposed that we should mount the horses and ride to Berwick. But this I would by no means agree to; and as my partner let me be the principal man and take the direction of our journey, I made the chaise be dragged on to Ayton, where we waited till the driver rode to Berwick and brought us a chaise. Never did I pass three hours more unhappily. We were set down in a cold ale-house in a little dirty village. We had a beefsteak ill-dressed and had nothing to drink but thick muddy beer. We were both out of humour so that we could not speak. We tried to sleep but in vain. We only got a drowsy headache. We were scorched by the fire on the one hand and shivering with frost on the other. At

erally controlled by "reason" so far as outward expression was concerned, were inwardly as enthusiastic and romantic as Sir Walter Scott's.

[1] See above, p. 8, the Soaping Club.

last our chaise came, and we got to Berwick about twelve at night. We had a slice of hard dry toast, a bowl of warm negus, and went comfortable to bed.

TUESDAY 16 NOVEMBER. We set off at six; breakfasted at Alnwick, where we had with us a Captain Elliot of the East Indies, and were hearty. Stewart and I began now to be acquainted and to talk about the Peace[2] and voyages and ways of living. We had a safe day, and got at night to Durham.

WEDNESDAY 17 NOVEMBER. We had a very good day of it, and got at night to Doncaster.

THURSDAY 18 NOVEMBER. We chatted a good deal. Stewart told me that some blacks in India were attacking their boat in order to plunder it, and that he shot two with his own hand. In the afternoon between Stamford and Stilton there was a young unruly horse in the chaise which run away with the driver, and jumping to one side of the road, we were overturned. We got a pretty severe rap. Stewart's head and my arm were somewhat hurt. However, we got up and pursued our way. During our two last stages this night, which we travelled in the dark, I was a good deal afraid of robbers. A great many horrid ideas filled my mind. There is no passion so distressing as fear, which gives us great pain and makes us appear contemptible in our own eyes to the last degree. However, I affected resolution, and as each of us carried a loaded pistol in his hand, we were pretty secure. We got at night to Biggleswade.

FRIDAY 19 NOVEMBER. It was very cold. Stewart was as effeminate as I. I asked him how he, who shivered if a pane of glass was broke in a post-chaise, could bear the severe hardship of a sea life. He gave me to understand that necessity made anything be endured. Indeed this is very true. For when the mind knows that it cannot help itself by struggling, it quietly and patiently submits to whatever load is laid upon it. When we came upon Highgate hill and had a view of London, I was all life and joy. I repeated Cato's

[2] See above, p. 17. The treaty was not actually signed until 10 February 1763, but hostilities had already ceased.

soliloquy on the immortality of the soul,[3] and my soul bounded forth to a certain prospect of happy futurity. I sung all manner of songs, and began to make one about an amorous meeting with a pretty girl, the burthen of which was as follows:

> She gave me *this*, I gave her *that*;
> And tell me, had she not tit for tat?

I gave three huzzas, and we went briskly in.

I got from Digges[4] a list of the best houses on the road, and also a direction to a good inn at London. I therefore made the boy drive me to Mr. Hayward's, at the Black Lion, Water Lane, Fleet Street. The noise, the crowd, the glare of shops and signs agreeably confused me. I was rather more wildly struck than when I first came to London. My companion could not understand my feelings. He considered London just as a place where he was to receive orders from the East India Company. We now parted, with saying that we had agreed well and been happy, and that we should keep up the acquaintance. I then had a bit of dinner, got myself shaved and cleaned, and had my landlord, a civil jolly man, to take a glass of wine with me. I was all in a flutter at having at last got to the place which I was so madly fond of, and being restrained, had formed so many wild schemes to get back to. I had recourse to philosophy, and so rendered myself calm.

I immediately went to my friend Douglas's, surgeon in Pall Mall, a kind-hearted, plain, sensible man, where I was cordially received.[5] His wife is a good-humoured woman, and is that sort of

---

[3] In Addison's famous play:

> It must be so—Plato, thou reasonest well!
> Else why this pleasing hope, this fond desire,
> This longing after immortality? . . .

[4] West Digges, leading man in the theatrical company at Edinburgh, had long been Boswell's ideal of manly bearing and social elegance. He was especially captivating in the part of Macheath in *The Beggar's Opera*. See below, p. 62.

[5] Boswell had made his acquaintance in 1760. Possibly a relative.

character which is often met with in England: very lively without much wit. Her fault is speaking too much, which often tires people. He was my great adviser as to everything; and in the mean time insisted that I should have a bed in his house till I got a lodging to my mind. I agreed to come there next day. I went to Covent Garden —*Every Man in His Humour*. Woodward played Bobadil finely. He entertained me much. It was fine after the fatigues of my journey to find myself snug in a theatre, my body warm and my mind elegantly amused. I went to my inn, had some negus, and went comfortably to bed.

SATURDAY 20 NOVEMBER. I got into a hackney-coach with my baggage and drove to Douglas's. We calculated my expenses, and I found that to live would require great economy.[6] However, I was upon honour to do my best. I strolled about all the forenoon calling for different people, but found nobody in. I went and saw a collection of wild beasts.[7] I felt myself bold, easy, and happy. Only I had a kind of uneasiness from feeling no amazing difference between my existence now and at Edinburgh. I dined at Douglas's; sat in all the afternoon and wrote letters.

SUNDAY 21 NOVEMBER. I got up well and enjoyed my good situation. I had a handsome dining-room and bed-chamber, just in Pall Mall, the finest part of the town; I was in pursuit of my commission, which I was vastly fond of; and I had money enough to live like a gentleman.

I went to Mayfair Chapel and heard prayers and an excellent sermon from the Book of Job on the comforts of piety. I was in a fine

[6] Boswell drew up a careful "Scheme of Living" on separate sheets. See below, p. 335. About this time he began also to write a series of memoranda, one octavo page every day, apparently jotted down the last thing before he went to bed or the first thing in the morning before he put on his clothes. In them he tells himself, always in the second person, what to eat, what to wear, what supplies to get in, what books to read; makes schedules for calls; gives directions for pleasures; orders himself to keep his journal posted; implores himself to try to attain to greater gravity. These memoranda are still for the most part unpublished. Some of them will be quoted later in these notes.

[7] Probably the royal menagerie in the Tower.

frame. And I thought that GOD really designed us to be happy. I shall certainly be a religious old man. I was much so in youth. I have now and then flashes of devotion, and it will one day burn with a steady flame.

I waited on Mr. George Lewis Scott, who was very kind and polite to me,[8] and on the Laird of Macfarlane, with whom I was a good deal diverted. He was keenly interested in the reigning contests between Scots and English. He talked much against the Union. He said we were perfect underlings; that our riches were carried out of the country; that no town but Glasgow had any advantage of trade by it, and that many others were hurt by it.[9]

I dined with Dr. Pringle,[1] where were Mr. Murdoch, the publisher, or rather the editor, of Thomson; Mr. Seymours, a travelling governor,[2] and some more, all Scotch. I found the Doctor in the way of discouraging me, which as from my father's friend I took patiently and intended to get the better of. The conversation was on indifferent common topics: the Peace, Lord Bute, footmen, and cookery.

I went to Douglas's and drank tea. I next went and called in Southampton Street, Strand, for Miss Sally Forrester, my first love, who lived at the Blue Periwig. I found that the people of the house

[8] Scott, born at Hanover of Scottish parents, a friend both of Lord Auchinleck and the poet James Thomson, author of *The Seasons,* had formerly been subpreceptor to George III. He was a brilliant mathematician, and at this time held appointment as one of the commissioners of excise.

[9] See above, p. 16. The Laird of Macfarlane, a renowned antiquary, was very stiff in his Scottishness. As will appear later (2 December), his wife, much younger than himself, was Andrew Erskine's sister.

[1] John Pringle, Physician General to the Army, has been called the founder of modern military medicine. He was at this time practising in London and building up a very considerable reputation as a scientist. Among his close friends were Lord Auchinleck and Benjamin Franklin. He was made a baronet in 1766.

[2] Boswell's spelling has been retained because the gentleman he refers to has not been identified, but the right spelling is probably Symers or Symmers. A travelling governor is a tutor who accompanies his pupil abroad.

were broke and dead, and could hear nothing of her. I also called for Miss Jeany Wells in Barrack Street, Soho, but found that she was fled, they knew not whither, and had been ruined with extravagance.[3] Good heaven, thought I, what an amazing change in two years! I saw in the year 1760 these young ladies in all the glow of beauty and admiration; and now they are utterly erased or worse. I then called on Love, and saw him and Mrs. Love and Billy.[4] I eat a tart there. He showed me a pantomime, called *The Witches*, of his.

Since I came up, I have begun to acquire a composed genteel character very different from a rattling uncultivated one which for some time past I have been fond of. I have discovered that we may be in some degree whatever character we choose. Besides, practice forms a man to anything. I was now happy to find myself cool, easy, and serene.

MONDAY 22 NOVEMBER. I strolled about all day looking for lodgings. At night I went to Drury Lane and saw Garrick play Scrub and the Farmer returned, and Love play Boniface, which brought the Canongate full in my head.[5] I was exceedingly well entertained.

TUESDAY 23 NOVEMBER. I went into the City and called for

[3] Miss Sally Forrester and Miss Jeany Wells are explained later, pp. 215, 236, 277. "Broke and dead" means "had gone bankrupt and had since died." For Barrack Street read Berwick Street. (In British pronunciation the two words are very similar.)

[4] James Dance, who took the name of Love when he went on the stage, had formerly been manager of the theatre at Edinburgh. He had long been a confidential friend of Boswell, who wrote his first journal at Love's request, and had lent Love money, as this journal somewhat tediously iterates. Earlier in the season Love had joined the company at Drury Lane. Some critics considered him the best Falstaff of the time. His son Billy (William Dance, at this time seven years old) attained some celebrity as a musician.

[5] For Garrick, see above, p. 29. "Scrub" and "Boniface" are parts in George Farquhar's popular comedy, *The Beaux' Stratagem*. *The Farmer's Return from London* was a farce by Garrick himself. The Edinburgh Theatre was in the Canongate.

George Home, Lord Kames's son.[6] As Lord Eglinton had used me neglectfully, and as I considered him as not to be depended upon, I determined to keep clear of him as a patron, but to like him as a companion; and if he offered to do me any service, good and well, but I should ask no assistance from him.[7] I called thrice, but he was out. This day I received a formal card of invitation to dine with him. I went, and was warmly received. Finding myself with him in the very dining-room where in my days of youthful fire I had been so happy, melted me much. Mylne the architect dined with us.[8] We talked on a rude and on a polished state of society. I kept up a *retenue* and spoke only when I was sure that I was right. I drank tea. I parted from him on a very good footing.

WEDNESDAY 24 NOVEMBER. I called on Dodsley, and found that although he had refused to take the hazard of publishing my *Cub*, that it had sold well, and that there was thirteen shillings of profit, which I made him pay me down.[9] Never did I set so high a value on a sum. I was much in spirits. I still went about seeking lodgings, but could find none that would answer. At night I called on Pringle. He was sour. Indeed, he is a good deal so, although a sensible learned man, a good philosopher, and an excellent physician. By the cheerful ease of my address I made him smile and be very kind to me. I consulted him about all my plans. I began to find that £200 a year was very little. I left him before twelve. I began to tire much of Mrs. Douglas, she spoke so much. And I was rather somewhat low-spirited.

[6] See above, p. 10. Lord Kames's name was Henry Home. "The City" is the part of London east of Temple Bar. Pall Mall, where Boswell was staying, is in Westminster.

[7] See above, pp. 6, 29. Boswell subjects Eglinton's character to minute analysis later in this journal.

[8] Robert Mylne (a Scotsman, of course) was at this time building Blackfriars Bridge.

[9] See above, p. 7. The poem had been published by the well-known booksellers Robert and James Dodsley, but Boswell's correspondence shows that he himself had guaranteed the costs. The Dodsley he met on this occasion was the younger brother, James.

THURSDAY 25 NOVEMBER. I had been in a bad situation during the night for I dreamt that Johnston did not care for me. That he came to see me set off on a long journey, and that he seemed dissipated and tired, and left me before I got away.[1] I lay abed very gloomy. I thought London did me no good. I rather disliked it; and I thought of going back to Edinburgh immediately. In short, I was most miserable.

I got up and breakfasted. I got a card from Lord Eglinton asking me to the House of Lords. I accordingly went and heard the King make his speech.[2] It was a very noble thing. I here beheld the King of Great Britain on his throne with the crown on his head addressing both the Lords and the Commons. His Majesty spoke better than any man I ever heard: with dignity, delicacy, and ease. I admired him. I wished much to be acquainted with him.

I went to Love's and drank tea. I had now been some time in town without female sport. I determined to have nothing to do with whores, as my health was of great consequence to me. I went to a girl with whom I had an intrigue at Edinburgh, but my affection cooling, I had left her. I knew she was come up. I waited on her and tried to obtain my former favours, but in vain. She would by no means listen.[3] I was really unhappy for want of women. I thought it hard to be in such a place without them. I picked up a girl in the Strand; went into a court with intention to enjoy her in armour.[4] But she had none. I toyed with her. She wondered at my size, and said if I ever took a girl's maidenhead, I would make her

---

[1] See above, p. 40, the beginning of the entry for 15 November. That Boswell was really deeply distressed by Johnston's failure to see him off is shown by his unpublished letters, now at Yale. He had especially counted on Johnston's company in his ritual farewell to Scotland (same entry).

[2] Opening the session of Parliament. It dealt with the Peace.

[3] She was probably a servant; the juxtaposition of references to her and to Love here and in the memoranda hints that she was a servant in Love's family. (Mrs. Love had just "come up" from Edinburgh.) In the memoranda and in earlier notes, where she is several times mentioned, she receives no other designation than the Greek character ϕ. Perhaps Phemie or Effie?

[4] That is, making use of a prophylactic sheath.

squeak. I gave her a shilling, and had command enough of myself to go without touching her. I afterwards trembled at the danger I had escaped. I resolved to wait cheerfully till I got some safe girl or was liked by some woman of fashion.

I went to Lord Eglinton's; John Ross Mackye was there. We had a little bit of supper, and I was easy. I have never yet mentioned General Douglas, whom I found to be a plain, civil man. I learnt that the Duke of Queensberry was not to be in town till Sunday, so that till then I could know nothing certain of my commission.[5]

FRIDAY 26 NOVEMBER. I waited on Lord Adam Gordon, who was very polite.[6] I liked to see a Colonel of the Guards in his elegant house. I was much difficulted about lodgings. A variety I am sure I saw, I dare say fifty. I was amused in this way. At last I fixed in Downing Street, Westminster.[7] I took a lodging up two pair of stairs with the use of a handsome parlour all the forenoon, for which I agreed to pay forty guineas a year, but I took it for a fortnight first, by way of a trial. I also made bargain that I should dine with the family whenever I pleased, at a shilling a time. My landlord was Mr. Terrie, chamber-keeper to the Office for Trade and Plantations. He was originally from the Shire of Moray. He had a wife but no children. The street was a genteel street, within a few steps of the Parade; near the House of Commons, and very healthful. I went to Mr. Cochrane, my banker, and received £25, my allowance every six weeks.

I then dined with Lord Eglinton. Lord Elibank was there, a

[5] John Ross Mackye was a Scots M.P. Boswell had been told before leaving home that Lieutenant-General Archibald Douglas, an officer with a distinguished military record and a relative of the Duke of Queensberry, could help him in getting a commission. For the Duke of Queensberry, see above, pp. 10, 33.

[6] Lord Adam was son of the Duke of Gordon. He had been recommended to Boswell "for introduction into life."

[7] Downing Street is widely known now as the street where the Prime Minister has his official residence. The house in which Boswell secured rooms has since been demolished.

man of great genius, great knowledge, and much whim, and Sir
James Macdonald, a remarkable young man of good parts and
great application. So that he knows a great deal. Also Sir Simeon
Stuart, much of a gentleman.[8] We had much ingenious talk. But
I am dull, and cannot recollect it. Before this I saw *The Witches*, a
pantomime. I felt composed, serene, happy.

SATURDAY 27 NOVEMBER. I walked into the City and or-
dered a remaining parcel of my *Cub* to be sent to Donaldson.[9] I then
breakfasted at Child's Coffee-house, read the political papers, and
had some chat with citizens.[1] On Sunday I had called at the Inner
Temple for my old friend Temple, but did not find him. This day
I called again. He was out of town. I longed to see him.[2]

I then went to Lord Eglinton's. Finding him very obliging, I
was glad to take the benefit of it. He carried me to Covent Garden
in a coach and bid me wait in the Bedford Coffee-house till he sent
for me. In a few minutes the famous Mr. Beard of Covent Garden
Theatre came for me and carried me up a great many steps to a
handsome room above the theatre, in which was met the Beefsteak
Club, a society which has subsisted these thirty years. The room
where it met was once burnt. The Gridiron (in Scotch, *brander*)
was almost consumed, but a thin image of it remained entire. That
they have fixed in the stucco in the roof. The president sits in a
chair under a canopy, above which you have in golden letters, *Beef
and Liberty*. We were entertained by the Club.[3] Lord Sandwich

[8] All Scots except Sir Simeon Stuart, who sounds Scottish but was actually a
Hampshire man. He was Chamberlain of the Exchequer. Johnson admired
Lord Elibank's conversation. Sir James Macdonald (Eglinton's nephew), at
this time an undergraduate at Oxford, was already called "the Marcellus of
the North" because of his learning. He died at Rome in 1766.
[9] Alexander Donaldson was Boswell's publisher in Edinburgh.
[1] See above, p. 23.
[2] See above, pp. 3, 34. He returned to London briefly in April, 1763, but not to
resume his legal studies. This journal reveals the rather surprising fact that
the correspondence between Boswell and his "dearest friend" had completely
lapsed for some months.
[3] Beard was the manager of Covent Garden. He was "famous" as an actor and

was in the chair, a jolly, hearty, lively man. It was a very mixed society: Lord Eglinton, Mr. Beard, Colonel West of the Guards, Mr. Havard the actor, Mr. Churchill the poet, Mr. Wilkes the author of *The North Briton*, and many more.[4] We had nothing to eat but beefsteaks, and had wine and punch in plenty and freedom. We had a number of songs.

Lord Eglinton and I talked a little privately. He imagined me much in the style that I was three years ago: raw, curious, volatile, credulous. He little knew the experience I had got and the notions and the composure that I had obtained by reflection. "My Lord," said I, "I am now a little wiser." "Not so much as you think," said he. "For, as a boy who has just learned the alphabet when he begins to make out words thinks himself a great master of reading, so the little advance you have made in prudence appears very great, as it is so much before what you was formerly." I owned that there was some justice in what he said. And I hoped that a little diffidence would help to keep me safe. I told him I was sorry that my dedication without leave to the Duke of York had been ill-taken, and I

---

singer. Handel composed some of his greatest tenor parts expressly for him. The Sublime Society of Beefsteaks was founded in 1735 by John Rich, the celebrated harlequin. This description of Boswell's furnishes details not otherwise recorded.

[4] The group Boswell names is certainly "mixed." Sandwich, an able but profligate man, was at this time closely associated with Wilkes and Churchill (see above, pp. 27, 35) in the orgies of the notorious Monks of Medmenham Abbey; a little later he earned the soubriquet of Jemmy Twitcher for impeaching Wilkes before the House of Lords for obscene and seditious libel. ("That Jemmy Twitcher should peach me, I own surprised me."—Macheath in *The Beggar's Opera*.) According to Horace Walpole, Sandwich himself was expelled from the Society of Beefsteaks as a consequence. Churchill in his *Rosciad* had pilloried Havard for his "easy vacant face" and general insipidity. We have Wilkes's own testimony that Eglinton was "a good-humoured, laughing fellow," but as a friend of Lord Bute and a Lord of the Bedchamber he must have had to refrain, in public at least, from any appearance of intimacy with Wilkes and Churchill. He was certainly offended by *The Prophecy of Famine*. See below, p. 166.

insisted that he should make it up and bring us together, which he half-assented to.[5]

My Lord's character is very particular. He is a man of uncommon genius for everything: strong good sense, great quickness of apprehension and liveliness of fancy, with a great deal of humour. He was neglected in his education, so that his knowledge from books is superficial. Yet he has picked up an infinite variety of knowledge from conversation. He has at the same time a flightiness, a reverie and absence of mind, with a disposition to downright trifling. Pope's lines may be applied to him:

> With too much quickness ever to be taught;
> With too much thinking to have common thought.

He is very selfish and deceitful, yet he has much good nature and affection. He now declared to me that he liked me as well as ever. And I believe he spoke truth. For I have such an opinion of myself as to imagine that nobody can be more agreeable company to him. Yet I kept aloof in some measure, and, finding myself too fond of him, I pulled the reins hard.

We parted at seven. I went to my lodging in Downing Street and put up my things, then went and saw the King and Queen pass from the Opera, and then saw the Guards drawn up in the court of the Palace while the moon shone and showed their splendour. I was all gentle felicity, and thought on an Edinburgh Saturday passed in a variety of amusing scenes. I had now got a genteel violet-coloured frock suit. I went home, sat a while with my landlord and landlady. They made too much work about me. I went to bed.

SUNDAY 28 NOVEMBER. I breakfasted with Mr. Douglas. I went to St. James's Church and heard service and a good sermon on

[5] See above, p. 7. H. R. H. Edward Augustus, Duke of York, a year and a half older than Boswell, was heir presumptive to the throne when Boswell met him in 1760. He was a violinist of some distinction, a rake, and what the eighteenth century called a "rattle." His friendly attentions quite turned Boswell's head. There is no record that Eglinton did bring the two together again. The Duke died of a fever at Monaco in 1767.

"By what means shall a young man learn to order his ways," in which the advantages of early piety were well displayed. What a curious, inconsistent thing is the mind of man! In the midst of divine service I was laying plans for having women, and yet I had the most sincere feelings of religion. I imagine that my want of belief is the occasion of this, so that I can have all the feelings. I would try to make out a little consistency this way. I have a warm heart and a vivacious fancy. I am therefore given to love, and also to piety or gratitude to God, and to the most brilliant and showy method of public worship.[6]

I then walked in the Park and went home to dinner, which was just a good joint of veal and a pudding. This they told me was their usual fare, which I approved of. I found my landlord rather too free. Therefore I carried myself with reserve and something of state.

At six I went to Mr. Sheridan's. He had been at Court and was splendidly dressed.[7] He met me at the door with a cordial warmth. I felt a little out, as his plan for me of the Temple was changed. He is a man of great genius and understands propriety of speech better than anybody. But he is rather too much of an enthusiast in favour of his darling study. He has read much and seen much and is very good company. I was introduced to Mrs. Sheridan, a woman of very homely looks, but very sensible and very clever, as appears from her *Memoirs of Miss Sidney Bidulph.*[8] I let myself appear by

[6] He had made plans for both church and fornication in his memorandum written that morning: " . . . to St. James's Church. . . . Then L.'s, as he's at club, and try old Canongate [girl]." The next day: "At eleven call L., and try all rhetoric old girl. . . . Concert with ϕ and vow eternal constancy and regard." (Much of this is in shorthand cipher.) The preacher's text (Ps. 119.9: "Wherewithal shall a young man cleanse his way") must have seemed uncomfortably apt.

[7] See above, pp. 8, 34. The Court had been held "to compliment his Majesty on the Preliminaries of Peace being ratified and exchanged between Great Britain, France, and Spain."

[8] "Mrs. Sheridan was a most agreeable companion to an intellectual man. She

degrees, and I found that I was agreeable to her, which flattered
me a good deal.

I asked for Mr. Samuel Johnson.[9] Sheridan said he now could
not bear him, because he had taken a pension of three hundred a
year from the Court, by the particular interest of Lord Bute, and
yet he still railed against the royal family and the Scots minister.
I said I imagined he put it upon this: that the pension was not a
favour but a reward *due* to his merit, and therefore he would show
still the same principles of opposition freely and openly. "No, Sir,"
said he. "Johnson took it as a favour; waited on Lord Bute, said he
could not find an English word to express what he felt, and was
therefore obliged to have recourse to the French: 'I am *pénétré*
with his Majesty's goodness.' This being the case, his business was
to be silent; or, if called upon to give his opinion, to say, 'Gentlemen, my sentiments are just the same that they were. But an obli-
gation forbids me to say much.' " It hurt me to find Sheridan abusing a man for whom I have heard him profess the greatest regard.
He added, "The bearish manners of Johnson were insupportable
without the idea of his having a good heart. But since he has been
made the object of royal favour, his character has been sifted and
is bad."[1] I drank tea and coffee and was very well. I came home and
went to bed.

MONDAY 29 NOVEMBER. I breakfasted with my landlord. I
then called at Love's, saw Mr. George Garrick (very like his
brother), admired Miss Pope of Drury Lane at the opposite win-

---

was sensible, ingenious, unassuming, yet communicative. I recollect with
satisfaction many pleasing hours which I passed under the hospitable roof
of her husband, who was to me a very kind friend. Her novel entitled *Memoirs of Miss Sidney Bidulph* contains an excellent moral . . . Johnson paid
her this high compliment upon it: 'I know not, Madam, that you have a
right, upon moral principles, to make your readers suffer so much' " (*Life
of Johnson*, beginning of 1763). *Miss Sidney Bidulph* was published in 1761.
[9] See above, p. 30.
[1] Boswell learned later that Sheridan had a more personal reason for his
change of heart with regard to Johnson. See below, p. 90.

dow,[2] sauntered a while, then dined Lady Frances Erskine's. Both
her sons were there, and Mr. Grant, son to Sir Ludovic. We were
very genteel and very dull. We just said the same things that everybody in town were saying. As I have no conversation of this day to
mark, I must be obliged to some former days.[3]

Lord Eglinton said that a savage had as much pleasure in eating his rude meals and hearing the rough notes of the bagpipe as a
man in polished society had in the most elegant entertainment and
in hearing the finest music. Mr. Mylne very justly observed that to
judge of their happiness we must have the decision of a being superior to them both, who should feel the pleasure of each; and in
that case it would be found that although each had his taste fully
gratified, yet that the civilized man, having his taste more refined
and susceptible of higher enjoyment, must be acknowledged to
have the greatest happiness.

Sir James Macdonald and Lord Elibank descanted much on the
character of Hannibal and admired him most for his thorough
knowledge of the people that he had to deal with. Lord Elibank is
a man of strong genius, great reading, and lively imagination. Sir
James Macdonald has natural quickness, and has led a life of hard
study these many years, so that he has got an excellent foundation.
How he will build upon it is hard to say. Mr. Sheridan said if he is
not able to throw out his knowledge with spirit it will not avail him
much. For a bookcase contains more learning than he. Sir James is
too much of the fellow of a college to be easy and agreeable in company, as he always introduces some learned subject. He has also the
appearance of too much haughtiness, which is disgusting. Lord
Eglinton said that he[4] knew nothing but men, women, and horses.
Sir James said that the proper knowledge of mankind was to be
gained from history. My Lord said that he who knew men only in
this way was like one who had got the theory of anatomy perfectly,
but who in practice would find himself very awkward and liable

[2] Miss Jane Pope, Drury Lane's great actress in soubrette roles "of the pert
order," was at this time only twenty. Churchill had given her high praise in
The Rosciad.   [3] 23, 26, and 28 November.   [4] That is, he himself.

to mistakes. That he again who knew men by observation was like one who picked up anatomy by practice, but who like all empirics would for a long time be liable to gross errors. In my opinion, history is more useful for understanding the great lines of men's characters when united in great societies, although, to be sure, the hearts and understandings of individuals are there in some measure displayed. But to know men, a long experience of life and manners is most useful. History and that together render the knowledge complete.

TUESDAY 30 NOVEMBER. I had young Douglas of Douglas[5] and young Douglas of Pall Mall, both Westminster scholars, to breakfast with me. I went with them and took a walk to Westminster Abbey; among the tombs was solemn and happy.

I dined with Mr. Sheridan. He was quite enthusiastic about oratory. He said Garrick had no real feeling; that his talents for mimicry enabled him to put on the appearance of feeling, and that the nicety of his art might please the fancy and make us cry, "That's fine." But as it was art, it could never touch the heart. Mr. Sheridan's distinction was just, but does not apply to Garrick, because he often has touched the heart and drawn tears from multitudes. After dinner, old Victor, many years joint-manager of the Dublin stage, poet laureate of Ireland and author of the *History of the Theatres*, came in. He is an honest, indolent, conversable man, and has a great many anecdotes. He told us that he was one day dining with Mr. Booth, when Mrs. Booth brought in a girl to sing some lively songs. She was much liked and taken into the theatre at twenty shillings a week, and who was this but Mrs. Pritchard, who had risen so high in dramatic fame.[6]

Sheridan said there were not three lines in a play spoke well on

[5] The dubious heir of the famous Douglas Cause, in which Boswell's feelings were later to be so deeply involved. He was at this time fourteen.
[6] Mrs. Hannah Pritchard (b. 1711) divided the honours in tragedy with Mrs. Susannah Maria Cibber. Johnson, though he considered her "a vulgar idiot" in private life, admitted that on the stage she "seemed to be inspired by gentility and understanding."

Drury Lane stage. Victor looked at me and shook his head. "With-out propriety of speech," said Sheridan, "all the powers of acting are nothing. It is just like time in dancing. And let a dancer play never so many tricks and feats of agility, he will not be applauded if he does not observe time." This comparison is not just. Because the greatest part of an audience have ear enough to judge of time, but very, very few can judge of propriety of speech, as that is a thing never taught them; and therefore the ornaments of action must please them independent of that. He inveighed much against the directors of his English scheme at Edinburgh, as if they thought from the beginning of knocking it on the head, and so had lost an opportunity of improvement and honour to their country.[7]

I was very easy, as he never mentioned my own plan, which I resolved by degrees to talk freely to him of. He asked me to come to his house in a family way whenever I had nothing to engage me elsewhere. I resolved to comply with his kind invitation. I found a good table, ease, and hospitality, and useful and agreeable con-versation there.

I thought my present lodgings too dear, and therefore looked about and found a place in Crown Street, Westminster, an obscure street but pretty lodgings at only £22 a year. Much did I ruminate with regard to lodgings. Sometimes I considered that a fine lodging denoted a man of great fashion, but then I thought that few people would see it and therefore the expense would be hid, whereas my business was to make as much show as I could with my small allow-ance. I thought that an elegant place to come home to was very agreeable and would inspire me with ideas of my own dignity; but then I thought it would be hard if I had not a proportionable show in other things, and that it was better to come gradually to a fine place than from a fine to a worse. I therefore resolved to take the Crown Street place, and told my present landlord that I intended to leave him. He told me that he was very sorry, and that he would allow me to make my own terms rather than quit his house; for he was in such circumstances that he was not obliged to let lodgings

[7] See above, p. 8.

for bread, and that as I was extremely agreeable to the family, he begged I would stay, and he would let me have my three rooms for £30. I thanked him for his good opinion of me, but told him that economy at present was my object, although I was very happy in his house; and that I could not ask him to let me have three rooms in a genteel street as cheap as two in an obscure one. He paused a while and then told me that I should have them at the same price. He only begged that I would not mention it, as he certainly let them below value. I therefore struck a bargain and settled myself for a year.

I do think this a very strong proof of my being agreeable. For here was I, a perfect stranger to my landlord, who showed so great regard for me. I thought my seeking a lodging was like seeking a wife. Sometimes I aimed at one of two guineas a week, like a rich lady of quality. Sometimes at one guinea, like a knight's daughter; and at last fixed on £22 a year, like the daughter of a good gentleman of moderate fortune. Now when fixed, I felt very comfortable, having got rid of the inconstant roving disposition of a bachelor as to lodging. However, I hope my choice of a wife will be more elegant. I hope that shall not be in haste. When I strolled in high spirits through London, full of gay expectation, I considered how much happier I was than if I had been married last year to Miss Colquhoun or Miss Bruce, and been a poor regular animal tied down to one.[8] I thanked Johnston for his kind advices.

WEDNESDAY 1 DECEMBER. The Duke of Queensberry was now come to town. I had called once or twice, but had never found him. Mrs. Douglas told me that Old Quant the porter would do nothing without the silver key. I therefore called today, and chatting a little with the surly dog, "Mr. Quant," said I, "I give you a great deal of trouble"; bowed and smiled, and put half a crown into his hand. He told me the Duke would be glad to see me next morning at nine.

On Tuesday I wanted to have a silver-hilted sword, but upon examining my pockets as I walked up the Strand, I found that I

[8] See above, p. 8.

had left the most of my guineas at home and had not enough to pay for it with me. I determined to make a trial of the civility of my fellow-creatures, and what effect my external appearance and address would have. I accordingly went to the shop of Mr. Jefferys, sword-cutter to his Majesty, looked at a number of his swords, and at last picked out a very handsome one at five guineas. "Mr. Jefferys," said I, "I have not money here to pay for it. Will you trust me?" "Upon my word, Sir," said he, "you must excuse me. It is a thing we never do to a stranger." I bowed genteelly and said, "Indeed, Sir, I believe it is not right." However, I stood and looked at him, and he looked at me. "Come, Sir," cried he, "I will trust you." "Sir," said I, "if you had not trusted me, I should not have bought it from you." He asked my name and place of abode, which I told him. I then chose a belt, put the sword on, told him I would call and pay it tomorrow, and walked off. I called this day and paid him. "Mr. Jefferys," said I, "there is your money. You paid me a very great compliment. I am much obliged to you. But pray don't do such a thing again. It is dangerous." "Sir," said he, "we know our men. I would have trusted you with the value of a hundred pounds." This I think was a good adventure and much to my honour.

Some time after I came to London, I met with Mr. Mayne from Scotland, who reminded me that he had got me admitted a member of the Society for the Encouragement of Arts and Sciences in the year 1760; that the subscription was two guineas a year, and that three years were now unpaid, so that I owed six guineas. This was a most alarming piece of news to a man who was trying to calculate a livelihood out of moderate finances. However, I put the best face on it: told Mayne that I imagined the neglect of payment for one year made a man lose his place, so that I had but two guineas to pay. However, if I found it otherwise, I should pay the whole. This was really my idea.

I went and called on Mr. Box, the collector (admirably named); found him a very civil man; told him that I had been in Scotland almost ever since my admission to the Society, and that

I was now uncertain how long I might stay in London. If therefore it was possible to have my name struck off the list so that I should never be considered as having been a member, and might afterwards when sure of settling in London be admitted a member of that elegant, useful, and noble Society, it would make me very happy. I treated him with so much complaisance and put the argument so home to him that he agreed to my proposal; and I left him with a cheerful heart at the thoughts of having six guineas to spend which I had given up for lost. This affair was transacted on the evening after I dined at the Beefsteak Club.

This afternoon I was surprised with the arrival of Lady Betty Macfarlane, Lady Anne Erskine, Captain Erskine, and Miss Dempster, who were come to the Red Lion Inn at Charing Cross.[9] It seems Lady Betty had written to the Laird that if he would not come down, she would come up; and upon his giving her an indolent answer, like a woman of spirit, she put her resolution in practice. I immediately went to them.

To tell the plain truth, I was vexed at their coming. For to see just the plain *hamely* Fife family hurt my grand ideas of London. Besides, I was now upon a plan of studying polite reserved behaviour, which is the only way to keep up dignity of character. And as I have a good share of pride, which I think is very proper and even noble, I am hurt with the taunts of ridicule and am unsatisfied if I do not feel myself something of a superior animal. This has always been my favourite idea in my best moments. Indeed, I have been obliged to deviate from it by a variety of circumstances. After my wild expedition to London in the year 1760, after I got rid of the load of serious reflection which then burthened me, by being always in Lord Eglinton's company, very fond of him, and much caressed by him, I became dissipated and thought-

[9] Captain (actually Lieutenant) Erskine is Andrew, Lady Betty Macfarlane and Lady Anne Erskine are his sisters; the fifth Earl of Kellie was their father and the sixth Earl is their brother. Miss Dempster is the sister and housekeeper of George Dempster, M.P., Boswell's other Scots crony, at this time unmarried.

less. When my father forced me down to Scotland, I was at first very low-spirited, although to appearance very high. I afterwards from my natural vivacity endeavoured to make myself easy; and like a man who takes to drinking to banish care, I threw myself loose as a heedless, dissipated, rattling fellow who might say or do every ridiculous thing. This made me sought after by everybody for the present hour, but I found myself a very inferior being; and I found many people presuming to treat me as such, which notwithstanding of my appearance of undiscerning gaiety, gave me much pain. I was, in short, a character very different from what GOD intended me and I myself chose. I remember my friend Johnston told me one day after my return from London that I had turned out different from what he imagined, as he thought I would resemble Mr. Addison. I laughed and threw out some loud sally of humour, but the observation struck deep. Indeed, I must do myself the justice to say that I always resolved to be such a man whenever my affairs were made easy and I got upon my own footing. For as I despaired of that, I endeavoured to lower my views and just to be a good-humoured comical being, well liked either as a waiter, a common soldier, a clerk in Jamaica, or some other odd out-of-the-way sphere. Now, when my father at last put me into an independent situation, I felt my mind regain its native dignity. I felt strong dispositions to be a Mr. Addison. Indeed, I had accustomed myself so much to laugh at everything that it required time to render my imagination solid and give me just notions of real life and of religion. But I hoped by degrees to attain to some degree of propriety. Mr. Addison's character in sentiment, mixed with a little of the gaiety of Sir Richard Steele and the manners of Mr. Digges, were the ideas which I aimed to realize.

Indeed, I must say that Digges has more or as much of the deportment of a man of fashion as anybody I ever saw; and he keeps up this so well that he never once lessened upon me even on an intimate acquaintance, although he is now and then somewhat melancholy, under which it is very difficult to preserve dignity; and this I think is particularly to be admired in Mr. Digges. Indeed, he and I never came to familiarity, which is justly said to beget contempt. The great art of living easy and happy in society is to study proper behaviour, and even with our most intimate friends to observe politeness; otherwise we will insensibly treat each other with a degree of rudeness, and each will find himself despised in some measure by the other. As I was therefore pursuing this laudable plan, I was vexed at the arrival of the Kellie family, with whom when in Scotland I had been in the greatest familiarity. Had they not come for a twelvemonth, I should have been somewhat established in my address, but as I had been but a fortnight from them, I could not without the appearance of strong affectation appear much different from what they had seen me. I accordingly was very free, but rather more silent, which they imputed to my dullness, and roasted me about London's not being agreeable to me. I bore it pretty well, and left them.

I then went to a play of Terence's (*The Eunuch*) performed by the King's Scholars of Westminster School. There was a very numerous audience, not one of whom I knew, except Churchill, and him only by sight.[1] Although I seldom understood them, yet I was entertained to see the boys play and hear them speak Latin with the English accent.[2] When Dr. Markham the Master came in, the scholars gave a loud clap. My mind was filled with many ideas of London, which relieved me from care.

THURSDAY 2 DECEMBER. At nine o'clock I waited upon the Duke. He received me with the greatest politeness. He is a man of the greatest humanity and gentleness of manners, has good plain sense, and is very cheerful notwithstanding of the severe shocks that he has met with.[3] He told me that he found it very difficult to get me a commission, but that he would try.[4] I was rather more bashful than I could have wished, although there was

---

[1] Churchill, as has been remarked above, had attended Westminster School.
[2] In Scotland the Continental pronunciation of Latin was taught.
[3] He had lost both his sons within a period of two years (1754–1756), one of them under the suspicion of suicide.   [4] See above, p. 19.

nobody with him. But I thought it was better to say little at the first interview. I did not sit long.

I then went and called on Colonel Gould, who is married to a daughter of General Cochrane's.[5] I had never seen either him or his lady. He was not up. So I went and waited on Mrs. Gould and breakfasted with her. I found her a genteel, affable woman. The house was very handsome, the furniture elegant. She was happy to hear of my coming into the Guards, and begged that I would make their house my own. She asked me to dine there next day, that she might present me to Mr. Gould; and she said that he would do everything to oblige me, and that it was of great advantage to a young man to have a good place where he can be easy at, and so shun bad company. I came away in fine spirits at having got so agreeable a home.

I then went to Leicester Street, where Lady Betty had a house taken. I pitied Macfarlane, who is very narrow, and had now house and footmen and coach and dress and entertainment of all kinds to pay. Captain Erskine said that he was past pity, for that he only knew the value of money in trifles; and he also said that to the length of five guineas the Laird might retain some degree of rationality, but when the sum exceeded that, he became perfectly delirious. What an absurd thing was it for this old clumsy dotard to marry a strong young woman of quality. It was certainly vanity, for which he has paid very heavily. Her marrying him was just to support herself and her sisters; and yet to a woman of delicacy, poverty is better than sacrificing her person to a greasy, rotten, nauseous carcass and a narrow vulgar soul.[6] Surely she who does that cannot properly be called a woman of virtue. She certainly wants feeling who can submit to the loathed embraces of a monster. She appears to me unclean: as I said to Miss Dempster,

[5] That is, Mrs. Gould was a first cousin of Boswell's mother.
[6] The Kellie fortune was small to begin with, and there were six children. In 1760 Lady Betty's brother, the sixth Earl, had sold all the estates except the mansion-house of Kellie. Andrew Erskine was always hard up and finally drowned himself in a fit of despair over his debts.

like a dirty table-cloth. I am sure no man can have the gentle passion of love for so defiled a person as hers—O my stomach rises at it!

FRIDAY 3 DECEMBER. I began now to be much at home in my lodgings and to get into a regular method. I resolved to want a servant for my first year and in every respect to be frugal, that I might learn the value of money, see what I could afford to do with my allowance, and rather live within than exceed my income. I am really surprised at the coolness and moderation with which I am proceeding. GOD grant I may continue to do well, which will make me happy and all my friends satisfied. (I have all along been speaking in the perfect tense, as if I was writing the history of some distant period. I shall after this use the present often, as most proper. Indeed, I will not confine myself, but take whichever is most agreeable at the time.) I never had a fire in my bedroom, but one in my parlour in the morning and one in my dining-room in the evening. I had my own tea and sugar, and got in bread and butter and milk as I wanted it. In short I regulate everything in the most prudent way. At the end of the year I shall subjoin a succinct account of my expenses.[7] Sure no minister of state could talk with more formality.

I had called once or twice and left my name at Northumberland House.[8] But hearing nothing from it, I began to think that they neglected me. However, I now received a card of invitation to the rout on Tuesday the 7. This raised my spirits, gave me notions of my consequence, and filled me with grandeur. Fain would I have got rich laced clothes, but I commanded my inclination and got just a plain suit of a pink colour, with a gold button.

[7] "Get quarto book to mark expenses. . . . Keep separate page each article, and mark the week's dinners, and pay each Saturday, and lodging each quarter. . . . Pay coal, candle, and butter, and cause milk be charged weekly. Pay bread also weekly" (Memoranda, 28, 29, 30 November 1762).
[8] See above, p. 33. He had secured a personal correspondence with the Countess early in 1761 by sending her a poem he had written on her son (*Verses on Lord Warkworth's Going a Volunteer to Germany, 1760*).

This day I dined at Colonel Gould's. I found him a sensible, genteel, obliging little man. Everything was in the best taste: quite ease and fashion. He was very kind to me; talked particularly of my commission, and gave me every hint that he could towards its succeeding. I really liked the man much. I thought to myself how curious it was that the master of this fine house, who lives in such warmth and splendour, might be called out to endure all the hardships of hunger and cold and confusion, and perhaps suffer the severest wounds or most violent death. It made all these things seem pretty easy to me, as I found they did not affect his happiness upon the whole.

He has a little daughter of seven year old, Miss Fanny, whom he is very fond of. She is an extraordinary child, very sagacious and very lively. The English children come very early to be rational, conversable beings. He has also a fine boy to his son, at Harrow School. Mrs. Gould has never had any children, but has a great affection for her husband's, which I admire much.

Gould told me that, as I was a single man, he hoped to see me very often at their family dinner, as they were almost always at home. We then had coffee and afterwards tea. It was just a Guard party: the Colonel and his lady, Mrs. Wynyard who has a son a colonel, Miss Gwynne who has a brother a colonel, and I who hope first to be an ensign and afterwards a colonel. We were pretty merry.

At nine I went to Lord Eglinton's but returned to Gould's at ten, as he insisted upon it, having invited Sir Alexander Gilmour of the First Regiment to meet me; but he did not come. We had a nice light bit of supper and were very happy. The Colonel talked of battles and dreadful wounds, which made us shudder. Really, these things are not to be talked of, for in cool blood they shock one prodigiously. He was on the expedition to St. Cast, but escaped unhurt.[9] He told me that his spirits kept up very well, but

[9] A minor Dunkirk. In August, 1758, an attack was made on the coast of France; the docks at Cherbourg were destroyed and a landing made in the Bay of St. Lunaire. Being warned of the approach of a superior French force

that sometimes he was in such a humour that fighting would have been very disagreeable to him. Here he spoke like a man of candour and a man of feeling. For the human mind even in the bravest is very variable.

SATURDAY 4 DECEMBER.[1] I breakfasted with Dempster.[2] He accompanied me into the City. He parted from me at St. Paul's, and I went to Child's, where there was not much said. I dined and drank tea with Lady Betty Macfarlane. We were but cold and dull. The Laird was low and disagreeable. I resolved to dine there no more; at least very, very seldom. At night, Erskine and I strolled through the streets and St. James's Park. We were accosted there by several ladies of the town. Erskine was very humorous and said some very wild things to them. There was one in a red cloak of a good buxom person and comely face whom I marked as a future piece, in case of exigency.[3]

SUNDAY 5 DECEMBER. I breakfasted with Ross Mackye, where I found the Duke of Queensberry, but did not mention a word of my commission.

from Brest, General Bligh ordered a retreat to St. Cast, where the British force was taken off by the fleet. The French arrived while the troops were re-embarking in flat-bottomed boats, shelled them from the heights above the bay, and finally attacked the Grenadier Guards, who were covering the retreat. Seven hundred fifty men were killed or taken prisoner.

[1] The reader, having been told of Boswell's daily memoranda, may like to compare one of them with the record of the same day in the journal. The entire memorandum for 4 December follows: "Breakfast first at home. Then in Bath [coat] and old grey [suit] and stick, sally to City. Send off *North Britons* to Digges. Get the one of the day. Go to Child's, take dish coffee, read *Auditor, Monitor, Briton.* Then come to Douglas's and inquire about parade. Then Leicester [Street], dine. Be comfortable yet genteel, and please your friend Captain Erskine. Drink tea. Then home, quiet, and wind up the week's journal in grey and slippers. Be always in bed before twelve. Never sup out. Breakfast R. Mackye Sunday and take franks." (Mackye, as a Member of Parliament, not only had the privilege of sending his own letters free of postage, but could also "frank" covers for other people to use.)

[2] See above, pp. 8, 29.

[3] See above, p. 25.

I then went to St. George's Church, where I heard a good sermon on the prophets testifying of Jesus Christ. I was upon honour much disposed to be a Christian. Yet I was rather cold in my devotion. The Duchess of Grafton attracted my eyes rather too much.[4]

In the evening I went to Douglas's, where I found a letter from my friend Johnston which gave me much satisfaction, brought many comfortable ideas into my mind, and put me on a regular plan of sending him my journal.

I then went to Dempster's, where I met with the Kellie family. I let myself out in humorous rhodomontade rather too much. We were very hearty. We disputed much whether London or Edinburgh was the most agreeable place to a Scotch gentleman of small fortune. Lady Betty said that it must be very cutting to find so many people higher than one's self and to see so many splendid equipages, none of which belong to one. "Lady Betty," said I, "you have the pleasure of admiring them. But your taste is too gross— you want to have the solid equipages themselves, to embrace and carry in your arms the thick tarry wheels."

In reality, a person of small fortune who has only the common views of life and would just be as well as anybody else, cannot like London. But a person of imagination and feeling, such as the Spectator finely describes, can have the most lively enjoyment from the sight of external objects without regard to property at all. London is undoubtedly a place where men and manners may be seen to the greatest advantage. The liberty and the whim that reigns there occasions a variety of perfect and curious characters. Then the immense crowd and hurry and bustle of business and diversion, the great number of public places of entertainment, the noble churches and the superb buildings of different kinds,

[4] Anne Liddell, some twenty-four years old. She attracted other eyes than Boswell's. She was separated from the Duke in 1765 and divorced by him in 1769, having in the mean time borne a son to the Earl of Upper Ossory, whom she married as soon as her marriage with Grafton was dissolved. She was one of Horace Walpole's favourite correspondents.

agitate, amuse, and elevate the mind. Besides, the satisfaction of pursuing whatever plan is most agreeable, without being known or looked at, is very great. Here a young man of curiosity and observation may have a sufficient fund of present entertainment, and may lay up ideas to employ his mind in age.

Dempster, talking of *Irene*, a tragedy written by Mr. Samuel Johnson, said it was as frigid as the regions of Nova Zembla; that now and then you felt a little heat like what is produced by touching ice.

MONDAY 6 DECEMBER. I waited on General Douglas, who told me that the Duke told him that he thought it would not be in his power to get me a commission. This was a discouraging piece of information. I left him in bad humour, cursed a state of waiting for anything from great men, and in short despaired a good deal of getting it. I called for Lord March,[5] who promised to keep the Duke in mind of it. I then went to Gould's, who kept up my spirits.

At one I went to the Duke's, and being in a kind of despair, I talked freely and boldly to him. He was gently informing me that the thing was very difficult. To show him that this did not affect me, "My Lord," said I, "it is as difficult as can be imagined, yet I should think your Grace's interest might do it." (I should have mentioned that I wrote a letter to him, some days ago, very fully.) "My Lord," said I now, and looked him in the face, "a state of suspense and hanging on is a most disagreeable thing. I have heard people talk of it, and I have read in the poets of it, but now I feel it. I have got an independent spirit, and I can assure your Grace that if I had not a good opinion of you as a man, upon my soul, I would not ask such a thing of you. It just comes to this; if your Grace is so generous as to make a push for me (which indeed I can scarcely ask), I believe the thing may do." I could see that the

[5] Queensberry's cousin and successor, a sporting peer and a friend of Eglinton. He is better known by his later soubriquet of "Old Q" or "the wicked Duke of Queensberry."

good old man was pleased with my spirit. He told me that he would do what he could with Lord Ligonier.[6]

I then asked him about Mr. Gay. He said he was a modest, quiet man, but when with people that he knew, was very entertaining. I told him that from reading Mr. Gay's writings, I had taken an affection to his Grace's family from my earliest years.[7] I then resumed my own affair, spoke a little, and took leave of him.

I drank tea at Macfarlane's. There was a most disagreeable set of women there. It was just one of the worst Edinburgh tea-drinking afternoons. Erskine and I sat out by ourselves and laughed immoderately just like two schoolboys. He went with me to Dempster's, where we sat a good while.

TUESDAY 7 DECEMBER. In the morning, I went to Lord Eglinton's, where was a breakfast, a concert, and a most elegant company: the Prince of Mecklenburg,[8] Duke of Kingston, Duke of Portland, Duke and Duchess of Ancaster, Duchess of Hamilton, Lord Lorne, Lord March, Lord Lichfield Chancellor of the University of Oxford, Lord and Lady Garlies, Lady Margaret Macdonald, Mr. Harris author of the essays on Poetry, Music, and Happiness, and a great many more. It was really a fine thing. Since ever I came up, I have resolved to preserve my own dignity and pay court to nobody, and rather have no communication with people than in any degree cringe to them. This morning I could observe Sir James Macdonald waiting till I should make up to him, which I did not do, but sat down by myself. He came and sat down beside me, and we chatted very well. I said I should wish to pass an hour or two with him. He said he would come and see me. This interview was very pleasing to me.

In the evening I went to Northumberland House, to the rout, which was indeed magnificent. Three large rooms and the gallery (a prodigious one) were full of the best company, between three and four hundred of them. The gallery is like one of the rooms in Holyroodhouse for size and richly adorned on the walls and ceiling

[6] The Commander-in-Chief in Great Britain and Colonel of the First Foot Guards.   [7] See above, p. 33.   [8] The Queen's brother.

with landscapes and gilding. The King and Lady Northumberland are exhibited in full length portraits, in their robes. As I was standing in pleasing reverie in the gallery musing on the splendid scene around me and joining with that the ancient ideas of the family of Percy, my Lady came up to me with the greatest complacency and kindness: "Mr. Boswell, I am very happy to see you. How do you do? I hope you are come to settle among us. I was very sorry that I was not at home when you called. I gave positive orders that you should be admitted whenever you called." This put me into the finest humour. I thanked her sincerely. I chatted easily. She then carried me to my Lord, who was very glad to see me and very civil to me. This is indeed a noble family in every respect. They live in a most princely manner, perfectly suitable to their high rank. Yet they are easy and affable. They keep up the true figure of old English nobility.

I felt a little awkward this night, as I scarcely knew anybody in the room. I told my Lady so. She said that would go off by degrees. I could observe people looking at me with envy, as a man of some distinction and a favourite of my Lady's. Bravo! thought I. I am sure I deserve to be a favourite. It was curious to find of how little consequence each individual was in such a crowd. I could imagine how an officer in a great army may be killed without being observed. I came home quiet, laid by my clothes, and went coolly to bed. There's conduct for you.

WEDNESDAY 8 DECEMBER. I sat in writing till one. I then strolled through the streets. I was somewhat dull and thought myself a poor sort of a being. At night I went to Covent Garden and saw *Love in a Village*,[9] a new comic opera, for the first night. I liked it much. I saw it from the gallery, but I was first in the pit. Just before the overture began to be played, two Highland officers came in. The mob in the upper gallery roared out, "No Scots! No Scots! Out with them!," hissed and pelted them with apples. My heart warmed to my countrymen, my Scotch blood boiled with indignation. I jumped up on the benches, roared out, "Damn you, you

[9] By Isaac Bickerstaffe.

rascals!," hissed and was in the greatest rage. I am very sure at that time I should have been the most distinguished of heroes. I hated the English; I wished from my soul that the Union was broke and that we might give them another battle of Bannockburn. I went close to the officers and asked them of what regiment they were of. They told me Lord John Murray's, and that they were just come from the Havana. "And this," said they, "is the thanks that we get—to be hissed when we come home. If it was French, what could they do worse?" "But," said one, "if I had a *grup o yin or twa o the tamd rascals I sud let them ken what they're about.*" The rudeness of the English vulgar is terrible. This indeed is the liberty which they have: the liberty of bullying and being abusive with their blackguard tongues. They soon gave over.[1] I then went to the gallery and was really well entertained with the opera.

THURSDAY 9 DECEMBER. I called on Erskine and related to him the history of the opera. I was in an immoderate flow of spirits and raged away. We then sauntered through the streets. He gave me a very sensible advice against repeating what people said, which may do much harm. I have an unlucky custom of doing so. I acknowledged my error and promised to be on my guard.

In the afternoon I drank tea at Macfarlane's. The ladies had now got everything in good order, and were pretty fond of London. I liked them better.

This was the great day of debate in the Houses of Parliament on the Peace.[2] But I could not get in. However, I was curious to hear how things were carried on. I went to Dempster's at twelve[3] to wait till he should come in. I stayed till three without him, and came home, cold and sleepy and wearied with waiting.

FRIDAY 10 DECEMBER. I went to Northumberland House in the forenoon. The porter told me there was nobody at home; but

[1] See above, p. 16.

[2] Fox by distribution of government favours had broken the Opposition led by Newcastle, Hardwicke, Devonshire, and Pitt. The terms of the Peace were carried by 319 votes to 65. The King's mother is said to have exclaimed, "Now is my son King of England." [3] Midnight, of course.

looking at me, "Sir," said he, "is your name Boswell?" Upon my answering, "Yes," "My Lady is at home, Sir," said he. Upon which I was shown up to her Ladyship, with whom I sat about twenty minutes in the most easy, agreeable way. She told me that she had a private party every Friday for particular friends, and that she would always be glad to see me there when I had nothing else to do. I exulted, and thanked her, and said that I could not think how I deserved all this, but that I hoped we should be better acquainted, and that I should run about the house like a tame spaniel. An old gentleman then came in. I sat a little longer and then withdrew, full of joy at being reckoned a particular friend of the heir of the great Percy and a woman of the first consequence in London. She mentioned my commission, and kindly desired me not to be impatient, and I would get it. If the Duke does not do it for me, she will be my next resource. But it is better to have but one patron at a time and stick close to him.

At night I went back to Northumberland House, about seven. We had tea and chatted for a while till the company (about twenty picked people) gathered. They then sat down to the card-tables. But I told my Lady that I never played, which she found no fault with.[4] A few did not play besides. However, I felt not so easy as those who did, and began to tire. I stayed there till eleven, and then came home.

SATURDAY 11 DECEMBER. I breakfasted with Macpherson, the translator of *Fingal*, a man of great genius and an honest Scotch Highlander.[5] It did my heart good to hear the spirit with which he talked. "The Highlanders," said he, "are hospitable and love society. They are very hardy, and can endure the inconveniences of life very well. Yet they are very fond of London when they get to it, and indulge as much in its pleasures as anybody. Let me," said he, "have something in perfection: either the noble rudeness of

[4] He had given Sheridan his word that he would not play for money.
[5] See above, p. 32. At the end of 1762 Macpherson was probably at the peak of his good fortune. *Fingal* had sold well and had received some extravagant praise. The charge of forgery had not yet become troublesome.

barbarous manners or the highest relish of polished society. There is no medium. In a little town you have the advantage of neither." He told me that he was very susceptible of tormenting love. But that London was the best place in the world to cure it. "In the country," said he, "we see a beautiful woman; we conceive an idea that it would be heaven to be in her arms. We think that impossible almost for us to attain. We sigh. We are dejected. Whereas here we behold as fine women as ever were created. Are we fond of one of them? For a guinea we get the full enjoyment of her, and when that is over we find that it is not so amazing a matter as we fancied. Indeed, after a moderate share of the pleasures of London, a man has a much better chance to make a rational unprejudiced marriage." Macpherson said he had strong and nice feelings, and therefore was easily made happy or miserable. "But then," said he, "nothing will make me either happy or the reverse above a day. It is hard," said he, "that we tire of everything."

I then took Dempster with me to the City, and to Child's. He did not enter into the spirit of it and went away soon. It is quite a place to my mind; dusky, comfortable, and warm, with a society of citizens and physicians who talk politics very fully and are very sagacious and sometimes jocular. "What is the reason," said one, "that a sole is not a good fish?" "Why, it is a good fish," said another, "if you dress it with a plain butter sauce. But you must have something so dev'lish high-seasoned. You might as well have a sauce of fire and brimstone." I shall hereafter for the sake of neatness throw our conversation into my journal in the form of a dialogue. So that every Saturday this my Journal shall be adorned with

A DIALOGUE AT CHILD'S.

1 CITIZEN. Pray now, what do you really think of this Peace?

2 CITIZEN. That it is a damned bad one, to be sure!

PHYSICIAN. Damned bad one? Pray what would you be at? Have not you had all that you wanted? Did you not begin the war to settle your boundaries in North America? And have not you got that done, as Mr. Pitt the great champion of the Opposition acknowledged in the House, better than could have been expected? Have not you got a large tract of country ceded to you? Is not the line of division plain and straight?

BOSWELL. Suppose, Sir, I went out a-hunting with intention to bring home a hare to dinner, and catch three hares. Don't you think that I may also bring home the other two? Now, Sir, I grant you that we began the war with intention only to settle our boundaries in America and would have been satisfied with that and nothing more. But, Sir, we have had uncommon success. We have not only got what we intended, but we have also picked up some other little things, such as the Havana, Guadeloupe, &c. I should be glad to know why we are to part with them?

PHYSICIAN. Because the French will not make peace except we do so. And we cannot carry on the war another year.

1 CITIZEN. But we can.

PHYSICIAN. From whence have you the money? Who will furnish that?

1 CITIZEN. The City of London.

PHYSICIAN. Where will you get the men?

BOSWELL. I own to you that is a difficulty.

PHYSICIAN. Lord, Sir! We could not raise men for another campaign. Consider how the country has been drained. Ay, ay, it is easy for a merchant in London to sit by his warm fire and talk of our army abroad. They imagine we have got a hundred thousand stout soldiers ready to march up against the enemy. Little do they know what the severities they have suffered produce. Indeed we have a very thin army. And those that remain, what are they? Why, like Jack Falstaff's scarecrows. No, no, no more war! Let us not sink ourselves so many more millions in debt, and let our contractors, like Dundas, bring home a couple of hundred thousand pounds.[6] We are now making a very good peace; let us be content.

[6] Sir Lawrence Dundas, a Scotsman, the contemporary type of profiteer, had been Commissary General and Contractor to the Army from 1748 to 1759. He died in 1781, "leaving an estate of £16,000 a year and a fortune of £900,000 in personalities and landed property." He had just been made a baronet, was a

3 CITIZEN. I do think it is better that anybody should bring home our money than leave it in Germany. I wish we could hear of more of it brought home.

I don't think this at all bad. My simile of the hares (my metaphor, rather) is pretty well. They might have answered me, "Suppose a man went out to shoot a hare for dinner, and not only shot that but a brace of partridges. The lord of the manor sees him, and is offended at him, and wants to take them all from him. Don't you think he is very well off if he gives the lord the partridges and trudges peaceably home with his hare on his shoulders, which is all that he wanted?"

The Spectator mentions his being seen at Child's, which makes me have an affection for it. I think myself like him, and am serenely happy there. There is something to me very agreeable in having my time laid out in some method, such as every Saturday going to Child's.

I also the same morning call at the pamphlet shop going into the Temple Exchange Coffee-house in Fleet Street, and buy *The North Briton*, which I send at night by commission, in a frank, to Digges. He is very grateful to me. He says it makes a great feast in his family circle, and when they have read it, they drink a bumper to the health of Mr. Boswell. He calls himself my poor correspondent, as he cannot make me a return for the valuable commodities of my letters. "Conversation," says he, "is the traffic of the mind; for by exchanging ideas, we enrich one another." Poor Digges! I really like him. He has been unlucky and has done many inexcusable things. But he is a pretty man, and has most amiable dispositions. Had he not been reduced, but had a plentiful fortune, he would have been a noble fellow, greatly admired.

I drank coffee at Macfarlane's. Erskine and he got into a dispute about the Peace and each told his antagonist that he was speaking arrant nonsense. They were seriously hot. I was much diverted at

---

Member of Parliament, and exerted a good deal of political power. His son was raised to the peerage; his later descendants were Marquesses of Zetland.

Captain Andrew's being so, who does not enter the least into common notions, and does not care a farthing whether there be peace or war or confusion in Europe, provided he and his own agreeable circle be safe and happy.

I must own that I am much of that way of thinking. I cannot help it. I see too far into the system of things to be much in earnest. I consider mankind in general, and therefore cannot take a part in their quarrels when divided into particular states and nations. I can see that after a war is over and a great quantity of cold and hunger and want of sleep and torment endured by mortals, things are upon the whole just as they were. I can see that Great People, those who manage the fates of kingdoms, are just such beings as myself: have their hours of discontent and are not a bit happier. This being the case, I am rather passive than active in life. It is difficult to make my feeling clearly understood. I may say, I act passively. That is, not with my whole heart, and thinking this or that of real consequence, but because so and so things are established and I must submit.

Meditating calmly and finding myself situated in this sublunary system, I do not know well what to make of it. I do not rightly understand it. GUARDIAN ANGEL. "Stop. How should you? GOD has formed men with very limited capacities." True. But still I cannot help enquiring and thinking, and viewing things in certain lights. "Certain shades, you should rather say," would be the reply of a man keenly bent on the pursuits of life.

The truth is with regard to me, about the age of seventeen I had a very severe illness.[7] I became very melancholy. I imagined that I was never to get rid of it. I gave myself up as devoted to misery. I entertained a most gloomy and odd way of thinking. I was much hurt at being good for nothing in life. The particular events of my romantic life since then, my friends well know. My lively fancy always remained. Many a struggle was in my mind between

[7] It has not previously been realized that Boswell suffered this illness (probably a nervous collapse). The absence of a matriculation record at the University of Edinburgh for the year 1757–1758 is now perhaps accounted for.

melancholy and mirth. I grew better and freer of my disorder. But I could not bear the law. Indeed, I had been so long accustomed to consider myself as out of the world that I could not think of engaging in real life. At last the Guards pleased me. I was opposed in this scheme. This made me fonder of it. I also was an enthusiast with regard to being in London. The charms of poetry also enchanted me. I became acquainted with Captain Erskine, which kept this turn alive. To get away from home, where I lived as a boy, was my great object. It was irksome beyond measure to be a young laird in the house of a father much different from me, of a mind perfectly sound, and who thought that if I was not a man of business, I was good for nothing. My worthy friend Johnston always comforted me; pointed out agreeable plans for me, and made me hope to be happy. Mr. McQuhae also did me much service.[8] He is a man of good parts, great and accurate knowledge, easiness of manners, and goodness of heart. I regard him much.

I used to have a degree of horror at the thoughts of the misery endured in war. Erskine relieved me from this. He goes upon system, which is just to keep himself as easy and happy as he can, and to make the best of everything. He does not suffer so much as others from his indifference and just yielding to the blasts of adversity. Thus he gets up in the morning and just tries to be as easy and happy as he can till night. Sometimes he feels elevation of spirit by lively company, or by reading a good poem, but he is rather still, and, like standing water, a little apt to be muddy and sour. The only fault that he has as a companion is now and then a little ill temper. If he were ordered abroad, he would just draw his legs after him and endeavour to get as good victuals (which, by the by, is his great source of satisfaction) and keep himself as warm and sleep as snugly as he could. Being with Erskine gives me a simplicity of sentiment and makes me very easy as to what men in general make such a work about.

I was mentioning Erskine's character to Sir James Macdonald, a young man who has made a great figure at Eton School and the

[8] See above, p. 3.

University of Oxford and is studying hard to fit himself for Parliament, being full of notions of the consequence of real life, and making a figure in the world, and all that. When he heard Erskine's sentiments (which, by the by, are much my own, and which I mentioned just to see what he would say), he was perfectly stunned. "Why," said he, "he must not be a man. He is unfit to live in human society. He is not of the species." I was really entertained. "Ah!" thought I, "little do you know of how small duration the pleasure is of making one of these great figures that now swell before your ambitious imagination."

Yet I do think it is a happiness to have an object in view which one keenly follows. It gives a lively agitation to the mind which is very pleasurable. I am determined to have a degree of Erskine's indifference, to make me easy when things go cross; and a degree of Macdonald's eagerness for real life, to make me relish things when they go well. It is in vain to sit down and say, "What good does it do to have a regiment? Is a general more happy than an ensign?" No. But a man who has had his desire gratified of rising by degrees to that rank in the Army, has enjoyed more happiness than one who has never risen at all. The great art I have to study is to balance these two very different ways of thinking properly. It is very difficult to be keen about a thing which in reality you do not regard, and consider as imaginary. But I fancy it may do, as a man is afraid of ghosts in the dark, although he is sure there are none; or pleased with beautiful exhibitions on the stage, although he knows they are not real. Although the Judgment may know that all is vanity, yet Passion may ardently pursue. Judgment and Passion are very different.

With these notions I am pushing to get into the Guards, where to distinguish myself as a good officer and to get promotion will be my favourite objects. If that does not succeed, I am at least living happily, I am seeing the world, studying men and manners, and fitting myself for a pleasing, quiet life in old age, by laying up agreeable ideas to feast upon in recollection. Thus shall I perhaps enjoy a serene felicity at the delightful Auchinleck, the ancient seat of a long line of worthy ancestors. Here will I end my days in calm devotion. If I shall be cut off before that time, I am satisfied. GOD is good; He will take care of me. O happy situation of mind which I now have! All things look well. I hope I shall be very happy. Let my mind be never so much distempered, I have devotion towards GOD and benevolence towards mankind. I have an honest mind and a warm friendship. Upon my soul, not a bad specimen of a man. However my particular notions may alter, I always preserve these great and worthy qualities.

Erskine and I went to Covent Garden and saw *Love in a Village*. We were well entertained. We got into a dispute, and said several very clever things. "Sir," said I, "when you and I get into a dispute, we give a smart rap against each other like two flints, and out fly sparks of fire. But Macfarlane and you come together like two thick-quilted chair-bottoms, and out comes a thick cloud of dust."

I went back with him to Macfarlane's. The ladies were in great dress; were getting into fashion and looked like the best idea of the Ladies of Kellie, daughters of a Scotch earl, descendants of the family of Mar. I did not think them vulgar but inwardly rejoiced at being in so friendly a way with them. However, after supper we had some altercation about standards of taste, and they grew hot and showed a strong example of the Edinburgh women's roughness of manners, which disgusted me. They have all a too-great violence in dispute, and are sometimes put quite out of humour by it.

I brought them to be pretty well again, and then went to Dempster's, where I was very well received. He and his sister Miss Jeanie have a great deal of gentleness of manners as well as cleverness. I sat till near one, which, as it was a transgression of my regular plan, gave me pain. This day makes a very good figure in my journal. It has been lucky, as I am happy.

SUNDAY 12 DECEMBER. I took a whim of dining at home every day last week, which I kept exactly to. The pleasure of gratifying whim is very great. It is known only by those who are whimsical. This day I was in a pleasing indolent humour. I sat at home writing till three, and then (as I am resolved to be at divine service

every Sunday) I then went and heard prayers in St. Margaret's
Church, Westminster. I dined at home very comfortably. I really
am very well situated in lodgings. My landlord is a jolly, civil man.
His wife a quiet, well-behaved woman, and his sister a neat-
handed, clever girl. They do everything to serve me. Mr. Terrie is
in a public office, so that he supplies me with paper and all materials for writing in great abundance, for nothing. Mrs. Terrie
gets all things that I want bought for me, and Miss sews the laced
ruffles on my shirts, and does anything of that kind. They have
always a good plain dinner. I have the art to be easy and chatty and
yet maintain a proper distance. In short, I live very comfortably.
I order any little alterations that I wish. For instance, there was no
communication between my dining-room and bedchamber. I ordered a door to be struck out, which was instantly done. I ordered
some large breakfast cups and a carpet to my bedchamber and a
bureau[9] to my dining-room. It is inconceivable with what attention
and spirit I manage all my concerns. I sat in all this evening calm
and indulgent. I had a fire in both my rooms above-stairs. I drank
tea by myself for a long time. I had my feet washed with milk-
warm water,[10] I had my bed warmed, and went to sleep soft and
contented.

MONDAY 13 DECEMBER. I waited upon the Duke, whom I
found rather in better humour about my commission, as Mr. Townshend had resigned, who was his great opposer.[1] "My Lord," said
I, "commissions are certainly got by interest, and I know nobody
who has better interest than your Grace." He told me he had not
seen Lord Ligonier, although he had called on him twice; but he
promised to see him, and also to make application soon to the new
Secretary at War,[2] which, he agreed with me, might do good. I
told his Grace that I would not relinquish the pursuit but wait for
my commission if it should be two years. My youthful impatience

[9] A writing desk (the usual meaning in England).
[10] One of Boswell's keenest sensual pleasures.
[1] Charles Townshend, Secretary at War.
[2] Welbore Ellis, appointed on 17 December.

was a little unsatisfied with the calm, diffident speech of the Duke, which, however, is in truth infinitely better than talking much and making me believe much more than is true.

This forenoon Mr. Sheridan was with me. I told him that I had great difficulty to get to London. "And how could it be otherwise," said he, "when you pushed the plan most opposite to your father's inclinations?" This immediately led us to talk fully on his scheme of the Temple, which I told him my father disapproved of, as my going to London at all was the thing that he could not think of. I told him that I could not study law, and being of a profession where you do no good is to a man of spirit very disagreeable. That I was determined to be in London. That I wanted to be something; and that the Guards was the only scene of real life that I ever liked. I feel a surprising change to the better on[3] myself since I came to London. I am an independent man. I think myself as good as anybody, and I act entirely on my own principles. Formerly I was directed by others. I took every man's advice, that I regarded; I was fond to have it. I asked it. I told all my story freely. But now I keep my own counsel, I follow the dictates of my own good sense, than which I can see no better monitor, and I proceed consistently and resolutely. I now spoke to Sheridan with a manly firmness and a conscious assurance that I was in the right. He said that application (by which he meant business) was necessary to keep a young man from being hurried down the stream. I swelled with satisfaction at the thoughts of showing him how well I should conduct myself as an officer of the Guards.

Sir James Macdonald then came in to wait upon me for the first time. I liked to see him and Sheridan together. They fell a-talking on tragedy. Sheridan said he thought there was no occasion for our modern tragedies to be in verse. That indeed it was necessary among the ancients, as they were then set to music; but amongst us we do not require that. And indeed the actor studiously disguises the measure in reciting, and therefore why labour so much in vain?

[3] A Scotticism.

Sir James said that for domestic distress prose might do, but for kings and heroes an elevation of language is necessary. "I don't know," says Sheridan, "if we may not have that in prose. Mr. Macpherson in his translation of *Fingal* has shown us what dignity the English language is capable of."

In his usual way he abused Garrick in tragedy, and said that he mimicked parts of all the good actors, but none entirely, and so appeared original. He said the taste of the age was terrible. That they would run to see an actor, being his first appearance, eagerly. "Now," said he, "it would be laughed at to advertise a solo to be performed by such a man, being his first time of playing on the fiddle, or a portrait to be sold by such a man, being his first attempt in painting. And yet the mechanical part of acting is at least as difficult as that of any of these two arts. If," said he, "I was manager of a theatre, nobody should be allowed to come on under seven years of apprenticeship and being regularly taught." He told us that he wanted Mrs. Sheridan to write a prose tragedy.

After they left me, I went to Gould's. The Colonel had been debauching the night before and was in bed, but Mrs. Gould insisted that I should eat a family dinner with her and the children, which I did very happily. Miss Fanny and I are now very good friends. "I am sure," said she, "Sir, if I like any man, I like you." She sat on the same chair with me after dinner, and sung and read very prettily. About six, Mr. Gould came down to us. I gave him a genteel lecture on the advantage of temperance, and made him acknowledge that the pain of rioting much exceeded the pleasure. He was heavy, but I was lightsome and entertaining, and relieved him. I drank tea and sat the evening, gay and happy, just in the way I could wish.

TUESDAY 14 DECEMBER. It is very curious to think that I have now been in London several weeks without ever enjoying the delightful sex, although I am surrounded with numbers of free-hearted ladies of all kinds: from the splendid Madam at fifty guineas a night, down to the civil nymph with white-thread stockings who tramps along the Strand and will resign her engaging person to your honour for a pint of wine and a shilling. Manifold are the reasons for this my present wonderful continence. I am upon a plan of economy, and therefore cannot be at the expense of first-rate dames. I have suffered severely from the loathsome distemper, and therefore shudder at the thoughts of running any risk of having it again. Besides, the surgeons' fees in this city come very high. But the greatest reason of all is that fortune, or rather benignant Venus, has smiled upon me and favoured me so far that I have had the most delicious intrigues with women of beauty, sentiment, and spirit, perfectly suited to my romantic genius.

Indeed, in my mind, there cannot be higher felicity on earth enjoyed by man than the participation of genuine reciprocal amorous affection with an amiable woman. There he has a full indulgence of all the delicate feelings and pleasures both of body and mind, while at the same time in this enchanting union he exults with a consciousness that he is the superior person. The dignity of his sex is kept up. These paradisial scenes of gallantry have exalted my ideas and refined my taste, so that I really cannot think of stooping so far as to make a most intimate companion of a groveling-minded, ill-bred, worthless creature, nor can my delicacy be pleased with the gross voluptuousness of the stews. I am therefore walking about with a healthful stout body and a cheerful mind, in search of a woman worthy of my love, and who thinks me worthy of hers, without any interested views, which is the only sure way to find out if a woman really loves a man. If I should be a single man for the whole winter, I will be satisfied. I have had as much elegant pleasure as I could have expected would come to my share in many years.

However, I hope to be more successful. In this view, I had now called several times for a handsome actress of Covent Garden Theatre, whom I was a little acquainted with, and whom I shall distinguish in this my journal by the name of LOUISA.[4] This lady

---

[4] The memoranda identify Louisa as one Mrs. Lewis, about whom, except for what we learn from Boswell himself (see below, pp. 135, 137–138), next to

had been indisposed and saw no company, but today I was admitted. She was in a pleasing undress and looked very pretty. She received me with great politeness. We chatted on the common topics. We were not easy—there was a constraint upon us—we did not sit right on our chairs, and we were unwilling to look at one another. I talked to her on the advantage of having an agreeable acquaintance, and hoped I might see her now and then. She desired me to call in whenever I came that way, without ceremony. "And pray," said she, "when shall I have the pleasure of your company at tea?" I fixed Thursday, and left her, very well satisfied with my first visit.

I then called on Mr. Lee,[5] who is a good, agreeable, honest man, and with whom I associate fine gay ideas of the Edinburgh Theatre in my boyish days, when I used to walk down the Canongate and think of players with a mixture of narrow-minded horror and lively-minded pleasure; and used to wonder at painted equipages and powdered ladies, and sing "The bonny bush aboon Traquair," and admire Mrs. Bland in her chair with tassels, and flambeaux before her.[6]

I did not find Lee at home. I then went to Love's. They were just sitting down to a piece of roast beef. I said that was a dish which I never let pass, and so sat down and took a slice of it. I was vexed at myself for doing it, even at the time. Love abused Mr. Digges grossly; said he was a worse player than the lowest actor in Covent Garden. Their vulgarity and stupid malevolence (for Mrs. Love

---

nothing is known. She played the Queen in *Hamlet* at Covent Garden on 27 September 1762, her first appearance there. On 20 October she played Mrs. Ford in the *Merry Wives*. Genest does not mention her again for the season.

[5] Former manager of the Edinburgh Theatre.

[6] "The bonny bush aboon Traquair" was a very popular Scots song the words of which were written by Robert Crawford (d. 1733) of the family of Craufurd of Auchenames. It makes no reference to the theatre or to players, but was probably associated with them by the boy Boswell merely because it was for him an epitome of everything romantically amorous. Mrs. Bland was the wife of General Humphrey Bland, Governor of Edinburgh Castle and Commander-in-Chief of the forces in Scotland.

also joined in the abuse) disgusted me much. I left them, determined scarcely to keep up an acquaintance with them, and in general to keep clear of the players, which indeed I do at present.

I dined at home. Whenever I don't mention my place of dining, it is to be understood that I dine at home. In my account of Mr. Terrie's family, I neglected to mention Molly the maid, whose pardon I most sincerely ask, as she is such a personage as one does not meet with every day. She is indeed one of the stupidest human beings that I ever met with. She has not, as the philosophers say, the *anima rationalis* in a great degree, but she rather has a kind of instinct by which she is actuated, by which, however, she goes on pretty well. She is very careful and diligent, and extremely good-natured and disposed to oblige, and, as she is ugly, her head is not taken off from her business.

WEDNESDAY 15 DECEMBER. The enemies of the people of England who would have them considered in the worst light represent them as selfish, beef-eaters, and cruel. In this view I resolved today to be a true-born Old Englishman. I went into the City to Dolly's Steak-house in Paternoster Row and swallowed my dinner by myself to fulfill the charge of selfishness; I had a large fat beefsteak to fulfil the charge of beef-eating; and I went at five o'clock to the Royal Cockpit in St. James's Park and saw cock-fighting for about five hours to fulfill the charge of cruelty.

A beefsteak-house is a most excellent place to dine at. You come in there to a warm, comfortable, large room, where a number of people are sitting at table. You take whatever place you find empty; call for what you like, which you get well and cleverly dressed. You may either chat or not as you like. Nobody minds you, and you pay very reasonably. My dinner (beef, bread and beer and waiter) was only a shilling. The waiters make a great deal of money by these pennies.[7] Indeed, I admire the English for attending to small sums, as many smalls make a great, according to the proverb.

[7] The sense would have been clearer if Boswell had written the preceding sentence in the form, "My dinner of beef, bread, and beer, with a penny for the waiter, cost only a shilling."

At five I filled my pockets with gingerbread and apples (quite the method), put on my old clothes and laced hat, laid by my watch, purse, and pocket-book, and with oaken stick in my hand sallied to the pit. I was too soon there. So I went into a low inn, sat down amongst a parcel of arrant blackguards, and drank some beer. The sentry near the house had been very civil in showing me the way. It was very cold. I bethought myself of the poor fellow, so I carried out a pint of beer myself to him. He was very thankful and drank my health cordially. He told me his name was Hobard, that he was a watch-maker but in distress for debt, and enlisted that his creditors might not touch him.

I then went to the Cockpit, which is a circular room in the middle of which the cocks fight. It is seated round with rows gradually rising. The pit and the seats are all covered with mat. The cocks, nicely cut and dressed and armed with silver heels, are set down and fight with amazing bitterness and resolution. Some of them were quickly dispatched. One pair fought three quarters of an hour. The uproar and noise of betting is prodigious. A great deal of money made a very quick circulation from hand to hand. There was a number of professed gamblers there. An old cunning dog whose face I had seen at Newmarket sat by me a while. I told him I knew nothing of the matter. "Sir," said he, "you have as good a chance as anybody." He thought I would be a good subject for him. I was young-like. But he found himself balked. I was shocked to see the distraction and anxiety of the betters. I was sorry for the poor cocks. I looked round to see if any of the spectators pitied them when mangled and torn in a most cruel manner, but I could not observe the smallest relenting sign in any countenance. I was therefore not ill pleased to see them endure mental torment. Thus did I complete my true English day, and came home pretty much fatigued and pretty much confounded at the strange turn of this people.

THURSDAY 16 DECEMBER. I called at the Duke's in the morning, but found that he was just setting out for Amesbury and could see nobody. This vexed me a little, as I was anxious to hear his suc-

cess this week. I sat at home writing all the forenoon. I received a
letter from McQuhae with an account of the death of his pupil, the
only son and comfort of his parents. I was much shocked with it.
Yet the consideration of the vanity of this life and the hopes of a
better made me easy.[8]

In the afternoon I went to Louisa's. A little black young fellow,
her brother, came in. I could have wished him at the Bay of Hon-
duras. However, I found him a good quiet obliging being who gave
us no disturbance. She talked on a man's liking a woman's company, and of the injustice people treated them with in suspecting
anything bad. This was a fine artful pretty speech. We talked of
French manners, and how they studied to make one another happy.
"The English," said I, "accuse them of being false, because they
misunderstand them. When a Frenchman makes warm professions
of regard, he does it only to please you for the time. It is words of
course. There is no more of it. But the English, who are cold and
phlegmatic in their address, take all these fine speeches in earnest,
and are confounded to find them otherwise, and exclaim against
the perfidious Gaul most unjustly. For when Frenchmen put a
thing home seriously and vow fidelity, they have the strictest
honour. O they are the people who enjoy time; so lively, pleasant,
and gay. You never hear of madness or self-murder among them.
Heat of fancy evaporates in fine brisk clear vapour with them, but
amongst the English often falls heavy upon the brain."

We chatted pretty easily. We talked of love as a thing that
could not be controlled by reason, as a fine passion. I could not
clearly discern how she meant to behave to me. She told me that a
gentleman had come to her and offered her £50, but that her brother
knocked at the door and the man run out of the house without say-

[8] "Poor McQuhae, he is just now in great affliction on account of the death of
his pupil, the only child of Mr. George Reid, a worthy old clergyman, and a
most amiable woman, a cousin of my father's and sister to the late Reverend
Mr. Campbell . . . They were very fond of this boy. He was a remarkable
genius" (Boswell to John Johnston, 21 December 1762). The Reverend George
Reid was minister of Ochiltree.

ing a word. I said I wished he had left his money. We joked much about the £50. I said I expected some night to be surprised with such an offer from some decent elderly gentlewoman. I made just a comic parody to her story. I sat till past eight. She said she hoped it would not be long before she had the pleasure of seeing me again.

This night I made no visible progress in my amour, but I in reality was doing a great deal. I was getting well acquainted with her. I was appearing an agreeable companion to her; I was informing her by my looks of my passion for her.

FRIDAY 17 DECEMBER. I engaged in this amour just with a view of convenient pleasure but the god of pleasing anguish now seriously seized my breast. I felt the fine delirium of love. I waited on Louisa at one, found her alone, told her that her goodness in hoping to see me *soon* had brought me back: that it appeared long to me since I saw her. I was a little bashful. However, I took a good heart and talked with ease and dignity. "I hope, Madam, you are at present a single woman." "Yes, sir." "And your affections are not engaged?" "They are not, Sir." "But this is leading me into a strange confession. I assure you, Madam, my affections are engaged." "Are they, Sir?" "Yes, Madam, they are engaged to you." (She looked soft and beautiful.) "I hope we shall be better acquainted and like one another better." "Come, Sir, let us talk no more of that now." "No, Madam, I will not. It is like giving the book in the preface." "Just so, Sir, telling in the preface what should be in the middle of the book." (I think such conversations are best written in the dialogue way.) "Madam, I was very happy to find you. From the first time that I saw you, I admired you." "O, Sir." "I did, indeed. What I like beyond everything is an agreeable female companion, where I can be at home and have tea and genteel conversation. I was quite happy to be here." "Sir, you are welcome here as often as you please. Every evening, if you please." "Madam I am infinitely obliged to you."

This is just what I wanted. I left her, in good spirits, and dined at Sheridan's. "Well," said he, "are you going into the Guards?" "Yes, Sir," said I; "the Temple scheme would not have done. It would only have been putting off time. I would not have applied. You cannot get a man to undergo the drudgery of the law who only want to pass his life agreeably, and who thinks that my Lord Chancellor's four and twenty hours are not a bit happier than mine.[9] Don't you think, Sir," said I, "that I am in the right to pursue the plan I like?" He replied, "I won't speak to you on the subject. But I shall always be glad to see you."

We talked of Johnson. He told me a story of him. "I was dining," said Johnson, "with the Mayor of Windsor, who gave me a very hearty dinner; but, not satisfied with feeding my body, he would also feed my understanding. So, after he had spoke a great deal of clumsy nonsense, he told me that at the last Sessions he had transported three people to the Plantations. I was so provoked with the fellow's dullness and impertinence that I exclaimed, 'I wish to GOD, Sir, I was the fourth.' " Nothing could more strongly express his dissatisfaction.

Mrs. Sheridan told me that he was very sober, but would sit up the whole night. He left them once at two in the morning and begged to be excused for going away so soon, as he had another visit to make. I like to mark every anecdote of men of so much genius and literature.

I found out Sheridan's great cause of quarrel with him was that when Johnson heard of his getting a pension, "What!" said he, "has *he* got a pension? Then it is time for me to give up mine." "Now," said he, "here was the greatest ingratitude. For it was I and Wedderburn that first set the thing a-going." This I believe was true.[10]

[9] Boswell's construction hesitates between the first person and the third.
[10] Ossian Macpherson had maliciously reported Johnson's remark to Sheridan, without telling him (what would perhaps not have mended matters) that Johnson, after a pause, had added, "However, I am glad that Mr. Sheridan has a pension, for he is a very good man." For Wedderburn, see below, p. 221 *n*.7. Sheridan had taught him pronunciation. In *The Life of Johnson* Boswell demurely remarks that Wedderburn's sister "was married to Sir Harry Erskine, an intimate friend of Lord Bute, who was the favourite of the King."

Mrs. Sheridan told me that she was travelling in a stage-coach, and had sat silent for a long time while a fellow was chattering away like a magpie and thought they were all admiring his brightness. At last he simpered and said, "An't I a most egregious coxcomb?" "Um?" cried an old deaf gentleman. Mrs. Sheridan bawled into his ear, "The gentleman, Sir, is a great coxcomb: he thinks we don't observe it, and he wants to tell us of it." This confounded him so that he did not speak a word for a long time.

Mr. Sheridan said that this age was (as Henry Fielding styled it) a trifling age. "In the reign of Queen Anne," said he, "merit was encouraged. Then a Mr. Prior was Ambassador, and a Mr. Addison Secretary of State. Then genius was cherished by the beams of courtly favour. But in the reigns of George the First and George the Second it was a disadvantage to be clever. Dullness and corruption were the only means of preferment. I knew several people when at school whose Juvenilia were equal to those of the great men of letters in Queen Anne's time; but as true great genius is always accompanied with good sense, they soon saw that being men of literary merit was not the way to rise; and therefore they turned lawyers and physicians and other employments, while the buds of genius withered away." I said I hoped we now lived in a better age, and that the reign of George the Third would give all due encouragement to genius. "Yes," said he, "we may now expect that merit will flourish." He observed that the bishops in particular were the great enemies of merit. That if a man could write well, they were of Captain Plume's opinion about the attorney: "A dangerous man; discharge him, discharge him."[1] He said Lord

---

[1] Farquhar's *Recruiting Officer,* Act I, Scene i:

KITE: I have listed the strong man of Kent, the King of the gipsies, a Scotch pedlar, a scoundrel attorney, and a Welsh parson.

PLUME. An attorney! Wert thou mad? List a lawyer! Discharge him, discharge him this minute.

KITE. Why, Sir?

PLUME. Because I will have nobody in my company that can write; a fellow that can write can draw petitions.—I say this minute discharge him.

Holdernesse with the greatest difficulty got Mr. Mason, the author of *Elfrida*, a living of £200 a year.

Mrs. Cholmondeley, wife to the Honourable and Reverend Mr. Cholmondeley, came to tea. Her husband was an ensign in the Guards, and at the battle of Fontenoy fairly hid himself; for which he was disgracefully broke at the head of the Army. He turned clergyman, and being an earl's brother, has done very well.[2] His lady is sister to the late Mrs. Woffington, the famous actress. She is a pretty-looking woman, lively and entertaining, with that fine gay polish of manners which is only to be acquired in the genteelest company.[3] Dr. Chamberlaine, brother to Mrs. Sheridan, a shrewd hearty man, was recollecting how long it was since he saw Mrs. Cholmondeley. "Just seven years, Sir," said she. "Madam," said he, "you mark time better than I do." "True, Sir," replied Sheridan, "but you must observe that time has not marked her."

Sheridan found fault with Francis's translation of Horace. "For," said he, "to give the literal meaning of Horace, it should be in verse. To give an idea of his manner and spirit, it should be imitation and applied to the present time, like Swift's two imitations, which are the only good ones." I mentioned Pope's. "He, Sir," said he, "has rather the gall of Juvenal than the delicate tartness of Horace." This Chamberlaine and I opposed, and indeed justly. Sheridan said that selfishness was the great cause of unhappiness, and that whenever a person made self the center, misery must ensue. I talked to him of Erskine's odd character. "Such people," said he, "must have diseased minds."

I really passed this afternoon very well, and with improvement as well as entertainment. I thought myself much happier than in the Kellie company, where mirth alone is the object; as if man was only formed a risible animal.

[2] Robert Cholmondeley, besides being son (not brother) to the Earl of Cholmondeley, was nephew to Horace Walpole. This story of his youthful disgrace (he was in his eighteenth year at the time of the battle of Fontenoy) turns up also in a letter by Joseph Jekyll written in 1831.

[3] Johnson called her "a very airy lady."

I mentioned to Sheridan how difficult it was to be acquainted with people of fashion in London: that they have a reserve and a forbidding shyness to strangers. He accounted for it thus: "The strangers that come here are idle and unemployed; they don't know what to do, and they are anxious to get acquaintances. Whereas the genteel people, who have lived long in town, have got acquaintances enough; their time is all filled up. And till they find a man particularly worth knowing, they are very backward. But when you once get their friendship, you have them firm to you."

I lamented to him the stiffness and formality of good company and the emptiness of their conversation. "Why, Sir," said he, "the people of fashion in England are very ill educated and can make no figure; to disguise this and prevent such as have got parts and application from shining, conversation is just reduced to a system of insipidity, where you just repeat the most insignificant commonplace things in a sort of affected delicacy of tone. I remember," said he, "when the late Lord Shelburne had been some time in London, he told me that he was a very unhappy man. That before he left Ireland he used always to have the conversation of men of genius and letters; but that here he was always in the best company, where he heard nothing and could say nothing. 'My Lord,' said I, 'will you come and eat a beefsteak with me, and I'll show you some good company.' He accordingly came, and I had some men of genius, taste, and learning for him; and he was quite transported and declared he had not passed a happy day before since he came to London." This Sheridan told me.

SATURDAY 18 DECEMBER. I should have mentioned yesterday that as I was sitting in my parlour after breakfast, Captain James Webster, newly arrived from Germany, came in.[4] He looked healthy and spirited notwithstanding of all the severities that he had endured. I was very glad to see him.

This day I was rather too late in going to Child's so that all

[4] Boswell's first cousin. He later served with distinction in the War of American Independence and died of wounds received at the battle of Guilford Courthouse.

the politics were over. I have therefore little or nothing from thence worth setting down. However, as I am a man who love forms, I shall always continue to present (such as it is) my Saturday's

DIALOGUE AT CHILD'S.

1 CITIZEN. Pray, Doctor, what became of that patient of yours? Was not her skull fractured?

PHYSICIAN. Yes. To pieces. However, I got her cured.

1 CITIZEN. Good Lord.

Enter 2 CITIZEN *hastily*. I saw just now the Duke of Kingston pass this door, dressed more like a footman than a nobleman.

1 CITIZEN. Why, do you ever see a nobleman, dressed like himself, *walking?*

2 CITIZEN. He had just on a plain frock. If I had not seen the half of his star, I should not have known that it was him. But maybe you'll say a half-star is sometimes better than a whole moon. Eh? ha! ha! ha![5]

There was a hearty loud laugh.

I then went to Louisa's. I was really in love. I felt a warmth at my heart which glowed in my face. I attempted to be like Digges, and considered the similarity of our genius and pleasures. I acquired confidence by considering my present character in this light: a young fellow of spirit and fashion, heir to a good fortune, enjoying the pleasures of London, and now making his addresses in order to have an intrigue with that delicious subject of gallantry, an actress.

I talked on love very freely. "Madam," said I, "I can never

[5] The Duke of Kingston was a Knight of the Garter, but as the First Citizen indicates, he would not have risked walking the street in court clothes. If he had, the mob would have considered him overdressed, and might have thrown mud at him. The Second Citizen's jest probably means no more than "half a loaf is better than none," the moon being a conventional symbol of something unattainable. But both "star" and "moon" were terms used in fortification, and terms of fortification were at this time much on the lips of wiseacres, as the contemporary satire of Sterne in *Tristram Shandy* shows.

think of having a connection with women that I don't love." "That, Sir," said she, "is only having a satisfaction in common with the brutes. But when there is a union of minds, that is indeed estimable. But don't think Sir, that I am a Platonist. I am not indeed." (This hint gave me courage.) "To be sure, Madam, when there is such a connection as you mention, it is the finest thing in the world. I beg you may just show me civility according as you find me deserve it." "Such a connection, Sir, requires time to establish it." (I thought it honest and proper to let her know that she must not depend on me for giving her much money.) "Madam," said I, "don't think too highly of me. Nor give me the respect which men of great fortune get by custom. I am here upon a very moderate allowance. I am upon honour to make it serve me, and I am obliged to live with great economy." She received this very well.

At night I went to Mr. Thomas Davies's shop and sat a while. I told him that I wanted much to see Johnson. "Sir," said he, "if you'll dine with me on Christmas day, you shall see him. He and some more men of letters are to be with me." I very readily accepted this invitation.

SUNDAY 19 DECEMBER. The night before, I drank tea and sat all the evening writing in the room with my landlord and landlady. They insisted that I should eat a bit of supper. I complied. I also drank a glass of punch. I read some of Pope. I sung a song. I let myself down too much. Also, being unaccustomed to taste supper, my small alteration put me out of order. I went up to my room much disgusted. I thought myself a low being.

This morning I breakfasted with Mr. Murray of Broughton, and then he and I went and waited on Lord and Lady Garlies, from whence we took Captain Keith Stewart with us and went to St. John's Chapel and heard a tolerable sermon on humility.[6] I was not so devout as I could have wished.

[6] Lord Garlies was the eldest son of the sixth Earl of Galloway; Keith Stewart (who later rose to be vice-admiral) was his younger brother; James Murray of Broughton was their brother-in-law. Boswell had seen all of them except Keith Stewart in Galloway on his harvest jaunt of the preceding autumn.

I then went to Macfarlane's. The ladies were indisposed. I could not see them. I had not been there nor seen one of the family all the week before. Captain Erskine is a most particular fellow. His indifference is amazing. He is vastly happy to have the company of people that he likes, yet he is not a bit troubled at their absence, nor will he take the smallest pains to be with them. I was really a little piqued that I had now been from him a week, that I had wished to see him, but that he had never once thought of me —which he told me. I must take him just in his own way. We were very cheerful and flighty. He abused the style of genteel company. We agreed in calling it *a consensual obliteration of the human faculties.*

I drank tea with *Louisa.* Her brother was there. I was very chatty and gay with looking at so fine a woman and thinking what delight I should have with her. She had a meeting with Mr. Stede, an old gentleman late Prompter and now in the Cabinet Council of Covent Garden Theatre. So I was obliged to leave her at seven.

I can come home in an evening, put on my old clothes, nightcap, and slippers, and sit as contented as a cobbler writing my journal or letters to my friends. While I can thus entertain myself, I must be happy in solitude. Indeed there is a great difference between solitude in the country, where you cannot help it, and in London, where you can in a moment be in the hurry and splendour of life.

MONDAY 20 DECEMBER. I went to Louisa's after breakfast. "Indeed," said I, "it was hard upon me to leave you so soon yesterday. I am quite happy in your company." "Sir," said she, "you are very obliging. But," said she, "I am in bad humour this morning. There was a person who professed the greatest friendship for me; I now applied for their assistance, but was shifted. It was such a trifle that I am sure they could have granted it. So I have been railing against my fellow-creatures." "Nay, dear Madam, don't abuse them all on account of an individual. But pray what was this favour? Might I know?" (She blushed.) "Why, Sir, there is a person has sent to me for a trifling debt. I sent back word that it was not convenient for me to let them have it just now, but in six weeks I should pay it."

I was a little confounded and embarrassed here. I dreaded bringing myself into a scrape. I did not know what she might call a trifling sum. I half-resolved to say no more. However, I thought that she might now be trying my generosity and regard for her, and truly this was the real test. I thought I would see if it was in my power to assist her.

"Pray, Madam, what was the sum?" "Only two guineas, Sir." Amazed and pleased, I pulled out my purse. "Madam," said I, "if I can do you any service, you may command me. Two guineas is at present all that I have, but a trifle more. There they are for you. I told you that I had very little, but yet I hope to live. Let us just be honest with one another. Tell me when you are in any little distress, and I will tell you what I can do." She took the guineas. "Sir, I am infinitely obliged to you. As soon as it is in my power, I shall return them. Indeed I could not have expected this from you." Her gratitude warmed my heart. "Madam! though I have little, yet as far as ten guineas, you may apply to me. I would live upon nothing to serve one that I regarded."

I did not well know what to think of this scene. Sometimes I thought it artifice, and that I was taken in. And then again, I viewed it just as a circumstance that might very easily happen. Her mentioning returning the money looked well. My naming the sum of ten guineas was rash; however, I considered that it cost me as much to be cured of what I contracted from a whore, and that ten guineas was but a moderate expense for women during the winter.

I had all along treated her with a distant politeness. On Saturday I just kissed her hand. She now sung to me. I got up in raptures and kissed her with great warmth. She received this very genteelly. I had a delicacy in presuming too far, lest it should look like demanding goods for my money. I resumed the subject of love and gallantry. She said, "I pay no regard to the opinion in the world so far as contradicts my own sentiments." "No, Madam, we are not to mind the arbitrary rules imposed by the multitude." "Yet, Sir, there is a decency to be kept with the public. And I must do so, whose bread depends upon them." "Certainly, Madam. But when may I wait upon you? Tomorrow evening?" "Sir, I am obliged to be all day with a lady who is not well." "Then next day, Madam." "What? to drink a dish of tea, Sir?" "No, no, not to drink a dish of tea." (Here I looked sheepish.) "What time may I wait upon you?" "Whenever you please, Sir." I kissed her again, and went away highly pleased with the thoughts of the affair being settled.

I dined at Macfarlane's. We were very hearty. I indulged in it much. Erskine and I walked down the Haymarket together, throwing out sallies and laughing loud. "Erskine," said I, "don't I make your existence pass more cleverly than anybody?" "Yes, you do." "Don't I make you say more good things?" "Yes. You extract more out of me, you are more chemical to me, than anybody." We drank tea at Dempster's.

I went and sat a while with Captain Webster. He told me that the fatigues of a German campaign are almost incredible. That he was fourteen nights running without being under cover, and often had scarcely any victuals. He said he never once repented his being a soldier, although he cursed the sad fatigues. "Men," said he, "are in that way rendered desperate; and I have wished for an action, either to get out of the world altogether or to get a little rest after it." We talked on a variety of old stories. He is a lively young fellow, and has humour. We were very merry. He returned me many thanks for my company and said it revived him.

TUESDAY 21 DECEMBER. I had resolved not to dine with my landlord, nor to see them much this week, in order to recover my proper dignity and distance. Another very good reason now glared me strong in the face. By my letting Louisa have two guineas, I had only thirteen shillings left; and my term of payment, as I have £25 every six weeks, was not till the 7 of January. I therefore could not afford a shilling, nor near so much, for dinner. So that I was put to my shifts, as I would not be indebted for dinner nor go and ask my allowance before it was due. I sat in till between four and five. I then went to Holborn, to a cheesemonger's, and bought a piece of 3 lb. 10 oz., which cost me 14½d. I eat part of it in the shop, with a halfpenny roll, two of which I had bought at a baker's. I then carried home my provision, and eat some more cheese with the other roll, and a halfpennyworth of apples by way of relish, and took a drink of water. I recollected that I had left a guinea of security at Noble's circulating library. I went and told him that he should put confidence in me, so got it back. This was a most welcome guest to my pocket and communicated spirit to my heart. But, alas, of short duration was this state of opulence. I was reminded by Miss Terrie of a pair of lace ruffles that I had bespoke, which came to 16s. "Very well," said I, and paid them. There was the genteel determined spirit. I comforted myself by thinking that I suffered in the service of my Mistress; and I was romantically amused to think that I was now obliged to my wits, and living on the profit of my works, having got just 13s. by my *Cub*.

I should have mentioned that on Monday Captain Douglas of Kelhead and Captain Maxwell of Dalswinton breakfasted with me.[7]

This evening I had a little adventure which took away the twenty-sixth part of my little stock. I was passing by Whitehall when a little boy came and told a girl who sold gingerbread nuts that he had just given her sixpence instead of a farthing. She denied this. Upon which the poor boy cried and lamented most bitterly. I thought myself bound to interfere in the affair. The boy affirmed the charge with the open keen look of conscious innocence, while the young jade denied it with the colour of countenance and bitterness of expression that betrayed guilt. But what could be done? There was no proof. At last I put it to this test: "Will you say, Devil take you, if you got his sixpence?" This imprecation the little gipsy roared out twice most fervently. Therefore she got

---

[7] Both cousins of Boswell, and for that matter, cousins of Captain James Webster.

off. No jury in any court could have brought her in guilty. There was now a good many people assembled about us. The boy was in very great distress. I asked him if the sixpence was his own. He said it was his mother's. I conceived the misery of his situation when he got home. "There, Sir," said I, "is the sixpence to you. Go home and be easy." I then walked on much satisfied with myself. Such a little incident as this might be laughed at as trifling. But I cannot help thinking it amusing, and valuing it as a specimen of my own tenderness of disposition and willingness to relieve my fellow-creatures.

WEDNESDAY 22 DECEMBER. I stood and chatted a while with the sentries before Buckingham House. One of them, an old fellow, said he was in all the last war. "At the battle of Dettingen," said he, "I saw our cannon make a lane through the French army as broad as that" (pointing to the Mall), "which was filled up in as short time as I'm telling you it." They asked me for a pint of beer, which I gave them. I talked on the sad mischief of war and on the frequency of poverty. "Why, Sir," said he, "GOD made all right at first when he made mankind. ("I believe," said the other, "he made but few of them.") But, Sir, if GOD was to make the world today, it would be crooked again tomorrow. But the time will come when we shall all be rich enough. To be sure, salvation is promised to those that die in the field." I have great pleasure in conversing with the lower part of mankind, who have very curious ideas.

This forenoon I went to Louisa's in full expectation of consummate bliss. I was in a strange flutter of feeling. I was ravished at the prospect of joy, and yet I had such an anxiety upon me that I was afraid that my powers would be enervated. I almost wished to be free of this assignation. I entered her apartment in a sort of confusion. She was elegantly dressed in the morning fashion, and looked delightfully well. I felt the tormenting anxiety of serious love. I sat down and I talked with the distance of a new acquaintance and not with the ease and ardour of a lover, or rather a gallant.

I talked of her lodgings being neat, opened the door of her bed-chamber, looked into it. Then sat down by her in a most melancholy plight. I would have given a good deal to be out of the room.

We talked of religion. Said she, "People who deny that, show a want of sense." "For my own part, Madam, I look upon the adoration of the Supreme Being as one of the greatest enjoyments we have. I would not choose to get rid of my religious notions. I have read books that staggered me. But I was glad to find myself regain my former opinions." "Nay, Sir, what do you think of the Scriptures having stood the test of ages?" "Are you a Roman Catholic, Madam?" "No, Sir. Though I like some parts of their religion, in particular, confession; not that I think the priest can remit sins, but because the notion that we are to confess to a decent clergyman may make us cautious what we do." "Madam," said I, "I would ask you to do nothing that you should be sorry to confess. Indeed I have a great deal of principle in matters of gallantry, and never yet led any woman to do what might afterwards make her uneasy. If she thinks it wrong, I never insist." She asked me some questions about my intrigues, which I nicely eluded.

I then sat near her and began to talk softly, but finding myself quite dejected with love, I really cried out and told her that I was miserable; and as I was stupid, would go away. I rose, but saluting her with warmth, my powers were excited, I felt myself vigorous. I sat down again. I beseeched her, "You know, Madam, you said you was not a Platonist. I beg it of you to be so kind. You said you are above the finesse of your sex." (Be sure always to make a woman better than her sex.) "I adore you." "Nay, dear Sir" (I pressing her to me and kissing her now and then), "pray be quiet. Such a thing requires time to consider of." "Madam, I own this would be necessary for any man but me. But you must take my character from myself. I am very good-tempered, very honest, and have little money. I should have some reward for my particular honesty." "But, Sir, give me time to recollect myself." "Well then, Madam, when shall I see you?" "On Friday, Sir." "A thousand thanks." I left her and came home and took my bread and cheese with great contentment, and then went and chatted a while with Webster.

I had not been at Lord Eglinton's for ten days. Last night I received a card from him: "Lord Eglinton presents his compliments to Mr. Boswell, and returns him a great many thanks for being so good as call on him so often. He is sorry he happened to be always out when Mr. Boswell called."

This he intended as a sharp reproof. However, as Lord Northumberland had called for me, I thought Lord Eglinton might do so, as I was quite independent of him. The card was not written with his own hand, which I was not pleased at. I am the easiest fellow in the world to those who behave well to me. But if a man has treated me with the least slight, I will keep him to every punctilio. I sent him for answer: "Mr. Boswell presents his compliments to Lord Eglinton; hopes he will excuse his writing this card with his own hand; he has not a secretary. Mr. Boswell has paid his respects to Lord Eglinton several times. He lodges at Mr. Terrie's in Downing Street."

This had a proper effect, for today he called when I was abroad, which satisfied me much.

I sat this evening a while with Webster. He entertained me and raised my spirits with military conversation. Yet he sunk them a little; as he brought into my mind some dreary Tolbooth Kirk ideas, than which nothing has given me more gloomy feelings.[8] I shall never forget the dismal hours of apprehension that I have endured in my youth from narrow notions of religion while my tender mind was lacerated with infernal horror. I am surprised how I have got rid of these notions so entirely. Thank GOD, my mind is now clear and elevated. I am serene and happy. I can look up to my Creator with adoration and hope.

THURSDAY 23 DECEMBER. I should have mentioned some

[8] Webster's father, the well-known Dr. Alexander Webster, was minister of the Tolbooth Church in Edinburgh and one of the leaders of the strict ("high-flying") party in the Church of Scotland.

days ago that Erskine and I took a walk in St. James's Park, on a fine, sunshine forenoon. I told him that if the Guards could not be got for me, I would just take a cornetcy of Dragoons. "I beseech you," said he, "never think of that. You would grow melancholy. You would destroy yourself. If you was sent by yourself to country quarters, I would not trust you with a basin of cold water to wash your hands, nor with the most awkward imitation of a penknife."

I had this day a walk there with Sheridan. Said he, "Our present plan of education is very bad. A young man is taught for a number of years a variety of things which, when he comes into the world, he finds of no manner of use. There is not one thing taught for the conduct of real life. The mind is ploughed and harrowed, but there is no seed sown. By cultivation the soil is made rich, and so when a young man comes into the world, whatever happens to be sown grows up in great luxuriance. A strong proof that the minds of the people of England are not formed is their instability. In Oliver Cromwell's time, they were all precise, canting creatures. And no sooner did Charles the Second come over than they turned gay rakes and libertines. In James the First's time, the Duke of Buckingham, who wanted to rival Cardinal Richelieu in everything, brought about a Parlimentary inquiry into the state of education, that he might do as much in that way as the great Minister of France; but by the Duke's death this did not take place, at least was not carried through. Without such a scheme, we cannot hope for a proper plan of education. But this I have reason to believe will be one of the first objects after the Peace. My plan would be that young people should be perfectly qualified to be good citizens in the first place, and that there should be particular opportunities of instruction for every particular way of life. There is one rank for which there is no plan of education, and that is country gentlemen. Surely, this is of great importance: that the landed interest should be well instructed." "Mr. Sheridan," said I, "I have thought a good deal upon education. I see so many difficulties that I despair of a good method. I take this state of being to be a jest; that it is not intended that we should do much here to the purpose; and therefore we must just go through it the best way we can." "Nay, Sir," said he, "we can do something to the purpose." Indeed, it is more agreeable to think of doing something than to consider ourselves as nothing at all.

I eat my cold repast today heartily. I have great spirits. I see how little a man can live upon. I find that Fortune cannot get the better of me. I never can come lower than to live on bread and cheese.

FRIDAY 24 DECEMBER. I waited on Louisa. Says she, "I have been very unhappy since you was here. I have been thinking of what I said to you. I find that such a connection would make me miserable." "I hope, Madam, I am not disagreeable to you." "No, Sir, you are not. If it was the first duke in England I spoke to, I should just say the same thing." "But pray, Madam, what is your objection?" "Really, Sir, I have many disagreeable apprehensions. It may be known. Circumstances might be very troublesome. I beg it of you, Sir, consider of it. Your own good sense will agree with me. Instead of visiting me as you do now, you would find a discontented, unhappy creature." I was quite confused. I did not know what to say. At last I agreed to think of it and see her on Sunday. I came home and dined in dejection. Yet I mustered up vivacity, and away I went in full dress to Northumberland House. There was spirit, to lay out a couple of shillings and be a man of fashion in my situation. There was true economy.

SATURDAY 25 DECEMBER. The night before I did not rest well. I was really violently in love with Louisa. I thought she did not care for me. I thought that if I did not gain her affections, I would appear despicable to myself. This day I was in a better frame, being Christmas day, which has always inspired me with most agreeable feelings. I went to St. Paul's Church and in that magnificent temple fervently adored the GOD of goodness and mercy, and heard a sermon by the Bishop of Oxford[9] on the publishing of glad tidings of great joy. I then went to Child's, where little was passing. However, here goes the form of a

[9] John Hume, D.D.

DIALOGUE AT CHILD'S.

1 CITIZEN. Why, here is the bill of mortality. Is it right, Doctor?
PHYSICIAN. Why, I don't know.

1 CITIZEN. I'm sure it is not. Sixteen only died of cholics! I dare
say you have killed as many yourself.

2 CITIZEN. Ay, and hanged but three! O Lord, ha! ha! ha!

I then sat a while at Coutts's,[10] and then at Macfarlane's, and
then went to Davies's. Johnson was gone to Oxford. I was introduced to Mr. Dodsley, a good, jolly, decent, conversable man,[1] and
Mr. Goldsmith, a curious, odd, pedantic fellow with some genius.[2]
It was quite a literary dinner. I had seen no warm victuals for four
days, and therefore played a very bold knife and fork. It is inconceivable how hearty I eat and how comfortable I felt myself after
it. We talked entirely in the way of Geniuses.

We talked of poetry. Said Goldsmith, "The miscellaneous
poetry of this age is nothing like that of the last; it is very poor.
Why there, now, Mr. Dodsley, is your *Collection*."[3] DODSLEY. "I
think that equal to those made by Dryden and Pope." GOLDSMITH.
"To consider them, Sir, as villages, yours may be as good; but let
us compare house with house, you can produce me no edifices equal
to the *Ode on St. Cecilia's Day*, *Absalom and Achitophel*, or *The
Rape of the Lock*." DODSLEY. "We have poems in a different way.
There is nothing of the kind in the last age superior to *The Spleen*."[4]
BOSWELL. "And what do you think of Gray's odes? Are not they
noble?" GOLDSMITH. "Ah, the rumbling thunder! I remember a
friend of mine was very fond of Gray. 'Yes,' said I, 'he is very fine
indeed; as thus—

[10] A well-known Scots banker in London.

[1] This Mr. Dodsley is Robert Dodsley, the elder and better known member of
the firm of R. & J. Dodsley (see above, 24 November). He had retired from
active business some years before.

[2] See above, p. 30. This is Boswell's first meeting with Goldsmith. It is hard
to tell from the tone of the entry whether Boswell knew any of his writings.

[3] Dodsley's *Collection* was a famous anthology of eighteenth-century verse
first published in 1748.   [4] By Matthew Green, first published in 1737.

Mark the white and mark the red,
Mark the blue and mark the green;
Mark the colours ere they fade,
Darting thro' the welkin sheen.'

'O, yes,' said he, 'great, great!' 'True, Sir,' said I, 'but I have made the lines this moment.' " BOSWELL. "Well, I admire Gray prodigiously. I have read his odes till I was almost mad." GOLDSMITH. "They are terribly obscure. We must be historians and learned men before we can understand them."[5] DAVIES. "And why not? He is not writing to porters or carmen. He is writing to men of knowledge." GOLDSMITH. "Have you seen *Love in a Village?*" BOSWELL. "I have. I think it a good, pleasing thing." GOLDSMITH. "I am afraid we will have no good plays now. The taste of the audience is spoiled by the pantomime of Shakespeare. The wonderful changes and shiftings." DAVIES. "Nay, but you will allow that Shakespeare has great merit?" GOLDSMITH. "No, I know Shakespeare very well." (Here I said nothing, but thought him a most impudent puppy.) BOSWELL. "What do you think of Johnson?" GOLDSMITH. "He has exceeding great merit. His *Rambler* is a noble work." BOSWELL. "His *Idler* too is very pretty. It is a lighter performance; and he has thrown off the classical fetters very much." DAVIES. "He is a most entertaining companion. And how can it be otherwise, when he has so much imagination, has read so much, and digested it so well?"

We had many more topics which I don't remember. I was very well. I then went to Macfarlane's. We were very merry. Erskine and I had some bread and wine and talked for near two hours. He told me that he was kept as a blackguard when he was a boy, then went to sea, and then came into the Army. And that he wondered how he had been turned out a tolerable being.

SUNDAY 26 DECEMBER. I went to Whitehall Chapel and

[5] Goldsmith here repeats a stricture on Gray's *Odes* that he had published five years earlier in *The Monthly Review*. A testimony, by the way, to the accuracy of Boswell's reporting.

heard service. I took a whim to go through all the churches and chapels in London, taking one each Sunday.

At one I went to Louisa's. I told her my passion in the warmest terms. I told her that my happiness absolutely depended upon her. She said it was running the greatest risk. "Then," said I, "Madam, you will show the greatest generosity to a most sincere lover." She said that we should take time to consider of it, and that then we could better determine how to act. We agreed that the time should be a week, and that if I remained of the same opinion, she would then make me blessed. There is no telling how easy it made my mind to be convinced that she did not despise me, but on the contrary had a tender heart and wished to make me easy and happy.

I this day received a letter from the Duke of Queensberry, in answer to one that I had wrote him, telling me that a commission in the Guards was a fruitless pursuit, and advising me to take to a civil rather than a military life. I was quite stupefied and enraged at this. I imagined my father was at the bottom of it.[6] I had multitudes of wild schemes. I thought of enlisting for five years as a soldier in India, of being a private man either in the Horse or Footguards, &c. At last good sense prevailed, and I resolved to be cheerful and to wait and to ask it of Lady Northumberland. At night I sat at Macfarlane's pretty well.

[6] The letter was as follows: "SIR:—I am sorry you have set your mind so much upon going into the Guards, because I am perfectly convinced you will now find it a fruitless pursuit, and therefore the best advice I can give you is to turn your thoughts some other way. My regard for your father's recommendation, and desire of gratifying your inclination, made me wish to obtain what I had very little hopes of doing, and you know from the beginning I never flattered you with any prospect of success; and therefore I hope you will the easier reconcile your mind to a civil instead of military occupation, especially when you consider that although you are a young man, yet you are above the age when an ensign's commission is thought desirable. I found it would be in vain to apply to my Lord Ligonier, having met with an intimate friend of his the day before I came out of town, who assured me it would be to no purpose to solicit him, nor indeed anybody else in the present state of the Army. I am, with much regard, Sir, Your obedient humble servant, QUEENSBERRY, &c. Amesbury, 22 December 1762."

MONDAY 27 DECEMBER. I went to Mrs. Gould's and told my lamentable story. I also told it to my friend Douglas. They advised me to apply to Lady Northumberland. I therefore wrote a letter to her Ladyship to the following purpose:

MADAM:—Your kindness to me upon many occasions makes me freely tell you anything that vexes me. Sympathy is the greatest cordial we can have. I have received a letter from the Duke of Queensberry informing me that a commission in the Guards cannot be got for me. What does your Ladyship think of a man who, notwithstanding of such a disappointment, can cry *vive la bagatelle!* and walk about contented, cheerful, and merry? Have not I spirit? Ought I not to be a soldier? Ought I not to have the honour of serving George the Third? When your Ladyship tore the skin of your leg and yet kept up your spirits, you had good reason to be vain.[7] I think I may be so too. Your Ladyship may remember that I observed to you that people often fell into a great mistake: because people of consequence liked them as acquaintances and showed them civility, they applied to them for substantial favours, which is quite a different sort of a thing. To come to the point, Madam, here am I anxious to get a commission in the Guards. If you and my Lord can do the thing for me, I shall be very happy. I have an independent spirit. I think a Welsh rabbit and porter with freedom of spirit better than ortolans and burgundy with servility. I will by no means cringe, not even to the ancient and honourable family of Northumberland. As a family I revere it. But I revere my own mind more. I can assure you, Madam, that I do not expect that

[7] " . . . the Duchess of Hamilton is so altered I did not know her. Indeed, she is big with child, and so big that, as my Lady Northumberland says, it is plain she has a camel in her belly; and my Lord Edgcumbe says it is as true that it did not go through the eye of a needle. That great vulgar countess has been laid up with a hurt in her leg; Lady Rebecca Poulett pushed her on the birthnight against a bench; the Duchess of Grafton asked if it was true that Lady Rebecca kicked her.—'Kicked me, Madam! When did you ever hear of a Percy that took a kick?' " (Horace Walpole to George Montagu, 23 December 1759.)

you are to take so much trouble for me. But I thought it was a chance, and I might try. I have got as much as I can live upon. But I want to be something, and I like nothing but the Army.

If your Ladyship tells me that it is not convenient, I shall neither be surprised nor fretted. I am much obliged to you for your goodness already. It just comes to this. If the representatives of the noble Percy choose to take a young man of a good old Scotch family by the hand, who will rather do credit to his friends than otherwise, and who will be very grateful, it will be extremely obliging. I remain, &c.

This I sent to her Ladyship.

I drank tea at Lady Betty's (for I will no longer name Macfarlane), and went with her and Lady Anne to Lady Frances Erskine's, where was a genteel company, tea and cards. I had been with Louisa in the forenoon, and I was always thinking of her. It must henceforth be taken for granted that I see her every day except when I mention the contrary. I came home with the ladies and supped. We were very merry. They owned that I was very well dressed.

TUESDAY 28 DECEMBER. I should have mentioned on Sunday last that I drank tea at Sheridan's, where was a Captain Maud[8] of the Blues, with whom he disputed on the propriety of theatrical action. He said that an actor ought to forget himself and the audience entirely, and be quite the real character; and that for his part, he was so much so that he remembered nothing at all but the character. This Mr. Maud opposed as wrong; because an actor in that case would not play so well, as he would not be enough master of himself. I think he was right.

This day I cast my eye on my old laced hat, which I saw would raise me a small supply. No sooner thought than done. Off it went with my sharp penknife. I carried it to a jeweller's in Piccadilly and sold it for 6s. 6d., which was a great cause of joy to me.

---

[8] Probably Mawhood (Captain Parravicini Mawhood, Royal Regiment of Horse Guards).

I drank tea at Dempster's. Erskine and the ladies were there. I laid open to them my poverty and my cheese adventures, which they were much entertained with. They sympathized with my distress and admired my resolution. They asked me to dine every day with them, which I refused till after my day of payment, as I would think myself obliged to them for a dinner. I don't know what to think of my discovering this affair to them. It was, to be sure, frank and agreeable to do so. But I am too open and have a desire to let all my affairs be known. This I must endeavour to correct.

I should have mentioned that I called at Love's this afternoon. We stayed and supped at Dempster's. I was rather dull and out of order.

WEDNESDAY 29 DECEMBER. I had Love at breakfast with me. He called up to my mind many theatrical ideas of Mr. Garrick, Old Cibber, &c. I then went to Lady Betty's. Lord Eglinton had long been wanting to be acquainted with Captain Andrew. He came there this forenoon, and I made them acquainted. My Lord said he fancied I was very busy, that I had not time to see my friends. "O, yes," said I, "there are many curious adventures in this town." Says he, "I had a very good party with me last night, amongst whom was Fingal, who is really a Highland claymore. If you was to scour him, you would spoil him. We were talking of Gray's fine *Elegy in a Churchyard*. 'Hoot!' cried Fingal, 'to write panegyrics upon a parcel of damned rascals that did nething but plough the land and saw corn.' He considered that fighters only should be celebrated." Erskine talked a little to him, but not much.

This day I had no dinner of any kind. At seven I went back to Lady Betty's. We went all in her coach a drive to Ludgate Hill, to a silk mercer's, where they bought a gown for Lady Jenny.[9] We returned and supped. We had a warm dispute about Lady Betty's style of living here. It was alleged that she had laid down a plan of living very private, which she had broke through, and that therefore she was unhappy, as she aimed at a way of life that she could

[9] The third of the Kellie ladies. She married Sir Robert Anstruther of Balcaskie a few months later.

not afford. She was really fretted at this, and she looked ugly and
ill-natured. I declared that I would either be the most splendid or
the most quiet being, for that happiness was seated either at the
head or the crampet[1] of the stick of life.

We sat till it was late. When I came home, I felt myself jaded
and stupid and uneasy. I was somewhat sick, and I had a headache.
I was vexed to find myself deviating from my scheme of sober
regularity and being really a rake, which I think sitting up a great
part of. I made myself easy by thinking that I had just raked three
nights during the holidays; and I resolved in time coming never
to be out at night, except on some very particular occasion.

THURSDAY 30 DECEMBER. I had Erskine with me at breakfast, after which he and I went to Lady Frances Erskine's, and then
I went to Lady Northumberland's. In my letter to her I mentioned
to her that I would not choose to be far from London; and therefore
I would choose no other corps but the Guards or the Blues; that is
to say, the Royal Horse Guards Blue.[2] "Madam," said I, "I took the
liberty to write you a letter." "Sir," said she, "I am sorry to find
these Guards so difficult to be got. I have been speaking to some
officers on that subject. I imagined that your father had wrote in
such a way to the Duke of Queensberry that he had not been in
earnest to get it. But I find that it really is a very difficult matter.
As to the Blues again, I should hope that may be easier; and when
the Marquis of Granby[3] comes over, I shall apply to him." "So
your Ladyship really intends to take a charge of me? Pray don't be
upon ceremony. I have no title to ask such a thing of you. I really
did not expect that you would have engaged in it." "Sir, I should
not say so if I did not intend it." "Madam, I am infinitely obliged to
you." "I shall certainly, Sir, recommend you to Lord Granby in the
strongest manner; and as the Blues are his own regiment, I should

---

[1] Iron guard at the end of a staff: "top or bottom."
[2] This is not the copy of the letter which he entered in the journal (above, 27
December).
[3] Commander-in-Chief of the British forces in Germany. His wife (recently
deceased) was Lady Northumberland's cousin.

think that they will not interfere but allow him to do what he pleases. I hope, Sir, you are living agreeably in the mean time, as you know one must wait for a vacancy." "I am, Madam. But I want to be something." "Really, Sir, I think you are right. There's my Lord Warkworth,[4] as his regiment is now to be broke, my Lord wrote to him to know if he chose to continue in the Army. He said, by all means. For he could not think of being idle. The Blues, Sir, will not be so good as the Guards, because your business does not lie in town. But it is a very fine corps, and you are always in the neighbourhood of London." "Madam, I shall be happy to be in it. I am just now living very well. Economy is all in all for a young man. I have but £200 a year, and yet I will be able to do. Your Ladyship's kindness has brought me into the best company, and nobody knows but I have a thousand a year." "Why, Sir, a young man has no occasion for elegant lodgings, a great many clothes, or being much in taverns." "I wish, Lady Northumberland, I could be of any service to you. It is possible it may be in my power. Well, Madam, shall I keep up my spirits?" "By all means." "I was thinking to enlist for five years in India. But that would have been a sad scheme. For at the end, I could but have had a commission; and I think, Madam, I can pass these five years better in London." We laughed heartily at this. I left her, in high glee at my success. This day may show on what a good footing I have the honour to be with this noble countess and excellent woman, for whom I have the highest regard and gratitude.

I called a little at Sheridan's. He said trifling was the greatest joy in life, provided that the mind was properly prepared to relish it, by hard study.

I then went to Louisa's. I told her my happy prospect, which she rejoiced much at. She was very gentle and rather low-spirited this day. I was much at home with her. I talked of love connections very freely. We insensibly slid into our own story without men-

[4] Lady Northumberland's son, later second Duke of Northumberland. Better known in America as the Earl Percy who commanded the retreat from Concord, 19 April 1775.

tioning parties. We said many tender delicate things. I told her that I was thinking according to our agreement. "Well, then," said she, "I hope you will think as I do." "Madam," said I, "I hope you will think as I do. However, we shall see when the time is elapsed."

FRIDAY 31 DECEMBER.[5] I waited on Louisa. The conversation turned upon love, whether we would or not. She mentioned one consequence that in an affair of gallantry might be troublesome. "I suppose, Madam," said I, "you mean if a third person should be interested in the affair. Why, to be sure, if such a person should appear, he must be taken care of. For my own part, I have the strongest principles of that kind." "Well, Sir," said she, with a sweet complacency. "But we won't talk any more on the subject."

I then went to Sheridan's upon an invitation to drink tea and spend the evening and hear a reading of *The Discovery*, a new comedy written by Mrs. Sheridan. He and she read alternately. I liked it much and was well entertained. Mrs. Cholmondeley was there, also a Captain Jephson, a lively little fellow and the best mimic in the world. Also Colonel Irwin, a genteel, well-bred, pretty man. He told us some little stories very well. We had some other people, and, with an elegant supper, the evening went very well on. Indeed, I was this night but a bad member of society. I was bashful and silent.

[5] The memorandum for this day is as follows: "Dress; then breakfast and be denied. Then journal and Hume, busy till three. Then Louisa; be warm and press home, and talk gently and Digges-like. Acquire an easy dignity and black liveliness of behaviour like him. Learn, as Sheridan said, to speak slow and softly. See not Kellies today. At six, Sheridan's. Be like Sir Richard Steele. Think on Prologue, and of being in the Blues, and so pushing your fortune fine. Write to Somerville about Kirk. Study calm and deliberate." Boswell had started reading Hume's *History of England;* he hoped to be allowed to write the prologue for Mrs. Sheridan's play. "Somerville about Kirk" is unexplained.

1763

DIALOGUE AT CHILD'S.

1 CITIZEN. Pray, Sir, have you read Mr. Warton's *Essay on the Life and Writings of Pope?* He will not allow him to be a poet. He says he had good sense and good versification, but wants the warm imagination and brilliancy of expression that constitute the true poetical genius. He tries him by a rule prescribed by Longinus, which is to take the words out of their metrical order and then see if they have the sparks of poetry. Don't you remember this?

2 CITIZEN. I don't agree with him.

1 CITIZEN. Nor I, neither. He is fond of Thomson. He says he has great force.

2 CITIZEN. He has great faults.

1 CITIZEN. Ay, but great force, too.

2 CITIZEN. I have eat beefsteaks with him.

3 CITIZEN. So have I.

I received for a suit of old clothes 11s., which came to me in good time. I went to Louisa at one. "Madam, I have been thinking seriously." "Well, Sir, I hope you are of my way of thinking." "I hope, Madam, you are of mine. I have considered this matter most seriously. The week is now elapsed, and I hope you will not be so cruel as to keep me in misery." (I then began to take some liberties.) "Nay, Sir—now—but do consider—" "Ah, Madam!" "Nay, but you are an encroaching creature!" (Upon this I advanced to the greatest freedom by a sweet elevation of the charming petticoat.) "Good heaven, Sir!" "Madam, I cannot help it. I adore you. Do you like me?" (She answered me with a warm kiss, and pressing me to her bosom, sighed, "O Mr. Boswell!") "But, my dear Madam! Permit me, I beseech you." "Lord, Sir, the people may

115

come in." "How then can I be happy? What time? Do tell me." "Why, Sir, on Sunday afternoon my landlady, of whom I am most afraid, goes to church, so you may come here a little after three." "Madam, I thank you a thousand times." "Now, Sir, I have but one favour to ask of you. Whenever you cease to regard me, pray don't use me ill, nor treat me coldly. But inform me by a letter or any other way that it is over." "Pray, Madam, don't talk of such a thing. Indeed, we cannot answer for our affections. But you may depend on my behaving with civility and politeness."

I drank tea at Lady Betty's. The Dempsters were there. Jocularity and loud mirth went round. After the elegant scene of gallantry which I had just been solacing my romantic imagination with, and after the high-relished ideas with which my fancy had been heated, I could consider the common style of company and conversation but as low and insipid. But the Fife tongue and the Niddry's Wynd address were quite hideous.[6] After the tender respect with which I had been treated by the adorable Louisa I could not brook the not-ill-meant though coarse gibes of this *hamely* company. I was hurt, but seemed easy. I left them at nine o'clock and went home.

SUNDAY 2 JANUARY. I had George Home at breakfast with me. He is a good honest fellow and applies well to his business as a merchant. He had seen me all giddiness at his father's, and was astonished to find me settled on so prudent a plan. As I have made it a rule to dine every Sunday at home, and have got my landlady to give us regularly on that day a piece of good roast beef with a warm apple-pie, I was a little difficulted today, as our time of dining is three o'clock, just my hour of assignation. However, I got dinner to be at two, and at three I hastened to my charmer.

Here a little speculation on the human mind may well come in.

[6] Niddry's Wynd was an alley in the Old Town of Edinburgh, extending from the High Street (near the Tron Church) to the Cowgate. The Musical Society of Edinburgh, in which the Earl of Kellie was a prominent member, held its concerts there. "Niddry's Wynd address" therefore probably means "Edinburgh society manners."

For here was I, a young man full of vigour and vivacity, the favourite lover of a handsome actress and going to enjoy the full possession of my warmest wishes. And yet melancholy threw a cloud over my mind. I could relish nothing. I felt dispirited and languid. I approached Louisa with a kind of an uneasy tremor. I sat down. I toyed with her. Yet I was not inspired by Venus. I felt rather a delicate sensation of love than a violent amorous inclination for her. I was very miserable. I thought myself feeble as a gallant, although I had experienced the reverse many a time. Louisa knew not my powers. She might imagine me impotent. I sweated almost with anxiety, which made me worse. She behaved extremely well; did not seem to remember the occasion of our meeting at all. I told her I was very dull. Said she, "People cannot always command their spirits." The time of church was almost elapsed when I began to feel that I was still a man. I fanned the flame by pressing her alabaster breasts and kissing her delicious lips. I then barred the door of her dining-room, led her all fluttering into her bedchamber, and was just making a triumphal entry when we heard her landlady coming up. "O Fortune why did it happen thus?" would have been the exclamation of a Roman bard. We were stopped most suddenly and cruelly from the fruition of each other. She ran out and stopped the landlady from coming up. Then returned to me in the dining-room. We fell into each other's arms, sighing and panting, "O dear, how hard this is." "O Madam, see what you can contrive for me." "Lord, Sir, I am so frightened."

Her brother then came in. I recollected that I had been at no place of worship today. I begged pardon for a little and went to Covent Garden Church, where there is evening service between five and six. I heard a few prayers and then returned and drank tea. She entertained us with her adventures when travelling through the country. Some of them were excellent. I told her she might make a novel. She said if I would put them together that she would give me material. I went home at seven. I was unhappy at being prevented from the completion of my wishes, and yet I thought that I had saved my credit for prowess, that I might through anxiety

have not acted a vigorous part; and that we might contrive a meeting where I could love with ease and freedom.

MONDAY 3 JANUARY. I begged Louisa to invent some method
by which we might meet in security. I insisted that she should go
and pass the night with me somewhere. She begged time to think
of it.

Webster and I dined at Gould's. The Colonel was not at home,
being upon guard. A Mrs. Douglas was there, lady to Captain
Douglas of the Guards, a mighty pretty, agreeable creature. She
asked me how long I had been from Scotland. If my name was Mr.
James Boswell, and if I remembered her at Moffat. She said if I did
not recollect her name then, she would not tell me. "Madam," said
I, "did it not begin with M?" She said it did. She proved to be a
Miss Mackay with whom I was deeply in love at thirteen, a passion
which Mr. Joseph Fergusson, then my tutor, ridiculed most roughly
by setting his teeth together and giving hard thumps on the knees of
his breeches. However, I certainly at that time felt all the pleasing
anguish of a genuine flame. I told Mrs. Gould, "This, Madam, is
a lady whom I was most desperately in love with." "Sir," said Mrs.
Douglas, "I never knew it." "No, Madam, I never declared my
hopeless passion." I diverted them by expatiating on this affair,
and we were very cheerful. She hoped to see me, she said, at her
house. Webster appeared in a poor light today. He seemed very
young. He was lively, but it was the liveliness of a boy.

TUESDAY 4 JANUARY. Louisa told me that she would go with
me to pass the night when she was sure that she would not be
wanted at the playhouse next day; and she mentioned Saturday as
most convenient, being followed by Sunday, on which nothing
is done. "But, Sir," said she, "may not this be attended with expense? I hope you'll excuse me." There was something so kind and
so delicate in this hint that it charmed me. "No, Madam, it cannot
be a great expense, and I can save on other articles to have money
for this."

I recollected that when I was in London two years ago I had left
a guinea with Mr. Meighan, a Roman-Catholic bookseller in

Drury Lane, of which I had some change to receive.[7] I went to him and got 5s. and 6d., which gave me no small consolation. Elated with this new acquisition of pecuniary property, I instantly resolved to eat, drink, and be merry. I therefore hied me to a beerhouse; called for some bread and cheese and a pint of porter.

Close by the fire sat an old man whose countenance was furrowed with distress. He said his name was Michael Cholmondeley, that he was a day-labourer but out of work, that he had laid out a penny for some beer, and had picked up a bit of bread in the street which he was eating with it. I immediately ordered such a portion of victuals and drink for him as I took for myself. He then told me he was a sad dog in his youth, run off from his friends to London, wrought here some time, and at last, wanting money, he had sold himself for a slave to the Plantations for seven years. "Upon my word," said I, "you are a most extraordinary genius. How much did you get?" CHOLMONDELEY. "Twenty pounds." BOSWELL. "And pray, what sort of a life had you there?" CHOLMONDELEY. "O, Sir, a very good life. We had plenty of meat and drink, and wrought but five hours a day." He said he then came back, and afterwards made voyages in lighters both to France and Spain. Poor creature! He had got falls and was sorely bruised, and often, even in severe weather, has been obliged to lie in the streets. I paid for his meal and gave him a penny. Why such a wretched being subsists is to me a strange thing. But I am a weak creature. I submit to GOD's will, I hope to know the reason of it some time.

I then bethought me of a place to which Louisa and I might safely go. I went to my good friend Hayward's at the Black Lion, told him that I had married, and that I and my wife, who was to be in town on Saturday, would sleep in his house till I got a lodging for her. The King of Prussia says in one of his poems that gallantry comprises every vice.[8] That of lying it certainly does, without

[7] Perhaps he had left a deposit to pay for books sent to his lodging, or to be sent after to him to Scotland?

[8] Perhaps *Épitre VIII, A Chasot (Sur la modération dans l'amour)*, though no lines in that poem correspond exactly to Boswell's paraphrase.

which intrigue can never be carried on. But as the proverb says, in love and war all is fair. I who am a lover and hope to be a soldier think so. In this instance we could not be admitted to any decent house except as man and wife. Indeed, we are so if union of hearts be the principal requisite. We are so, at least for a time. How cleverly this can be done here. In Scotland it is impossible. We should be married with a vengeance.[9] I went home and dined. I thought my slender diet weakened me. I resolved to live hearty and be stout. This afternoon I became very low-spirited. I sat in close. I hated all things. I almost hated London. O miserable absurdity! I could see nothing in a good light. I just submitted and hoped to get the better of this.

WEDNESDAY 5 JANUARY. I was agreeably surprised at breakfast with the arrival of my brother John in good health and spirits, although he had been for three months lately in a most terrible way. I walked with him in the Park. He talked sensibly and well.[1]

[9] Because in Scotland no more was necessary for a legal marriage than for a marriageable couple to acknowledge themselves man and wife in the presence of two witnesses. I am told, however, that Boswell shows himself either weak in law or troubled in conscience in assuming that this escapade would have made him a married man against his will if it had happened in Scotland. For a marriage of this kind to be held valid by a court in case of any question arising, the court would have had to be satisfied that the parties truly intended to contract marriage. In this case, the assumption of false names (see below, pp. 137–138) belied any such intent.

[1] John Boswell was at this time a lieutenant in the Thirty-first Regiment of Foot. Boswell had heard on 26 October 1762 that he was "ill" at Plymouth, and was "really hurt a great deal," no doubt because the illness was mental. On 8 February he wrote to Johnston, "My brother John was very bad this winter at Plymouth. He was confined by a severe disorder. He was quite delirious. Good GOD, how alarming! But it was occasioned by a fall from a stair. He is now quite well, is in London, and goes to Scotland this week. . . . If you hear the story of his illness mentioned, pray let the fall be known." John suffered periodically from insanity all the rest of his life. He retired from active service in 1764 but remained on the half-pay list until 1798, which was probably the year of his death. Boswell's unfailing kindness to his sullen and at times dangerous brother is one of the most attractive features of his journal.

I then went to Lady Betty's. I was rather in the low-spirited humour still. She was by herself. I talked of my schemes. I owned my unsettled views, which indeed are only so at times, as I have preserved almost an uninterrupted constancy to the Guards. She asked me to dine. I told her I now had money to support me till Friday, was not obliged by a dinner, and therefore would come. I went and had some elegant conversation with Louisa; told her all was fixed for Saturday. She sweetly acquiesced. I like her better and better every day.

I was very hearty at dinner, but was too ridiculous. This is what I ought most to guard against. People in company applaud a man for it very much, but behind his back hold him very cheap. I have a strange knack at inventing odd phrases. We were talking of Mr. Garrick's power of making plays run. "Ay," said I, "he never takes a calf by the tail but he makes it run." This we made a common byword of. I had this morning sent a letter to Lord Eglinton as follows:

MY LORD:—Your Lordship's card, which came safe, was received by me with different feelings.[2] At first I talked very cava-

[2] Eglinton had made a riposte to Boswell's stately note of 22 December (above, p. 102), but Boswell had omitted to enter it in his journal or even to record its receipt, probably because of chagrin at having come off so badly in the interchange. After thinking the matter over, he has allowed his natural candour to assert itself. Eglinton's card was as follows: "Lord Eglinton presents his compliments to Mr. Boswell, and returns him a great many thanks for being so good as to teach him good breeding.—He did not know he had been upon ceremony with Mr. Boswell, otherwise he would have done himself the honour to have waited on Mr. Boswell sooner.—Lord Eglinton may be mistaken, and submits it to Mr. Boswell's better judgment, but he always looked on ceremony to be certain rules for the conduct of those who had not sense to guide them, and never to be used by a man of true nobleness but to keep impertinence at a distance.—As to the message sent Mr. Boswell being wrote *by his secretary*, as he is pleased to call it, Lord Eglinton begs leave to assure Mr. Boswell it was not from want of respect; but as the Duc de Nivernois, the Duke of Kingston, &c., &c., generally send messages to him wrote by the footman or the porter, he thought he might

lierly: "Upon my word, the man has brought himself well off."
But on a second perusal and a discovery of the poignant ridicule, I
was obliged to acknowledge that you had used me as Mr. Moodie
did the Devil: *left me no the likeness o' a cat.*[3] However, I contrive
to get an indirect compliment by being the cause (as Falstaff says)
of something so clever. You know we have often disputed whether
or not I am a poet. I have sent you an ode.[4] Lord Elibank thought
it good. I think so too.

As we were at dinner I got his answer as follows:

DEAR JAMIE,—I received your note, and am very glad you are
got right again. I like your ode much. There was no need of that
to convince me you had genius. I wish I was as sure of your judgment of men and things. I know you think yourself as well acquainted with both as Mr. Moodie's elders think him with GOD and
the Devil. I agree you are upon a par, but I differ from the chosen
ones. Yours,

E———.

Pray sup with me tonight. I have a choice spirit or two. Bring the

---

venture to send one to Mr. Boswell wrote by his valet de chambre. Queen
Street, December 22.—Lord Eglinton sends this by a servant out of livery."
(That is, he delivered it himself.)

[3] Probably some anecdote of the spiritual prowess of the Reverend Alexander
Moodie of Riccarton, immortalized by Burns in *The Holy Fair:*

> Now a' the congregation o'er
> 　Is silent expectation:
> For Moodie speels [enters] the holy door,
> 　Wi' tidings o' salvation.
> Should Hornie, as in ancient days,
> 　'Mang sons o' GOD present him,
> The vera sight o' Moodie's face
> 　To's ain het hame had sent him
> 　　Wi' fright that day.

[4] See later in the entry for his day. No copy of the *Ode to Ambition* has as yet
been recovered. Boswell seems to have thought it his best achievement in
verse, for he wrote it out for Voltaire when he visited him at Ferney.

Captain with you. We'll rub him up, and you shall have leave to laugh at him for not knowing the world. Lady Macfarlane's brother, I mean.

This was really so good that they all agreed I should go, which the Captain complied with; so we sent our compliments, and we would wait on him. We then resumed our free jollity. I said I was happy. Indeed, after my gloom yesterday, it was a great odds. "But," said Lady Betty, "his weakness is that he would prefer Mrs. Gould's to this." "Indeed," said I. "I like your company much. But then I want to be among English people and to acquire the language." They laughed at that. I declaimed on the felicity of London. But they were cold and could not understand me. They reasoned plainly like people in the common road of life, and I like a man of fancy and whim. Indeed, it will not bear reasoning. But I can hear the rude attacks of people on my notions, and pursue them with complacency and satisfaction. Indeed, as to the happiness of life, it is neither in this thing nor that thing. It is in everything. Reason is not the sole guide. Inclination must chiefly direct us; and in this, one man's inclination is just as good as another's. For my own part, I shall always endeavour to be as happy as I can.

I represented Michael Cholmondeley's case and got three shillings for him. I drank tea with my landlord.

At nine Erskine and I went to Lord Eglinton's. His choice spirits were Lord Advocate,[5] Sir James Macdonald, and Captain Johnstone of the Navy,[6] son to Sir James. Erskine and I were most amazingly bashful and stupid. The conversation was all about the banks of

---

[5] The Lord Advocate of Scotland, Thomas Miller, later Lord Justice-Clerk, Lord President of the Court of Session, and baronet. He was in town as Member of Parliament for Dumfries. The Lord Advocate is the principal law-officer of the Crown; much the same thing as Attorney General in England.

[6] George Johnstone, later Commodore, Governor of West Florida, 1763; one of the commissioners appointed in 1778 to treat with the American colonies. In the course of the negotiations he attempted to bribe one of the American members and was forced by a resolution of Congress to withdraw from the Commission.

Scotland; a method to burn ships at a distance, as by burning glasses; and other topics out of our way entirely. In short, we appeared to horrid disadvantage. Let never people form a character of a man from being a night in his company, especially a man of wit. George Selwyn, one of the brightest geniuses in England, of whom more good sayings are recorded than anybody, is often the dullest fellow that can be seen. He was a droll dog when at Oxford, and kept up a most earnest and grave correspondence with a reverend bishop on a point of controversial divinity: whether, after receiving the Communion before Confirmation, he was in a reprobate state or in a state of grace. He kept up the disguise of mystical religion long, and tormented the worthy prelate with his many grievous doubts. The letters he has by him. He was at last expelled the University for a piece of gross profanity, giving the sacrament to a dog. He did it literally, to a degree of craziness. He cut his arm and made the dog drink his blood, saying, "This is my blood, &c."[7]

Lord Eglinton and Sir James disputed about vanity. Sir James said it always made a man disagreeable. My Lord said vanity did not, because a vain man in order to be flattered always pays you great court. But a proud man despises you. The vain man piques himself on some qualities which you must know and admire. The proud man piques himself on being quite above you; so the lower he can thrust you, the higher he is himself; and of all things a purse-proud man is the most terrible. Sir James mentioned a disagreeable pride of understanding, which I thought very applicable to himself. My Lord mentioned poetry. Sir James said it was just personification, animating every object and every feeling, and that measure was not necessary. Erskine agreed with him. I maintained that personification was only one requisite in poetry, and that measure was absolutely necessary, without which it ceased to be

[7] The usual (and more probable) story is that Selwyn was rusticated for using a chalice at a wine-party, and took his name off the books to avoid expulsion. Because of his public reputation for wit of a bizarre and macabre sort, anecdotes of him are likely to be distorted or apocryphal.

poetry and must be denominated some other work of the imagination. That indeed it might be called poetical, as it partook of the nature of poetry. This was all the show that I made tonight in the way of speech. But my Lord produced me in writing, saying he had got a new poem (which was my *Ode to Ambition*). I asked him when he got it. He said it was lying in the pocket of a coat that he wore last year.[8] Sir James read it aloud. He praised it upon the whole. He said the author wanted correctness, which is the least fault in a poet. He said these lines,

> When Fancy from its bud scarce peep'd,
> And Life's sweet matins rung,

were poor. But I think them two beautiful allusions. So speaks the author.

There was a simile which Captain Johnstone said was what the French call *une simile*[9] *avec une longue queue*, a simile with a long tail. Sir James said, "The author of this does not want either poetical imagination or ambition." Such a scene would have disconcerted some people. But I sat by with the most unconcerned ease. My Lord took me by the hand. "I hope we are very good friends." "My Lord, I hope we never were otherwise."

We stayed till near three. I was really uneasy going home. Robberies in the street are now very frequent. The night air, too, is very bad for the health, and always hurts me. I resolved to be determined against suppers, and always to be at home early, in spite of every temptation.

THURSDAY 6 JANUARY. My brother breakfasted with me. This was Twelfth-day, on which a great deal of jollity goes on in England, at the eating of the Twelfth-cake all sugared over. I

[8] Not altogether clear; the marks of parenthesis surrounding "which . . . *Ambition*" have been added by the editor. Eglinton produced the poem without naming the author, and Boswell pretended ignorance in order to get Sir James to talk freely about it?

[9] Read *comparaison* or *similitude*. If there were a French word *simile*, it would be masculine. Boswell's French at this time was very imperfect.

called at Gould's. Mrs. Gould chid me for not being oftener there, and said jestingly that if she did not see me more, she would write to my father that I was idle. I then walked into the City. I took a whim that between St. Paul's and the Exchange and back again, taking the different sides of the street, I would eat a penny Twelfth-cake at every shop where I could get it. This I performed most faithfully.

I then dined comfortably at Dolly's Beefsteak-house. I regretted much my not being acquainted in some good opulent City family where I might participate in the hearty sociality over the ancient ceremony of the Twelfth-cake. I hope to have this snug advantage by this time next year.

I drank tea at Dempster's. Erskine and Lady Anne were there. We laughed a good deal.

FRIDAY 7 JANUARY. Captain Maxwell and my brother breakfasted with me. I then waited on Louisa. She informed me that Saturday could not be the hoped-for time to bestow perfect felicity upon me. "Not," said she, "that I have changed my mind. But it cannot be." In short, I understood that Nature's periodical effects on the human, or more properly female, constitution forbade it. I was a little uneasy at this, though it could not be helped. It kept me longer anxious till my ability was known. I have, together with my vivacity and good-humour, a great anxiety of temper which often renders me uneasy. My grandfather had it in a very strong degree.

I dined at Dr. Pringle's, where was a Scotch company, none of whom were of much note. We had however a kind of cordiality of conversation that did very well. I drank tea at Douglas's, and then, though very indolent, went home and dressed, and went to the private party at Lady Northumberland's. I was not there last Friday, and as my Lady knows I have nothing very important to take me up, it would look ill not to be often there, since she has been so kind as to ask me there.

Indeed, as I do not play, I am at a disadvantage, as people get much easier acquainted when set round a card-table and mixing a little chat while the cards are dealt. But I am under a promise to Sheridan not to play for five years. He relieved me from game distress when he was at Edinburgh by lending me five guineas. Happy is it for me that I am thus tied up; for with my warmth and impetuosity of temper, I might go to the greatest lengths and soon involve myself in ruin and misery. There is no setting bounds to gaming when one engages keenly in it; and it is more genteel to say you never play than to refuse playing for whatever sums the company choose. The acquaintances made in this way are very slight. One made by a man who does not play is worth a hundred of them. Because in the one case it is only for the respect due to his money that he is known. In the other it is for the respect due to himself. This night I was badly off, I being the only person in the room who was not engaged at play. So that I was a little awkward and uneasy.

SATURDAY 8 JANUARY. I forgot to mention that upon Thursday I went to Michael Cholmondeley and gave him four shillings, three from the Kellie family and one of my own. The creature did not seem so thankful as I could wish. An old woman who stood by (for I gave him it in a little court) grumbled that I might have bestowed my charity better, and presently a young one said that people who had both been worthless and would be idle should not be encouraged. Michael's choler rose, he raged in blackguard exclamation. The young jade said he had fifty wives or thereabouts, and such as encouraged him would choose to have the like. By this time a number of miscreants was gathered round us. I was sorely beset, and stood like the unhappy stag at bay, considering how it should come about that I should be thus rendered uneasy when in the exercise of that most Christian grace, charity. A Scotch Seceder or an English Methodist would make out many mystical conjectures on this subject. They would affirm that it was a temptation of Satan in order to try my steadfastness, and if possible drive me from the practice of goodness. Or perhaps that Providence had permitted the infernal enemy of souls to assault me, on purpose to teach me that I should be more judicious and less whimsical in the exercise

of my benevolence. I endeavored to expostulate with the two in-
censed females in terms mild and gentle. "You see," said I, "this
poor old man. We shall not dispute whether his conduct has been
good. But you see him ragged, hungry, and cold; and surely I did
right in trying to relieve a fellow-creature in such circumstances."
I then stole away slowly from them. Their malevolence and hard-
ness of heart I detested, yet I imagine the creature Cholmondeley
must have been worthless. I asked a decent tradesman before whose
shop we stood what character he had. "Sir," said he, with a kind of
waggery, "he is a very honest man from head to foot."

This day I was rather late at Child's. There was nobody almost
there, and no dialogue. So this day must want that garnish, as I am
resolved to adhere strictly to fair truth in this my journal. Indeed
it vexes me a little to be put out of my regular plan, for which I
have a most rooted affection. I do think my love of form for its own
sake is an excellent qualification for a gentleman of the Army,
where there is such a deal of form and variety of attitude.

I dined at Gould's. Mrs. Douglas was there. She and I chatted
away with much vivacity. I feel myself now quite easy at Colonel
Gould's. He is a most amiable man. I like him much for his great
degree of indolence. He loves to lie abed dearly, and gently
grumbles at the thoughts of undergoing the fatigue of dressing.
This is a pretty sort of account of my good friend. But I believe I
have already mentioned his being a man of good sense, good temper, and regular conduct. I wish I could do him any good. He and
I are growing better together every day. I asked him if he was
severe upon the men. "No," said he, "I have too great an aversion
at trouble myself to give them any." Mrs. Gould is a most agreeable
woman, quite of the first fashion, yet kind and affectionate. I am
sure I have good reason to say so. She is excessively good to me,
wants me to be much at her house, is anxious that I should get my
favourite commission, yet soothes me to patience and keeps up my
spirits. She is also to introduce me to some good families where I
can pop in now and then easily. This to so quiet a fellow as me who

have no love for riot, no ambition to be a buck, is of very great consequence.

Young Buckley, the son, takes me by the hand as his friend and there we talk away most intimately and most keenly. Miss Fanny runs smiling to me, sets her chair close by mine, directs her lively prattle with a most engaging vehemence to me, asks me many questions, and has a great respect for my opinion. And then we will read together a little tale, or a fable of Gay's, and sing some smart lively song. She is a very fine child, and will probably be one of the first beauties and clever women in England. She has a grandmother who may give her a very handsome fortune, and in that case she will be a most elegant match for a man of spirit. I call her sometimes Mrs. Boswell. She is very angry, to be sure; crests up her little head and tells me I am very impertinent. Then by and by takes me by the hand and throws out a sparkling sally of life. Were many people to read this leaf of my journal, they would hold me in great contempt as a very trifling fellow. But surely what Mr. Churchill calls *the grave triflers*[1] are neither so wise nor so happy as he who can give his time and attention now and then to the rising sprouts of humanity and derive simplicity of feeling and gaiety of heart from children.

Mrs. Gould cautioned me against Mrs. Cholmondeley. I insinuated that if she was a woman of intrigue, why not have that amusement with her? She did not answer that, but said she had the character of a jilt, that she had given encouragement to a certain lord, got many presents from him, at last consented to an assignation, and when he attempted to use freedoms, her husband came in. My Lord swore it must have been concerted between them, damned her for a jilting bitch, and flung out of the room. I told her she need not be afraid of me.

Mrs. Gould and Mrs. Douglas and I went in the Colonel's char-

---

[1] "What the grave triflers on this busy scene,
When they make use of this word REASON, mean,
I know not."—*The Apology*, ll. 410–12.

iot to the Haymarket. As we drove along and spoke good English, I was full of rich imagination of London, ideas suggested by the Spectator and such as I could not explain to most people, but which I strongly feel and am ravished with. My blood glows and my mind is agitated with felicity. My friend Temple feels this greatly, so does Johnston in some measure, also so does McQuhae. I am a good deal disappointed at the want of Temple here this winter. He and I were great friends in youth. We have yet the same dispositions and the same turn to fancy and whim. I have not yet learned where he is. I hope to have his company in London next winter, when we shall be very happy.

In this pleasing humour I was set down at the foot of the Haymarket and went straight home and sat in well pleased all the evening.

SUNDAY 9 JANUARY. I heard an excellent sermon at St. Martin's Church by Mr. Sumner, Master of Harrow School. His text was, "My yoke is easy." He showed that although religion might in some respects be called a yoke, as it laid some restraint upon the inclinations and passions of men, yet to a mind properly trained it was easy, nay delightful. The happiness of genuine piety he displayed in elegant language enforced by just and animated action.

After church I went in sober yet gay humour to Louisa and got her to fix Wednesday without fail as the happy night. I then called for Mr. Craufurd of Auchenames in Ayrshire and Errol in Fife, who received me with uncommon kindness, told me that he heard I was wanting to get into the Guards, and if he could do me any service, I might command him. That he knew Lord Rothes well, who commands the Third Regiment, and that he would introduce me to him. These professions would have looked like deceit from most people, but Craufurd is a very honest and a very generous man. He saved my Lord Rothes's estate by advancing a large sum of money. Consequently he has a good deal to say with him.

I dined at home and drank tea with my brother. We were very merry talking over the days when we were boys, the characters of

Mr. Dun, Mr. Fergusson, Mr. McQuhae, and Mr. Gordon[2] and the servants who were then in the family. In short, an infinite number of little circumstances which to ourselves were vastly entertaining.

MONDAY 10 JANUARY. I waited on Lady Northumberland and expressed my joy at hearing that the Marquis of Granby was in a fair way of recovery, and would soon be over.[3] "I hope, Madam," said I, "you will not forget me." "No, Sir," said she, "you may be sure I will not." As I hope to have the honour of a forenoon's conversation with her Ladyship every week, I shall enrich my journal with it in the form of the original dialogue.

LADY NORTHUMBERLAND. There was a gentleman presented yesterday on his getting a commission in the Guards. I thought of you, Mr. Boswell.

BOSWELL. Ay, the Guards, Madam; that is the thing. Really, I have been thinking on the subject since I saw you, and must tell your Ladyship that the Guards is the particular thing that I have always been fond of, just like the woman that a man is in love with. At the same time I mentioned the Blues, as to be sure I should rather choose to serve there than not at all. But I beg leave to speak plain and let your Ladyship know exactly what my views are, that in case you did me the honour to put me into the Blues, you might not be surprised or think me an odd changeable fellow if after half a year I should beg to have it changed for a commission in the Guards.

LADY NORTHUMBERLAND. Why, Sir, I wish we may get you into the Guards.

BOSWELL. Indeed, Madam, I should be sorry that you had to say, "This man does not know what he would be at. I got him into the Blues, which he was very desirous of, and now he is discontent and wants to change." The thing is this, that I am anxious to live in London, and besides the exercise of the Horse would be disagree-

---

[2] The domestic tutor who succeeded Mr. McQuhae in Lord Auchinleck's household. See above, p. 2.

[3] He had long been dangerously ill of a fever.

able to me; whereas in the Guards my duty would be quite a pleasure to me.

LADY NORTHUMBERLAND. Indeed, Sir, that is of a good deal of consequence. I shall therefore present you to the Marquis as a friend of mine who is very desirous to serve in the Guards, and next to that in his own corps. He is a good-natured man and is therefore ready to give his promise.

BOSWELL. I hope, Madam, we will keep him in mind of it. I wish I was introduced to him.

LADY NORTHUMBERLAND. Why, to be sure, Sir, I will very naturally say, "My Lord, you will give me leave to present Mr. Boswell to you"; and then you can keep him in mind of it.

BOSWELL. I am extremely obliged to your Ladyship. Indeed, I set a higher value on the countenance you show me than anybody could do. For, Madam, I have the old notions about families. I think of

> The Percy out of Northumberland
> And a vow to GOD made he.[4]

Indeed, Madam, these notions are much out now.

LADY NORTHUMBERLAND (well pleased). Really, Sir, they are too much out, as people show by the strange connections that they make.

BOSWELL. I wish I had this commission of mine.

LADY NORTHUMBERLAND. I wish you had. Could not you have the thing mentioned to your countryman, Lord Rothes?

BOSWELL. I was yesterday, Madam, with a Scotch Member, a brother of General Craufurd's, who is very intimate with Lord Rothes and promised to introduce me. But you know, Madam, there is a delicacy in talking to a colonel when a man is not to purchase, as he gets the profits of the commissions that are sold.

LADY NORTHUMBERLAND. Indeed, Sir, it would be the best thing for you to purchase if you could.

BOSWELL. But then, Madam, my father is rather averse to the

[4] The opening lines of the old ballad of *Chevy Chase.*

scheme and would not advance the money; and by borrowing it, I should bring myself into difficulties. Indeed, I am determined to purchase if I cannot get in without it. But I think it is worth while to wait a twelvemonth.

LADY NORTHUMBERLAND. It is so, Sir.

BOSWELL. I did not know whether or not to apply to Lord Rothes. It is not everybody one would be obliged to. And I reckon myself very happy in depending on your Ladyship, whom I am very happy to be obliged to.

LADY NORTHUMBERLAND. O Sir!

BOSWELL. I did not know but your Ladyship might be displeased at my speaking to anybody else.

LADY NORTHUMBERLAND. Not at all, Sir.

BOSWELL. Pray, Madam, could you do anything with Mr. Ellis, the Secretary at War?

LADY NORTHUMBERLAND. Sir, I tell you honestly what I can do and what I cannot. I have asked a favour from Mr. Ellis and have not yet got it, so that I have not much to say with him. I assure you, Sir, I have all the inclination in the world to serve you. I beg you may not judge of my inclination by my success.

BOSWELL. Madam, I will not if it be bad. But I will if it be good.

LADY NORTHUMBERLAND. It was a bad night for you, Mr. Boswell, last Friday, as you was the only person that did not play. I hope we shall have more company for you next Friday.

BOSWELL. Indeed, it was a little dull for me.

LADY NORTHUMBERLAND. Why don't you go to Court, Mr. Boswell? I'm sure that's a cheap diversion; it costs you nothing, and you see all the best company, and chat away. It is the best coffeehouse in town.

BOSWELL. But ought I not, Madam, to be introduced first?

LADY NORTHUMBERLAND. You should, Sir. To be sure, some people do go and stand there without being presented. But that would not be right for *a man of your rank*.

BOSWELL. I shall pay my respects to my Lord Northumberland and be obliged to him to take me there.

LADY NORTHUMBERLAND. He will present you to the Queen.[5] But one of the Lords of the Bedchamber must do it to the King. Your friend Lord Eglinton will do that.

BOSWELL. I shall certainly go there.

LADY NORTHUMBERLAND. You should.

BOSWELL. Do you know, Madam, that Lord Eglinton really used me ill? He encouraged me much in my scheme of the Guards; and when I applied to him, put me off in a most shameful manner. Now, Madam, I would upon no account ask his interest.

LADY NORTHUMBERLAND. To be sure, Sir. Pray is your house in the country finished?

BOSWELL. It is, Madam.

LADY NORTHUMBERLAND. It is a very good house; and then the Old Castle is very fine.

BOSWELL. Indeed, Madam, there are more romantic beauties there than at any place I know. (Rising.) Your Ladyship's most obedient. You are very good to me. I hope you won't give the porter orders to deny you.

LADY NORTHUMBERLAND. Sir, I gave him particular orders to let you in.

BOSWELL. Madam, your most obedient. (Shutting the door.) You won't forget me?

LADY NORTHUMBERLAND. No, Sir.

This is the substance of our conversation today, I dare say I was half an hour with her. Her kindness made me very happy. I dined at home. One Faucit a singer was with us. We had some good songs.

At night I went to Drury Lane pit and saw the Second Part of *King Henry IV*, where Mr. Garrick in the pathetic scene between the old King and his son drew tears from my eyes. The entertainment was *The Witches*, a pantomime by Love. It is but a dull thing.

TUESDAY 11 JANUARY. I am amazed how I have neglected

[5] Lord Northumberland was Lord Chamberlain to the Queen.

last Friday to mention a circumstance so very material to me as
the payment of my allowance, which indeed elevated me to a most
extraordinary pitch. Many a time did I lay the lovely shining
pieces upon my table, count them over, put them in rank and file
like the Guards, and place them in many different sorts of figures.
In short, a boy at school could not be more childishly fond of sugar
plums than I was of golden guineas.

This day I had some agreeable conversation with my dear
Louisa. All was now agreed upon. I had been at Hayward's on Saturday morning and told that we could not be there that night,
as my wife was not come to town. But that we would be there next
week and take our chance for a bed. And here a hint or two of
Louisa's history may well come in. She was born of very creditable
parents in London. But being too strictly confined, she ran off and
married heedlessly. She was obliged for subsistence to go upon
the stage, and travelled in different companies. Her husband
proved a harsh, disagreeable creature, with whom she led a terrible life; at last, as it was discovered that they were illegally married, they parted by consent, and she got into Covent Garden
Theatre.

I dined with Coutts in the Strand, my banker, a jolly, plentiful
dinner with a Scotch company, and free, easy conversation. I
drank tea with my brother and then went home cool and serene,
looking forward with joy to next day.

WEDNESDAY 12 JANUARY. Louisa and I agreed that at eight
at night she would meet me in the Piazzas of Covent Garden. I was
quite elevated, and felt myself able and undaunted to engage in
the wars of the Paphian Queen.

I dined at Sheridan's very heartily. He showed to my conviction that Garrick did not play the great scene in the Second Part
of *King Henry* with propriety. "People," said he, "in this age know
when particular lines or even speeches are well spoke; but they do
not study character, which is a matter of the utmost moment, as
people of different characters feel and express their feelings very
differently. For want of a knowledge of this, Mr. Barry acted the

distress of Othello, the Moorish warrior whose stubborn soul was hard to bend, and that of Castalio, the gentle lover who was all tenderness,[6] in the self-same way. Now Mr. Garrick in that famous scene whines most piteously when he ought to upbraid. Shakespeare has discovered there a most intimate knowledge of human nature. He shows you the King worn out with sickness and so weak that he faints. He had usurped the crown by the force of arms and was convinced that it must be held with spirit. He saw his son given up to low debauchery. He was anxious and vexed to think of the anarchy that would ensue at his death. Upon discovering that the Prince had taken the crown from his pillow, and concluding him desirous of his death, he is fired with rage. He starts up. He cries, 'Go chide him hither!' His anger animates him so much that he throws aside his distemper. Nature furnishes all her strength for one last effort. He is for a moment renewed. He is for a moment the spirited Henry the Fourth. He upbraids him with bitter sarcasm and bold figures. And then what a beautiful variety is there, when, upon young Harry's contrition, he falls on his neck and melts into parental tenderness."

I yielded this point to Sheridan candidly. But upon his attacking Garrick as a tragedian in his usual way, I opposed him keenly, and declared he was prejudiced; because the world thought him a good tragic actor. "So do I, Sir," said he; "I think him the best I ever saw." BOSWELL. "Except yourself, Mr. Sheridan. But come, we shall take this for granted. The world then think him near equal or as good as you in what you excel in." SHERIDAN. "Sir, I am not a bit prejudiced. I don't value acting. I shall suppose that I was the greatest actor that ever lived and universally acknowledged so, I[7] would not choose that it should be remembered. I would have it erased out of the anecdotes of my life. Acting is a poor thing in the present state of the stage. For my own part, I engaged in it merely as a step to something greater, a just notion of

---

[6] In Otway's *The Orphan*.

[7] Probably a shift of construction from "I shall suppose" to "Suppose." A page ends with "so."

eloquence." This was in a good measure true. But he certainly talked too extravagantly.

An old Irish maid, or rather an Irish old maid (O most hideous character!) dined with us. She was indeed a terrible Joy.[8] She was a woman of knowledge and criticism and correct taste. But there came to tea a Miss Mowat who played once on the stage here for a winter or two, a lovely girl. Many an amorous glance did I exchange with her. I was this day quite flashy with love. We often addressed our discourse to each other. I hope to see her again; and yet what have I to do with anybody but dear Louisa?

At the appointed hour of eight I went to the Piazzas, where I sauntered up and down for a while in a sort of trembling suspense, I knew not why. At last my charming companion appeared, and I immediately conducted her to a hackney-coach which I had ready waiting, pulled up the blinds, and away we drove to the destined scene of delight. We contrived to seem as if we had come off a journey, and carried in a bundle our night-clothes, handkerchiefs, and other little things. We also had with us some almond biscuits, or as they call them in London, macaroons, which looked like provision on the road. On our arrival at Hayward's we were shown into the parlour, in the same manner that any decent couple would be. I here thought proper to conceal my own name (which the people of the house had never heard), and assumed the name of Mr. Digges. We were shown up to the very room where he slept. I said my cousin, as I called him, was very well. That Ceres and Bacchus might in moderation lend their assistance to Venus, I ordered a genteel supper and some wine.

Louisa told me she had two aunts who carried her over to France when she was a girl, and that she could once speak French as fluently as English. We talked a little in it, and agreed that we would improve ourselves by reading and speaking it every day. I

---

[8] "The use of the word joy [as a term of friendly address] . . . is so common among the lower classes of the Irish that the words 'dear joy' are often used by way of derision to signify an Irishman" (Joseph Wright, *English Dialect Dictionary*). Scots "jo" is the same word.

asked her if we did not just look like man and wife. "No," said she, "we are too fond for married people." No wonder that she may have a bad idea of that union, considering how bad it was for her. She has contrived a pretty device for a seal. A heart is gently warmed by Cupid's flame, and Hymen comes with his rude torch and extinguishes it. She said she found herself quite in a flutter. "Why, really," said I, "reason sometimes has no power. We have no occasion to be frightened, and yet we are both a little so. Indeed, I preserve a tolerable presence of mind." I rose and kissed her, and conscious that I had no occasion to doubt my qualifications as a gallant, I joked about it: "How curious would it be if I should be so frightened that we should rise as we lay down." She reproved my wanton language by a look of modesty. The bells of St. Bride's church rung their merry chimes hard by. I said that the bells in Cupid's court would be this night set a-ringing for joy at our union.

We supped cheerfully and agreeably and drank a few glasses, and then the maid came and put the sheets, well aired, upon the bed. I now contemplated my fair prize. Louisa is just twenty-four, of a tall rather than short figure, finely made in person, with a handsome face and an enchanting languish in her eyes. She dresses with taste. She has sense, good humour, and vivacity, and looks quite a woman in genteel life. As I mused on this elevating subject, I could not help being somehow pleasingly confounded to think that so fine a woman was at this moment in my possession, that without any motives of interest she had come with me to an inn, agreed to be my intimate companion, as to be my bedfellow all night, and to permit me the full enjoyment of her person.

When the servant left the room, I embraced her warmly and begged that she would not now delay my felicity. She declined to undress before me, and begged I would retire and send her one of the maids. I did so, gravely desiring the girl to go up to Mrs. Digges. I then took a candle in my hand and walked out to the yard. The night was very dark and very cold. I experienced for some minutes the rigours of the season, and called into my mind many terrible ideas of hardships, that I might make a transition from such dreary thoughts to the most gay and delicious feelings. I then caused make a bowl of negus, very rich of the fruit, which I caused be set in the room as a reviving cordial.

I came softly into the room, and in a sweet delirium slipped into bed and was immediately clasped in her snowy arms and pressed to her milk-white bosom. Good heavens, what a loose did we give to amorous dalliance! The friendly curtain of darkness concealed our blushes. In a moment I felt myself animated with the strongest powers of love, and, from my dearest creature's kindness, had a most luscious feast. Proud of my godlike vigour, I soon resumed the noble game. I was in full glow of health. Sobriety had preserved me from effeminacy and weakness, and my bounding blood beat quick and high alarms. A more voluptuous night I never enjoyed. Five times was I fairly lost in supreme rapture. Louisa was madly fond of me; she declared I was a prodigy, and asked me if this was not extraordinary for human nature. I said twice as much might be, but this was not, although in my own mind I was somewhat proud of my performance. She said it was what there was no just reason to be proud of. But I told her I could not help it. She said it was what we had in common with the beasts. I said no. For we had it highly improved by the pleasures of sentiment. I asked her what she thought enough. She gently chid me for asking such questions, but said two times. I mentioned the Sunday's assignation, when I was in such bad spirits, told her in what agony of mind I was, and asked her if she would not have despised me for my imbecility. She declared she would not, as it was what people had not in their own power.

She often insisted that we should compose ourselves to sleep before I would consent to it. At last I sunk to rest in her arms and she in mine. I found the negus, which had a fine flavour, very refreshing to me. Louisa had an exquisite mixture of delicacy and wantonness that made me enjoy her with more relish. Indeed I could not help roving in fancy to the embraces of some other ladies which my lively imagination strongly pictured. I don't know if that was altogether fair. However, Louisa had all the advantage. She said she was quite fatigued and could neither stir leg nor arm. She begged I would not despise her, and hoped my love would not be altogether transient. I have painted this night as well as I could. The description is faint; but I surely may be styled a Man of Pleasure.

THURSDAY 13 JANUARY. We awaked from sweet repose after the luscious fatigues of the night. I got up between nine and ten and walked out till Louisa should rise. I patrolled up and down Fleet Street, thinking on London, the seat of Parliament and the seat of pleasure, and seeming to myself as one of the wits in King Charles the Second's time. I then came in and we had an agreeable breakfast, after which we left Hayward's, who said he was sorry he had not more of our company, and calling a hackney-coach, drove to Soho Square, where Louisa had some visits to pay. So we parted. Thus was this conquest completed to my highest satisfaction. I can with pleasure trace the progress of this intrigue to its completion. I am now at ease on that head, having my fair one fixed as my own. As Captain Plume says, the best security for a woman's mind is her body.[9] I really conducted this affair with a manliness and prudence that pleased me very much. The whole expense was just eighteen shillings.

I called at Louisa's and seemed to be surprised that she was abroad. I then went and called at Drury Lane Playhouse for Mr. Garrick. I had called for him at his house, but had never found him.[1] He met me with great civility and even kindness; told me that he had bowed to me in the House of Lords when I had not

[9] "SILVIA [disguised as a man]. . . . So, before I list, I must be certified that this girl is a virgin.

"PLUME. Mr. Wilful, I can't tell you how you can be certified in that point till you try; but, upon my honour, she may be a vestal for aught that I know to the contrary. I gained her heart, indeed, by some trifling presents and promises, and, knowing that the best security for a woman's soul is her body, I would have made myself master of that too, had not the jealousy of my impertinent landlady interposed" (George Farquhar, *The Recruiting Officer*, IV.i).   [1] Boswell had made his acquaintance in 1760.

observed him; said he would be glad to contribute to my happiness, and asked me if I was come to stay. I told him that I hoped to get into the Guards. "To be sure," said he, "it is a most genteel thing, and I think, Sir, you ought to be a soldier. The law requires a sad deal of plodding. But" said he, "has your father got over the pangs of your forsaking his scheme?" I told him he was pretty well reconciled. I told him I wanted much to pass some time with him. He said he always breakfasted at nine and would be glad to see me whenever I chose to come and let Mrs. Garrick make tea for me. He then carried me to see the paintings of Mr. Zoffany in the Piazzas, where Mr. Garrick is shown in several different ways.[2] "Take care, Zoffany," said he, "you have made one of these heads for me *longer* than the other, and I would not willingly have it shortened." In the theatre there was a fine large dog chained. "This," said he, "is Johnston's (the boxkeeper's) bear, though I don't know which of 'em is the greatest *bear*."

I dined nowhere, but drank tea at Love's, and at night went to Covent Garden gallery and saw *The Jovial Crew*.[3] My frame still thrilled with pleasure, and my want of so much rest last night gave me an agreeable languor. The songs revived in my mind many gay ideas, and recalled in the most lively colours to my imagination the time when I was first in London, when all was new to me, when I felt the warm glow of youthful feeling and was full of curiosity and wonder. I then had at times a degree of ecstasy of feeling that the experience which I have since had has in some measure cooled and abated. But then my ignorance at that time is infinitely excelled by the knowledge and moderation and government of myself which I have now acquired. After the play I came home, eat a Bath cake[4] and a sweet orange, and went comfortably to bed.

FRIDAY 14 JANUARY. I drank tea with Louisa. There was one

[2] That is, in several of his dramatic *rôles*.

[3] By Richard Brome, first produced in 1652; altered to a very successful comic opera by additional songs and brought again on the stage in 1731.

[4] So named from the city of Bath: a large fruit bun with sugared top.

of the least men I ever saw at tea with us, on whom Louisa threw out many diverting jokes. At night I went to Lady Northumberland's. There was a very full meeting, and many people of my acquaintance, so that I was at my ease and had plenty of conversation. I strutted up and down, considering myself as a valiant man who could gratify a lady's loving desires five times in a night; and I satisfied my pride by considering that if this and all my other great qualities were known, all the women almost in the room would be making love to me. This evening I was accosted by a lady of quality whom I was a little acquainted with, and to whom I shall give the name of Lady Mirabel.[5] Thus went our conversation:

LADY MIRABEL. You don't play, Mr. Boswell.

BOSWELL. No, Madam, I never do; and yet I am very well amused here. I can have a great deal of entertainment just by looking around me. A man, Madam, who can be happy thus must either be very stupid or more clever than ordinary.

LADY MIRABEL. Indeed, Sir, he must be extremely clever.

BOSWELL. Well, Madam, I think I have made out what I wanted very well. But pray don't you think the meetings here of people of fashion very dull? There seems to be no communication between men and women. They seldom speak to each other.

LADY MIRABEL. True, but when they do speak, they speak to the purpose.

BOSWELL. Bravo! Indeed they do that. But they want sentiment.

---

[5] Not certainly identified; the memoranda (which are missing for this date) also employ the pseudonym. From various hints too minute to detail here, I think it possible that she was Lady Mary Coke, daughter of the second Duke of Argyll, born in 1726 and since 1753 widow of Edward, Viscount Coke, son of the Earl of Leicester. She was a countrywoman of Boswell's, was a friend of Lord Eglinton, and was intimate with the Duke of York, to whom she afterwards tried to persuade people she had been secretly married. She kept a voluminous and useful diary, of which only a part has been printed. The published diary does not mention Boswell, but she no doubt was much less conscious of him than he was of her.

LADY MIRABEL. And therefore it is that their connections last only for a winter. It is very different abroad.

BOSWELL. You must know, Madam, I run up and down this town just like a wild colt.

LADY MIRABEL. Why, Sir, then, don't you stray into my stable, amongst others?

BOSWELL. Madam, I shall certainly have that pleasure.

From this conversation and Lady Mirabel's looks, I entertained some notion that an intrigue would not be disagreeable to her Ladyship. Lady Mirabel is a widow of middle age, has a jointure sufficient to live genteelly upon; although not pretty she has a fine air and is very agreeable. In short, whether I succeed or not, this may be an amusing pursuit.

Sir Harry Erskine[6] bowed often and spoke much to me this night, in expectation, as I supposed, that I would pay court to him and ask his interest for my commission. Instead of that I pushed him much, or rather represented strongly to him, that my friend and his cousin Erskine should have a company. "I wish, Sir," said he, "that it was in *my* power to get him a company." He no doubt imagined that I would have said, "If it is not in *your* power, Sir Harry, who can do such things?" But I was resolved to beat him in a smart way, so replied, "Um, I don't know, Sir Harry. You may help." He bowed and smiled more than once and withdrew (as I thought) like my inferior.

Lord Eglinton really paid court to me. He asked me how I had been this long time, and hoped that I heard of his being at my door several times. He insisted that I should sup with him. He said he had several very clever fellows, amongst whom was Erskine. But I told him that I never was abroad at night, for that I was in love with a fine woman and wanted to keep myself healthy, stout, and strong. I asked him if Erskine had spoke more to him yet. He said, "No. But he must be forced to it. For a man has no more a

---

[6] Lord Bute's favourite, or at least considered to be so. He was a major-general in the Army.

right not to furnish his share of conversation than not to pay his club." I went home in good time and in good spirits.

SATURDAY 15 JANUARY. I breakfasted with Dempster in exceeding lively spirits. I then hied me to the City, blithe and gay. As I passed Water Lane, I superstitiously took off my hat and bowed to the Black Lion.

DIALOGUE AT CHILD'S.

PHYSICIAN. Do, Sir, stand a little to one side that we may see the fire.

1 CITIZEN. Sir! I think I make atonement for my error by leaving it.

PHYSICIAN. Have not you observed a certain gentleman with a broad backside who frequents this coffee-house, have not you seen him clap his backside to the fire, so as to cover it from us and almost to burn his own clothes, if not called to?

2 CITIZEN. Why the devil is he called to? Why not let him burn his clothes?

PHYSICIAN. That would be uncharitable.

I then called at Louisa's, and begged to be allowed what I most desired. She would not consent today, as everybody was at home, but said that next day at one her landlady would be abroad, and I might come then. I begged to know if she had any intrigues since she parted with her husband. She confessed that she had one, but that it was now over, and the gentleman was not in Britain. My being afraid of a rival was a sure sign of a sincere passion.

I dined at Mrs. Douglas's, where I met Mr. and Mrs. Gould and young Webster. Hunger was my predominant inclination this day, and a most hearty dinner I did eat. In the afternoon some strangers came to tea. I disliked them. I went home soon, but, I don't know how, had got into bad humour.

SUNDAY 16 JANUARY. I heard service and sermon in the New Church in the Strand,[7] which insensibly relieved me from

[7] St. Mary Le Strand.

my cloudy spirits. I had not been at Lady Betty's since Thursday sennight, as I wanted to have nothing but English ideas, and to be as manly as I possibly could. However, I thought they might take amiss my being absent for so long a time without being able to assign them any rational reason for it. I therefore went there after church and found them at breakfast. They were glad to see me, and very kind. I hoped they were not angry at me for running through London whimsically so long without ever calling on them. They said, by no means. For they had now got a method to account for all my actions, which was just to say, "It is part of his plan"; and that they would always be glad to see me. I said I valued them much more after being some time absent from them. I really liked them this day better than ever.

I then went to Louisa and was permitted the rites of love with great complacency; yet I felt my passion for Louisa much gone. I felt a degree of coldness for her and I observed an affectation about her which disgusted me. I had a strong proof of my own inconstancy of disposition, and I considered that any woman who married me must be miserable. Here I argued wrong. For as a licentious love is merely the child of passion, it has no sure ground to hope for a long continuance, as passion may be extinguished with the most sudden and trifling breath of wind; but rational esteem founded on just motives must in all probability endure, especially when the opinion of the world and many other considerations contribute to strengthen and preserve it. Louisa and I began this day to read French. Our book was a little light piece of French gallantry entitled *Journal Amoureux*. She pronounced best and I translated best. Between us we did very well.

MONDAY 17 JANUARY. Louisa and I continued our study of French, which was useful as it gave us some employment and prevented us from tiring on account of conversation becoming insipid from a sameness that must necessarily happen when only two people are much together. I this day again had full fruition of her charms. I still, though, found that the warm enthusiasm of love was over. Yet I continued to mention my fears of her having some other favourite. I first said that I would watch her carefully, and would come at different times and by surprise if possible, that I might find out the truth. But I recovered myself and said I was sure I had no reason, so would not anxiously inquire. "Indeed, Sir," said she, "it is better not. For it is a maxim with me, where there is no confidence, there is no breach of trust."

I dined at Lady Betty's. Erskine was not there. We were very happy and in a better style than I ever knew us in. We were in a composed and sensible and at the same time a lively style. We talked of happiness, as we then owned that we were much so. I said that of making money was certainly great, as it lasted for ever, and as you had always something to show. I lamented that the happiness of the mind was so very transient, and that you had nothing left. For that a man may have a great quantity of happiness today, and tomorrow it is all gone, and what a man had avails him nothing. "True," said Lady Betty, "but you must consider, though you are thus a bankrupt, yet you may quickly again be worth ten thousand pound."

We then fell upon political topics, and all agreed in our love of the Royal Family of Stuart and regret at their being driven from Britain. I maintained that their encroachments were not of so bad consequence as their being expelled the throne. In short, the substance of our conversation was that the family of Stuart, although unfortunate, did nothing worthy of being driven from the throne. That their little encroachments were but trifles in comparison of what Oliver Cromwell did, who overturned the whole Constitution and threw all into anarchy; and that in a future period King William, who came over the defender of our liberties, became a most domineering monarch and stretched his prerogative farther than any Stuart ever did. That by the Revolution we got a shabby family to reign over us, and that the German War, a consequence of having a German sovereign, was the most destructive thing this nation ever saw. That by the many changes and popular confusions the minds of the people were confused and thrown loose from ties of loyalty, so that public spirit and national principle were in a great measure destroyed. This was a bold and rash way of talking; but it had justice, and it pleased me.[8]

I liked the Kellie family vastly this day. I considered that I was happy in the intimate acquaintance of ladies of quality of a good family, genteel and ingenious. They were now talking of going for Scotland in a fortnight. This made them appear more valuable. I told them I would dine with them every day while they stayed. They made me welcome with that easy kindness which cannot be feigned. "Indeed," said Macfarlane, "you are welcome on your own account. But suppose that was not the case, I owe your father as many dinners." I drank tea there.

TUESDAY 18 JANUARY. Lord Eglinton sent me the following card: "Lord Eglinton presents his compliments to Mr. Boswell (I believe I should only have said Boswell, for, as the Gascon said to Monsieur Tallard,[9] nobody ever said Mr. Horace), and takes the liberty to acquaint his Poetship that he has called twice and lives in Queen Street, Mayfair."

I wrote for answer: "To the Earl of Eglinton, one of the Lords of his Majesty's Bedchamber, Boswell the Poet, sole Lord of his own, sends such compliments as men of the world generally send to each other. The honour that Lord Eglinton has done him in calling twice is most properly felt; and he begs leave to acknowledge himself much out of his duty in not paying his respects in Queen Street before now; although between the ladies celestial and terrestrial he has for some time past been kept in pretty good

---

[8] The Kellie family came by its "love of the Royal Family of Stuart" somewhat more legitimately than Boswell. The fifth Earl of Kellie, father of Boswell's friends, joined the Rebellion of '45 as a colonel of the Jacobite army, and was detained in the Castle of Edinburgh for three years after the uprising was put down. He escaped worse punishment, it is said, only because his fortune was small and his understanding suspect. His wife was daughter of Dr. Archibald Pitcairne, the celebrated Jacobite physician and poet.
[9] Eglinton's card actually reads, "Marchall Talard." The reference is probably to the Maréchal Tallard, a French general defeated and captured by the Duke of Marlborough at the Battle of Blenheim, but the source of the anecdote which Eglinton is quoting has not yet been found.

employment both of mind (which I mention first as the most exalted part of our nature) and body; which, let metaphysicians talk as they may, has no small share in human felicity. Boswell will very soon wait of[1] Lord Eglinton."

This way of corresponding that the Earl and I have got into is something very clever and entertaining.

This day being the Queen's birthday, I was amused by seeing multitudes of rich-dressed people driving in their splendid equipages to Court. Really, it must be confessed that a court is a fine thing. It is the cause of so much show and splendour that people are kept gay and spirited. I recollected all the stories of the old Scottish magnificence when our monarchs resided at Holyroodhouse, and I wished to see such days again. In short, I had more pleasing ideas tramping along the pavement than those who rattled by me in gilded chariots.

I went and waited on Lady Margaret Macdonald. Amongst other subjects we talked of her brother, Lord Eglinton. She said he was ruined by having never had a fixed plan in life. I mentioned to her his usage of me. "Sir," said she, "don't you be at the trouble to take it amiss from him, for I can assure you that he has used me as ill. He insisted that I should bring up my two youngest sons, and made the strongest promises of regard—nay, went so far as to say that if he did not do more for them than all their friends in Scotland put together, he would refund the expense of their education. They were accordingly brought up, and yet he never once minded them nor did anything for them." This indeed is the strongest proof that I ever heard of Lord Eglinton's want of firmness, just owing to his sad dissipation.

I told Lady Margaret that I believed I took his behaviour to me in too serious a light, and by being pretty much angry and keeping at a distance, I lost a great deal of pleasure from his agreeable company. "Indeed, Sir," said she, "you are wrong. Have no dependence upon him, but go to his house often, just as you would to a play." This was a most candid and a most sensible advice. For I lose a deal

[1] A Scotticism.

of satisfaction, and the thoughtless Earl does not much mind my stateliness; although it must be owned that I have made him very attentive to me of late and made myself of more consequence in his opinion.

I then called for Lady Mirabel. She seemed to like me a good deal. I was lively, and I looked like the game.[2] As it was my first visit, I was very quiet. However, it was agreed that I should visit her often. This elated me, as it afforded a fine, snug, and agreeable prospect of gallantry. Yet I could not think of being unfaithful to Louisa. But, then, I thought Louisa was only in the mean time, till I got into genteel life, and that a woman of fashion was the only proper object for such a man as me. At last delicate honour prevailed, and I resolved for some time at least to keep alive my affection for Louisa.

I this day began to feel an unaccountable alarm of unexpected evil: a little heat in the members of my body sacred to Cupid, very like a symptom of that distemper with which Venus, when cross, takes it into her head to plague her votaries. But then I had run no risks. I had been with no woman but Louisa; and sure she could not have such a thing. Away then with such idle fears, such groundless, uneasy apprehensions! When I came to Louisa's, I felt myself stout and well, and most courageously did I plunge into the fount of love, and had vast pleasure as I enjoyed her as an actress who had played many a fine lady's part. She was remarkably fond of me

[2] Amorous sport or play, quoting Shakespeare's *Troilus and Cressida*, IV, v. 62:

> Fie, fie upon her!
> There's a language in her eye, her cheek, her lip,
> Nay, her foot speaks; her wanton spirits look out
> At every joint and motive of her body.
> O these encounterers, so glib of tongue,
> That give a coasting welcome ere it comes,
> And wide unclasp the tables of their thoughts
> To every tickling reader! Set them down
> For sluttish spoils of opportunity
> And daughters of the game.

today, and sighing said, "What will become of me if I lose you now?"

I dined at Lady Betty's. I said I sometimes contracted my plan. Says Erskine, "You should contract nothing but debt." To which Macfarlane added, "And marriage." We were very merry. They declared their hearty joy at this scheme of dining every day chancing to become part of my plan.

At five I left them for an hour and went to Sheridan's. In order to explain my errand there, I must give a narration of several sentences. Mrs. Sheridan some weeks ago asked me to write a prologue to her new comedy. She said there were very few good poets in this age; and she said that if they had been in good terms with Johnson, she would have asked him. Her applying to me after this no doubt flattered me a good deal. She said there were few who had sense and temper enough to allow a fair criticism on their verses, as they were too much attached to their favourite productions. But I told her she need be under no apprehension of making me angry, for that I was perfectly easy in that respect. Indeed, my ease proceeds not from the good sense it might be imputed to, but from a carelessness of fame and a happy indifference, from a thorough conviction of the vanity of all things. As I had written no verses for some months, the task appeared very formidable. However, I wrote one which she said had good lines but was too general. I therefore wrote another, which she said was near the mark, and with a little polishing would do.[3] The thing now pleased me exceedingly. I thought it fine to have my lines spoken by Mr. Garrick and resounding through Drury Lane. I mentioned it to the Kellies and the Dempsters, and walked about elated, but would not let them hear it. To get a definite answer about this prologue was now my errand to Sheridan's. I must observe that from the first Sheridan himself never seemed hearty in the thing. I bid Mrs. Sheridan not show it him, as he was a severe critic. After sitting a little, he said, "Why, Sir, you

[3] Both versions are preserved in the large manuscript collection of Boswell's verses now in the Bodleian Library, but they are not of enough general interest to warrant publication in this edition.

don't ask about your prologue?" "Indeed," said I, "I am too indifferent."

SHERIDAN. Well, but prepare your utmost philosophy.

BOSWELL. How so?

SHERIDAN. It is weighed in the balances and found light.

BOSWELL. What, is not good?

SHERIDAN. Indeed, I think it is very bad.

BOSWELL. Pray, Mrs. Sheridan, what is the meaning of this?

MRS. SHERIDAN. Mr. Sheridan, Sir, does not like it, and he has insisted upon me to write one which he thinks will do.

"Oho!" thought I, "is this it?" I then desired to hear the faults of mine. Sheridan pointed them out with an insolent bitterness and a clumsy ridicule that hurt me much, and when I answered them, bore down my words with a boisterous vociferation. It is incredible with what seeming good humour I behaved. I declared that I must either be a man of the finest temper or the nicest art. He then read Mrs. Sheridan's, which was much duller, as I thought.[4]

We disputed about poems. Sheridan said that a man should not be a poet except he was very excellent; for that to be a *mediocris poeta*[5] was but a poor thing. I said I differed from him. For the greatest part of those who read poetry have a mediocre taste; consequently one may please a great many. Besides, to write poems is very agreeable, and one has always people enough to call them good; so that a man of a tolerable genius rather gains than loses.

I returned to Lady Betty's at six really a good deal mortified, and in that sort of humour that made me consider writing as a dangerous thing and wish that I had never wrote and think I would not write again. I really have still a great degree of imbecility of mind; I am easily persuaded by what other people say, and cannot have a firm enough judgment. I told them my lamentable story.

[4] It is surprising that he does not add (as he could have) that Mrs. Sheridan's prologue not only borrowed its ideas from his but also lifted one of his couplets.

[5] Horace, *Ars Poetica*, l. 372. ("Middling poets were never tolerated by gods, by men, or by booksellers.")

They were really angry, and sympathized with my vexation. I repeated my prologue, which they thought very good; and I repeated Sheridan's criticisms, which they thought puerile and stupid, and declared they always thought him a dull fellow. This had a most pleasing effect and put me again into good humour, although a little of my former uneasiness still remained.

Now did I ponder most seriously with myself how to behave to Sheridan. I was certainly used ungenteelly. Yet to take notice of it was low, and made him triumph in having been able to vex me. So is human nature constituted that I now had an aversion at Sheridan. I saw his bad taste, his insolence, his falsehood, his malevolence in the strongest light. I was sorry that I had been so much with him, and I resolved to take an opportunity of breaking off acquaintance and then lashing him for a presumptuous dunce, like as my friend Erskine and other people do in great abundance. But then I thought I was entertained in his company, so had better keep in with him. I just resolved that I would be upon a sort of indifferent footing. Be diverted with him, and not care a straw how he thought of me.

WEDNESDAY 19 JANUARY. This was a day eagerly expected by Dempster, Erskine, and I, as it was fixed as the period of our gratifying a whim proposed by me: which was that on the first day of the new tragedy called *Elvira's* being acted, we three should walk from the one end of London to the other, dine at Dolly's, and be in the theatre at night; and as the play would probably be bad, and as Mr. David Malloch, the author, who has changed his name to David Mallet, Esq., was an arrant puppy, we determined to exert ourselves in damning it.[6] I this morning felt stronger symptoms

[6] David Mallet enjoyed general and deserved unpopularity for having accepted a large sum of money from the Duchess of Marlborough to write a life of the Duke, of which he never penned a line; for being the author of a discreditable party pamphlet against the unfortunate Admiral Byng; and for having courted Pope with fulsome flattery, and then having attacked him after he was dead. He was also a sceptic whose public declaimings against Christianity Hume thought indecent. His chief offenses in the eyes of Scotsmen were that he had changed his distinctively Scots name of Malloch, and

of the sad distemper, yet I was unwilling to imagine such a thing.
However, the severe exercise of today, joined with hearty eating
and drinking, I was sure would confirm or remove my suspicions.

We walked up to Hyde Park Corner, from whence we set out at
ten. Our spirits were high with the notion of the adventure, and
the variety that we met with as we went along is amazing. As the
Spectator observes, one end of London is like a different country
from the other in look and in manners. We eat an excellent breakfast at the Somerset Coffee-house. We turned down Gracechurch
Street and went upon the top of London Bridge, from whence we
viewed with a pleasing horror the rude and terrible appearance of
the river, partly froze up, partly covered with enormous shoals of
floating ice which often crashed against each other.[7] Dempster said
of this excursion from the road that our Epic Poem would be somewhat dull if it were not enlivened by such episodes. As we went
along, I felt the symptoms increase, which was very confounding
and very distressing to me. I thought the best thing I could do was
not to keep it secret, which would be difficult and troublesome, but
fairly to own it to Dempster and Erskine and ask their advice and
sympathy. They really sympathized, and yet they could not help
smiling a little at my catching a tartar so very unexpectedly, when
I imagined myself quite safe, and had been vaunting most heroically of my felicity in having the possession of a fine woman, to
whom I ascribed so many endearing qualities that they really

that he had learned to speak English so well that even Johnson (who despised him) had to admit that he had never caught him in a Scotch accent.
Boswell, Erskine, and Dempster also felt that his arrogant manners were not
becoming in one who was the son of a tenant farmer, and who had served for
a time in his youth as janitor in the High School of Edinburgh.
[7] "The frost here has been quite intense for some time past. It is likely to be
a most severe winter, which is very hard on the poor people" (Boswell to
John Johnston, written this same day). "In London the severity of the cold
has been such that two soldiers were frozen to death on their duty; and in
other parts several that have lost their way in the night have been found
frozen to death in the morning" (20 January 1763 in the Historical Chronicle
of the *Gentleman's Magazine*).

doubted of her existence, and used to call her my *ideal lady*. We went half a mile beyond the turnpike at Whitechapel, which completed our course, and went into a little public house and drank some warm white wine with aromatic spices, pepper and cinnamon. We were pleased with the neat houses upon the road.

We met a coach loaded with passengers both within and without. Said I, "I defy all the philosophers in the world to tell me why this is."[8] "Because," said Erskine, "the people wanted a quick carriage from one place to another." So very easily are the most of the speculations which I often perplex myself with refuted. And yet if some such clever answerer is not at hand, I may puzzle and confound my brain for a good time upon many occasions. To be sure this instance is too ludicrous. But surely, I and many more speculative men have been thrown into deep and serious thought about matters very little more serious. Yet the mind will take its own way, do what we will. So that we may be rendered uneasy by such cloudy reveries when we have no intention to be in such a humour. The best relief in such a case is mirth and gentle amusement.

We had a room to ourselves, and a jolly profusion of smoking juicy beefsteaks. I eat like a very Turk, or rather indeed like a very John Bull, whose supreme joy is good beef. We had some port, and drank damnation to the play and eternal remorse to the author. We then went to the Bedford Coffee-house and had coffee and tea; and just as the doors opened at four o'clock, we sallied into the house, planted ourselves in the middle of the pit, and with oaken cudgels in our hands and shrill-sounding catcalls in our pockets, sat ready prepared, with a generous resentment in our breasts against dullness and impudence, to be the swift ministers of vengeance.[9] About five the house began to be pretty well filled. As is usual on first nights, some of us called to the music to play *Roast Beef*.[1] But they did not comply with our request and we were not numerous enough to turn that request into a command, which in a London theatre

[8] Boswell found it hard to understand why passengers were riding outside in such cold weather?   [9] See above, p. 25.

[1] A popular patriotic song from Henry Fielding's *Grub-Street Opera*.

is quite a different sort of public speech. This was but a bad omen for our party. It resembled a party's being worsted in the choice of praeses[2] and clerk, at an election in a Scotch county.

However, we kept a good spirit, and hoped the best. The prologue was politically stupid. We hissed it and had several to join us. That we might not be known, we went by borrowed names. Dempster was Clarke; Erskine, Smith; and I, Johnston. We did what we could during the first act, but found that the audience had lost their original fire and spirit and were disposed to let it pass. Our project was therefore disconcerted, our impetuosity damped. As we knew it would be needless to oppose that furious many-headed monster, the multitude, as it has been very well painted,[3] we were obliged to lay aside our laudable undertaking in the cause of genius and the cause of modesty.

After the play we went to Lady Betty's, and as they were not disposed to eat and we were very hungry after our fatigues, we were set down in the parlour by ourselves to an excellent warm supper. We were in high glee, and after supper threw out so many excellent sallies of humour and wit and satire on Malloch and his play that we determined to have a joint sixpenny cut,[4] and fixed next day for throwing our sallies into order. The evening was passed most cheerfully. When I got home, though, then came sorrow. Too, too plain was Signor Gonorrhoea. Yet I could scarce believe it, and determined to go to friend Douglas next day.

THURSDAY 20 JANUARY. I rose very disconsolate, having rested very ill by the poisonous infection raging in my veins and anxiety and vexation boiling in my breast. I could scarcely credit my own senses. What! thought I, can this beautiful, this sensible, and this agreeable woman be so sadly defiled? Can corruption lodge

[2] Presiding officer, moderator.

[3] It was Pope (*Satires,* V. 305) who spoke of the "many-headed monster of the pit."

[4] Apparently "a jointly written sixpenny pamphlet intended to wound Mallet's feelings deeply." "Cut" in this sense is perfectly plausible (see Boswell's use of the word below, p. 298), but the Oxford English Dictionary gives no exactly parallel examples.

beneath so fair a form? Can she who professed delicacy of sentiment and sincere regard for me, use me so very basely and so very cruelly? No, it is impossible. I have just got a gleet by irritating the parts too much with excessive venery. And yet these damned twinges, that scalding heat, and that deep-tinged loathsome matter are the strongest proofs of an infection. But she certainly must think that I would soon discover her falsehood. But perhaps she was ignorant of her being ill. A pretty conjecture indeed! No, she could not be ignorant. Yes, yes, she intended to make the most of me. And now I recollect that the day we went to Hayward's, she showed me a bill of thirty shillings about which she was in some uneasiness, and no doubt expected that I would pay it. But I was too cautious, and she had not effrontery enough to try my generosity in direct terms so soon after my letting her have two guineas. And am I then taken in? Am I, who have had safe and elegant intrigues with fine women, become the dupe of a strumpet? Am I now to be laid up for many weeks to suffer extreme pain and full confinement, and to be debarred all the comforts and pleasures of life? And then must I have my poor pocket drained by the unavoidable expense of it? And shall I no more (for a long time at least) take my walk, healthful and spirited, round the Park before breakfast, view the brilliant Guards on the Parade, and enjoy all my pleasing amusements? And then am I prevented from making love to Lady Mirabel, or any other woman of fashion? O dear, O dear! What a cursed thing this is! What a miserable creature am I!

In this woeful manner did I melancholy ruminate. I thought of applying to a quack who would cure me quickly and cheaply. But then the horrors of being imperfectly cured and having the distemper thrown into my blood terrified me exceedingly. I therefore pursued my resolution of last night to go to my friend Douglas, whom I knew to be skillful and careful; and although it should cost me more, yet to get sound health was a matter of great importance, and I might save upon other articles. I accordingly went and breakfasted with him.

Mrs. Douglas, who has a prodigious memory and knows a

thousand anecdotes, especially of scandal, told me that Congreve the poet lived in the family of old Lord Godolphin, who is yet alive, and that Lady Godolphin was notoriously fond of him. In so much that her lord having gone abroad upon an embassy for two years, on his return she presented him with a fine girl by the author of *Love For Love*, which he was so indulgent as to accept of; nay, after Congreve's death, he joined with her in grief, and allowed her to have an image of him in wax daily set at table and nightly in her bedchamber, to which she spoke, believing it through heat of fancy, or believing it in appearance, to be Congreve himself. The young lady was most tenderly educated, and it is a certain fact that she was never suffered to see the moon for fear she should cry for it. She is now Duchess of Leeds, and has turned out extremely well.[5]

After breakfast Mrs. Douglas withdrew, and I opened my sad case to Douglas, who upon examining the parts, declared I had got an evident infection and that the woman who gave it me could not but know of it. I joked with my friend about the expense, asked him if he would take a draught on my arrears,[6] and bid him visit me seldom that I might have the less to pay. To these jokes he seemed to give little heed, but talked seriously in the way of his business. And here let me make a just and true observation, which is that the same man as a friend and as a surgeon exhibits two very opposite characters. Douglas as a friend is most kind, most anxious

[5] Lady Godolphin was eldest daughter of the great Duke of Marlborough, at whose death she became Duchess of Marlborough in her own right. She was certainly fond of Congreve to the point of insanity, and built a monument for him in Westminster Abbey with an inscription of her own composing. In it she commemorated "the happiness and honour she enjoyed in the sincere friendship" of Congreve. The "scandal" did not originate with Mrs. Douglas. Pope characterizes the Duchess in very blunt terms ("Chaste to her husband, frank to all beside, A teeming mistress, but a barren bride. . . . In another fit She sins with poets through pure love of wit"), and Horace Walpole preserves a story that the old Duchess (Sarah Jennings), misquoting her daughter's epitaph for Congreve, said, "I know not what *pleasure* she might have in his company, but I am sure it was no *honour*."

[6] "Take my note for what I was unable to pay."

for my interest, made me live ten days in his house, and suggested every plan of economy. But Douglas as a surgeon will be as ready to keep me long under his hands, and as desirous to lay hold of my money, as any man. In short, his views alter quite. I have to do not with him but his profession.

As Lady Northumberland was to have a great rout next day, I delayed beginning my course of medicine till Friday night. Enraged at the perfidy of Louisa, I resolved to go and upbraid her most severely; but this I thought was not acting with dignity enough. So I would talk to her coolly and make her feel her own unworthiness. But hearing the Duke of Queensberry was in town, I thought I would go and have one more brush at him and hear what he had to say.

When I entered, he looked somewhat abashed and timid, which encouraged me. "My Lord," said I, "I got your Grace's letter, and was sorry for the contents. Your Grace was pleased to mention my following a civil life. I should be glad to know what. The law I am not able for. If indeed I could be put upon the civil list for about a thousand a year, as Sir Francis Wronghead[7] says, I should like it very well." At this he laughed. He then talked of the difficulty of getting a commission. "Certainly," said I, "my Lord Duke, it is very difficult. But your Grace has never yet mentioned me to Lord Ligonier. I should be sorry to give your Grace a great deal of trouble, but I should think that it would not be much to mention the thing once, so as I might be put upon Lord Ligonier's list." He promised to me that he would mention it. In short, I find that indolence was the matter with him, and that he must be pushed, although I have but little hopes from him.

I then went to Louisa. With excellent address did I carry on this interview, as the following scene, I trust, will make appear.

LOUISA. My dear Sir! I hope you are well today.

BOSWELL. Excessively well, I thank you. I hope I find you so.

---

[7] A simple country gentleman in *The Provok'd Husband,* a comedy by Vanbrugh and Cibber.

LOUISA. No, really, Sir. I am distressed with a thousand things. (Cunning jade, her circumstances!) I really don't know what to do.

BOSWELL. Do you know that I have been very unhappy since I saw you?

LOUISA. How so, Sir?

BOSWELL. Why, I am afraid that you don't love me so well, nor have not such a regard for me, as I thought you had.

LOUISA. Nay, dear Sir! (Seeming unconcerned.)

BOSWELL. Pray, Madam, have I no reason?

LOUISA. No, indeed, Sir, you have not.

BOSWELL. Have I no reason, Madam? Pray think.

LOUISA. Sir!

BOSWELL. Pray, Madam, in what state of health have you been in for some time?

LOUISA. Sir, you amaze me.

BOSWELL. I have but too strong, too plain reason to doubt of your regard. I have for some days observed the symptoms of disease, but was unwilling to believe you so very ungenerous. But now, Madam, I am thoroughly convinced.

LOUISA. Sir, you have terrified me. I protest I know nothing of the matter.

BOSWELL. Madam, I have had no connection with any woman but you these two months. I was with my surgeon this morning, who declared I had got a strong infection, and that she from whom I had it could not be ignorant of it. Madam, such a thing in this case is worse than from a woman of the town, as from her you may expect it. You have used me very ill. I did not deserve it. You know you said where there was no confidence, there was no breach of trust. But surely I placed some confidence in you. I am sorry that I was mistaken.

LOUISA. Sir, I will confess to you that about three years ago I was very bad. But for these fifteen months I have been quite well. I appeal to GOD Almighty that I am speaking true; and for these six months I have had to do with no man but yourself.

BOSWELL. But by G—D, Madam, I have been with none but you, and here am I very bad.

LOUISA. Well, Sir, by the same solemn oath I protest that I was ignorant of it.

BOSWELL. Madam, I wish much to believe you. But I own I cannot upon this occasion believe a miracle.

LOUISA. Sir, I cannot say more to you. But you will leave me in the greatest misery. I shall lose your esteem. I shall be hurt in the opinion of everybody, and in my circumstances.

BOSWELL (to himself). What the devil does the confounded jilt mean by being hurt in her circumstances? This is the grossest cunning. But I won't take notice of that at all.—Madam, as to the opinion of everybody, you need not be afraid. I was going to joke and say that I never boast of a lady's *favours*. But I give you my word of honour that you shall not be discovered.

LOUISA. Sir, this is being more generous than I could expect.

BOSWELL. I hope, Madam, you will own that since I have been with you I have always behaved like a man of honour.

LOUISA. You have indeed, Sir.

BOSWELL (rising). Madam, your most obedient servant.

During all this conversation I really behaved with a manly composure and polite dignity that could not fail to inspire an awe, and she was pale as ashes and trembled and faltered. Thrice did she insist on my staying a little longer, as it was probably the last time that I should be with her. She could say nothing to the purpose. And I sat silent. As I was going, said she, "I hope, Sir, you will give me leave to inquire after your health." "Madam," said I, archly, "I fancy it will be needless for some weeks." She again renewed her request. But unwilling to be plagued any more with her, I put her off by saying I might perhaps go to the country, and left her. I was really confounded at her behaviour. There is scarcely a possibility that she could be innocent of the crime of horrid imposition. And yet her positive asseverations really stunned me. She is in all probability a most consummate dissembling whore.

Thus ended my intrigue with the fair Louisa, which I flattered myself so much with, and from which I expected at least a winter's safe copulation. It is indeed very hard. I cannot say, like young fellows who get themselves clapped in a bawdy-house, that I will take better care again. For I really did take care. However, since I am fairly trapped, let me make the best of it. I have not got it from imprudence. It is merely the chance of war.

I then called at Drury Lane for Mr. Garrick. He was vastly good to me. "Sir," said he, "you will be a very great man. And when you are so, remember the year 1763. I want to contribute my part towards saving you. And pray, will you fix a day when I shall have the pleasure of treating you with tea?" I fixed next day. "Then, Sir," said he, " the cups shall dance and the saucers skip."

What he meant by my being a great man I can understand. For really, to speak seriously, I think there is a blossom about me of something more distinguished than the generality of mankind. But I am much afraid that this blossom will never swell into fruit, but will be nipped and destroyed by many a blighting heat and chilling frost. Indeed, I sometimes indulge noble reveries of having a regiment, of getting into Parliament, making a figure, and becoming a man of consequence in the state. But these are checked by dispiriting reflections on my melancholy temper and imbecility of mind. Yet I may probably become sounder and stronger as I grow up. Heaven knows. I am resigned. I trust to Providence. I was quite in raptures with Garrick's kindness—the man whom from a boy I used to adore and look upon as a heathen god—to find him paying me so much respect! How amiable is he in comparison of Sheridan! I was this day with him what the French call *un étourdi*. I gave free vent to my feelings. Love was by, to whom I cried, "This, Sir, is the real scene." And taking Mr. Garrick cordially by the hand, "Thou greatest of men," said I, "I cannot express how happy you make me." This, upon my soul, was no flattery. He saw it was not. And the dear great man was truly pleased with it. This scene gave me a charming flutter of spirits and dispelled my former gloom.

I dined at Lady Betty's, as I resolved to live well these two days, knowing that severe starving would be my lot for some weeks after. I was now very sick and in very great pain. Yet we were merry enough.

After dinner, Erskine produced our observations on *Elvira* thrown into a pamphlet size. We corrected it, and I copied it out. We resolved to take it to Flexney, near Gray's Inn, Holborn, who, being Mr. Churchill's bookseller, was well known. To give ourselves a good air, we took Lady Betty's coach, and away we drove between nine and ten; called upon Flexney, whom we found a fine, lively, affable little man. Erskine said he conceived an affection for him from the first moment that he saw him. We explained our business, and he readily undertook it. Both I and Erskine behaved with good address.

We came back and supped. The Dempsters were there. We were very hearty and well. I said Erskine was wonderfully improved. For that he used to be like a burthen to me: I had him to carry, and now and then set him down and had a good entertainment out of him. But that now he was become animated, and could go about himself, and was more entertaining than ever. Indeed, my good friend is much altered to the better this winter. He is more content, has more constant spirits and greater ease of manners than ever he had. He candidly owns that I have contributed greatly towards making him a better member of society. When I got home, I felt myself very bad.

FRIDAY 21 JANUARY. Between nine and ten I went to Mr. Garrick's. He received me with particular kindness. Mrs. Garrick made breakfast for us. She is an Italian lady, was a famous dancer on the stage, and when she married Mr. Garrick, Lord Burlington gave her £10,000. She is a genteel, agreeable, unaffected creature. Love was there, also Dr. Brown, author of *Athelstan*, *The Estimate*, &c. I entertained them with some of our remarks on *Elvira*. We talked of the works of Ossian, which Brown extolled to the skies. Brown, instead of being the severe pedant that I expected, is an easy, lively, entertaining man.

I quite forgot my distemper. It was a fine morning. We had a genteel breakfast, which I think the most agreeable meal, in ease and plenty. I was sitting with the great Roscius of the age and with a very good poet.[8] In short, this was a period of felicity. I was happy, I could not tell how. We walked into Mr. Garrick's library, which is a handsome room with a pretty large collection of good books and some busts and pictures. As he was obliged to attend rehearsal in the forenoon, we were too soon deprived of his company. He asked me to come whenever I could. I rejoiced. This is really establishing myself in a charming place. I shall there see all the men of genius of the age. Let me indulge the pleasing prospect of the many happy hours which I shall pass there when I again am blessed with health.

I then called on Lord Eglinton—no, I mistake, it was yesterday that I was there. I am scrupulous to a nicety about truth. He discovered by my looks that I was ill. I went with him into another room and confessed my misfortune. He was going to blame my rashness at first, but upon my telling him that my Dulcinea was an actress, he was silent. I told him I have had several intrigues within these two years, and that if I was taken in but once in four or five times, I was not unlucky. He agreed to all this. He was really kind today. I loved him; and I could see that it was in vain for me to carry it high with him, for he did not understand it. He said he wished I could be kept at a mediocrity of spirits, neither too high nor too low. But he was afraid I was low, as I had not come near him for some time. "Nay, my Lord," said I. "I am high, and don't require you." Said he, "You should have half a dozen of your friends to whom you should come regularly." I asked him to come and sit an afternoon with me. He promised he would.

This forenoon I thought that our pamphlet was too abusive, so Dempster and I went and got it back. Flexney said, very like a gentleman, that he thought it had less cleverness than scurrility.

[8] Brown's best-known work, *An Estimate of the Manners and Principles of the Times* (1757), was a prose attack on contemporary luxury. But he had also written successful poems and verse tragedies.

But if it were made more genteel, it would do. We agreed to do so. Erskine at first was somewhat sulky. But at last he consented, and it was polished and sent back for the press in a day or two.

I dined at Macfarlane's pretty hearty, and drank tea at Dempster's. I next went to Lady Northumberland's grand rout. I was in severe distress and grew very low-spirited. I cared for nothing, and I thought life very tiresome. I chatted a little with Lady Mirabel, but she was dissipated by the crowd and hurry. I got no speaking to Lady Northumberland, and I could scarce keep my dreary humour from persuading me that she despised me, a sure sign of the spleen, which makes us always imagine that we are despised. I chatted a while with Lord Eglinton. He promised that when I got sound, he would introduce me to some women of intrigue of the highest fashion. I came home in bad situation both of body and mind. I had informed my landlord of my misfortune, that everything might be got convenient for me, about which he was very obliging. I laid by my hat and sword, begun to take medicine, and coolly resolved to endure my ill chance patiently.

SATURDAY 22 JANUARY. Calmly and considerately did I sit down in my arm-chair this morning and endeavour to call up all the philosophy that I could. A distemper of this kind is more dreadful to me than most people. I am of a warm constitution: a complexion, as physicians say, exceedingly amorous, and therefore suck in the poison more deeply. I have had two visitations of this calamity. The first lasted ten weeks. The second four months. How severe a reflection is it! And, O, how severe a prospect! Yet let me take courage. Perhaps this is not a very bad infection, and as I shall be scrupulously careful of myself, I may get rid of it in a short time. Then, as Smith[9] used to observe, a time of indisposition is not altogether a time of misery. There is a softness of disposition and an absence of care which attend upon its indolent confinement. Then, I have often lamented my ignorance of English history. Now I may

[9] Adam Smith, later author of *The Wealth of Nations*. He was professor of moral philosophy at the University of Glasgow during the year that Boswell spent there.

make up that want. I may read all Hume's six volumes.[1] I may also be amused with novels and books of a slighter nature.

I gave orders to say at the door that I was gone to the country, except to a few friends. Dempster, Erskine, and my brother were with me today. Though bad, my spirits did not flag. Yet to be kept from comfortable Child's is somewhat hard. However, I will be patient.

SUNDAY 23 JANUARY. I was very dull this day. I considered the Guards as a most improper scene of life for me. I thought it would yield me no pleasure, for my constitution would be gone, and I would not be able to enjoy life. I thought London a bad place for me. I imagined I had lost all relish of it. Nay, so very strange is wayward, diseased fancy that it will make us wish for the things most disagreeable to us merely to procure a change of objects, being sick and tired of those it presently has. I thought I would go immediately down to Edinburgh, and would be an advocate in the Parliament House, and so lead a comfortable life. I was vexed to find all my gay plans vanished, and I had a struggle between hope and despair.

My friend Captain Erskine came in. I told him my strange conceits. He reminded me of the uneasy situation I had been in when at home. This settled me a little. In the afternoon, my brother came. He brought many low old Sunday ideas when we were boys into my memory. I wanted to indulge my gloom in solitude. I wearied of him. I showed it. I was angry at myself. I was peevish. He was good enough to say he would go and come just as I chose. He left me. I remained ill.

MONDAY 24 JANUARY. I was somewhat better, and had some hope of being happy again. I received the following card from Lord Eglinton:

DEAR JAMIE,—I am sorry it has not been in my power to pay

[1] David Hume is best known now as a sceptical philosopher, but he made his fortune with a *History of England* which long remained the standard work on the subject. It had been completed only two years before.

my respects to you as I promised, but will call on you soon. If you are not engaged, pray dine with me tomorrow. Yours,

.

EGLINTON.

I wrote for answer:

MR. BOSWELL presents his compliments to Lord Eglinton, and is sorry he cannot comply with his Lordship's kind invitation, being confined to the house. But when he gets well, he hopes to be oftener with his Lordship, for indeed, my Lord, we love each other. Yours,

BOSWELL.

This card was a little effusion of the love which I cannot help having for this very agreeable nobleman who first brought me into life and taught me the joys of splendour and gaiety.—What will now become of my journal for some time? It must be a barren desert, a mere blank. To relate gravely that I rose, made water, took drugs, sat quiet, read a book, saw a friend or two day after day, must be exceedingly poor and tedious. My journal must therefore, like the newspapers, yield to the times. Yet I may have some incidents to insert. At any rate, I shall soon again be roaming abroad in search of amusing adventures.

TUESDAY 25 JANUARY. Lord Eglinton came to me this forenoon. We talked of Churchill. My Lord owned he was a very clever fellow, but must in some degree be either a fool or a knave to abuse the Scotch so grossly. He said it was a pity he had taken such a turn. I asked my Lord to frank some covers.[2] "Certainly," said he, "I am your scribe, and everything else that you please." As he was writing, I could not help beginning upon my difference with him, as I felt my old love for him. Our dialogue was as follows:

BOSWELL. Upon my word, my Lord, you and I ought to be upon a good footing. But we are not.

[2] That is, to write "Free, Eglinton" on pieces of paper that Boswell would later use as envelopes, thus securing his correspondents from the payment of postage. Eglinton enjoyed the privilege of franking as one of the sixteen Scots peers elected to sit in the House of Lords.

EGLINTON. I am sorry for it, Jamie. But it is not my fault. I am sure I forgive you all your little follies.

BOSWELL. But, my Lord, I don't forgive you.

EGLINTON. How so now? Let me hear your complaints. Tell your story.

BOSWELL. Why then, my Lord, to begin and go regularly through. You know I left Scotland abruptly and came up to London two years ago in an odd enough way. Your Lordship was kind enough to take particular notice of me. You took me into your own house. And you brought me right. You pulled me out of the mire, washed me and cleaned me and made me fit to be seen. I was told by some friends that the cause of all this was the election in Ayrshire being then in dependence. But I was convinced not. No, no, I was a fine fellow. It was all on my own account. Well, my Lord, you then pointed out to me a most agreeable way of life, which was to be an officer of the Guards; indeed, the only real employment that I ever liked; and you promised to use all your interest for me. My father then came up and I was hurried down to Scotland, confined to live in my father's family, and pressed to study law, so that my situation was very unhappy. Your Lordship in the mean time continued to profess a regard for me and promised me your assistance. Nay, my Lord, you went so far as to say to me, "Jamie, to be sure, I cannot do so much for you as your father; but if you and he cannot agree, come to me, and I will do all I can for you." Now, my Lord, this was saying the strongest thing you could say. It was making me more indifferent as to breaking with my father. At last I got my father's consent. I immediately applied to you. And you know, my Lord, how you used me, how you put me off. It was very hard.

EGLINTON. Now, Jamie, I acknowledge all this true that you have said. Have not I heard you patiently? I hope you will hear me in the same way.—When you was first in London, I found that you had been much hurt by being forced to studies contrary to the natural bent of your genius, and been obliged to live with your parents, who, though very good people, had a strictness and confined way of thinking which a man of your strength of imagination and natural freedom of sentiment could not put up with. I pointed out the Guards to you, as I thought the gaiety of a military life was the best thing in the world to keep off that melancholy to which you was a little subject. Upon my going down to Scotland, I found your father much averse to it, and I need not tell you that he did all he could to thwart and oppose it. Now, you must allow that it would have been very disagreeable for me just directly to oppose him.

BOSWELL. I grant you this, my Lord. But then—

EGLINTON. Allow me to go on. You wrote to me in May last that you had got your father's consent, and therefore you hoped I would now get you into the Guards. But then you desired expressly that your commission might be in one of the battalions at home. Now, will you consider what sort of a demand this was? No doubt, it would have been the utmost difficulty for me to get such a thing at any rate; and I would have required every argument, and among the rest, that the young man was anxious to go upon service. But how could I possibly ask for one at home? And you know, Jamie, I wrote you this very strongly.

BOSWELL. You did so, my Lord. But you should have done it more gently.

EGLINTON. I confess to you that my letter was too harsh from a man to his friend. But then you must consider that I was really in a passion for your having brought me into a sad scrape by publishing your *Cub* and dedicating it to the Duke of York without his leave. I can assure you he was very angry.

BOSWELL. I think, my Lord, he was wrong there. For in my opinion I paid him a compliment.

EGLINTON. So I think indeed.

BOSWELL. Well, but, my Lord, you know I answered your letter and told you that I was willing to go abroad.

EGLINTON. You did so. But it was in such a way that I could not imagine it anything else than a genteel evasion, and what I should have expected from a man of your sense and genius if you did not want flatly to refuse going upon service, but yet chose to shun it. I have your letters yet to show you. I put that point very home to you. I expected an explicit answer. And you only said that no doubt you would be very willing to go if your regiment went. But this was what no man could refuse to do except he would declare himself an arrant poltroon. He would rather go and take the chance of not coming to action.

BOSWELL. Well, I assure you, my Lord, that my meaning was this: that my great plan in getting into the Guards was not so much to be a soldier as to be in the genteel character of a gentleman; and therefore I would have rather chose that my commission should have been in one of the battalions at home. But I should certainly have rather gone abroad than not get in.

EGLINTON. Indeed, Jamie, I did not understand you so. You wrote me two letters. The first treated the thing slightly. In the second you seemed very angry. I assure you, I took it in this light, that I thought you would not accept a commission in a battalion in Germany.

BOSWELL. Then, my Lord, all this has just been a mistake. But I think my taking your behaviour so ill is a proof that I really meant as I say, to go abroad if that should be necessary.

EGLINTON. It is so. But I hope I have explained my conduct to you. No doubt, as you took it, you had great reason to blame me and think I had broke my promise to you. But you see how it was.

(Here my heart melted with tenderness, genuine candour, and joy.)

BOSWELL. My Lord, I did not intend to have spoke on the subject at all to you. I was quite convinced of your bad usage. I intended just to be off with you. But, my Lord, I am happy we have had this conversation. I see you was not to blame. (Taking him by the hand.) I suffered very much in thinking myself so deceived.

EGLINTON. Well, I hope all is over now, and we're just where we were.

BOSWELL (almost weeping). We are indeed, my Lord. I rejoice at my being ill at present, as it has given us this opportunity. Even when I was most angry, I could not help now and then having returns of fondness for you as strong as ever.

EGLINTON. Like what one feels for a mistress, was it not?

BOSWELL. Just so, my Lord.

EGLINTON. I assure you, Jamie, I have the same regard for you I ever had. I have made allowance for you all this time. Writing me such cards and never coming near me was enough to make me break with you. But I made allowance for your mistakes. Had you been a man of as much prudence and discernment as you take yourself to be, I would not have forgiven it. Though I believe you now know your own character pretty well. I will own to you that I have too much resentment in my disposition, more than a man of a noble mind ought to have. Your liveliness of fancy and warmth of heart, Jamie, are the qualities most ready to lead a man wrong.

BOSWELL. I believe that is very true.

EGLINTON. Believe me, I was always ready to serve you, and I will help you at this time.

BOSWELL. Will you, my Lord?

EGLINTON. Indeed will I.

I then told him all my different expectations about my commission: the Duke of Queensberry, Lady Northumberland, the Marquis of Granby. He said he would take me to Lord Bute's levee, and I should push at all hands. All would help. We went on:

BOSWELL. Do you think, my Lord, it is worth my while to please myself with the idea of having a regiment by the time I am sixty?

EGLINTON. Ay, by the time you're forty. It is agreeable to have a prospect before one.

BOSWELL. Yes, my Lord, but what will you say to a man who is philosopher enough to know that a man, even before he gets the first step, can enjoy his bottle, his girl, and his friend just as well as when he comes to be a general? That is my case.

EGLINTON. I'll tell you what I would do. When things go well, I would encourage the ideas of rising; and when they go ill, I would be the philosopher.

BOSWELL. Your Lordship is right.

EGLINTON. Well, Jamie, I must go. Now think seriously on what I have said to you, and I am sure you will see it stronger and stronger.

We embraced each other cordially, and he left me. Here now is a very material period in my journal. I was deeply offended with the behaviour of this nobleman. I had resolved to give up all regard for him; and now, by our coming to an explanation, I am perfectly convinced that he was not to blame. I hope this acknowl- edgment is not owing to mere goodness and easiness of temper. For his facts and arguments, which are all just, are very strong in his favour. I think my candid soul is to be admired for yielding my resentful feelings to truth. This event makes me very happy. I shall now enjoy his elegant company and conversation as fully and freely as formerly. We shall be intimate companions.

Yet, let me moderate these sallies of gladness and kindness. Let me not all at once make a transition too violent. Certain it is that although Lord Eglinton might mean to act honestly with respect to me, yet it is certain that he is very selfish and very dis- sipated, and therefore a man who depends upon him must have a great deal of trouble and vexation. He also sets a high value on his favours, so that he treats people who are obliged to him with a degree of contempt. Let me therefore be in this style with him: just an agreeable lively companion who is much at his house amongst other men of wit and spirit. This is not being obliged to him more than he is to me. I will thus have a great deal of pleas- urable conversation, and at the same time maintain my own con- sequence. There is another consideration of some importance, which is keeping myself independent of him in Ayrshire. Elections are very nice things. Nobody can tell what accidents may happen. I have a good family interest. I may indulge the idea of representing the County. Well, then, let me keep this in mind, and I shall do very well.

This afternoon, by taking too much physic, I felt myself very ill. I was weak. I shivered, and I had flushes of heat. I began to be apprehensive that I was taking a nervous fever, a supposition not improbable, as I had one after such an illness when I was last in London. I was quite sunk. I looked with a degree of horror upon death. Some of my intrigues which in high health and spirits I valued myself upon now seemed to be deviations from the sacred road of virtue. My mind fluctuated, but grew more composed. I looked up to the beneficent Creator. I was resigned and more easy, and went to bed in hope.

WEDNESDAY 26 JANUARY. Erskine came and dined with me. I was much better, and I felt a hearty satisfaction in entertaining my friend.

THURSDAY 27 JANUARY. Our performance entitled *Critical Strictures on the New Tragedy of "Elvira," written by Mr. David Malloch* pleased me greatly. I felt just the satisfaction that a man does on the first time of seeing himself in print. We were very severe on Malloch without souring our own good humour.[3] Er-

---

[3] *Critical Strictures*, a pamphlet of twenty-four pages in large type, is one of the rarest of Boswell's works. The following paragraph (which sounds much more like Erskine than like Boswell) is a fair sample: "In the fifth act we were melted with the sight of two young children which the king embraced, which the prince embraced, which Elvira embraced. Mr. Addison in the 44th number of *The Spectator* has some remarks so judicious and lively on the practice of introducing children on the stage that we must beg leave to transcribe the passage. . . . We would suggest to Mr. Malloch the useful hint of introducing in some of his future productions the whole Foundling Hospital, which, with a well-painted scene of the edifice itself, would certainly call for the warmest tears of pity and the bitterest emotions of distress; especially when we consider that many of the parents of these unfortunate babes would probably be spectators of this interesting scene."— *Elvira* had a moderate success, and the reviews were very severe on the pamphlet. *The Critical Review* dismissed it with a single sentence: "We

skine drank tea with me. Our conversation was rather sensible and composed than lively and witty. I continued in a good way, and was not discontent.

FRIDAY 28 JANUARY. Mr. Ward, a physical young man[4] who attends my brother, breakfasted with me. The day went on tolerably well.

SATURDAY 29 JANUARY. I amused myself with writing letters. I continued in a good way. I have lived all this week on bread and tea. I would fain say something to keep up the practice of writing journal, like the Highlander who stole his pockets full of hay to keep his hand in use. I put down mere trifles. I have now one great satisfaction, which is reading Hume's *History*. It entertains and instructs me. It elevates my mind and excites noble feelings of every kind.

SUNDAY 30 JANUARY. I regretted much my being kept from divine service. I was not so well. I had more inflammation, so I caused Douglas blood me,[5] which gave me relief. I now began to take a little better diet. I had a pound of veal made into a large bowl of weak broth. This gave me better spirits, and cherished my nerves.

MONDAY 31 JANUARY. The Martyrdom of King Charles falling on a Sunday this year, this day was kept as the fast on that occasion. This tragical event is an indelible stain on the British nation. Worthy, though misguided Monarch! May thy soul rest in peace. I could have wished to hear some of the sermons this day. I found myself in a good way.

TUESDAY 1 FEBRUARY. I began to write a little comic piece.[6]

---

shall bestow no further notice on these strictures than to say they appear to be the crude efforts of envy, petulance, and self-conceit." This provided one epithet for each of the authors, and Boswell says they entered into a humorous contention as to which adjective belonged to which.
[4] That is, a young medical practitioner.
[5] "Made Douglas draw a quantity of blood from the vein in my arm"— standard eighteenth-century practice for fevers and inflammations.
[6] Nothing is known of this piece except that it was called "Taylors"—presumably, *The Tailors.*

This diverted me, and made me form many pleasing reveries of its success on the stage.

WEDNESDAY 2 FEBRUARY. I had a visit of Captain Erskine, eldest son to Lady Frances.[7] Dempster drank tea with me. We talked of the House of Commons, and schemes of rising in the world. Dempster said he had a great deal of ambition, and yet much contentment. I asked him what his ambition extended to. He answered, "To be the first man in the Kingdom"—a fine idea no doubt but a chimerical one. I hinted that servility to the Court might be necessary: to stoop in order to rise. But he maintained that a man who kept himself quite independent, and who showed that he resolutely acted according to his conscience, would acquire respect, and would make his way honourably. He said that a Member who sets up on that footing must be laughed at for some time, because all the Patriots have at last come in, for proper considerations; at least, the exceptions are very few.[8] But he declared to me upon his word that he was determined to persevere in rectitude, let the consequence be lucky or the reverse. He put me into excellent spirits. They lasted me all the evening. I read, wrote, and played on my violin with unusual satisfaction.[9] And did not repine.

THURSDAY 3 FEBRUARY. I was not so well as yesterday. I was somewhat morose. I thought the treacherous Louisa deserved

[7] John Francis Erskine, in whose person (1824) the earldom of Mar was restored. It had been forfeited in 1716 when his grandfather joined the Pretender.

[8] That is "All the Members who made a great parade of their incorruptible devotion to liberty and their unalterable opposition to tyranny have swung into line with the Government when the bribe got large enough." The fact that "Patriot" was at this time the cant term of a self-seeking political group needs to be kept in mind in assessing Johnson's famous remark, "Patriotism is the last refuge of a scoundrel."

[9] It must seem rather odd that Boswell has not previously mentioned the fact that he could play the violin, or that he had a violin with him. At various times in his life he played the violin, the flute, and the bass viol, but probably none of them very well, for there is no record of his playing with others. He loved to sing, and had a good ear and a good voice.

to suffer for her depravity. I therefore wrote her the following letter:

MADAM:—My surgeon will soon have a demand upon me of five guineas for curing the disease which you have given me. I must therefore remind you of the little sum which you had of me some time ago. You cannot have forgot upon what footing I let you have it. I neither *paid* it for prostitution nor *gave* it in charity. It was fairly borrowed, and you promised to return it. I give you notice that I expect to have it before Saturday sennight.

I have been very bad, but I scorn to upbraid you. I think it below me. If you are not rendered callous by a long course of disguised wickedness, I should think the consideration of your deceit and baseness, your corruption both of body and mind, would be a very severe punishment. Call not that a misfortune which is the consequence of your own unworthiness. I desire no mean evasions. I want no letters. Send the money sealed up. I have nothing more to say to you.

JAMES BOSWELL.

This, I thought, might be a pretty bitter potion to her. Yet I thought to mention the money was not so genteel. However, if I get it (which is not probable), it will be of real service to me; and to such a creature as her a pecuniary punishment will give most pain. Am not I too vindictive? It appears so; but upon better consideration I am only sacrificing at the shrine of Justice; and sure I have chosen a victim that deserves it.

This day was the first representation of Mrs. Sheridan's comedy, *The Discovery*. As Dempster, Erskine, and I had made a resolution to be present at every first night, I determined to venture abroad, although I could not but hesitate for fear of being the worse of it. I had this forenoon visits from Lord Advocate and Dr. Pringle, so that I had two chariots in one day at my door. I told Lord Advocate that I could not do without employment; and that if I could not get into the Guards, I would go back to Scotland and join his society. But that in the mean time, I would take a full

career of London, and perhaps roam a while abroad in France and
Italy.

At three I swallowed an apple-tart, then wrapped myself well
up in two pair of stockings, two shirts, and a greatcoat; and thus
fortified against the weather, I got into a snug chair[1] and was
carried to Drury Lane. I took up my associates at the Rose Tavern,
and we went into the pit at four, where, as they had not dined,
they laid down their hats, one on each side of me, and there did I
sit to keep their places. I was amused to find myself transported
from my room of indisposition to the gay, gilded theatre. I put
myself as much as possible into proper humour for seeing the
play. Luckily, Dr. Goldsmith came into the seat behind me. I
renewed my acquaintance with him, and he agreed to keep the
same place for the night. His conversation revived in my mind
the true ideas of London authors, which are to me something
curious, and, as it were, mystical.

In my opinion, perfect simplicity and intimate knowledge of
scenes takes away the pleasing sort of wonder and awe that we
have for what is not clear to us: as the seers of old got reverence by
concealing the whole of their transactions. People in that case
imagine more in things than there really is. This makes the great
difference between people that are raw and those that know the
world. When we know exactly all a man's views and how he comes
to speak and act so and so, we lose any respect for him, though we
may love and admire him; at least we lose that kind of distant respect which is very agreeable for us to feel and him to receive. I
wish I may make myself understood upon this subject. The ideas
are perhaps odd and whimsical; but I have found them with respect to my own mind just and real. As an instance of this, my
agreeable family of Kellie from their plain *hameliness* (to use
Lord Elibank's expression with respect to the ladies of Scotland)
do not inspire that awe that women with less parts and good looks
than they have would do, provided they have studied address and
learned the nice art of neither being too free nor too reserved;

[1] A sedan chair. See above, p. 23.

who know exactly and who practice their knowledge of how much they ought to show and how much to conceal. Politeness is just what gives that. All its merit consists in that. There is indeed a kind of character perfectly disguised, a perfect made dish, which is often found, both male and female, in London. This is most disgusting: plain nature is infinitely better. What I admire is nature improved by art, for art certainly may and does improve nature.

I had but a troublesome occupation keeping two seats while my companions were enjoying themselves over a bottle and lolling at their ease, in no hurry to come in. However, I had the satisfaction to see them well punished, for by staying so late they could scarcely squeeze through the crowd, and with the utmost difficulty got to their places. The evening went finely on. I felt a little pain when the prologue was spoke, considering how near I was to have had mine sounding away. We had several judicious and lively people round us, and kept up a clever enough chat. I wrought myself up to the imagination that it was the age of Sir Richard Steele, and that I was like him sitting in judgment on a new comedy.

This gave me much pleasure, in so much that I could have wished my two companions absent from me, as they brought down my ideas and made me imagine myself just at Edinburgh, which, though a kind of a comfortable idea, was not so high as what I was indulging. I find that I ought not to keep too much company with Scotch people, because I am kept from acquiring propriety of English speaking, and because they prevent my mind from being filled with London images, so that I might as well be in Scotland. For there is little or no difference between being with an entire Scotch company in a room in London and a room in Edinburgh. Yet, as I am in such a degree of intimacy with the Kellies and the Dempsters, and as they are in reality as good society as any, it will require the nicest conduct to act as I would choose. In the mean time, till I get into the Guards, I may be much there. They will probably be gone after this winter. When I become an officer, I shall have more occupation, be more in the great world, and so have a very good title to have a little alteration in my conduct. There is a fine scheme. I wish I may be able to realize it.

This long digression has carried me quite away from the play. However, I may be glad now of any tolerable materials to furnish my journal with. The play really acted heavily. Dempster proposed its damnation. I would have agreed, had not I been tied up, as it would look like revenge for refusing my prologue. It was therefore allowed to jog through. Goldsmith said many smart acrimonious things. I stole quietly into a chair. As I was carried along and viewed the streets by the light of the lamps, I was amused by considering the variety of scenes going on in this metropolis with which I was now wholly unconnected during my state of confinement. Upon my coming home, I felt myself not so well. I dreaded the worst, and went to bed.

FRIDAY 4 FEBRUARY. I had been very bad all night, I lay in direful apprehension that my testicle, which formerly was ill, was again swelled. I dreamt that Douglas stood by me and said, "This is a damned difficult case." I got up today still in terror. Indeed, there was a little return of inflammation. I had catched some cold. However, before night I was pretty easy again.

SATURDAY 5 FEBRUARY. I continued better. Erskine for the first time this day was absent altogether from me. My brother drank tea with me.

SUNDAY 6 FEBRUARY. Erskine drank tea with me. I affirmed that flattery was a very good thing, and when we flatter a man, we do him a kindness. "To be sure," said Erskine. "For applause is the thing we are all eagerly seeking after. Now, when a man is flattered, he gets his praise in ready money. Future fame from the world is but like an Edinburgh bank-bill, optional and not payable at sight." He might have added the many chances against merit's being heard of—and the danger of a slight piece of paper's being blown away. My opinion of flattery is this: that it may be made a very fine thing. I would not say to a man what I don't think. But surely it is humanity, it is benevolence, to hide from a man the faults which he cannot help and to enumerate all the perfections that he evidently has.

This evening I praised Erskine's poetry exceedingly. I gave him just reasons for my opinion, and he owned himself obliged to me for my agreeable flattery. We were in the very best spirits: comfortable and lively and happy. I told him I wondered how Mr. Lloyd got so much poetry for his magazine.[2] "I wonder," said he, "that he does not get much more of such poetry. It is as if one were making a collection of whinstones in Scotland, where you may get them on every field." We talked with relish on publishing and on the profits made by books and pamphlets. We both agreed that if we could get something worth while by our works, we would be very glad. Money got this way would be highly valued by us, and we would enjoy the pleasures which it purchased, with peculiar satisfaction. It is very agreeable to look forward and imagine that we shall probably write much, get much fame, and much gold.

I had now and then mentioned my journal to him. I read him a little of it this evening. To be sure it is very carelessly wrote, which he freely took notice, and said it might become a habit to me to write in that manner, so that I would learn a mere slatternly style. He advised me to take more pains upon it, and to render it useful by being a good method to practice writing: to turn periods and render myself ready at different kinds of expression. He is very right. I shall be more attentive for the future, and rather give a little neatly done than a good deal slovenly.

MONDAY 7 FEBRUARY. Douglas told me he had just been with Lord Eglinton, who was indisposed and had been blooded, and had desired Douglas to tell me so and make that apology for his not having been again to see me. He said my Lord talked of me with great regard; explained our difference fully; and upon Douglas's saying that his Lordship had now an opportunity to

[2] Robert Lloyd, poet and friend of Churchill (he had been Churchill's schoolfellow at Westminster), was editing *The St. James's Magazine*.

make perfectly up an affair which was not quite clear, he declared he would do all for me in his power. I was pleased with this new instance of the Peer's sincere liking to me, and I wrote him the following epistle:

My Dear Lord:—Mr. Douglas delivered me your kind message today, for which accept of my sincere love in return. Indulgent Fancy, my Lord, is now bringing back to my mind those pleasing days when our intimacy first began, when your Lordship first showed me the brilliant scenes of life and inspired me with the gay ideas which I have ever since admired and fondly pursued. I had formerly been a stranger to Pleasure. The Goddess had been debarred access to my mind, which Nature had formed capable of being made a temple worthy of her residence. A dark curtain had been drawn between me and her charms. It was Lord Eglinton who opened to me the enchanted palace. Delightful prospect! What lively impressions did it make on my youthful imagination! How sweetly did I revel in delicious enjoyment! But those days did not last. Hurried into the bleak northern shade, the blissful visions fled. Gloom and Melancholy succeeded. Dismal I sat. I looked around, but fair Hope would not approach me. Spirited Resolution came and lent his friendly hand. Encouraged by him, I pushed my way; and here I am again in the sunshine. Reflect, O thou who wast once my affectionate guardian, whom I can never think of without the feelings of tender regard, reflect on all the circumstances of the unhappy coldness that has for some time been between us. We have already communed together freely; and, thanks to the propitious stars! we are no longer at variance. But upon serious reflection, I must be allowed to give my opinion that thou hast acquitted thyself fully at the tribunal of Justice; yet thou hast not given entire satisfaction in the more delicate court of Friendship.

My dear Lord! You bid me think of our dispute with attention. I have done so; and I have spoke freely. Your Lordship may be assured that we shall now be very good friends.

I am very sorry to hear of your being ill. Pray take care of yourself. I wish you were as good a patient as me. Whenever you come abroad, I hope for the honour of seeing you. I shall get well again soon, and then for days of felicity together. Yours,

BOSWELL.

I beg leave to remind your Lordship of a little sketch which I drew of you at Newmarket in the year 1760. I appealed to you as an honest man if it was like; you owned it was.

LORD EGLINTON
A Lord whose swift-discerning eye
The nicest strokes of wit can spy;
Whose sterling jests, a sportive train,
Flow warmly genuine from the brain,
And with bright poignancy appear
Original to ev'ry earl
BOSWELL *fecit.*

I am in spirits, you see. David Hume and John Dryden are at present my companions. Surely I am a man of genius. I deserve to be taken notice of. O that my grandchildren might read this character of me: "James Boswell, a most amiable man. He improved and beautified his paternal estate of Auchinleck; made a distinguished figure in Parliament; had the honour to command a regiment of footguards, and was one of the brightest wits in the court of George the Third."

I was certain this epistle would please him much. I was pleased with writing it. I felt myself quite serene and happy, my mind unclouded and serenely gay. I never remember to have passed more agreeable moments. All looked fine in my blest imagination.

TUESDAY 8 FEBRUARY. I should have mentioned yesterday that Mr. Lee of Drury Lane Theatre breakfasted with me. He recalled to my mind my first ideas of plays and players in the days of my youth at Edinburgh.

This forenoon Mr. Sheridan came and stayed an hour with me.

I told him openly and smartly who had wrote the critical strictures on Malloch's play. He said they were laughable, and sneered. I was in fine humour and in such a degree of spirits that I thought myself a match for any man. I therefore dexterously tickled the Professor of Oratory: "Do you know, Mr. Sheridan, that we intend regularly to have strictures on every new play, and as the boy always reminded Philip of Macedon that he was a man, so shall we remind the authors that they are dull." I then repeated to him many severe taunts on his wife's comedy, but with so smiling a countenance that he could not show any anger. I must remark that I have a most particular art of nettling people without seeming to intend it. I seldom make use of it, but have found it very useful.

Erskine came in, and he and Sheridan talked very well upon the poems of Ossian, whom Sheridan said he preferred to all the poets in the world, and thought he excelled Homer in the Sublime and Virgil in the Pathetic. He said Mrs. Sheridan and he had fixed it as the standard of feeling, made it like a thermometer by which they could judge of the warmth of everybody's heart; and that they calculated beforehand in what degrees all their acquaintances would feel them, which answered exactly. "To be sure," said he, "except people have genuine feelings of poetry, they cannot relish these poems. But if a man does not feel himself, he never imputes it to his own deficiency, but persuades himself that it is all a pretence in those who say they do. Thus a man who is short-sighted will maintain that there is no such object as other people declare that they see plainly; and he would continue obstinate in his denial did not the application of a glass to his eyes impress him with irresistible conviction. This allusion holds good in the case we are now upon. But we have not the same assistance to show people their mistakes. We have no glasses for the mind. I consider it too," said he, "as a great discovery in another respect. These poems give us great light into the history of mankind. We could not imagine that such sentiments of delicacy as well as generosity could have existed in the breasts of rude, uncultivated people."

Sheridan is really a fellow who knows a great deal; and his conversation is more instructive and classical than that of most people.
Yet he has an Irish wrongheadedness and a positive singularity that
is very disgusting; and, for all that he says, I am apt to imagine that
he has no real feeling of poetical beauty. I rather take him to be a
man of very great art who wants to disguise it under the appearance
of nature. He had asked me to dine with him two Sundays ago. He
asked me next. But I resolved to keep the house till out of danger.
His invitation showed that he still continued on good terms with
me. I shall be upon the same with him.

As I formerly mentioned my giving orders to say that I was
gone to the country, it may appear surprising that I should yet have
so many visitors. But that surprise will soon vanish when I tell that
these orders were countermanded. I found a little intercourse with
the living world was necessary to keep my spirits from sinking into
lethargic dulness or being soured to peevish discontent. My brother
dined with me today. We did very well as companions.

WEDNESDAY 9 FEBRUARY. I got up excellently well. My present life is most curious, and very fortunately is become agreeable.
My affairs are conducted with the greatest regularity and exactness. I move like very clock-work. At eight in the morning Molly
lights the fire, sweeps and dresses my dining-room. Then she calls
me up and lets me know what o'clock it is. I lie some time in bed
indulging indolence, which in that way, when the mind is easy
and cheerful, is most pleasing. I then slip on my clothes loosely,
easily, and quickly, and come into my dining-room. I pull my bell.
The maid lays a milk-white napkin upon the table and sets the
things for breakfast. I then take some light amusing book and
breakfast and read for an hour or more, gently pleasing both my
palate and my mental taste. Breakfast over, I feel myself gay and
lively. I go to the window, and am entertained with the people
passing by, all intent on different schemes. To go regularly through
the day would be too formal for this my journal. Besides, every day
cannot be passed exactly the same way in every particular. My day
is in general diversified with reading of different kinds, playing on

the violin, writing, chatting with my friends. Even the taking of medicines serves to make time go on with less heaviness. I have a sort of genius for physic and always had great entertainment in observing the changes of the human body and the effects produced by diet, labour, rest, and physical operations.

My landlord took a great anxiety that I should read the news, thought it would divert me much, and begged me to take in one of the papers. I expressed my fondness for his scheme, but said I did not choose to be at the expense of it. So I put it off. However, his anxiety was so great that he made a bold push at the Office, where a number of the papers are taken in, and regularly every day does he bring home *The Public Ledger*, which is most duly served up to me. I joked with him and said, "You see, Sir, when I put you to your shifts what you can do." "Indeed," said he, "I did not know before that I could do such a thing. But I find it is very easy."

As I am now in tolerable health, my appetite is very good, and I eat my slender bit of dinner with great relish. I drink a great deal of tea. Between eleven and twelve my bed is warmed and I go calmly to repose. I am not at all unsatisfied with this kind of existence. It is passing my portion of time very comfortably. Most philosophically do I reason upon this subject, being certainly the most important one to me at present. I consider that although I want many pleasures which are to be had by being abroad, yet I also want many pains. I am troubled with no dirty streets nor no jostling chairmen. Multitudes of ideas float through my fancy on both sides of the question. I shall now and then put some of them down as they strike me strongly.

I now made a very near calculation of my expenses for the year, and found that I would be able to save £50 out of my allowance. This sum would be requisite for immediate necessaries in case of my getting a commission in the Guards, and I would have a pride to furnish it without any extraordinary assistance from my father, which it is reasonable he should allow in that event, as everybody thinks he should rig me out. However, if I can do without him, I must be called an excellent manager. Not satisfied with saving £50,

I went to work still nearer, wishing to save £20 more, and with great thought and assiduity did I compute. In short, I found myself turning very fond of money and ruminating with a kind of transport on the idea of being worth £70 at the year's end. The desire of being esteemed a clever economist was no doubt mixed with it, but I seriously think that sheer love of coin was my predominant principle.

While I was strongly possessed with this inclination, my landlord came to wait on me, and renewed a proposal which he had formerly mentioned; and that was that if I would give up one of my rooms, there should be a reasonable abatement made of my rent. He said that a Mr. Smith, a gentleman of good fortune, with his lady and son, wanted to take three rooms. I told him that I should be glad to do what was convenient for him and at the same time of advantage to myself; and that I considered my having two rooms above was unnecessary, as I had the parlour below to entertain my company in. I therefore agreed to the proposal, and he engaged to have a handsome tent-bed with green and white check curtains put up in the room to the street. By this means I can save several pounds a year. The thing happened most opportunely while I was so much enamoured of the money-making scheme. It gratified my passion while it was strong, which is quite the nice requisite for pleasure. A drink when a man is dry is highly relished. And in other gratifications, the analogy holds good. I have observed in some preceding period of this my journal that making money is one of the greatest pleasures in life, as it is very lasting and is continually increasing. But it must be observed that a great share of anxiety is the constant concomitant of this passion, so that the mind is as much hurt in one way as it is pleased in another. I felt this now very plainly. For while I hugged myself with the prospect of my golden possessions, I was in pain lest I should not be able to fulfil my conjecture, and had disagreeable struggles between the love of many amusing schemes that gaily started up to my imagination and my principal scheme of saving.

It is a good deal diverting to consider my present views. A

young fellow of life and spirit, with an allowance extremely moderate, in so much that most people declare it must be wonderful management that can make it support a genteel appearance, yet is this fellow gravely laying down plans for making rich and being a man of wealth. The love of property is strongly implanted in mankind. Property, to be sure, gives us a power of enjoying many pleasures which it can purchase; and as society is constituted, a man has a high degree of respect from it. Let me, however, beware of allowing this passion to take a deep root. It may engross my affections and give me a meanness of spirit and a cold indifference to every manly and spirited pursuit. And when we consider what one gains, it is merely imaginary. To keep the golden mean between stinginess and prodigality is the point I should aim at. If a man is prodigal, he cannot be truly generous. His money is foolishly dissipated without any goodness on his part, and he has nothing to be generous with. On the other hand, a narrow man has a hard, contracted soul. The finer feelings are bound up, and although he has the power, he never can have the will to be generous. The character worthy of imitation is the man of economy, who with prudent attention knows when to save and when to spend, and acts accordingly. Let me pursue this system. I have done so hitherto since my setting out upon my own footing. Let me continue it. Let me lay out my money with ease and freedom, though with judgment and caution; and if at the year's end I should have a genteel sum remaining as a reward of my economy, let me congratulate myself on my felicity.

Upon my word my journal goes charmingly on at present. I was very apprehensive that there would be a dreary vacancy in it for some weeks, but by various happy circumstances I have been agreeably disappointed. I think, too, that I am making a good use of the hint which Captain Erskine gave me, and am taking more pains upon it, and consequently writing it in a more correct style. Style is to sentiment what dress is to the person. The effects of both are very great, and both are acquired and improved by habit. When once we are used to it, it is as easy to dress neatly as like a sloven;

in the same way, custom makes us write in a correct style as easily as in a careless, inaccurate one.

Some time ago I left off the pamphlet shop in the passage to the Temple Exchange Coffee-house, and took *The North Briton* from the publisher of it, Mr. Kearsley in Ludgate Street, hard by Child's. I have it now sent to me regularly by the Penny Post, and read it with vast relish. There is a poignant acrimony in it that is very relishing. Noble also sends me from time to time a fresh supply of novels from his circulating library, so that I am very well provided with entertainment.

How easily and cleverly do I write just now! I am really pleased with myself; words come skipping to me like lambs upon Moffat Hill; and I turn my periods smoothly and imperceptibly like a skilful wheelwright turning tops in a turning-loom. There's fancy! There's simile! In short, I am at present a genius: in that does my opulence consist, and not in base metal.

My brother drank tea with me and took a cordial farewell, being to set out for Scotland next day. We parted on excellent terms. He is as fond of being at home as I am of ranging freely at a distance. My friend Erskine came and supped with me. I am excellently lodged. I get anything dressed vastly well. We had a very good evening of it.

THURSDAY 10 FEBRUARY. This forenoon a maid from Louisa left a packet for me. It was most carefully sealed up, "by the hands of attention," but was not addressed to me. I opened it up and found my two guineas returned, without a single word written. I felt a strange kind of mixed confusion. My tender heart relented. I thought I had acted too harshly to her. I imagined she might—per-haps—have been ignorant of her situation. I was so foolish as to think of returning her the money and writing her a letter of atone-ment. I have too much of what Shakespeare calls "the milk of human kindness." I mentioned the thing to Dempster. He said it was just a piece of deep artifice in her. I resolved to think no more on the matter, and was glad that I had come off two guineas better than I expected.

Before I left Scotland, I had a long conversation with Sir David Dalrymple on my future schemes of life.[3] Sir David is a man of great ingenuity, a fine scholar, an accurate critic, and a worthy member of society. From my early years I used to regard him with admiration and awe, and look upon him as a representative of Mr. Addison. Since I came to London I have found his name much respected in the literary world. He is also a great friend of my father's, is one of two witnesses to an important transaction between my father and me,[4] and is a sincere well-wisher to the family of Auchinleck. Upon all these considerations, I thought his advice and correspondence would be of service to me and also give me pleasure. I therefore wrote to him, telling him how my affairs went on, and that I wanted to be rationally happy, yet easy and gay, and hoped he would take a charge of me; would let me know what books to read, and what company to keep, and how to conduct myself. This was paying him a high compliment. I thought his precepts might do me much good, and that I might follow them just as far as I thought them right. The views of things, too, which he would send me would place them in new lights and give me the dear pleasure of variety. I proposed to him that I would write to him on a Saturday, once a fortnight, as I was a man much devoted to form. I offered to send him any pamphlets he might choose to have, and execute any other little commissions he might have in London. I don't know what success my proposal may meet with, but I think it is a good one.

FRIDAY 11 FEBRUARY. Nothing worth putting into my journal occurred this day. It passed away imperceptibly, like the whole life of many a human existence.

SATURDAY 12 FEBRUARY. When I began first to keep the house with this distemper which now confines me, it was a most severe frost. Luckily, this did not last long after I was laid up, for cold is very bad for venereal complaints. The weather, I always

---

[3] See above, p. 28.
[4] That is, to the "infamous deed," 7 March 1762, by which Boswell gave his father power to put him under trustees. See above, p. 9.

find, has a sensible effect upon me. It has been mild and gentle for some time. This day it turned worse, and I got a little splenetic. However, I submitted quietly, and in the afternoon the foul fiend left me.

SUNDAY 13 FEBRUARY. This was a most terrible day. None of my friends could come abroad to see me. I was really a good deal low-spirited all the forenoon. In the evening my mind cleared up. I was pleased and lively, and my genius was in fine humour for composition. I wrote several fanciful little essays, which pleased me highly.[5] Well, the human mind is really curious: I can answer for my own. For here now in the space of a few hours I was a dull and a miserable, a clever and a happy mortal, and all without the intervention of any external cause, except a dish of green tea, which indeed is a most kind remedy in cases of this kind. Often have I found relief from it. I am so fond of tea that I could write a whole dissertation on its virtues. It comforts and enlivens without the risks attendant on spirituous liquors. Gentle herb! Let the florid grape yield to thee. Thy soft influence is a more safe inspirer of social joy.

MONDAY 14 FEBRUARY. Erskine drank tea with me. We were in a luscious flow of spirits and vastly merry. "How we do chase a thought," said Erskine, "when once it is started. Let it run as it pleases over hill and dale and take numberless windings, still we are at it. It has a greyhound at its heels every turn." The distemper was now almost over. I was free from pain, and had pleasurable ease. This night my new tent-bed was put up. I liked it much. It gave a snug yet genteel look to my room, and had a military air which amused my fancy and made me happy.

TUESDAY 15 FEBRUARY. I had the pleasure to receive a very cordial answer from Sir David Dalrymple, in which he approved much of my proposal of writing to him regularly, and insisted that

---

[5] Several years ago Dr. Joseph L. Walsh found one of these among the Wilkes papers in the British Museum. Boswell had sent it for publication in *The North Briton*, where, however, it never appeared. It is a rather feeble comparison of the contemporary manoeuvres in British politics to a vulgar Scots game called hop-romp.

it should be every Saturday. This gave me much satisfaction and a good opinion of myself, to find that a man of so much true worth and even piety had my interest at heart and was willing to keep a correspondence with me.⁶ Erskine drank tea with me. I don't know what was the matter, but we did not talk nor laugh with great glee. We were coldish and somewhat tired. We have not the command of our faculties.

WEDNESDAY 16 FEBRUARY. Dempster and Erskine had the night before put a trick upon me. A lad whose name is Fletcher (a cousin of Dempster's), at whom I had a very great antipathy, was the instrument which they employed. They forged a letter from

⁶ "I like your fancy of returns, but I would wish to have them oftener than once a fortnight. Bailie Lawson said (when he lived or where is not material to the story), 'I wonder how any one can be so wicked as to sleep in church on Sunday when he has not balanced his books on Saturday night.' Being partly of Bailie Lawson's opinion, I desire that your return may be once a week.—I thank you for your theatrical intelligence. *Elvira* is dull, to be sure, but I wish my name had not been mentioned in the Preface to the *Strictures*, for I do sincerely blame myself for mixing my publication with a private pique principally occasioned by Mr. Mallet's treatment of his friend Thomson in the Preface to his *Alfred*.—When Members of Parliament write pamphlets, I think they might frank them or cause them to be franked, otherwise a friend pays a shilling for what an enemy might have at sixpence. I cannot help thinking that Mr. Mallet's conduct in his play is like that of Lucky Spence (the Mother Douglas of other times), who, when she left one of her lasses with a he-creature, always said, 'Between you and your own consciences be it, for I wash my hands of it.' The poet brings his people into critical situations and then leaves them to their own consciences, for he does not aid nor abet them when they are once there." (Sir David Dalrymple to Boswell, undated. In the Advertisement to the *Strictures* the authors had said, "We have followed the authority of Sir David Dalrymple and Mr. Samuel Johnson in the orthography of Mr. Malloch's name, as we imagine the decision of these gentlemen will have more weight in the world of letters than even that of the said Mr. Malloch himself." Johnson, in the abridgment of his dictionary, 1756, had defined *Alias* as "A Latin word signifying otherwise; as Mallet, *alias* Malloch; that is, otherwise Malloch." Dalrymple's slur has not been located.)

David Hume to me containing some genteel compliments and recommending Fletcher to me, who was come up to go out to the East Indies. He accordingly delivered it, and I, suspecting no deceit, was vastly pleased. They expected that I would be much distressed at having a being so disagreeable recommended to me, but so great was my vanity that it put me into exceeding good humour even with a being very odious. They came this forenoon and told me the artifice, at which I was really vexed. I could not dissemble my resentment of it. I told them it was what I would not have done to them, and that I did not think it genteel in them to give such a miscreant as Fletcher an opportunity of laughing at me as much as themselves. I told Erskine that I would henceforth consider him and Dempster not in the light of friends, and in short was quite chagrined. It was surprising how such a thing should have given me so much pain; yet to have my vanity so sadly balked and to be made the sport of them and their emissary was very galling.

And here I must observe that my connections with Erskine and Dempster are really not those of friendship. We are in the style of companions. It is only fancy that cements us. It is only because we are entertaining to one another that we are so much together. Dempster I do not know thoroughly. Erskine has too much selfishness and too bad a temper to be what I call a friend. Thank heaven! I have some true friends. Johnston is most strictly so. Temple is also one. Honest McQuhae is also one. To these I can unbosom my anxious mind; from these I am sure of sympathy and kindness. Besides, these all agree with me in many things which are of consequence. They all, with me, look forward to another world, which Dempster and Erskine never think of. They have all strong ideas of real life and manners, which Erskine and Dempster see in fanciful and ludicrous lights and are not in earnest about. Such distinctions are very nice and are better felt than explained. I dare say if I was to talk in this way to the gentlemen I have mentioned, they would laugh most heartily; and, what is more, their ridicule would not only silence but in some measure convince me. That is really a weakness about me, that I am easily overcome in any dispute, and even (as Dr. Brown has it) vanquished by a grin.[7] I ought therefore seldom to engage in argument, especially upon matters so very nice and delicate. I am also much made by the company which I keep. I should be very cautious in my choice. I almost determined to break with Dempster and Erskine. Yet I had a disagreeable struggle of mind about it.

THURSDAY 17 FEBRUARY. My resentment abated and I resolved to laugh the thing off, but at the same time to be more reserved with Dempster and Erskine in time coming. Dempster came and sat a while in the evening. I told him all was now over. I certainly won by this. For to have broke with them just now would have given them opportunity to make me ridiculous; and if I find it convenient, it is very easy to get out of acquaintance (or rather familiarity) with them. For they are very agreeable acquaintances. But when a man is familiar with many people he must expect many disagreeable familiarities. Another shocking fault which I have is my sacrificing almost anything to a laugh, even myself; in so much that it is possible if one of these my companions should come in this moment, I might show them as matter of jocularity the preceding three or four pages, which contain the most sincere sentiments of my heart; and at these would we laugh most immoderately. This is indeed a fault in the highest degree to be lamented and to be guarded against. I am firmly resolved to amend it. I shall be most particularly wary. I shall rather err on the other, which is the safer, side.

FRIDAY 18 FEBRUARY. By having come down to my parlour the day before, I had got some cold and felt myself rather worse. I was very low-spirited and had the most dreary and discontented imaginations. All things looked black. I thought I should never be well again. I could encourage no prospect in life. After dinner I grew better and was seized with a whim of making my quarrel

[7] "And coxcombs vanquish Berkeley with a grin."—Dr. John Brown, *Essay on Satire*, l. 212.

with my companions a good reason for obtaining the correspondence of David Hume. I wrote therefore the following letter to him:

DEAR SIR:—Dempster and Erskine (both of whom you probably have some acquaintance of) have served me a trick which they consider as a very high joke, but which I (like the frogs in the fable) consider in a very different light. They caused the enclosed letter to be delivered to me as if from you; and you will believe that it wound up my vanity to a pitch more than ordinary. After amusing themselves a little with my elevation of spirits occasioned by a fond but very excusable credulity, they informed me of the deceit, which brought me as low as before I had been high, and afforded them still greater subject for mirth. I will own to you, Sir, that all the little philosophy which I possess was not sufficient to preserve my temper unruffled. I was really chagrined: I indulged the morose and resentful feelings, and I almost resolved to break off all intercourse with men who had used me so ill. However, *the milk of human kindness*, as Shakespeare tenderly expresses it, was not long destroyed by this acrimony. My natural sweetness of disposition returned and I freely forgave them. Although I still feel some degree of uneasiness from the severe ridicule which I underwent, yet that is greatly overbalanced by a conscious pride of having had goodness enough to excuse it. Permit me now, Sir, to solicit the honour of your correspondence. You will administer consolation to me in my uneasiness, and will bestow a reward on my welldoing. You will give me a triumph over my facetious tormentors when they find that I really possess what I was so vain of in imagination; and in short you will give much happiness to your, &c.,

JAMES BOSWELL.

P.S. This is a mere memorial.[8] It might very well be given in as a representation to the Lords of Session. If you will agree to cor-

[8] A written statement of facts concluding with questions asking for an advocate's opinion in the form of answers—a very common term in Scots law. Hume, though not a lawyer, had studied law and had been Librarian of the Advocates' Library.

respond with me, you shall have London news, lively fancies, humorous sallies, provided that you give me elegant sentiments, just criticism, and ingenious observations on human nature. I should gladly endeavour to return you now and then something in your own style, which I am ambïtious enough not to despair of doing.

This letter amused me in writing. Perhaps I may reap advantage by it. The correspondence of distinguished men is very much to be valued. It gives a man a dignity that is very desirable.

At night I fell back into my melancholy mood. I was quite harassed with anxious discontent. I thought I would return to Scotland and drudge as a lawyer, which would please my father and gain me a character of prudence and also get me money and enable me to do good; and as I would not flatter myself with the expectation of much felicity, I would not be disappointed. But then I considered this scheme as the unripe fruit of vexatious thought and as what I would soon repent of. Then it pained me to the heart to think that all the gay schemes which I had planned were to prove abortive, and that all my intentions of seeing the world should be frustrated. Never was any man more upon the fret than I now was. I never thought (or rather would not allow myself to believe) that all these clouds were produced by my sickly confinement. At last I thought I would weather out a year in this way and then return to Scotland. Alas, alas, poor Boswell! to what an abject situation art thou now reduced! Thou who lately prided thyself in luxuriance of health and liveliness of imagination art now a diseased, dull, capricious mortal. Is not this a just punishment for thy offences? It is indeed; I submit to it. Sometimes I thought I would go down to Oxford and pass some weeks privately in that august seat of learning. But then it would cost me money; and besides I am not fit for travelling. Alas! this sad distemper again comes across me. However, this is Sir James Macdonald's last winter at Oxford, and he asked me to come down and said he would show me everything. I should not lose the opportunity. Perhaps, when I get well again and the fine weather comes in, I may make a trip to it. What is a sure sign of my not being right just now is my having dismal dreams almost every night. I hope to be better ere long.

SATURDAY 19 FEBRUARY. This morning my guardian angel smiled upon me and whispered soft notes into my glad ears. I loved the Guards and I longed for my commission. The Marquis of Granby had now been come home some time. I regretted my losing this fresh occasion of reminding Lady Northumberland of her promise. I considered that time was now precious, and as I thought an apology necessary for my long absence, I wrote her this letter:

MADAM:—I have been indisposed and confined to the house for some weeks, which has prevented me from having the honour and pleasure of paying my duty to your Ladyship. I am now better and hope to be abroad soon. In the mean time, Madam, as my Lord Granby is now come over, permit me to put your Ladyship in mind of my commission. I have the honour to be, Madam, your obliged and faithful humble servant,

JAMES BOSWELL.

Webster was with me a while. Though he got a company the other day, he was discontented, and repined and talked forsooth of retiring from the world. I told him he was much in the wrong. "Retire! Why, am not I in retirement? And a pretty spectacle I am." He was pretty lively and agreed with me that everybody had their portion of infelicity. "Now," said he, "Calcraft the great agent who makes such an opulent fortune every year might be allowed pretty happy; and yet he is at this moment perfectly miserable. Mr. Fox, his great patron, has sent to see him immediately on express business, and he in this great hurry has lost one of his knee-buckles, which cannot be found." This was very well hit off.

Crookshanks, who is Lord Eglinton's steward in England, comes now and then to see me. He came this forenoon and entered just on the same subject of the unhappiness of mortals. He is a spirited fellow, has read a good deal, and is much of a gentleman, but has at the same time much of what is called a *rattle*. He went on thus. "Damn me if I can see why God Almighty has created us all, just to complain and vex ourselves. By the Lord, I don't see who's happy, not I. And yet one may be happy with anything. I have been happy with buying a new gun, and have been in high spirits for a week with a new dog. By the Lord, Mr. Boswell, you have fine means of happiness by your turn for writing. I would rather have written the preface to that *Cub* than had a good sum." In this manner did he run on, much to my amusement. He does not want fancy and has a generous heart.

I must observe that we are not affected by the complaints of a genteel agreeable man against life. The agreeable ideas which he inspires serve as an antidote to gloom, and we cannot believe his murmurings to be serious. Everybody must feel this from experience. When we see a fine lady before us and hear her venting discontented exclamations, we are apt to imagine them words of course; or if we think her really distressed, we solace ourselves by thinking that distress is not so terrible and may be endured with a good deal of complacency, considering that a person may present us with so pleasing an appearance, who is distressed. This is a nice observation, but I am persuaded that it must be allowed a just one by those who have delicacy of sentiment.

In the evening Dempster and Erskine were with me. My rancour was quite gone. We were very happy together. Yet I determined in my own mind to behave to them henceforth with more reserve.

SUNDAY 20 FEBRUARY. I passed the day very comfortably. Captain Erskine was with me in the forenoon and we were very well together. Honest Captain Andrew! I must keep well with him. This forenoon I read the history of Joseph and his brethren, which melted my heart and drew tears from my eyes. It is simply and beautifully told in the Sacred Writings. It is a strange thing that the Bible is so little read. I am reading it regularly through at present. I dare say there are many people of distinction in London who know nothing about it. Were the history of Joseph published by some genteel bookseller as an Eastern fragment and circulated amongst the gay world, I am persuaded that those who have any genuine taste might be taken in to admire it exceedingly and so by degrees have a due value for the oracles of GOD. I have a great mind to make the experiment. Were I a man more known and of more consequence, it might do very well. Sir Richard Steele published his *Christian Hero* when he was an officer of the Guards, in the Coldstream Regiment. I had this day the honour of a message from the Countess of Northumberland inquiring how I was. She is indeed an excellent woman. I cannot enough regard her.

I have heard nothing from Lord Eglinton this long time, a strong proof how little he is to be depended upon. After the interesting scene which we had together, it might have been expected that he would have been somewhat more attentive to me than ordinary. But that confounded dissipation of his ruins all his other good qualities, so that although we may love him for a little now and then, yet he can never be valued.

I set apart this day for taking medicine most effectually and keeping very warm, so was denied to everybody but those who were upon the footing of making good their way upstairs, notwithstanding of all my injunctions. I was quite in earnest to get quite free of this most terrible malady, which in my opinion is really a serious evil. I am sure it is so to me. But what I am most anxious about is to get it entirely eradicated, that I may recover perfect soundness of constitution and may not bring a race of poor sickly human beings into the world.

I employed the day in reading Hume's *History*, which enlarged my views, filled me with great ideas, and rendered me happy. It is surprising how I have formerly neglected the study of history, which of all studies is surely the most amusing and the most instructive. As I am now begun to it in earnest, I hope to make good progess. I write my father regularly my observations on each volume, which is of great service to me and gives much satisfaction to him.

MONDAY 21 FEBRUARY. There has more than once been calling for me a tall gentleman in black, when I was denied; he never would leave his name. I this morning received the following letter from him:

ARRAH now by my shoul, my dear Shoy,[9] you are much in the wrong in the midst of your melancholy to shut the door against your acquaintances and deprive yourself of the comforts of friendly confabulation. Who in the performance of a manly part would not wish to get *claps?* The brave only are wounded in front, and heroes are not ashamed of such scars. Yours are the offspring of fun and merriment, and would you make them the parents of dolour and care? I intend to laugh and breakfast with you tomorrow. Pray give the necessary orders for my admission; otherwise, *pox* take you. Yours.

I sent him for answer that he would be very welcome. I could not conceive who it was. I formed multitudes of conjectures. Erskine drank tea with me, and we chatted very comfortably.

TUESDAY 22 FEBRUARY. Who did this strange tall gentleman in black turn out to be but Mr. William Cochrane, Judge Advocate for Scotland.[1] Upon my word, I did not think he had humour enough to write such a letter, and I told him so. He told me he was come up to study English law and be called to the bar here. I was put into good humour with him. His company was a fine variety to me. He put me in mind of Bruntsfield Links and Mondays after the spring sacrament at Edinburgh, when the Meadow swarms with preachers and others taking their walks.[2]

WEDNESDAY 23 FEBRUARY. This week I feel myself greatly better. I come always down to my parlour, which is more cheerful for me; and I have my hair dressed every day, which gives me an idea of being well. I have an excellent hairdresser. His name is Chetwynd. He lives just opposite to me. He is a genteel chatty

[9] See above, p. 137 *n.* 8.   [1] Second cousin to Boswell's mother.
[2] Because he was dressed in black? Bruntsfield Links (a very ancient playing-ground for golf) and the adjoining Meadows are promenades on the South Side of Edinburgh.

fellow, like the generality of his profession, who, by being so much among gentlemen, acquire something of their manners.

THURSDAY 24 FEBRUARY. Dr. McQuhae[3] had sent me a letter enclosed in mine to Mr. Alexander Macdonald, surgeon to the *Lord Mansfield* Indiaman.[4] This young fellow has been long intimate with McQuhae, who has often given him an excellent character; and as he is besides a Highlandman from the Isle of Skye, I thought I would like to see him. I accordingly sent to him and begged he might come here. He came this morning to breakfast.[5] He was going out to India on his first voyage. In a few minutes he and I were as easy and chatty as could be. The Highlanders have all a vivacity and a frankness that is very agreeable. I was in fine spirits, and I thought of many agreeable ideas. I found him warmly attached to the family of Stuart; and he said the Scotch Jacobites had yet great hopes of a restoration, in which they were confirmed by a dream which he had. He told me it and he promised to write it out for me. It was really very fanciful and strongly allegorical. He repeated it to me with the greatest enthusiasm. It was very entertaining to see the superstitious warmth of an old Highland seer mixed with the spirited liveliness of a neat clever young fellow. He had a picture of Mary Queen of Scots set in a ring, which he wore with much affection. I really took a liking to the lad. He passed the forenoon with me, and he promised to call again before he sailed. It gave me pleasure to see him animated with the prospect of making a fortune and then returning to Scotland.

This afternoon I was very high-spirited and full of ambition.

[3] See above, p. 3. Boswell's "Dr." is jocular, McQuhae at this time not even having been ordained.

[4] That is, the East India Company's vessel, *The Lord Mansfield.*

[5] "Be fine with Macdonald. Think on McQuhae, Countess of Eglinton. Breakfast sunshine, marmalade. Highland hills—tartan plaids—Jacobites—Cairnie—Miss Macleod—Sandy's making fortune and coming home. Go on with Hume and *Letters,* &c." (Memorandum for this day. "Miss Macleod" is unexplained. Boswell will presently provide the explanation of *"Letters"* himself.)

I wanted much to be a man of consequence, and I considered that I could only be that in my own country, where my family and connections would procure it. I also considered that the law was my plain road to preferment. That if I would go to the Scotch bar I would soon be well employed, and as this confinement has made me see that I can sit in and labour very well, I thought I might be able very well to do business. By this means I would make money which would enable me to jaunt about wherever I pleased in the vacations. I would have an opportunity of being of much real use, of being of service to my friends by having weight in the country, and would make my father exceedingly happy. I considered that the law seemed to be pointed out by fate for me. That the family of Auchinleck had been raised by it. That I would soon be made Advocate Depute on the circuits and in all probability be made a Baron of Exchequer, and by this means have respect and yet an easy life—*otium cum dignitate.*[6] I considered that my notions of an advocate were false. That I connected with that character low breeding and Presbyterian stiffness, whereas many of them were very genteel people. That I might have the wit and humour of Sir David Dalrymple, the jollity of Duncan Forbes, the whim of Baron Dalrymple, the show of Baron Maule, and the elegant taste of Baron Grant. I thought I might write books like Lord Kames and be a buck like Mr. James Erskine. That I might keep a handsome machine. Have a good agreeable wife and fine children and keep an excellent house. That I might show all the dull, vulgar, plodding young lawyers how easily superior parts can outstrip them. That I might keep them at a distance, have my own few select friends, and that Johnston and I might enjoy life comfortably

[6] An advocate depute is a deputy of the Lord Advocate, the principal law-officer of the Crown in Scotland. The American equivalent would perhaps be assistant prosecuting attorney. Boswell is probably remembering his trip on the North Circuit in the autumn of 1758 when Sir David Dalrymple went as Advocate Depute. The Court of Exchequer had supreme jurisdiction in revenue cases. Boswell presumably prefers it to the Court of Session because some of the barons were English, and because the Court usually followed the forms of the law of England.

together. I thought I might go to the Church-of-England Chapel, like Pitfour;[7] and, in short, might live in the most agreeable manner.

I viewed this plan in every favourable light and became exceedingly fond of it. As I am most impetuous in whatever I take a fancy for, I was beginning to determine that I would write to my father and propose the thing to him, on condition that he made me a handsome settlement; that is to say, continued my £200 a year and agreed that I should have lodgings of my own and be quite an independent man. But then such a step taken precipitantly would not be the thing. I therefore thought I had better get his permission to go abroad for a year or two to Holland, where we have some Dutch relations, to France and to Italy; after which I would be better satisfied and more settled. So great was my impatience to be a man of consequence that I thought this would keep me too long from the Session House. So very violent an inclination could not last, as will appear hereafter.

FRIDAY 25 FEBRUARY. I continued in exceeding high spirits. Variety of fine cheering ideas glanced athwart my blest imagination, ideas which gave me exquisite sensations at the time but which are so very nice that they elude endeavours to paint them. A man of similar feelings with me may conceive them. The law scheme appeared in another light. I considered it as bringing me back to a situation that I had long a rooted aversion to. That my father might agree to let me be upon the footing of independence, but when he had me under his eye, he would not be able to keep to it. I considered that I would at once embark myself for all my life in a labyrinth of care, and that my mind would be harassed with vexation. That the notion of being of consequence was not much, for that just now I knew from experience that just by strength of imagination I could strut about and think myself as great as any man. That the Guards was a situation of life that had

[7] James Fergusson of Pitfour, Episcopalian and reputed Jacobite, one of the great lawyers at the Scots bar. He was long passed over because of his politics, but was finally raised to the bench in 1764.

always appeared most enchanting to me, as I could in that way enjoy all the elegant pleasures of the gay world, and by living in the Metropolis and having plenty of time, could pursue what studies and follow what whims I pleased, get a variety of acquaintances of all kinds, get a number of romantic adventures, and thus have my satisfaction of life. That if a man who is born to a fortune cannot make himself easier and freer than those who are not, he gains nothing. That if I should suddenly relinquish my favourite schemes, I should deservedly be considered as a man of no stability but inconstant and wavering with every breath. I considered that at present I was not a fair judge of a question of so much importance; that by a long course of confinement and medicine my animal spirits were necessarily tamed and my relish for pleasure and amusement and whim evaporated. That the mere satisfaction of ease after a situation of pain and the happy prospect of a recovery of health had elevated me too much and made me imagine nothing too difficult for me to compass. That indeed I had laboured hard, but it had been in writing my journal, letters, and essays, which were all works chiefly of the imagination. But that I would find it very irksome to sit for hours hearing a heavy agent explain a heavy cause, and then to be obliged to remember and repeat distinctly the dull story, probably of some very trivial affair. I considered that when I should again go about and mix in the hurry and bustle of life and have my spirits agitated with a variety of brilliant scenes, this dull legal scheme would appear in its usual colours.

Such were my reasonings upon both sides of this question, which are, in my own opinion, very ingenious. It is strange to consider that the same man who could waver so much could produce them. I was somewhat uneasy at the consideration of my indetermined state of mind, which argues a degree of imbecility. I wished much for some of my sincerely affectionate friends to whom I might unbosom myself, and whose kind counsel might relieve and direct me. I had much ado to keep myself from mentioning the thing to people who must laugh at me and had not my interest deeply at heart. However, I resolved to keep my own counsel, and I was sure it was a thing that nobody would suspect. I was anxious a little about my commission, and thought I should be disappointed in it and become peevish and turn a sort of misanthrope. But I summoned up more cheerful ideas and imagined that my noble Countess was pushing for me. At any rate, I determined to give it a year's run; and after that time I would be fully able to judge what to think of great people and what plan of life I should pursue.

SATURDAY 26 FEBRUARY. Last night Dempster came to me between ten and eleven and sat till one. He is really a most agreeable man: has fine sense, sweet dispositions, and the true manners of a gentleman. His sceptical notions give him a freedom and ease which in a companion is very pleasing, although to a man whose mind is possessed with serious thoughts of futurity, it is rather hurting to find them considered so lightly. He said he intended to write a treatise on the causes of happiness and misery. He considered the mind of man like a room, which is either made agreeable or the reverse by the pictures with which it is adorned. External circumstances are nothing to the purpose. Our great point is to have pleasing pictures in the inside. To illustrate this: we behold a man of quality in all the affluence of life. We are apt to imagine this man happy. We are apt to imagine that his gallery is hung with the most delightful paintings. But could we look into it, we should in all probability behold portraits of care, discontent, envy, languor, and distraction. When we see a beggar, how miserable do we think him! But let us examine his pictures. We will probably find merriment, hope, a keen stomach, a hearty meal, true friendship, the newspaper, and a pot of porter. The great art is to have an agreeable collection and to preserve them well.

This is really an ingenious and lively fancy. We gave some examples. Lord Elibank has just a cabinet of curiosities, which are well ranged and of which he has an exact catalogue. Macpherson has some bold portraits and wild landscapes. Lord Eglinton has had a variety of pieces, but they have been mostly slightly painted and are fading, so that his most frequent picture is Regret. The

mind of a young man (his gallery I mean) is often furnished different ways. According to the scenes he is placed in, so are his
pictures. They disappear, and he gets a new set in a moment. But
as he grows up, he gets some substantial pieces which he always
preserves, although he may alter his smaller paintings in a moment. I said that he whose pictures shifted too often, like the
glaiks,[8] was too light-headed, and so in Scotland he is called
glaiked, an expression perfectly of a piece with this system.

I passed this day in writing a great many letters, particularly
a long one to McQuhae, whom I regard much. He has excellent
parts, and has had a most accurate education. He has a good heart,
fine dispositions, and an agreeable vivacity of manners. He had
a high relish for the scenes of active life and a great natural share
of spirited ambition. But considering the uncertainties and the
hazards of a soldier of fortune, he coolly checked his aspiring ideas,
determined to embrace a sure competency and live contented as
a country clergyman. He has formed a scheme of passing his time
pretty much to his mind with the duties of his station, the pursuit
of elegant literature, and the enlivening pleasures of society,
which, though not in profusion, are yet to be enjoyed in the country. I regret my want of power to serve such men as him according to his merit; however, I hope to make him tolerably happy.

Erskine came and sat some hours at night. We diverted ourselves with making ludicrous parodies on *The Cure of Saul*, a sacred ode by Dr. Brown.

SUNDAY 27 FEBRUARY. I had now kept the house five complete weeks, except that night when I was carried to *The Discovery*.
My disorder was now over. Nothing but a gleet remained, which
gave me no pain and which could be removed in three days. But
I chose to give it a little longer time, that I might get clear of
every the least tincture of infection. I thought, since I had been
so much in earnest hitherto to have a complete cure, I would undoubtedly complete it. Douglas gave it as his opinion that I should
confine myself no longer. There was now no danger; and he

[8] Gleams or reflections of light; a trick or illusion of the eyes.

thought a little air, exercise, and amusement would be of great use both to my health and spirits. This day the sun shone prettily, yet I doubted as to going abroad. However, a battalion of the Guards from Germany were this day to march into town; and when I heard the beat of their drums, I could not restrain my ardour, and thought this the happiest occasion for me to emerge from obscurity and confinement, to light and to life.

George Home was with me. I wrapped myself up in my great-coat, and taking my staff in my hand, he accompanied me while I walked out to the Park. The Battalion was not drawn up on the Parade, as I expected, but was marched up to Lincoln's Inn Fields, so I lost that show. However, I was much obliged to my soldiers for bringing me fairly out. I might really have got a habit of laziness and become mopish altogether. The sweet elevation of spirits which I now felt is scarcely to be conceived. I was quite in an ecstasy. O how I admired all the objects around me! How I valued ease and health! To see the variety of people in the Park again put me all in a flutter. The sight of the Parade and the splendid Guards brought back my love to that profession with re-doubled force. I was convinced that it was indeed the genuine object of my inclinations, and the only station in real life which (at least for some years) I could fill with pleasure.

And now I swear that this is the true language of my heart. O why can I not always preserve my inclinations as constant and as warm? I am determined to pursue it with unremitting steadi-ness. I don't despair of having a regiment. O why don't my friends encourage me in it? Surely I ought not to languish in idleness. And surely so delicate a mind as I have cannot be greatly blamed for wavering a little when such terrible obstacles oppose my fa-vourite scheme. I now see the sickly suggestions of inconsistent fancy with regard to the Scotch bar in their proper colours. Good heaven! I should by pursuing that plan have deprived myself of felicity when I had it fairly in my power, and brought myself to a worse state than ever. I shudder when I think of it. I am vexed at such a distempered suggestion's being inserted in my journal, which I wished to contain a consistent picture of a young fellow eagerly pushing through life. But it serves to humble me, and it presents a strange and curious view of the unaccountable nature of the human mind. I am now well and gay. Let me consider that the hero of a romance or novel must not go uniformly along in bliss, but the story must be chequered with bad fortune. Aeneas met with many disasters in his voyage to Italy, and must not Boswell have his rubs? Yes, I take them in good part. I am now again set a-going; let me be content and cheerful and pursue the chase of happiness.

Mr. William Cochrane was with me today. I tired of him. He was affected, vulgar, and snappish. Love drank tea with me. He brought to my mind many old agreeable ideas. Dempster sat an hour tonight and was very agreeable.

MONDAY 28 FEBRUARY. I walked about half an hour in the Park very sweetly. The languor attendant on a man enfeebled with sickness has something in't not disagreeable to me. Then the taking care of one's self is amusing. At night I received the following letter from David Hume, Esq.

YOU MUST KNOW, Mr. James Boswell, or James Boswell, Esq., that I am very much out of humour with you and your two companions or co-partners. How the devil came it into your heads, or rather your noddles (for if there had been a head among you, the thing had not happened; nor are you to imagine that a parcel of volatile spirits enclosed in a skull, make a head)—I repeat it, how the devil came it into your noddles to publish in a book to all the world what you pretend I told you in private conversation? I say *pretend I told you*; for as I have utterly forgot the whole matter, I am resolved utterly to deny it. Are you not sensible that by this *étourderie*, to give it the lightest name, you were capable of making a quarrel between me and that irascible little man with whom I live in very good terms? Do you not feel from your own experience that among us gentlemen of the quill there is nothing of which we are so jealous (not even our wives, if we have any) as the honour of our productions? And that the least touch of blame on that head puts us into the most violent fury and combustion? I reply nothing to your letter till you give me some satisfaction for this offence, but only assure you that I am not, Sir, your most obedient and most humble servant,

DAVID HUME.

Edinburgh, 24 February 1763.

This letter was occasioned by a paragraph in our strictures on Mr. Malloch's *Elvira* which ran thus: "We heard it once asserted by David Hume, Esq., that Mr. Malloch was destitute of the Pathetic." This was actually true. He said so to Captain Erskine and me just before I left Scotland. The conversation is to be found at large in the Journal of my Harvest Jaunt, 1762.[9] Indeed, to repeat a private conversation and that in so very public a manner was rather using Mr. Hume ungenteelly. But we were all alive for sharp criticism, and thought this so fine a hit that it is no wonder we did not advert to the impropriety we were guilty of. Mr. Hume seems by his letter to have been seriously offended, although he has been so good-natured as to lighten his reproof by blending it with an agreeable pleasantry. I agreed to write him an answer.

Erskine told me that he was in Becket's shop[1] this forenoon, where was Mr. Murphy, the dramatic writer, who told an anecdote of the Reverend Dr. Brown, author of *An Estimate of the Manners and Principles of the Times*. Sir Hanbury Williams lived some weeks at a house in the country where Brown had lodged, and where he discovered there was a pretty girl whom the Doctor was fond of and had even attempted to offend with. "Well," said Erskine, "I think since he railed against the effeminacy of the age, he was right to show that he himself had some vigour left."

TUESDAY 1 MARCH. I was made acquainted with the quarrels and commotions of my landlord's family. He is a fellow of a high Scotch spirit, very passionate and very easily persuaded. His sister

[9] In the entry for 4 November.
[1] Thomas Becket was a bookseller and publisher.

who stayed in the house with us and other two who are in London are wicked malicious beings, and have always endeavoured to make a difference between him and his wife, who is a mild, agreeable creature as can be, but whom they hate. Poor Molly the maid, having been born at Norwich (which is the town her mistress came from), was for that reason an object of their hatred; and they have provoked Mr. Terrie against her so much that she is to leave us next month. This led me to the knowledge of all the broils. For poor Mrs. Terrie with the tear in her eye related to me all the mischiefs occasioned by the malevolence of the sisters, by whose instigation Mr. Terrie formerly behaved so harshly to her that she parted from him and went and lived as a kind of better servant with a lady in Ireland for near a twelvemonth. But told me how her husband was just as glad to get her back again. She has now turned the other sister out of the house, which I rejoice at. She proved to be an abominable, cunning, revengeful little wretch. There is really in Scotland a species of low insidious wicked women worse than any creatures in the world. Terrie is a sad harsh dog, but not a bad fellow in the main. However, I shall always have a worse opinion of him, and have less acquaintance with him, though I shall make him very serviceable to me, as usual.

At night I wrote to David Hume as follows:

My Dear Sir,—The heavy charge which you have given us demands a reply of proportionate weight of mettle. We are equally surprised and afflicted at your imagining that we meant you when we mentioned David Hume, Esq. To be sure, Sir, you are *the* David Hume, Esq., but you are not the sole one. He whose authority we have made bold to quote is a bookseller at Glasgow, who from his employment must be supposed to be well known in the world of letters. He is a man of very good understanding and more genius than most of his brethren, but his contempt for Mr. Malloch's abilities as a tragic poet almost exceed belief. He will not so much as allow his works to stand in his shop, and he constantly affirms that he is destitute of the Pathetic.

Now, Sir, we shall suppose that we really meant you; and in that case we are ready to make oath either before Sir John Fielding or Mr. Saunders Welch[2] that we heard you utter that very expression. As to the consequences of this affair: we are very sorry that you live in good terms with Mr. Malloch, and if we can make a quarrel between you, it will give us infinite pleasure. We shall glory in being the instruments of dissolving so heterogeneous an alliance; of separating the mild from the *irascible*, and the divine from the *bestial*.

We know very well how sore every author is when sharply touched in his works. We are pleased with giving acute pain to Mr. Malloch. We have vast satisfaction in making him smart by the rod of criticism, as much as many a tender bum[3] has smarted by his barbarous birch when he was janitor of the High School at Edinburgh.

As to the giving you satisfaction for the offence, you may receive full gratification by reading the Reviews on our performance. You will there find us held forth both as fools and as knaves; and if you will give us any other abusive appellations, we shall most submissively acquiesce. I hope this affair is now perfectly settled. I insist upon your writing to me in your usual humane style, and I assure you most sincerely that *I am*, my dear Sir, your most obedient humble servant,

Boswell & Co.

This letter I think a very good one; it is well expressed and has a proper mixture of compliment and spirit and jocularity. Erskine and Dempster were much pleased with it, and their praise now was more agreeable than their trick was disagreeable. I am now in very good terms with them, and I shall be on my guard and hope to meet with no more rubs.

WEDNESDAY 2 MARCH. I called at Northumberland House,

[2] Justices of the Peace for Westminster. Sir John was brother to the novelist. See below, the entry for 6 July.
[3] Buttocks.

but my Lady was not at home. I now wished much for my commission, and hoped to push it with success. While I have been confined, Colonel Gould's family has been some time out of town, and when they returned I had a message to come and dine. But I sent my excuse of indisposition. I was afraid that they might be taking my absence amiss. I shall soon wait on them and make all right again.

THURSDAY 3 MARCH. I called again at Northumberland House. But my Lady was again abroad. The porter promised to let her know that I had been there and would call again next day. He is a fine civil fellow.

FRIDAY 4 MARCH. I called at Northumberland House a little after ten. The porter said my Lady was not stirring, but would be up in half an hour. I said I would call again. I then went to my banker's and received a term's allowance. I had not such an exquisite relish for gold now as last time, after my extreme poverty. At eleven I called again at Northumberland House but was told my Lady was just gone out but would be glad to see me in the evening. This looked very ill. She could not possibly be gone out so soon after she rose. She has found that she could not *easily* do me any service with the Marquis of Granby, and so wants to shun a conversation with me; and has asked me to come in the evening, as she is then surrounded with company and I can have no opportunity to talk to her.

I was much vexed and fretted, and began to despair of my commission altogether and to ruminate whether it would not be better just to lay aside thoughts of it. However, I plucked up spirit and determined to give it the twelvemonth's run. I thought I behoved to go to my Lady's at night, but I thought I might make my apology and so just be six weeks absent from her house. I encourage whims of this kind too much and often deprive myself of pleasures for some conceit about times and numbers and seasons.

Donaldson the painter drank tea with me. He reminded me of former days at Edinburgh, when he drew Johnston's picture in the Lawnmarket, where my friend then lived and where I could wish he still had lived, rather than down in Don's Close; though indeed his having an agreeable buxom landlady and having a view of the Lomond Hills from his windows are very great inducements. Donaldson is a kind of a speculative being, and must forsooth controvert established systems. He defended adultery, and he opposed revealed religion. I could not help being much diverted with his abusing Edinburgh and saying it was a place where there was no company. However, he observed very justly that there is a degree of low cunning and malevolence amongst the vulgar, and a want of humour and spirit. As also, amongst the better sort a deal of ill-bred coarse raillery and freedom of abusive speech.

SATURDAY 5 MARCH. I breakfasted with Dr. Pringle. He was pleased with my paying him my first visit. He gave me wholesome reproof for having been ill, and gave me a merry pun which I never heard before: he that runs may read. He advised me to read all I could in English, and declared that the Latin was a very bad language from the confusion of cases and inversions. He said David Hume was a man of a fine imagination but did not write correct English.

I walked this day, as indeed I did yesterday, as far as Holborn. I formerly, as it were, only coasted it, in the Park. But now I launched into the wide ocean. I exulted in moving again freely about. I was rather too keen, and had too great a hurry of spirits.

SUNDAY 6 MARCH.[4] I heard prayers and sermon at Spring Garden Chapel; I felt a calm delight in again being at divine service. I then went and presented myself at Lady Betty's, where I was received with the greatest kindness. I was very lively, and chatted with my former ease and volatility; and they joked with

[4] "Breakfast on fine muffins and [enjoy] good taste of flour. Have hair dressed, and if the day is moderate, go to Whitehall Chapel and Lady B.'s. But if it be cold, stay in comfortable and write journal, short this week, and account of 4 volume of Hume. Have Erskine today and tell him the story and inspirit him. Pray remember—and mark it on separate paper—how happy you now are in the full enjoyment of liberty. Summer will come when all Scots will be gone. Then you'll grow more English and fine." (Memorandum for this day. The "story" he was to tell Erskine is explained later.)

great good humour on my keeping the house. Erskine and I then walked through the Park and over Westminster Bridge. It was a delightful day. He came in the evening and drank tea with me. The time passed swiftly away in a kind of indolent, amusive listlessness, yet with vivacity.

MONDAY 7 MARCH. I breakfasted at Lady Betty's, and then Erskine and I walked to Holborn and were very hearty. I passed the evening at home.

TUESDAY 8 MARCH. I breakfasted at Lady Betty's. Then Lady Anne, Erskine, and I drove out in the coach to Brompton, where we left Lady Anne. It was a charming day. We were very fine, and Lady Anne owned that London was infinitely preferable to Edinburgh. Erskine and I then returned in the coach through Hyde Park, and then dined at Lady Betty's very happily.

WEDNESDAY 9 MARCH. The exceeding great change of life which I have now experienced cannot fail to make me very giddy. A man who has been confined to the house, suffering gloominess and pain, for six weeks—when he gets abroad and enjoys all the pleasure of freedom and bustle and variety, he must be quite intoxicated. I went this day to Lord Eglinton's. He insisted that I should dine, which I agreed to. Sir James Macdonald and some more company were with us. I was pretty happy, yet a little dull. In the evening Sir James and I walked to Covent Garden together. I had a long conversation with him, in which I discovered that his seeming pride was not real haughtiness. We talked in such a way that we parted with a good opinion of each other and a desire to be more together. I then met my Lord, with whom I walked a little. He said he would do everything he could with Lord Bute to get my commission.

THURSDAY 10 MARCH. I breakfasted with Lord Eglinton. He generally breakfasts with his family above stairs, whom I shall now paint. It consists of three. In the first place, Miss or Mrs. Brown, who has lived with him seven or eight years. She is a good-looking woman, and I dare say is the best of her profession that ever existed. She is quiet, good-humoured, and diligent at slight pretty work. She is neither avaricious nor extravagant. She has a degree of laughing simplicity that is agreeable so far, but when she shows it too much it appears foolish. Next, there is Mrs. Reid the housekeeper, who has been a great many years with my Lord. She is a good hearty wife, tells an old story, and looks after the family affairs most diligently. She is a Jacobite and a keen church-woman, yet is she wantonly enough minded, and is not displeased that young people of different sexes should solace themselves with the enjoyment of each other. The third is Mr. Charles Crook-shanks. He had his education with my Lord, and has been his steward in England fifteen or sixteen years. He is a very excellent fellow. He is honest, faithful, and generous. He has very good sense, a great deal of fancy, and is much of a gentleman. He and I are very good friends, and I find myself very happy in his company.

This forenoon Sir James Macdonald and I walked a long time in the Green Park. I found him very good company. We now begin to understand one another, and he likes me.

FRIDAY 11 MARCH. Dempster took me into the House of Commons. The novelty of being in the High Court of Parliament which I had heard so much about pleased me exceedingly. My respect for it was greatly abated by seeing that it was such a tumultuous scene. Yet I felt an ambition to be a speaker there. I wish that may be the case. It must afford very high satisfaction to make a figure as an orator before an assembly of so much consequence. At night I was at Lady Northumberland's. She said that she had as yet only seen Lord Granby in public, but would not forget me. She spoke rather slightly, and I imagined she had no more thoughts of serving me. I was really depressed.

SATURDAY 12 MARCH. This was one of the blackest days that I ever passed. I was most miserably melancholy. I thought I would get no commission, and thought that a grievous misfortune, and that I was very ill used in life. I ruminated of hiding myself from the world. I thought of going to Spain and living there as a silent morose Don. Or of retiring to the sweeter climes of France and

Italy. But then I considered that I wanted money. I then thought of having obscure lodgings, and actually looked up and down the bottom of Holborn and towards Fleet Ditch for an out-of-the-way place. How very absurd are such conceits! Yet they are common. When a man is out of humour, he thinks he will vex the world by keeping away from it, and that he will be greatly pitied; whereas in truth the world are too busy about themselves to think of him, and "out of sight, out of mind."

I again went to my good Child's, which gave me some comfort. I felt a warmth of heart to it after so long an absence. I then dined at Lord Eglinton's. Sir James and Lord Advocate were there. I was very dreary. I had lost all relish of London. I thought I saw the nothingness of all sublunary enjoyments. I was cold and spiritless.

I went to Lady Betty's. Lady Anne only was at home. She gave me some tea and we chatted gently. Then the rest came in. I valued them, as they were to go for Scotland on Monday. I stayed supper, after which we talked of death, of theft, robbery, murder, and ghosts. Lady Betty and Lady Anne declared seriously that at Allanbank they were disturbed two nights by something walking and groaning in the room, which they afterwards learnt was haunted. This was very strong. My mind was now filled with a real horror instead of an imaginary one. I shuddered with apprehension. I was frightened to go home. Honest Erskine made me go with him, and kindly gave the half of his bed, in which, though a very little one, we passed the silent watches in tranquillity.[5]

SUNDAY 13 MARCH. I got up rather out of order. I am very easily disconcerted. I could never submit with patience to the inconveniences of a marching corps. The want of my own bed and my own nightcap, and being confined to stretch myself in a small space, hurt my cogitations. We went over to Lady Betty's immediately, and breakfast relieved me. As I was rather in bad frame, and

[5] In the sketch of his life which he wrote later for Rousseau, Boswell confessed that he had been so much afraid of ghosts that he could not sleep alone until he was eighteen. The fear, though somewhat moderated, persisted throughout his life.

as it was the last day of the ladies' being in London, I stayed at home from church. Erskine and I took a walk to Covent Garden, and I carried him to Southampton Street and showed him the house in which I first paid my addresses to the Paphian Queen, where I first experienced the melting and transporting rites of Love.[6] We then returned to dinner, after which the ladies went out, and the afternoon was passed round the fire by Macfarlane, myself, Erskine, and the Laird of Spottiswoode, a very curious exhibition. He is quite a *braid-Scots man.* His conversation was diverting from being so very unlike anything that I have heard for a good time. He is half-brother to Macfarlane, and they have a great similarity. They are both crammed with knowledge of families and places in Scotland, and have both a sort of greasy drollery. In the evening I walked early and quietly home, and felt a most comfortable degree of sensation upon getting into my neat warm bed and resigning myself to repose.

MONDAY 14 MARCH. This forenoon was quite a scene of confusion at Lady Betty's. We had a good breakfast, though, and made as merry as we could. The bills were now coming in upon her Ladyship; they fell around her like flakes of snow. They lighted upon the Laird. They rendered him frigid, and their whiteness was by reflection transferred to his Honour's face. The black lines upon them were indeed a black sight to him. I thought a little jocularity would be useful. I made the sun of good humour to smile, and to warm and cheer the Chieftain.[7] I declared that these confounded bills were satires upon marriage, lampoons upon conjugal felicity. The Laird did not choose that the holy state should be censured. He therefore with no small keenness embraced the cause of the lady.

[6] The lodging of Miss Sally Forrester. See above, p. 46; below, pp. 236, 277.
[7] Macfarlane was head of the clan and jealous of his dignities. "Where races are thus numerous, . . . none but the Chief of a clan is addressed by his name. . . . The late Laird of Macfarlane, an eminent genealogist, considered himself as disrespectfully treated if the common addition was applied to him. 'Mr. Macfarlane,' said he, 'may with equal propriety be said to many; but I, and I only, am Macfarlane' " (Johnson's *Journey to the Western Islands*).

(O could he but embrace her person! or as a friend desire me to
do it!) He asserted that men spent their money more foolishly,
which, after a little opposition, I acquiesced in. About four they
set out. Erskine and I trotted along till we saw them fairly on the
north side of London. We then took leave of them. I insulted over
them a little; desired them to recollect that they were leaving all
the magnificence and splendour and gaiety of the Metropolis, and
were *gaein down to Halkerston's Wynd and wigs and roundabouts.*[8]

They deserved a little chastisement for pretending not to be
fond of London, though indeed it might really be so. For to ladies,
London can never be agreeable till they have been there a long
time and have a numerous circle of acquaintances. They have not
the same advantages of indulging passion and whim and curiosity
that men have. Besides, women who have been in the habit of
living in a place where they are well known and, being the Earl of
Kellie's sisters, are just as good as anybody, must be hurt to find
themselves just poor lasses whose names are hardly known.

There was a proposal made that Erskine and I should take a
chaise and convoy them as far as Barnet and stay a night and make
merry. This proposal was much approved of by the Captain but
declined by me, partly to save money, partly because I felt no inclination for a jaunt. The Captain therefore did not go.

I then went to Lord Eglinton's. He had a large company with
him, so I would not see him, but went up to Mrs. Brown's and had
some of the dainties from his board. There was a degree of meanness in this, and I felt it at the time. Yet I made it appear like a
frolic. I felt a little regret at the ladies of Kellie being gone altogether. It was a very comfortable society for me. I drank tea with

[8] Halkerston's Wynd had plenty of historic associations, and before the North
Bridge was built, was the main thoroughfare for anyone wishing to cross the
North Loch from the High Street, but what it meant specially for the ladies
of Kellie is not clear. Macfarlane's house was in the Canongate. A wig is a
kind of cake or bun; a roundabout is either a fire-place detached from the
wall so that people can sit round it on all sides, or (more probably because of
the association with wigs) an oatcake of circular form, pinched all around
with the finger and thumb (*English Dialect Dictionary*).

Mrs. Brown. I was diverted with a little English girl who had been educated in France.[9]

TUESDAY 15 MARCH. I breakfasted with Colonel Skene. I then went to Gould's, where I had been once last week. I was very happy to find myself in their elegant house again.

I then went to Lord Eglinton's; he and I sauntered about all the forenoon. I had formed a scheme of writing a letter to Lord Bute about my commission, but thought it a wild conceit, so kept it to myself. Luckily Lord Eglinton hit upon the same, and proposed it to me. I appointed to meet him at his house this evening at eleven, when we might talk my affair over fully. He promised he would do everything in his power for me with Lord Bute. "But," said he, "Jamie, after all you will perhaps not believe me." "No, my Lord," said I. "Be not afraid of that. I always believe your Lordship in the past tense but never in the future. When you say, 'I *have* done so and so,' I make no doubt of it. But when you say, 'I *will* do so and so,' your Lordship must excuse me. I believe you intend to do what you say, but perhaps the song of *Three blind mice* comes across you and prevents you from thinking of it."[1] He smiled. We are now very well together. I told him, "My Lord, you first put it into my head that I might enjoy felicity. Now, don't you think yourself obliged to make my existence happy?" He replied, "I do think myself obliged to do all in my power to make you happy."

We parted, and I waited on Mrs. Schaw, formerly Miss Thomson, who was very happy to see me.[2] She is a woman of a good deal of knowledge, pretty good sense, much vivacity, and a prodigious flow of words.

[9] A deliberately cryptic sentence which perhaps should be paragraphed by itself as having no connection with what precedes; the memoranda give no assistance. Hardly a daughter of the Earl and Mrs. Brown, for they were both Scots.

[1] Eglinton was a prominent member of the Catch Club and was very fond of catches and glees. See below, 23 March.

[2] A young woman with whom he had thought himself much in love the year before. She had married Captain Frederick Bridges Schaw less than four months before.

I then called for my Lord at a Mrs. Carwardine's, where he was sitting for his picture in miniature. She is a very good-looking, agreeable woman; unmarried, but I imagine virtuous. I was again in pleasant spirits. The fine arts enliven me exceedingly. I never went into a good painter's but I became happy. There is a sweetness and gentleness in this art which most of all soothes the mind to peaceful tranquillity. My Lord then went to dress and go abroad to dinner.

I sauntered about, and came at three and chatted with my friend Crookshanks, who has just the same opinion of my Lord that I have. Said he, "My Lord desires you just to be one of the family. Have a care. If you go upon that footing, it will be disagreeable. He sets a value upon saving you a shilling for dinner. Keep clear and independent." However, he insisted that I should dine with Mrs. Brown that day. I asked him if I was not doing wrong. He owned it, but said for that day I must comply. We were very cheerful at dinner. I left them after it, but returned to tea.

At night my Lord came as he promised. I ordered everything just as I pleased. I made it just an evening which we passed when I was first in London, which I described in my letter to his Lordship which was published in *The Scots Magazine:* "We sat down in the dining-room, to an enlivening bottle of old hock."[3] I showed him a

[3] " . . . Undoubtedly [in the Coronation] you have had a noble show of grandeur. But, if I mistake not, my Lord, you and I have run through more agreeable scenes together, when I had the honour of living under your Lordship's roof and patronage at London. I say *living*, for at that time, by enjoying, I really knew the value of life. Your Lordship convinced me that this same existence of ours, bad as some philosophers and divines may call it, is yet worth the having; ay, and thanking GOD Almighty for too if we will but make the most of it. I believe, my Lord, when you and I, after a pleasant drive in the chariot from Ranelagh, have sat down by ourselves in your dining-room to an enlivening bottle of old hock, and with all imaginable gaiety have resumed the adventures of the day—sometimes indeed the former night, too, has dropped into the scales—I believe then, my Lord, our sentiments of *all things under the sun* were somewhat different from that illustrious monarch's, who, to be sure, was a very wise man, but who, for the very reason that he was a man, might chance to fall into a little mistake.—Is not this a

letter that I had written to Lord Bute, which he declared too long, too personal, and too circumstantial. He therefore wrote the following, which I just copied out:

My Lord:—I am ashamed to trouble your Lordship, having nothing to recommend me but being the eldest son of a Scotch judge who is thought to serve his country honestly: I mean my Lord Auchinleck.

My father insisted on my following the law. I passed trials to please him, but having an utter detestation at that profession, beg your Lordship would recommend me to his Majesty to have a commission in the Army; which will be conferring the highest favour on one who is, with highest respect and esteem, my Lord, your Lordship's most obedient humble servant,

James Boswell.

I thought this letter not plain enough nor free enough, but my Lord said he would explain all the affair. So I resolved to be for once the real courtier, and so most gravely signed this letter. This anecdote will amuse me much afterwards. I told my Lord I would have nothing but the Guards. "Sir," said he, "I think you should catch at any string." "Nay, my Lord," said I, "another commission would be a rope wherewith to hang myself; except you can get me one that is to be broke, and then I am not forced from London."[4]

---

lounging length of sentence? It is so" . . . (*Scots Magazine*, September, 1761).

[4] "Except you can get me one that is to be broke" means, "unless you can get me a commission in a regiment that is about to be disbanded." The memoranda for the days ensuing show Boswell violently repenting of having authorized this letter. 16 March: "Breakfast Douglas's, then Erskine's, and take him with you to Eglinton's and settle affair, and not to send letter by any means, as you will write." 17 March: " . . . Then Eglinton's and settle no letter sent." 20 March: " . . . Then Eglinton's and consult, and determine nothing out of London but what is broke, and insist on seeing Lord Bute, so then you can tell him your story." 21 March: " . . . After Fergusson, Lord Eglinton, and be spirited, and say you will have nothing but Guards, and you've made a vow not to quit London, as you'd be miserable. Keep to pur-

We sat till near three. Honest Crookshanks saw me half way home.

WEDNESDAY 16 MARCH. I breakfasted at Douglas's. I then called for Erskine and we went and saw the exhibitions of pictures in the Strand.[5] I was jaded with sitting up, and rather in bad spirits. I went by myself and dined in a chop-house near the New Church in the Strand. I have not yet learnt its proper name.[6] But I shall soon, as I shall resort to it pretty often. My spirits grew better there. Really good sustenance dispels the vapours. I should now dislike dining with my landlord. There is something confined and vulgar in it. The worst thing about me at present is, that, having been accustomed during my confinement to live very cheap, I grudge even a shilling for dinner. I must mention another strange thing, as it now occurs. From having been so long and so lately under strict family discipline at home, whenever I have been a little too

pose, don't be imbecile, and ask to see Lord Bute." 23 March: " . . . Don't go Lord Bute, as Eglinton forbid it; so let him take his own way entirely." See below, the entry for 21 March.

[5] "The prize pictures were opened at the Society's office in the Strand, the subjects of which were as follows: Canute reproving his flattering courtiers; for this piece the painter has been adjudged the first prize of 100 guineas. The death of General Wolfe; this piece was put in competition for the first prize, but was adjudged inferior to the former in merit; and as it could not be admitted for the second prize, a compliment of five and twenty guineas was paid the painter as an encouragement to merit. Caractacus before the Roman Emperor Claudius. Edward the Black Prince introducing his prisoner, the French king, to his father, Edward III. Edward the Confessor plundering his mother of her effects; for this piece the author received the second premium of 50 guineas. There are besides ten landscapes, their merits not yet determined." (Historical Chronicle in the *Gentleman's Magazine*, Friday 11 March 1763. "The Society" was the Society of Arts. The winner of the first prize was Robert Edge Pine, of the second, John Hamilton Mortimer. "The Death of General Wolfe" was the picture by which George Romney first attracted public notice. He is said to have believed that he had originally been given the second prize, but that the judges were influenced by Reynolds to reverse their verdict.)

[6] St. Clement's Chop-house? See the entries for 4 and 9 April. (But "New Church Chop-house" appears again in the entry for 14 April.)

late abroad at night, I cannot help being apprehensive that Terrie my landlord will reprove me for it next morning. Such is the force of custom.

THURSDAY 17 MARCH. Erskine and I breakfasted with young Pitfour, who gave us a very copious meal, and put us into good humour with his oddity. I dined at Lord Advocate's, where was an invited contrived formal company. I was but dull. Wedderburn was there, who was overbearing and flippant.[7] Mrs. Miller's abominable Glasgow tongue excruciated me. I resolved never again to dine where a Scotchwoman from the West was allowed to feed with us.[8] At six I left them and met Erskine at Dempster's, where our society over the pleasant tea was very agreeable. Time galloped along. We stayed and had a little supper, and then getting into a deep speculative conversation about the immortality of the soul, human nature, the pursuits of men, and happiness, we did not part till near three, to the severe mortification of Maid Molly, who was obliged to sit up for me. Poor being!

FRIDAY 18 MARCH. Finding myself much dissipated and having a good deal to write, I kept the house all day and did my work, and became serene.

SATURDAY 19 MARCH. Erskine and I breakfasted at Dempster's. He then accompanied me to Child's, where I was not quite so comfortable as when there by myself. I can however now again furnish something like a

DIALOGUE AT CHILD'S.

1 CITIZEN. What changeable weather have we had!

PHYSICIAN. One day this week was like December and another like midsummer.

[7] Alexander Wedderburn, later Chief Justice and Lord Chancellor with the peerage titles of Lord Loughborough and Earl of Rosslyn, was at this time, at thirty, on the threshold of his public career. Having abandoned the Scots for the English bar six years before, he was now, through the influence of Bute (his intimate friend) M.P. for the Ayr burghs, and King's Counsel. Most people, like Boswell, disliked his conceit and resented his success. See above, p. 90.   [8] Yet he later married one.

2 CITIZEN. Bless me! how this play, *The Fall of Mortimer*, has sold, and all for the Dedication.

PHYSICIAN. Yes, 'tis an old play and not worth sixpence.[9]

2 CITIZEN. I remember when the common price of new plays was sixpence, and no more.

We then walked to the Exchange, and sauntered into Guildhall. I was in good London humour and comfortable enough. We dined at Dolly's Beefsteak-house; then went to Saint Paul's Church and heard the choir chanting. In short, this was a day of great variety. We next walked into the Temple. It looked well. I thought of living there some time perhaps. We then walked round by Holborn and came to Dempster's and drank tea. Erskine then went home with me and stayed till I dressed for a grand rout at Northumberland House. He was in lively spirits. We kept up a pretty sharp platoon of raillery, to the no small entertainment of Mr. Chetwynd. "Boswell," said the Captain, "your hair will be very well dressed; but people will think it ill dressed, by seeing it upon your head." The rout this night was very splendid. I stayed till near one looking at very deep play, which made me shudder.

SUNDAY 20 MARCH. I was at St. Clement's Church, which gave me very devout ideas. I then called on Sir James Macdonald, with whom I stayed an hour and was very easy. I then dined at Chapman's Eating-house in Oxford Road. I am resolved to have a variety of dining places. I am amused this way. I shall by degrees see many a one. This is a kind of curiosity whimsical enough. I drank tea with Mrs. Schaw, where we were pretty lively and agreeably entertained.

[9] Isabella, queen of Edward II of England, having entered into an adulterous intimacy with Roger Mortimer, Earl of March, deposed her husband and procured his murder, she and her lover ruling the realm in the name of her son Edward III, a boy of fourteen. In *The North Briton*, Wilkes had "ostentatiously deprecated" a comparison between the Princess Dowager of Wales and Isabella, between Bute and Mortimer, between George III and Edward III. He had now published an adaptation of an old play by William Mountfort, *The Fall of Mortimer*, with an ironical dedication to Bute.

MONDAY 21 MARCH.[1] I breakfasted with Fergusson. He said he had been constantly happy all his life, except one year that he was sick and three days that he was in love. He said he had a rule that he would never do anything for any man which he would not do for him. I then called for Lord Eglinton. We walked together. He told me that he had presented my *Ode on Ambition* to Lord Bute, which he read and liked. That he also presented my letter and told my story in the most favourable manner; but that Lord Bute told him it was impossible to give me a commission in the Guards, as people of the best parliamentary interest were pushing to purchase them. He then asked a commission in another regiment for me, which Lord Bute promised I should have.

BOSWELL. I hope, my Lord, you insisted on its being in a young corps.[2]

EGLINTON. I could not mention it so particularly.

BOSWELL. I thought your Lordship had just talked freely with Lord Bute, as I do with you.

EGLINTON. So I do. But a minister of state is so much taken up that he has not time to talk so much. Although there is no man that I have a greater regard for than you, yet if I were a minister of state, I could not talk so much to you.

BOSWELL. Then, my Lord, I am glad you are not one; and I am glad I am not one, for I could not talk so much to you.

EGLINTON. If you get your commission in a young regiment,

---

[1] "Dress and go and breakfast Pitfour. . . . After Fergusson [i.e., "Pitfour," which is a territorial designation], Lord Eglinton, and be spirited and say you will have nothing but Guards, and you've made a vow not to quit London, as you'd be miserable. Keep to purpose, don't be imbecile, and ask to see Lord Bute. Then call Lady Mirabel and propose fairly, and say you'll do all in your power to make happy. At three, Sheridan's, and be *retenu*, and never mention *Discovery* nor be back for five weeks. Tuesday, in all day." (Memorandum for this day. That for 20 March contains the direction, "Then go Lady Mirabel's and try siege fairly. Then saunter till five, and then Mrs. Schaw.")

[2] One of the more recently constituted corps. As usual, the younger organizations were being disbanded, the older kept as a peacetime army.

you will be broke of course. If in an old, you will get numbers who will be willing to exchange a half-pay commission for yours and give you some money into the bargain.

BOSWELL. Well, my Lord, remember you must settle the affair for me, for London leave will I not.

In this situation are my affairs at present. This may be a step towards my favourite situation, the Guards. At any rate, it can do no harm, as I can throw it up immediately when I feel the least inconvenience from it. We sauntered about this forenoon, and went to Mrs. Carwardine's, where my Lord sat again for his picture. I then parted from him, dined in a pastry shop, and drank tea with Mrs. Brown and Mr. Crookshanks.

When I went home in the evening, I felt myself quite dissipated by running about so much. I was indolent and careless and could not fix to anything. Even this my journal was in danger of being neglected. Near a whole week had elapsed without my writing a single page of it. By way therefore of penance for my idleness, and by way of making up for the time lost and bringing up my business, I determined to sit up all this night; which I accordingly did, and wrote a great deal. About two o'clock in the morning I inadvertently snuffed out my candle, and as my fire was long before that black and cold, I was in a great dilemma how to proceed. Downstairs did I softly and silently step to the kitchen. But, alas, there was as little fire there as upon the icy mountains of Greenland. With a tinder-box is a light struck every morning to kindle the fire, which is put out at night. But this tinder-box I could not see, nor knew where to find. I was now filled with gloomy ideas of the terrors of the night. I was also apprehensive that my landlord, who always keeps a pair of loaded pistols by him, might fire at me as a thief. I went up to my room, sat quietly till I heard the watchman calling, "Past three o'clock." I then called to him to knock at the door of the house where I lodged. He did so, and I opened it to him and got my candle relumed without danger. Thus was I relieved and continued busy till eight next day.

TUESDAY 22 MARCH. What a curious creature is man! With what a variety of powers and faculties is he endued! Yet how easily is he disturbed and put out of order! This night's watchfulness (or rather last night's) has quite stupefied and confused me. However, the day must be weathered out.

I went with Erskine and breakfasted at Slaughter's Coffee-house, and then we walked to Holborn, which did me good. We then came to Douglas's and saw from his windows the procession of the heralds and all the other pageants up Pall Mall in their way to the City to proclaim the Peace.[3]

We then went with Dempster to the House of Commons, where the Cider Bill was in agitation.[4] Mr. Fox spoke, as did several others. But at last Mr. Pitt got up, and then indeed I heard oratory. The ease, the fluency, the grace with which he spoke was amazingly fine. He kindled an ardour in my breast to distinguish myself as he did.[5] Erskine and I stayed in the House till past dinner-time. We then drank tea with Miss Dempster.

I felt myself pleasingly sleepy, and at nine went home and went to bed with great joy. It is worth while to want the comforts of life a little, to have the satisfaction of recovering them again.

I should have mentioned last Sunday that I called at Mr. Gar-

---

[3] "The . . . proclamation was read at St. James's Gate, Charing Cross, Temple Bar, the end of Wood Street, Cheapside, and at the Royal Exchange. The usual officers and heralds attended, but the joy usually expressed on reading such proclamations was not observable on reading this" (Historical Chronicle in the *Gentleman's Magazine*, 22 March 1763).

[4] Sir Francis Dashwood, Chancellor of the Exchequer, had just presented his budget, which was proving to be very unpopular. Its provision for a new excise on cider caused riots in the cider counties.

[5] Boswell dwelt at greater length on this in one of his French themes written at Utrecht a year later: "I heard him there [the House of Commons] speak on the cider tax, and I shall never forget it. He gave me for the first time an example of true eloquence such as I had imagined in reading those great masters Quintilian and Cicero. I shall never forget the elegant force of his expressions, the clean arrangement of his arguments, the melody of his voice, the ease and grace of his gestures" (Translated).

rick's, who said there were half a dozen as clever things in the *Strictures on Elvira* as he ever had read.

WEDNESDAY 23 MARCH. I breakfasted with Lord Eglinton, who was very good to me. He said nobody liked me better than he did. He begun and taught me to sing catches, of which he is very fond. He gave me much encouragement, and said there were not five people in the whole Catch Club who had a better ear than I have. I dined at Harris's Eating-house in Covent Garden, and then called on Erskine, with whom I walked in the Park. We compared the authors of Great Britain to sheep. For instance, the wool of Johnson is coarse but substantial. Hume's fine but slight. We then went to Miss Dempster's and drank tea. Dempster said he had been drunk the night before, and this morning his tongue rattled in his mouth like two dice in a box. "True," said his sister, "and your head ached like a backgammon table."

THURSDAY 24 MARCH. Erskine and I breakfasted with Captain Maxwell of Dalswinton and then walked to Holborn. After sauntering about, I went to Sheridan's, where I dined. I had called there a few minutes one day before; and both at that time and this I never mentioned *The Discovery*, which I thought the best way to pique them a little. This day he at last said to me, "You saw *The Discovery* only the first night?" "No more," said I. SHERIDAN. "O, then you did not see it to half the advantage." BOSWELL. "What, was it lightened?" (Garrick said, "We lightened it.") In this manner did I nettle them. It appeared strongly upon my asking him if he had read Captain Erskine's *Odes to Indolence and to Impudence*.[6] "No, no," said he, "he is no poet. Neither you nor he are poets." This was somewhat impertinent.

FRIDAY 25 MARCH. Erskine breakfasted with me. We parted in the forenoon, and I sauntered up and down the streets rather out of spirits. I drank tea at Sheridan's, where was Old Victor. We disputed much on systems of government. Sheridan stood up for monarchy, and Victor mumbled some stuff in favour of a republic.

[6] Published by Dodsley in a quarto pamphlet, June, 1762.

Surely a regular limited royal government is the best and the most conducive to the happiness of mankind. A republic is in my opinion a most confused, vulgar system, whereas a monarchy inspires us with gay and spirited ideas.

As I was coming home this night, I felt carnal inclinations raging through my frame. I determined to gratify them. I went to St. James's Park, and, like Sir John Brute, picked up a whore.[7] For the first time did I engage in armour, which I found but a dull satisfaction. She who submitted to my lusty embraces was a young Shropshire girl, only seventeen, very well-looked, her name Elizabeth Parker. Poor being, she has a sad time of it!

I supped at Lord Eglinton's. Sir James was there. He invited me very kindly to come to Oxford, and promised to show me everything to the best advantage. I shall certainly go and pass a week there.

SATURDAY 26 MARCH. Erskine and I sauntered up and down some hours. I should have mentioned some time ago that I said to him that if venereal delight and the power of propagating the species were permitted only to the virtuous, it would make the world very good. Our pulpits would then resound with noble descriptions of conjugal love. Preachers would incite the audience to goodness by warmly and lusciously setting before their imaginations the transports of amorous joy. This would render the pleasures of love more refined and more valuable, when they were participated only by the good. Whereas at present it is the common solace of the virtuous and the wicked, the man of taste and the man of brutality.

I was somewhat averse to my City walk today. But Erskine encouraged me in it, and said it would give my ballocks the venerable rust of antiquity. Such wild ludicrous sallies will we sometimes throw out. Child's was this day a silent meeting, as the Quakers say. I was too late to hear a Dialogue. *The North Briton* is

[7] Sir John Brute is a character in Vanbrugh's *Provok'd Wife*; Boswell is quoting from Act IV, Scene 3.

now never published till four o'clock, so that I shall dine in the City every Saturday, so as to have it fresh from the press. Erskine and I met at Dempster's and drank tea.

SUNDAY 27 MARCH. I heard service at St. Dunstan's Church. I then called on Erskine, and he and I walked in the Park till four, and then went to Dempster's, where we were engaged to dine. We expected an agreeable party with him and his sister, but we were hurt by two cousins who were there. Dempster has a tribe of dismal relations who are about him, and he himself is not sensibly affected by disagreeable company, so that he does not discourage them. We stayed and drank tea. I then left them and came home.

MONDAY 28 MARCH. I wonder how I forgot to mention yesterday that just as I was going out to church a gentleman called upon me; and who was this but Derrick, who is now Master of the Ceremonies at Bath. I unluckily got acquainted with this creature when I was first in London,[8] and after I found him out to be a little blackguard pimping dog, I did not know how to get rid of him. I now took care to let him see that I did not choose to renew my acquaintance with him. I shifted all his proposals of meeting with me. Yet I asked him to breakfast this day, in order to show him to Erskine. However, he did not come.

Erskine and I walked to Holborn, and he convoyed me up Snow Hill as far as to Cheapside. I then went to Jeffrey Square beyond Cornhill and dined with Mr. William Cochrane, merchant.[9] He has got an excellent house and lives well. He asked me to come and dine with him as often as I could. He is a good, plain, comfortable Scots fellow; and his wife, though a lean existence, is a quiet civil being. He is entrusted by my father to pay me my allowance, and being his great friend, takes upon him to lecture me on my idle views of life. I could not answer him, and yet I thought myself right from feeling, which is the great test to every man. I stayed and drank tea.

TUESDAY 29 MARCH. I was in miserable spirits. All was dark. I dined with Webster, who treated me as his guest at a military

[8] In 1760. See above, p. 6.   [9] Almost certainly another cousin.

mess at the Tilt Yard. Really it must be observed that officers live rather better than any other society. They have less to do, so it is a more important object. I had this day the satisfaction of a very good dinner, genteelly served up in an elegant room, and a good company round me. Yet was I melancholy. I considered them all as unhappy, tired, slavish beings singled out from the rest of mankind for toil and pain. I disliked the idea of being a soldier. I thought of refusing a commission.

I went and drank tea at Douglas's. He said he was low-spirited, that he was quite sunk, and that his wig was too heavy for his head. Mrs. Douglas joked us both about that disease, and said it was people's own fault, for that it might be easily prevented or driven away. She has a clear constant flow and never feels it. They talked much of Sir Alexander Jardine and his melancholy and whims, and what a pretty, agreeable man he was at the same time. This relieved me, and by degrees I grew easy and cheerful. Douglas said that Sir Alexander used to disappear and hide himself in bed for weeks here. Colonel Caesar of the Guards used to do the same.[1]

WEDNESDAY 30 MARCH. Erskine and I dined with Lord Eglinton, where we were very happy.[2] My Lord and the Captain are

[1] Sir Alexander Jardine of Applegirth (1712–1790) resided principally abroad. He had become a Roman Catholic and had been elected one of the Knights of Malta, a celibate military order. At Milan in 1765 Boswell met the Dominican friar (Giuseppe Allegranza) who had converted Sir Alexander, "of whom," he says at that point in his journal, "I have thought so very much." He had no doubt thought about Sir Alexander at the time when he himself was proposing to retire to a monastery.

[2] On this day, probably, Eglinton gave Boswell a brief note or "card" that he had received from Bute: "Lord Bute presents his compliments to Lord Eglinton, and acquaints his Lordship that he mentioned to the King Mr. Boswell's case, and that his Majesty will not fail to order that he should have a pair colours. South Audley Street, March 26, 1763." Boswell mentioned this in a letter to Johnston, 5 April 1763: "I am now resolved to accept of an ensigncy in a marching regiment, and to exchange it immediately with a half-pay one, and so have that pretence to push for the Guards. [These technicalities are explained above, pp. 219, 223.] Lord Eglinton advised me to take it. I am sure of having it. I enclose you Lord Bute's card, sealed with his own large

growing better acquainted. We drank tea. We talked on human happiness. I said I wondered if any man ever passed a whole day pleasantly. Sir James said that a man in the gay life of London could scarcely do it, because a thousand accidents may cross and disappoint him. But that he had passed such days at Oxford, because his time was regularly laid out. Exactly at such hours he did such and such things, the doing of which in that manner was his pleasure, and could scarcely be interrupted, as he moved like clockwork.

I really believe the college life in England is the least painful of any. If the mind is not much agitated with joy, neither is it shaken with grief. But although the boisterous enjoyment of life is not here, there is quiet, gentle meditation, pleasing exercise of the mental powers; perhaps there is a silent preying misery too. In short, we cannot pronounce where felicity deigns to fix her residence; I hope in the world that is above. We supped here. Colonel Maxwell of Kingsley's,[3] who commanded a brave battalion of Genadiers in Germany, was with us; a fine bold Scot, an open, brave, honest soldierly fellow.

THURSDAY 31 MARCH. Erskine this morning exhibited in a new capacity—that of a landlord. He promised me a breakfast; and a most excellent breakfast did he give, entertaining me not only with plenty of good tea and bread and butter but with that admirable viand, marmalade.

We were very cheerful and very cordial. I sauntered about all the day. I did not dine and was somewhat lowish. At night I strolled

---

seal. His mention of his Majesty is only a form; it means the Secretary at War." In a postscript he asks to have Bute's letter back. He later endorsed it: "The Prime Minister's note that I was to have an ensigncy. But as I liked only the Guards, I declined it."

[3] The Twentieth Foot, named from its colonel, Major- (later Lieutenant-) General William Kingsley. It was very prominently engaged at the battle of Minden (1 August 1759), and suffered such losses that it was excused from all further duty. The Regiment is said to have fought in a rose-garden, and its members are reported still to wear "Minden roses" in their caps on each anniversary of the battle.

into the Park and took the first whore I met, whom I without many
words copulated with free from danger, being safely sheathed. She
was ugly and lean and her breath smelt of spirits. I never asked her
name. When it was done, she slunk off. I had a low opinion of this
gross practice and resolved to do it no more. I went and sat a while
with Webster.

FRIDAY 1 APRIL. This being Good Friday, I endeavoured to
excite in my mind a devout and solemn frame. In my opinion the
annual return of such holy seasons is of great use. Men are thus
kept in mind of religion, and their affections are improved. The
Churches of Rome and England in this particular have a great advantage over the Presbyterians. Regularity and ceremony are of
much advantage.

I don't know how it happened, but a sort of listlessness seized
me; and instead of going to church I strolled up and down all day.
As Love owed me a bill of £40, I was anxious to have it paid, which
makes me call much oftener for him than I otherwise would do. I
drank tea there tonight, and I was very gloomy. At nine I went to
Dempster's. Erskine was there. I was hungry and eat a good supper,
which was a sort of solace to me.

SATURDAY 2 APRIL. I have often and often made inquiry for
my friend Temple. On Sunday last I heard of him and wrote to him
immediately. I breakfasted this day at Dempster's. Erskine, Pitfour,
and other jolly Scots were there. I then set out for the City. Just at
St. Paul's Church-yard whom should I meet but Temple. We met
with a kind of confused joy at our unexpected interview. I engaged
to breakfast with him next day. I was a little afraid that he and I
might not find ourselves so happy together as we formerly were.
We have not met for these five years, except one day at Cambridge.[4]
In so long a time we may have acquired new habits of thinking
and living. When we were together, we were both very studious
and scrupulously moral. Now I am pretty idly disposed. I have not
the same high opinion of learning that I had when at college. I am
more fond of conversation and amusement. I am also much more

[4] During Boswell's London jaunt of 1760.

of a libertine. Tomorrow will convince me how we shall be. I am anxious till it comes.

I dined at Cochrane's. He had two or three Scotch people with him, and we were very hearty. After dinner I sauntered in a pleasing humour to London Bridge, viewed the Thames's silver expanse and the springy bosom of the surrounding fields. I then went up to the top of the Monument.[5] This is a most amazing building. It is a pillar two hundred feet high. In the inside, a turnpike stair runs up all the way. When I was about half way up, I grew frightened. I would have come down again, but thought I would despise myself for my timidity. Thus does the spirit of pride get the better of fear. I mounted to the top and got upon the balcony. It was horrid to find myself so monstrous a way up in the air, so far above London and all its spires. I durst not look round me. There is no real danger, as there is a strong rail both on the stair and balcony. But I shuddered, and as every heavy wagon passed down Gracechurch Street, dreaded that the shaking of the earth would make the tremendous pile tumble to the foundation. I then got *The North Briton* and read it at Child's. I shall do so now every Saturday evening. I then came to Dempster's, where Erskine and I drank tea. This seems now to be an established rule on Saturdays.

SUNDAY 3 APRIL. I went at nine and breakfasted with Temple. I found him in pleasant agreeable chambers, with everything neat and genteel about him. We got into an easy style of conversation, mentioned old stories, compared our ideas, and found that we were pretty near just as similar as when we parted. Though my friend was still studious and moral, yet he was more gay in his pursuits and more liberal in his notions than ever. This was really a matter of much consequence to us both. It so seldom happens in this world

[5] Designed by Sir Christopher Wren; erected to mark the spot where the Great Fire of London broke out in 1666. It formerly bore an inscription stating that the fire was started by the Roman Catholics. Hence Pope's lines, "Where London's column, pointing at the skies, Like a tall bully, lifts the head and lies."

that men of delicate feelings meet with agreeable friends that such a society cannot be enough valued.

Poor Temple has been unfortunate in the world. His father's affairs went wrong, and Temple is obliged to give up about a half of an independent estate of between £3 and 400 a year in order to relieve his parent from shame and distress. He talks of it like a philosopher, and says that out of the wrecks of his fortune he will be able to pick as much as will support him in studious retirement, which is the life that he likes. He is not yet fixed whether he shall go into the Church. I shall encourage him in that scheme. He will be just the clergyman in *The Spectator*. We were so happy and so pleasingly forgetful of everything but the immediate participation of cordial friendly discourse that we did not go to church, although it was Easter Day, that splendid festival.

I dined with my friend Douglas. We had a hearty English dinner. I have particular agreeable ideas annexed to dining there on a Sunday which I affixed to it when I was first in London. I drank tea there, and was really substantially happy. At night, at home, I read the Church service by myself with great devotion.

MONDAY 4 APRIL. Temple breakfasted with me. I found him much more liberal in all his notions than when we were formerly together. We then walked in the Park a good time. We parted, and I went to Gould's, where I explained my scheme of accepting an ensigncy in a marching regiment. He pushed me to get it changed to a cornetcy, from which I might easily step into the Guards. Erskine and I dined at St. Clement's Chop-house very hearty, and then drank tea at Dempster's, where was Captain Archibald Erskine, whom Johnston and I used to call the Owl.[6]

TUESDAY 5 APRIL. I breakfasted with Mrs. Brown. Lord Eglinton was at Newmarket this week. I dined and drank tea at Dempster's with the two Captain Erskines. I recollect nothing that passed.

WEDNESDAY 6 APRIL. Temple breakfasted with me. We

[6] Andrew's brother, later seventh Earl of Kellie.

talked much of learning and philosophy. We then walked into the City, and then strolled about the Temple, which is a most agreeable place. You quit all the hurry and bustle of the City in Fleet Street and the Strand, and all at once find yourself in a pleasant academical retreat. You see good convenient buildings, handsome walks, you view the silver Thames. You are shaded by venerable trees. Crows are cawing above your head. Here and there you see a solitary bencher sauntering about. This description I take from the Reverend Dr. Blair,[7] who is now come to town. To select all these circumstances shows a fine imagination.

Blair is a very amiable man. In my earliest years I admired him while he was Minister in the Canongate. He is learned and ingenious, and has a degree of simplicity about him that is extremely engaging. He and I went this day to Sheridan's and dined.[8] Pitfour was there. It was diverting to see Tommy and Blair. No sooner was the Doctor set down than he gave him a cart-load of compliments on his *Dissertation on the Poems of Ossian.* Poor Blair sat quietly and took it all like a Scotch fornicator when rebuked on the stool of repentance; and when Tommy was done, he just began to lay on the colour of adulation upon Mrs. Sheridan's comedy. However, he did it with a gentle and moderate hand.

Sheridan in his usual way railed against Mr. Garrick, and I as strenuously defended him against Tommy's attacks. He gave us, however, a most ingenious dissertation on the character of Hamlet that atoned for all his wrong-headed abuse of the great modern Roscius. He made it clear to us that Hamlet, notwithstanding of his seeming incongruities, is a perfectly consistent character. Shakespeare drew him as the portrait of a young man of a good heart and fine feelings who had led a studious contem-

---

[7] Hugh Blair, well-known preacher and Professor of Rhetoric in the University of Edinburgh.

[8] " . . . Then home, read Hume, and then dress in frock suit and five-shilling diced stockings and clean shirt, and sally at three to Sheridan's. Be home before twelve. Thursday, breakfast Temple, and give over dissipation. Restrain . . . " (Memorandum for this day).

plative life and so become delicate and irresolute. He shows him in very unfortunate circumstances, the author of which he knows he ought to punish, but wants strength of mind to execute what he thinks right and wishes to do. In this dilemma he makes Hamlet feign himself mad, as in that way he might put his uncle to death with less fear of the consequences of such an attempt. We therefore see Hamlet sometimes like a man really mad and sometimes like a man reasonable enough, though much hurt in mind. His timidity being once admitted, all the strange fluctuations which we perceive in him may be easily traced to that source. We see when the Ghost appears (which his companions had beheld without extreme terror)—we see Hamlet in all the agony of consternation. Yet we hear him uttering extravagant sallies of rash intrepidity, by which he endeavours to stir up his languid mind to a manly boldness, but in vain. For he still continues backward to revenge, hesitates about believing the Ghost to be the real spirit of his father, so much that the Ghost chides him for being tardy. When he has a fair opportunity of killing his uncle, he neglects it and says he will not take him off while at his devotions, but will wait till he is in the midst of some atrocious crime, that he may put him to death with his guilt upon his head. Now this, if really from the heart, would make Hamlet the most black, revengeful man. But it coincides better with his character to suppose him here endeavouring to make an excuse to himself for his delay. We see too that after all he agrees to go to England and actually embarks. In short, Sheridan made out his character accurately, clearly, and justly. Blair and I stayed supper. Whately, a lawyer, was there; a fine, honest, open, sensible, agreeable man. I conceived a great esteem and liking for him.

THURSDAY 7 APRIL. I breakfasted with Temple. This day was afterwards passed in dissipation which has left no traces on my brain.

FRIDAY 8 APRIL. This morning Erskine introduced me to Colonel Tayler of his regiment. We breakfasted with him. He is a man of good sense, vivacity, and humour, an excellent cheerful temper, and speaks English more properly and easily than most people; which even in an Englishman is a very rare thing. I then went to Temple's, walked a while, then dined at Clifton's Chophouse. I drank tea at Dempster's.

SATURDAY 9 APRIL. Dr. Blair came and sat a while with me. I then went with Erskine to Holborn. At three I called on Blair, as we were engaged to go together to the English Opera of *Artaxerxes.* Nairne[9] was with us. I conducted them to St. Clement's Chop-house, where we dined. I was diverted at walking the streets of London with Dr. Blair. I marched him down Southampton Street in the Strand, from the whimsical idea of passing under the windows of my first London lady of the town with an Edinburgh minister whom I had so often heard preach in the New Church. We were in good frame and talked agreeably serious.

The house at Covent Garden was much crowded;[1] so I left my

[9] William Nairne (later a Lord of Session and a baronet) was one of Boswell's closer friends among the Faculty of Advocates.

[1] "At Mr. Tytler's I happened to tell that one evening a great many years ago, when Dr. Hugh Blair and I were sitting together in the pit of Drury Lane playhouse, in a wild freak of youthful extravagance I entertained the audience prodigiously by imitating the lowing of a cow. A little while after I had told this story, I differed from Dr. Johnson, I suppose too confidently, upon some point which I now forget. He did not spare me. 'Nay, Sir,' said he, 'if you cannot talk better as a man, I'd have you bellow like a cow.' " To this (which appears in the printed *Journal of a Tour to the Hebrides* as of November, 1773) Boswell adds the following note: "As I have been scrupulously exact in relating anecdotes concerning other persons, I shall not withhold any part of this story, however ludicrous.—I was so successful in this boyish frolic that the universal cry of the galleries was, '*Encore* the cow! *Encore* the cow!' In the pride of my heart I attempted imitations of some other animals, but with very inferior effect. My reverend friend, anxious for my *fame,* with an air of the utmost gravity and earnestness, addressed me thus: 'My dear sir, I would confine myself to the *cow!*' " This escapade could not have happened on this night unless Boswell is wrong in saying it occurred at Drury Lane, but is mentioned here because this is the only unambiguously recorded occasion on which he and Blair appear in a playhouse together. The complete absence of the cow story from the present journal is surprising. *Artaxerxes* was by Thomas Arne.

place to Nairne, went and drank tea with Mrs. Brown, then came to the Park, and in armorial guise performed concubinage with a strong, plump, good-humoured girl called Nanny Baker. I then went to Drury Lane gallery and saw the entertainment of *Thomas and Sally*,[2] in which Mrs. Love appeared for the first time, with pretty good applause. After the play I met Blair and Nairne at the great Piazza Coffee-house, where we had some negus and solaced our existences.

SUNDAY 10 APRIL. I breakfasted with Temple and then went to the Temple Church and heard a very good sermon on "Set thy house in order, for thou shalt shortly die." This with the music and the good building put me into a very devout frame, and after service my mind was left in a pleasing calm state. I returned to my friend's chambers, and we read some of Mr. Addison's papers in *The Spectator* with infinite relish. We then dined at Clifton's, and drank coffee at Tom's. I drank tea at Dempster's, from whence Erskine and I went to Lord Eglinton's and supped.

John Home was there; he was forward and priggish, but clever.[3] I was arguing for the benefit of philosophy; how it soothed us in distress, and how, by hoping for future ease and pleasure, we might bear up under present distress. Said he, "If you was broiling upon a gridiron all this night, it would be no great consolation to you to know that you would be easy tomorrow." "Nay," said I, "but philosophy may be used to heal the mind as oil does a burnt finger." "But I'm afraid," said Home, "that philosophy is not such a specific as oil." "The true way," said Erskine, "to determine the thing, would be to burn both fingers and take philosophy to the one and oil to the other, and see which of them was first healed." Lord Eglinton said that the women of Italy were worthy of a man's fixing his affections on them, because they can intrigue and yet have principle, as it is the custom of the country. But in this country, a woman must be quite abandoned.

[2] By Isaac Bickerstaffe.
[3] The author of *Douglas*. He was private secretary of Lord Bute and had been tutor to George III when he was Prince of Wales.

MONDAY 11 APRIL. I passed the forenoon with Lord Eglinton, sauntering about, and sitting at Mrs. Cadwaldin's the painter (for I believe her name is spelled thus).[4] It was now fixed that Lord Northumberland should go Lord Lieutenant to Ireland. This I considered as a very fortunate thing for me, as I could go over as an aide-de-camp, get promotion in the Army in Ireland, and from thence step easily into the Guards. Lord Eglinton promised to do what he could to forward this scheme; and this forenoon we met my Lady Northumberland in her chair. Lord Eglinton stopped her and proposed the thing to her. She said she should like it much, but did not yet know whether my Lord and she were to go to Ireland. This looked ill, as if she wanted to shift doing anything. O these Great People! They are a sad set of beings. This woman who seemed to be so cordially my friend and promised me her good offices so strongly is, I fear, a fallacious hussy. Thus do I philosophize, and thus do I lash such unworthy proceedings. However, let me not yet be too certain. She may perhaps be honest. I dined at Lord Eglinton's. Erskine and I drank tea and supped at Dempster's, where we were pretty merry; only Erskine lost a little money at cards.

TUESDAY 12 APRIL. This was the greatest day that Erskine and I ever saw: the day of the publication of our *Letters*. We used to write lively humorous letters to one another. I thought we might make a very entertaining little volume of them, and proposed the scheme to Erskine, who at first opposed it much. But at last the inclination seized him and he became as fond of it as I. During my confinement the thing was resolved upon and set a-going. Flexney was pitched upon for bookseller and Mr. Chandler for printer. And this was the reason of our taking so many walks to Holborn, so often mentioned in this my journal, for both Flexney and Chandler live there. For a while we were in a sort of anxiety about

[4] He was right the first time (see above, p. 218): Penelope Carwardine or Cawardine. She was a friend of Sir Joshua Reynolds and his sister, and appears about 1772 to have married a Mr. Butler, organist of Ranelagh and of St. Margaret's and St. Anne's, Westminster.

the thing; dreaded censure and exposing ourselves; but by degrees we became well pleased with the plan. We were entertained with the printing of it. We kept our secret to a miracle. Not a single soul knew a word of it till it appeared in the newspapers.[5]

Erskine went out of town today to St. Albans, where his regiment was to be broke.[6] I went a little way in the chaise with him. He was more concerned this day by much than I was, and rejoiced at his being absent for the first week after the publication. For my part, I was pretty easy, and resolved just to bear the brunt. At night I called on my friend Temple, with whom I talked over the affair. I began to be a little uneasy. He said he was vexed, but soothed me.

[5] On 10 February Boswell wrote to John Johnston, asking Johnston to open a sealed parcel of papers left in his care and to send on the copies which Boswell had kept of his letters to Erskine. From that date forward the memoranda furnish an almost daily commentary on the progress of the book. Erskine, as Boswell says, disliked the scheme and had to be won over; Flexney was wary because of the small sale of *Critical Strictures;* and a great deal of time had to be spent in rewriting the letters and in correcting the proofs. When it is considered that the preparation of copy was not begun until some time after 10 February and that the book was published on 12 April, it will be seen that Boswell had not been as idle in the interval as the journal would lead one to suppose. Two of the memoranda will serve to represent the whole: "Write letters out by degrees. It will amuse, and it will bring you gold to jaunt to Oxford and about the dusty roads round London" (21 February). "Be denied to all but Flexney. Talk to him of *Strictures.* Pamphlets sell ill. But books how? Better, I suppose. Then mention publication scheme gradually and temperately. Open it to him fully and clearly, and see what he offers. Then ask all terms, consult as to size and see specimen, what time it will take and what expense, and how to get proofs; and to see his printer, &c. Think on true London authors: men of wit, praise, pleasure, and profit" (28 February). *Letters between the Honourable Andrew Erskine and James Boswell, Esq.* is a pretty little book of 156 pages containing 42 letters, the earliest dated in August, 1761, the last in November, 1762, on the eve of Boswell's departure for London. The letters, which are impudent, frothy, and strenuously facetious, will be found not bad reading by those who retain some taste for childish things.
[6] All infantry regiments junior to the Seventieth Foot were being disbanded. Erskine had the hard luck to hold a commission in the Seventy-first. He remained on half-pay until 1765.

He entertained me with a temperate repast of toast and negus, which he always takes in the evening.

WEDNESDAY 13 APRIL. Who is now come to town but the Great Donaldson?[7] I breakfasted with him this morning, and then we went to Flexney's, where he took a parcel of the *Letters*, and then to the booksellers in Paternoster Row, whom he engaged to befriend us. In these matters the favour of *the trade* (as the booksellers call themselves) is a prodigious point. Temple and I dined at Clifton's, a very good chop-house in Butcher Row, near the Temple. We then went to Drury Lane gallery and saw *Macbeth*. We endeavoured to work our minds into the frame of the Spectator's, but we could not. We were both too dissipated. Indeed, Temple has some reason; for a gentleman lives with him in his chambers who is quite his reverse: a prig, a fop, an idler.[8] He will soon be rid of him, and then he will be at ease. The fellow is in the main a good enough lad, but his manners are very opposite and disagreeable to ours.

Macbeth was played by Holland, who played it but poorly and affected us little. I went home with Temple and sat till near twelve, and was very happy. I should have mentioned last night that I met with a monstrous big whore in the Strand, whom I had a great curiosity to lubricate, as the saying is. I went into a tavern with her, where she displayed to me all the parts of her enormous carcass; but I found that her avarice was as large as her a—, for she would by no means take what I offered her. I therefore with all coolness pulled the bell and discharged the reckoning, to her no small surprise and mortification, who would fain have provoked me to talk harshly to her and so make a disturbance. But I walked off with the gravity of a Barcelonian bishop. I had an opportunity tonight of observing the rascality of the waiters in these infamous sort of taverns. They connive with the whores, and do what they can to fleece the gentlemen. I was on my guard, and got off pretty

[7] See above, p. 51. Boswell calls him "the Great" and "the Immense" because of his ambitious publishing schemes and his lordly manner.
[8] No clues are given for identifying this gentleman.

well. I was so much in the lewd humour that I felt myself restless, and took a little girl into a court; but wanted vigour. So I went home, resolved against low street debauchery.

THURSDAY 14 APRIL. Captain Maxwell breakfasted with me. Temple and I dined at the New Church Chop-house, and then he drank tea with me. He talked to me seriously about fixing on some plan of life, about which I find I am as yet uncertain. I went to Lady Northumberland's rout. I was easier this night than I have been at any. I called up all my fortitude of mind to stand the jokes on my *Letters*. After the run of the book is over, I shall in this my journal give an abstract of the different observations made upon them.[1] I chatted a good deal with Lady Margaret Hume, a woman pretty clever, but snappish.

FRIDAY 15 APRIL. Temple and I dined together at Clifton's. I remember nothing more.

SATURDAY 16 APRIL. I dined with Dempster. After dinner he went out; and I sat and drank tea *tête à tête* with his sister. We were in the most agreeable style; calm, sensible, and entertaining, without flashiness. We talked of love and marriage, on which she

[1] He did make such an "abstract," but on separate sheets of paper. Eglinton's remarks, dated as of this day, will serve as a specimen: "LORD EGLINTON. How do you do, Jamie? Why, Jamie, you have been playing the very devil, you and Erskine. You have been publishing private letters between you. BOSWELL. My Lord, is it not something very terrible? EGLINTON. Upon my soul, Jamie, I would not take the direction of you upon any account, for as much as I like you, except you would agree to give over that damned publishing. Lady N—— would as soon have a raven in her house as an author. By G—, I heard it asserted today in a public assembly that you had done it for money. Your father would give you none, and Erskine's regiment was going to be broke. I wonder really at Erskine, for he seems to be a douce, sagacious fellow. BOSWELL. Poor fellow! My Lord, I've led him into the scrape. I've persuaded him. EGLINTON. He cannot be very sensible if you have persuaded him. You must get it suppressed, or put in an advertisement in the papers denying it. By the Lord, it's a thing Dean Swift would not do—to publish a collection of letters upon nothing. Nor Madam Sévigné either. BOSWELL. My Lord, hers are very fine. EGLINTON. Yes, a few at the beginning; but when you read on, you think her a d—nd tiresome bitch."

threw out many elegant sentiments, which gave me a more favourable opinion of her than I ever had.

SUNDAY 17 APRIL. Temple and I went to St. Bride's Church, where the parson was so very heavy and drawling that my friend tired, and we came away before the sermon. We were rather unsettled and in bad humour.

MONDAY 18 APRIL. Temple and I went to the Tower to see the landing of the Venetian ambassadors. It was very elegant to see the fine barges; and then the procession of their coaches, music, and attendants was exceedingly splendid.[2]

I was introduced to a namesake in the Guards. He spells it Bosville, but it is the same with Boswell, and he told me it used to be spelt the latter way in his family. They are both derived from the French Boisville, our ancestor who came over with William the Conqueror. Never were two Highlanders of the same clan happier to meet in a strange place than he and I were to meet here. He told me that he was the eldest son of an ancient family with a good estate in Yorkshire. He is about eighteen; a genteel, well-looked, agreeable young man. He was very civil to Temple and me; took us to his apartment and attended us till the show was over. He promised to call for me, and we agreed to be better acquainted.[3] Temple and I dined at Dolly's comfortably.

TUESDAY 19 APRIL. I supped with the renowned Donaldson

[2] "Their excellencies M. Quirini and Morosini, ambassadors extraordinary from the Republic of Venice, made their public entry in a most magnificent manner. . . . The Venetian ambassadors continued their public entry from Somerset House to St. James's, where they were received by his Majesty sitting on his throne under a rich canopy. From St. James's they returned to their house in Ormond Street" (18 and 22 April in the Historical Chronicle for April, *Gentleman's Magazine*).

[3] Lieutenant William Bosville of the Guards attained sufficient fame as a *bon vivant* to win a place in the *Dictionary of National Biography*. Boswell met his father, Godfrey Bosville of Thorpe and Gunthwaite, in 1766, did homage to him as his chief, and established with him one of the pleasantest intimacies of his entire life.

and his wife, whom he has brought to see London. I was very easy and snug somehow.

WEDNESDAY 20 APRIL. I breakfasted with Captain Webster, who was very high in spirits. At night Temple and I went to Covent Garden and heard the English opera of *Artaxerxes*. We were in pretty good frame, so relished the music. After the opera, I went home with Temple and had an agreeable conversation. It is a fine comfortable idea, having a friend in the Temple.

THURSDAY 21 APRIL. I breakfasted with our Scotch Judge Advocate.[4] I made a mistake in mentioning *Artaxerxes* yesterday; it was tonight.

FRIDAY 22 APRIL. To make a fair trial of Lady Northumberland I had written to her as follows:

MADAM:—I am soon to have a commission in the Army. I beg leave to offer my attendance on Lord Northumberland to Ireland. Your Ladyship has it now in your power to serve me very much. I hope to be honoured with an answer. I am, &c.

This day I had her answer as follows:

SIR:—It is with very great pleasure I hear you are likely so soon to get a commission in the Army. I hope it is in the Guards, as I know that will be the most agreeable to you. My Lord is as well as myself extremely thankful to you for your polite offer of accompanying us into Ireland. Our establishment there was completed for some time before the King's destination of my Lord to the Lieutenancy of that Kingdom was made public; nor indeed is there any post in the Household fit for the acceptance of a man in your situation in life; but should anything happen in our power, we should be very happy to show our inclination to serve you, which I assure you we much wish to do. I am, with great truth, Sir, your most obedient humble servant,

ELIZABETH NORTHUMBERLAND.

[4] William Cochrane; see above, p. 198.

This letter I by no means liked. I showed it to Lord Eglinton, who said it was very polite, but just "three blue beans in a blue bladder." However, he said he would try if she would do anything.

Temple and I had a stroll in the streets this forenoon, and amused ourselves by building many aerial castles of future felicity when he would be with me at Auchinleck.

I dined at Lord Eglinton's, where was John Home, with whom I argued against war for making so much bloodshed. "True," said he, "but consider by the exercise of how many virtues this bloodshed is brought about: by patience, by honour, by fortitude. And as to all the severities of a campaign, one day of the *ennui*, the low spirits of a man, in London is worse than them all." I don't know how far he was right. I am afraid that in a campaign I should have the low spirits and the severities into the bargain. I am sure I always feel myself rendered melancholy by any degree of these hardships.

I had now fixed next day for my jaunt to Oxford.[5] So this evening I took Mr. Chetwynd as my guide and baggageman to the Blue Bell and Crown in Holborn, where the machine puts up. I ordered a bed here, that I might be ready in time next morning. So very delicate am I that I was hurt at the bed's not being so neat and agreeable as my own.

SATURDAY 23 APRIL. Between five and six we set out. I imagined myself the Spectator taking one of his rural excursions. We had as passengers a fellow of Magdalen College, Oxford, called Hawkins, and a Mr. Smith near Oxford. A lady left us because we would not allow her son too to stay in. We had a very good journey, and we chatted a good deal. I got to Oxford about six.

[5] "This is the day before you go to Oxford, so employ it well. Call Dempster a moment first. Then home, get ink, and fall to journal, and be denied to all but Temple. Bring up journal short and neat. Then have Chetwynd and take advice about what to take with you. If you can get small portmanteau, good and well; if not, just bundle. Have shirts, stocks, stockings, and slippers. Leave shoes to be soled. Either go to bed at five and rise eleven, or go to inn and lie; 'twill be but shilling. Be fine and composed" (Memorandum for this day).

The ideas which I had conceived of that noble university were realized when I saw it.

I sauntered about for an hour before I could find Sir James Macdonald, which flattened my spirits a good deal; and from my old notions of a college taken from those at Edinburgh and Glasgow, I had a kind of horror upon me from thinking of confinement and other gloomy circumstances. Sir James received me with much politeness and carried me to sup with Dr. Smith of St. Mary Hall, a gentleman born at Maybole in Ayrshire, but who has been nineteen years at Oxford and gives lectures on anatomy, and is also well employed as a physician. He had with him a Mr. Pepys of Devonshire, a Mr. Cornwallis, Mr. Eden of the County of Durham, and a Mr. Foote.[6] They were all students and talked of learning too much; and in short were just young old men without vivacity. I grew very melancholy and wearied. At night I had a bed at the Blue Boar Inn. I was unhappy to a very great degree.

SUNDAY 24 APRIL. I got up in miserable spirits. All my old high ideas of Oxford were gone, and nothing but cloud hung upon me. I breakfasted with Sir James, and then wrote a few letters to friends, which amused me a little. Sir James and I then walked about and saw the many different colleges, which, to be sure, are very noble. I also dined with him. Dr. Smith and Pepys were with us. Smith is a learned, clever, agreeable man. Pepys is also learned,

[6] Sir James Macdonald had probably picked three of the four guests (Pepys, Cornwallis, and Eden were, like Sir James himself, of Eton and Christ Church), and Sir James, a remarkable young man, was likely to have remarkable young men for friends. William Weller Pepys (Boswell seems to have been mistaken in connecting him with Devonshire) became Master in Chancery, was a friend of the Bluestockings, and was created a baronet. His son rose to be Lord Chancellor and was made an earl. James Cornwallis, later fourth Earl Cornwallis, became Bishop of Lichfield and Coventry. William Eden, later first Baron Auckland, distinguished himself as statesman and diplomat. "Mr. Foote" (George Talbot Hatley Foote, 1744–1821), the one representative of St. Mary Hall, became a barrister-at-law of Lincoln's Inn but seems not to have got into biographical dictionaries.

but too rusty. I now thought that human happiness was quite visionary, and I was very weary of life. After dinner we walked about the place. I tried to work myself up to a little enthusiasm, and took a draught of the water of Isis so much celebrated in poetry, but all in vain. We supped with Pepys, and I continued very bad.

MONDAY 25 APRIL. I breakfasted with Sir James. Pepys was there. I thought them two very dull and unhappy existences. In short, I could form no idea of happiness, and was vexed at having deprived myself of the venerable ideas which I had of Oxford. Even London seemed dull to my dreary mind. However, I took a place in the machine for next morning, which was a sort of relief to me. Sir James and I went to the Theatre,[7] which is indeed a noble edifice, yet I could not relish it. We dined at Dr. Smith's, where I was just as bad as ever.

In the midst, however, of my dulness, I recollected a Mr. Shepherd of Corpus Christi College, author of *Odes Descriptive and Allegorical* and of *The Nuptials*, a didactic poem. I had read extracts from his odes in *The Scots Magazine* a summer or two ago, in fine weather, when I was in serene and pleasant spirits, and so had elegant ideas of them. I could find nobody who was acquainted with him, which I thought a good sign of him. Sir James said he was a very good sort of man, very retired, and that he had seen him walking by himself in deep meditation, with the distracted look of a poet. I took a vast desire to be acquainted with him; and I said I would just call upon him and pay my respects as an admirer of his genius. They thought this a most extraordinary proposal. I drank tea with Mr. Thomson, brother to Miss Thomson (now Mrs. Schaw).

At six there was a concert, which I did not go to. So I had an hour or two by myself. I went and knocked at Mr. Shepherd's rooms, but he was not at home. My curiosity to see him was so great that I wrote him the following card: "A gentleman from

[7] The Sheldonian Theatre, the building at Oxford used for great public ceremonies. It was the gift of Archbishop Gilbert Sheldon (1598–1677), and was built by Sir Christopher Wren.

London who has received much pleasure from Mr. Shepherd's *Odes* is now in Oxford, and is to leave it early tomorrow morning. He is to sup with Mr. Foote of Christ Church, so cannot be his own master till eleven o'clock. If after that time Mr. Shepherd will honour him with his company at the Blue Boar, it will be very obliging. He hopes Mr. Shepherd will excuse this freedom from a stranger."

I got for answer: "Mr. Shepherd's compliments to the gentleman from whom he was favoured with a note, and wishes he might have had the pleasure of waiting on him at his rooms tomorrow; as that cannot be, he will do himself the pleasure of waiting on him at the time appointed tonight."

I was as much pleased with this as most courtiers would have been with a letter assuring them of a place or pension. I strolled about by myself in the walks, went to Pembroke College, where Whitefield[8] was educated, and to Lincoln College, where Hervey was educated. I surveyed them with a degree of enthusiasm, especially Lincoln, in which the amiable and ingenious Hervey lived, whose *Meditations* breathe the most genuine piety and are full of fancy, taste, and elegance. This night I passed the only pleasant hours during my stay at Oxford.

At supper we met at Mr. Foote's of St. Mary Hall (and not of Christ Church), where the very same dulness clouded me. One thing that contributed to this was full living. I observe when I am bad that I grow very voracious; and here we had great dinners and great suppers, and I just clogged my faculties. It is but justice to observe that the young Oxonians are very hospitable and civil to strangers. I experienced that very much.

At eleven I hastened to my inn and waited Mr. Shepherd's arrival with impatience, and with a degree of concern as to my behaviour to him. When he came, I was freed from my apprehensions by finding him a quiet, modest, diffident man. I fell into his way with great address and we soon chatted quite easily. I told him my name and where I came from; and he spoke with the utmost free-

[8] George Whitefield, the great evangelist.

dom, told me he was fellow of a college, but it was but a poor pittance which that yielded him; and besides, that it kept him from active life, which was the sphere he loved most; in particular the Army. So strangely do people mistake themselves! Mr. Shepherd is exactly in the quiet serene life that is proper for him, and yet he has some fanciful ideas of the charms of a scarlet coat and the respect which is shown to a military man who has seen the world, as the phrase goes. I remember Mr. Smith[9] at Glasgow once told me that his friends had cut his throat in not allowing him to be a soldier. In him such an idea is completely ridiculous. For he is quite a learned, accurate, absent man. Poor Shepherd would like to have been born to an estate. He signified as much, and quoted Martial, who reckons *"Fortuna non parta labore"*[1] as one of the requisites of happiness. He had so much simplicity that he offered to pay the wine. "No, no, Mr. Shepherd," said I, "that would neither be descriptive nor allegorical." He was much pleased. He promised to call on me when he came to town, and said he would wish to cultivate an acquaintance with me. I was really pleased with this night's adventure.

TUESDAY 26 APRIL. Early in the morning I set out. My companions were a Mr. Head of Hertford College, Mr. Crisp an old gentleman, and a jolly surgeon to a man-of-war. I was much out of order and very gloomy, but by degrees we grew hearty and I turned better. We had a very good journey. I was a little afraid of highwaymen, but we met none. When I got to London I could not view it in the usual light. My ideas were all changed and turned topsyturvy. Old Crisp asked us all to come and see him at his house in Pall Mall Court. I came to Dempster's and drank tea and made all my complaints. I retained the most gloomy ideas of the University. My mind was really hurt by it. I thought every man I met had a black gown and cap on, and was obliged to be home at a certain hour.

WEDNESDAY 27 APRIL. I found myself quite unhinged. At

[9] Adam Smith. See above, p. 164.
[1] "A fortune not the result of toil"—that is, inherited property. (The Latin actually reads *Res*, not *Fortuna*.)

night I went to the Temple and was pretty happy with my friend. He sympathized with my distress. I went also to *The Cure of Saul*.

THURSDAY 28 APRIL. Temple and I passed the day mostly together. I was very unhappy. Erskine was now come; and he and I dined with Captain Archibald Erskine.

FRIDAY 29 APRIL.[2] The two Captain Erskines breakfasted with me. Captain Andrew and I dined with Houstoun Stewart. We were too extravagant in the ludicrous style, and I was not happy.

SATURDAY 30 APRIL.[3] I breakfasted with Captain Cordwell, who formerly lodged in the same house with me at Edinburgh. I sauntered up and down all the day, very low-spirited, and in the afternoon Erskine and I drank tea and coffee at the Turk's Head Coffee-house.

SUNDAY 1 MAY. I breakfasted with Macpherson, who had just returned from a trip through Holland and France with Lord Elibank. He said his ideas of this country were lessened by seeing the gaiety and splendour of France and the opulence and cleanliness of Holland. At the same time he said that to retain our high ideas of anything, we should not see it. He said too that few, if any, people were happy.

I was so bad this day that I could not settle to go to public worship. I met my friend Temple, who introduced me to his brother, a

[2] In the memorandum for this day Boswell instructs himself to "buy another *Chronicle*": i.e., another copy of *The London Chronicle*, which in the number for 26–28 April contains a long and highly laudatory review of the Erskine-Boswell *Letters*. The concluding paragraph begins, "Upon the whole, we would recommend this collection as a book of true genius, from the authors of which we may expect many future agreeable productions." This would fill one with admiration for the perspicacity of a critic who was able thus early to hail the genius of James Boswell if the memoranda did not provide that critic's name. Boswell wrote the review himself.

[3] " . . . Then Erskine, then Flexney, then Donaldson; then home and just have tea and bring up fortnight's journal and letters, so as to be clear on May Day. Now be sure to do this. . . . " (Memorandum for this day. The discrepancy between counsel and performance is often complete, as this memorandum hints.)

genteel, agreeable young man, a lieutenant in the Royal Volunteers. Temple sympathized much with my distress and forgave my not calling on him for some days. I dined at Douglas's, where was Captain Blair. This dinner was comfortable and hearty, and relieved me a good deal. Honest Blair was very good company. In the evening I called at Dempster's, where was Erskine.

MONDAY 2 MAY.[4] This morning Erskine and I expected the reviews on our letters. So we breakfasted at Dempster's. However, our time was not yet come. Dempster this day gave us an excellent dinner. We went with him and saw his Honour lay out half a guinea in the article of fish. Johnston the advocate was one of the guests. He pleased me by talking about a man's having vigour of mind. Indeed, there is such a kind of human beings; and happy are they in comparison with the feeble and fluctuating. We drank tea here. Yet I still remained very low-spirited.

TUESDAY 3 MAY. I walked up to the Tower in order to see Mr. Wilkes come out. But he was gone.[5] I then thought I should see pris-

[4] "Dress just queue; then leave clothes with Chetwynd, and see Terrie and settle about letters, and tell Dempster the story today. This is GREAT DAY. Go to Erskine immediately and send for both reviews. Then Dempster's and read. Then Eglinton's and Temple's: you could not settle till now. So at night home and bring up. L[ove']s this forenoon. Be at *Lear* solus. Be now *retenu* and never out at night" (Memorandum for this day).

[5] " . . . Then up to Tower and see show and think on King Charles' days" (Memorandum for this day). *The North Briton* No. 45, which had appeared on 23 April, had characterized certain references to the Peace in the recent speech from the throne (19 April) as "the most abandoned instance of ministerial effrontery ever attempted to be imposed on mankind," and had insinuated that the King, in consenting to read the speech, had countenanced a deliberate lie. The Government, with the hearty approval of the King, ignored the convention that the responsibility for a speech from the throne rests with the ministers, and ordered the prosecution of the writer of the paper. Since it was ostensibly anonymous, proceedings in the ordinary course were impossible. The two secretaries of state accordingly issued a "general" warrant (i.e., one not naming any one specifically) for the apprehension of the authors, and on this warrant Wilkes was taken into custody (30 April). The legality of a general warrant in any case would have been

oners of one kind or other, so went to Newgate. I stepped into a sort of court before the cells. They are surely most dismal places. There are three rows of 'em, four in a row, all above each other. They have double iron windows, and within these, strong iron rails; and in these dark mansions are the unhappy criminals confined. I did not go in, but stood in the court, where were a number of strange blackguard beings with sad countenances, most of them being friends and acquaintances of those under sentence of death. Mr. Rice the broker was confined in another part of the house. In the cells were Paul Lewis for robbery and Hannah Diego for theft. I saw them pass by to chapel. The woman was a big unconcerned being.[6] Paul, who had been in the sea-service and was called Captain, was a genteel, spirited young fellow. He was just a Macheath. He was dressed in a white coat and blue silk vest and silver, with his hair neatly queued and a silver-laced hat, smartly cocked. An acquaintance

---

questionable, and the use of such a warrant for the arrest of a Member of Parliament made the matter doubly grave. A writ of *habeas corpus* was applied for, but as there was some delay in issuing the writ, the secretaries committed Wilkes to the Tower of London and kept him there incommunicado. His house was ransacked and his personal papers seized, and at the King's express orders his commission in the militia was cancelled. This, of course, was playing into the hands of an extremely adroit demagogue who knew how to make the most of what was undoubtedly a high-handed and illegal proceeding. On the morning of 3 May Wilkes was taken from the Tower and brought before the bar of the Court of Common Pleas. The hearings not being completed on that day, he was offered his liberty on bail. On his refusing to provide bail, he was sent back to the Tower, but his friends were allowed to see him.

[6] Rice, a prosperous broker, had forged a power of attorney and sold a client's stock to cover losses incurred partly by defaulting clients, partly by his own speculations. He had escaped to France, but had been extradited. Lewis, a young man of twenty-four or less, a clergyman's son, had served in the Navy (as Boswell says) with great intrepidity, but had a bad character. On 12 March he had held up a farmer named Brown on the highway, and had pulled the trigger twice on him, missing the first time and getting only a flash in the pan the second; whereupon he had been ignominiously overpowered by his intended victim. Hannah Diego had stolen "the household goods of Eleanor Hussey, being all the poor woman had in the world."

asked him how he was. He said, "Very well"; quite resigned. Poor fellow! I really took a great concern for him, and wished to relieve him. He walked firmly and with a good air, with his chains rattling upon him, to the chapel.[7]

Erskine and I dined at the renowned Donaldson's, where we were heartily entertained. All this afternoon I felt myself still more melancholy, Newgate being upon my mind like a black cloud. Poor Lewis was always coming across me. I felt myself dreary at night, and made my barber try to read me asleep with Hume's *History*, of which he made very sad work. I lay in sad concern.

WEDNESDAY 4 MAY. My curiosity to see the melancholy spectacle of the executions was so strong that I could not resist it, although I was sensible that I would suffer much from it. In my younger years I had read in the *Lives of the Convicts* so much about Tyburn that I had a sort of horrid eagerness to be there. I also wished to see the last behaviour of Paul Lewis, the handsome fellow whom I had seen the day before. Accordingly I took Captain Temple with me, and he and I got upon a scaffold very near the fatal tree, so that we could clearly see all the dismal scene. There was a most prodigious crowd of spectators. I was most terribly shocked, and thrown into a very deep melancholy.[8]

I went to Lord Eglinton and begged he would try to relieve me. He made me dress and dine with him, and said he would take me at night to Ranelagh and introduce me to some pretty women. Dress and dinner gave me spirits. But at seven, he proposed to take a little boy, one Barron, in the coach with us. This is a boy of great genius both as a painter and a musician, and he will probably be a man of great eminence. But at present he is a little black trifling being, so that his being in my company is a punishment to me. My Lord therefore having gone out and promised to call with the coach and

[7] Macheath, the hero of *The Beggar's Opera*, is a captain in the Army, a gallant, a highwayman, and at the end of the play is shown in chains in the condemned hold at Newgate. In one way or another the figure of Macheath dominates this entire journal.

[8] Hannah Diego got her hands loose and struck the executioner.

take us up, I made my escape very quietly. This was perhaps being too nice and capricious.

I went home and changed my clothes. But gloomy terrors came upon me so much as night approached that I durst not stay by myself; so I went and had a bed (or rather half a one) from honest Erskine, which he most kindly gave me.

THURSDAY 5 MAY. This was a Thanksgiving day for the Peace. But I did not go to church. Dempster, Erskine, and I walked out to Kensington to look for country lodgings to the great Orator (i.e., Dempster). It was a fine day, and the walking in the Garden delicious. We dined at the C-House,[9] and came to Dempster's and passed the evening. I was still in horror, and so slept this night with him.

FRIDAY 6 MAY. I awaked as usual heavy, confused, and splenetic. Every morning this is the case with me. Dempster prescribed to me to cut two or three brisk capers round the room, which I did, and found attended with most agreeable effects. It expelled the phlegm from my heart, gave my blood a free circulation, and my spirits a brisk flow; so that I was all at once made happy. I must remember this and practice it. Though indeed when one is in low spirits he generally is so indolent and careless that rather than take a little trouble he will just sink under the load.

This morning the famous Wilkes was discharged from his confinement and followed to his house in Great George Street by an immense mob who saluted him with loud huzzas while he stood bowing from his window.[1]

I should have mentioned on the 29th of last month that Dr. Blair and some more of us went and saw the British Museum, the

---

[9] The manuscript reads, "dind at ye C-House"—a crowded interlinear addition. Probably Colby House, Kensington, a stately brick mansion "facing the palace gates, at the entrance of the High Street." But Boswell may actually mean the Red Lion Inn close by.

[1] Early on the morning of 6 May Wilkes was taken again before the Court, which discharged him on the ground of his privilege as a Member of Parliament. Lord Chief-Justice Pratt delivered the opinion.

numerous curiosities of which amused me a good deal. I forgot also to mention on Tuesday last that I breakfasted with Mr. Garrick. Colman, the author of *The Jealous Wife*, was there. He is a sensible, clever, agreeable little man. Mr. Garrick was very obliging today and told me that his doors were always open to me.

I then went to Temple's, where I had not been for some days. He said he excused my unhappy dissipation, and just thought, "Poor man! He can't help it!" But he hoped I would become composed. He and I and Bob (the Captain) dined at Clifton's, where we intend always to dine. When I went home at night, I was tired and went to bed and thought to sleep. But I was still so haunted with frightful imaginations that I durst not lie by myself, but rose and sallied straight to Erskine, who really had compassion on me, and as before shared his bed with me. I am too easily affected. It is a weakness of mind. I own it.

SATURDAY 7 MAY. The immense Donaldson and I sat a while at Dempster's this morning. I then went to the City and dined with Mr. Cochrane and drank tea. I was very comfortable. My mind was recovering its tone. I went home at night, after sauntering with Dempster up and down Fleet Market, and I went to bed quietly and slept soundly.

SUNDAY 8 MAY. I went to Audley Chapel, but was still so dissipated that I could not fix my attention, so I came out after part of the service was over. I then stepped into a Romish Chapel[2] and was filled with most romantic ideas. I dined with Lord Eglinton, where was Lord Thanet and Abel.[3]

MONDAY 9 MAY. My gloom was gone, but my spirit of dissipation still remained, so that I was not solidly happy. I dined at Lord Eglinton's. We had an exceeding good company, amongst whom were Mr. Harris of Salisbury, Dr. Blair and Mr. Macpherson and Sir James Macdonald. I felt myself happy in such a set, and really felt gratitude to Lord Eglinton for his kindness. He was not pleased

[2] No doubt the Portuguese Chapel (chapel of the Portuguese ambassador), which stood in South Audley Street.

[3] Karl Friedrich Abel, the celebrated player on the viola-da-gamba.

for my shunning to go to Ranelagh. He said it was very difficult to make me go on right. "Jamie," said he, "you have a light head, but a damned heavy a—; and, to be sure, such a man will run easily down hill, but it would be severe work to get him up." This illustration is very fine. For I do take lively projects into my head, but as to the execution, there I am tardy.

Macpherson and I took a turn as far as Charing Cross. The night was bad and it affected us both, and we groaned and said we were wretched. He said he had no relish for anything in life except women, and even these he cared but little for. We returned to my Lord's and lay on the couch an hour in a lounging way, till he and Sir James came home. So we supped and were pretty well.

TUESDAY 10 MAY. What greater proof need be given of dissipation than my forgetting to mark in my journal of yesterday that the hours between one and three were passed in the Little Theatre in the Haymarket under the auspices of Mr. Foote? There did I laugh at his *Orators* very heartily. I was in the first row of the gallery; and immediately behind us sat Mr. Apreece, the original Cadwallader. Foote has his manner very much, but the excessive caricatura that he makes him is altogether unjust and unnatural.[4]

I dined this day with my friend at Clifton's. At night I waited at Lord Eglinton's till he should come in. But the twelfth hour did not bring him. I therefore would wait no longer. At the bottom of the Haymarket I picked up a strong, jolly young damsel, and taking her under the arm I conducted her to Westminster Bridge, and then in armour complete did I engage her upon this noble edifice. The whim of doing it there with the Thames rolling below us amused me much. Yet after the brutish appetite was sated, I could

---

[4] See above, p. 24. Foote, who was an extraordinary mimic, made his reputation in so-called comedies of his own in which he took off living persons. "Mr. Apreece" was one of his own friends. Boswell can hardly mean that he saw Foote play Cadwallader this afternoon, for Cadwallader is not in *The Orators* but in another piece called *The Author*. What he presumably means is that now that he has seen Apreece, he can judge the aptness of a performance of Cadwallader which he had once seen Foote give. This might have been in 1759, when Foote visited Edinburgh.

not but despise myself for being so closely united with such a low wretch.

When I knocked at my lodgings, I could not get in. The poor girl, despairing of my approach, had gone to bed and fallen asleep. I returned to Lord Eglinton's, as Mr. Crookshanks was out of town and I might have his room. Accordingly, I was just shown into my old little chamber, which I slept in when I first lived at Lord Eglinton's. I was happy to get into it. But when I compared my ideas then with those I had now, the present seemed very dim and very tasteless. I went to bed at three. My Lord was still abroad.

WEDNESDAY 11 MAY. My Lord made me very welcome, and immediately he and I began singing catches, which is really a most enlivening thing. There is some lively sentiment well accompanied with suitable music, and when sung in parts a fine harmony is produced. I take a lesson from him whenever I can, and I make very good progress.

I had a letter some time ago from Bruce Campbell, in which he told me that he had once drank a bottle of sherry in London for me; and he insisted that I should call on a lady of the town named Miss Watts and treat her with another of the same. I waited on her last night and found her a sensible, quiet, well-behaved girl. But as she was engaged, I could not have her company. I promised to call again.

This day I dined at Dempster's. Then dressed and at seven went to Lord Eglinton's, and with Mrs. Brown and Mrs. Reid went in his coach to Ranelagh. I felt a glow of delight at entering again that elegant place. This is an entertainment quite peculiar to London. The noble Rotunda all surrounded with boxes to sit in and such a profusion of well-dressed people walking round is very fine.[5] My spirits were now better. Temple was here tonight. I went home with my Lord and his family, and took my bed freely and snugly.

THURSDAY 12 MAY. I went to Drury Lane and saw Mr. Garrick play *King Lear*. So very high is his reputation, even after play-

[5] See above, p. 26.

ing so long, that the pit was full in ten minutes after four, although the play did not begin till half an hour after six. I kept myself at a distance from all acquaintances, and got into a proper frame. Mr. Garrick gave me the most perfect satisfaction. I was fully moved, and I shed abundance of tears. The farce was *Polly Honeycomb*, at which I laughed a good deal.[6] It gave me great consolation after my late fit of melancholy to find that I was again capable of receiving such high enjoyment.

FRIDAY 13 MAY. I breakfasted with Mr. Garrick. I was proud at being admitted to the society of so great an actor. O'Brien the player was there, a lively little fellow, but priggish. Mr. Garrick was pleased to hear that Donaldson had set up a shop for cheap books, and he walked out with me to the shop, where I introduced Donaldson to him. The prodigious Vendor of Literature was very proud of this. It was really curious to see Mr. Garrick in Donaldson's shop, and the two talking away busily. Mr. Garrick and I then walked to Lincoln's Inn, where he went to call for Colman. He said he would undoubtedly go to Scotland some one summer and play a night for each of the charities at Edinburgh. I told him that he would be adored as something above humanity.

I parted with him, and then dined at Clifton's with Temple. We then went to his chambers, where he introduced me to a particular friend of his, a Mr. Nicholls who had been with him at Cambridge.[7] I never saw anybody who engaged me more at the very first than this gentleman. He discovered an amiable disposition, a sweetness of manners, and an easy politeness that pleased me much. We went to Tom's and had a pot of coffee, and sat there for two hours. Our conversation took a literary turn. We talked of Helvétius, Voltaire, Rousseau, Hume. Mr. Nicholls I found to be sensible and elegantly learned; with an agreeable moderation of sentiment intermixed, his character was finely completed. I talked really very well. I have not passed so much rational time I don't know when. The degree of distance due to a stranger restrained me from my effusions of

[6] By George Colman the Elder, whom Boswell had met on 3 May.

[7] Norton Nicholls, a friend also of Gray. He later took holy orders.

ludicrous nonsense and intemperate mirth. I was rational and composed, yet lively and entertaining. I had a good opinion of myself, and I could perceive my friend Temple much satisfied with me. Could I but fix myself in such a character and preserve it uniformly, I should be exceedingly happy. I hope to do so and to attain a constancy and dignity[8] without which I can never be satisfied, as I have these ideas strong and pride myself in thinking that my natural character is that of dignity. My friend Temple is very good in consoling me by saying that I may be such a man, and that people will say, "Mr. Boswell is quite altered from the dissipated, inconstant fellow that he was. He is now a reserved, grave sort of a man. But indeed that was his real character; and he only deviated into these eccentric paths for a while." Well, then, let me see if I have resolution enough to bring that about.

I went to Lord Eglinton's and supped, together with Sir James, with whom I am now on an excellent footing. I ordered my bed and took up my quarters as usual.

SATURDAY 14 MAY. Every time that I sleep at the Earl's, I never fail to breakfast before I leave his house. I am really on an excellent plan at his house. I believe he is as fond of me as dissipation will allow him to be of any man. I must however complain against fate that Mrs. Brown stays in his house. For I really find her to be such a gawky, and so much of a low censorious Scots lass that I am just in a rage, or rather in a discontent, with her.

This forenoon I met Dempster. He has now taken country lodgings at Kensington for himself and sister. He and I called on Dr. Blair, where was Sir James, who asked if they could understand such a strange thing as this: Boswell and Macpherson got into a coach together; both exclaimed they were miserable; and both burst out in loud peals of laughter. This was literally true. Indeed, I have often found that when I vented my complaints of melancholy, it appeared somewhat ludicrous and I could not but laugh. Blair said that Macpherson must be miserable, because he was absolutely void of curiosity. Blair asked him why he was fond of

[8] The manuscript reads, "attain & constancy & dignity."

staying in England, as he surely could not like John Bull. "Sir," said he, "I hate John Bull, but I love his daughters."

I walked out to Kensington with Dempster and dined with him. I was glad to see Miss Dempster once more. He is charmingly lodged here, and the fellow enjoys it much. We came all in to London together. They were going to the country, and set me down at Hyde Park Corner.

SUNDAY 15 MAY. I was in an excellent calm and serious mood. I attended divine service in Ludgate Church with patience and satisfaction, and was much edified. I then dined at honest Cochrane's, after which he and I and two other gentlemen went to Dr. Fordyce's meeting in Monkwell Street and heard Dr. Blair preach. I thought this would have done me good. But I found the reverse. Blair's New Kirk delivery and the Dissenters roaring out the Psalms sitting on their backsides, together with the extempore prayers, and in short the whole vulgar idea of the Presbyterian worship, made me very gloomy. I therefore hastened from this place to St. Paul's, where I heard the conclusion of service, and had my mind set right again.

I should have mentioned that I breakfasted this morning with the illustrious Donaldson. In the evening I went to Temple's; he brought me acquainted with a Mr. Claxton, a very good sort of a young man, though reserved at first.[9] Mr. Nicholls was there too. Our conservation was sensible and lively. I wish I could spend my time always in such company.

MONDAY 16 MAY.[1] Temple and his brother breakfasted with

[9] Temple's other intimate Cambridge friend; also, like Temple and Nicholls, a friend of Thomas Gray. He was a lawyer and an antiquary. Temple named his third son John James after Claxton and Boswell.

[1] The memorandum for this day is remarkable for what it does *not* contain—the most important single event in Boswell's life. He plans the relinquishment of his military scheme, but of course could not foresee that he would meet Samuel Johnson: "Send breeches mend by barber's boy. You are now on good plan. Breakfast neat today, toast, rolls, and butter, easily and not too laughable. Then Love's and get money, or first finish journal. Keep plan in mind and be in earnest. Keep in this fine frame, and be directed by Tem-

me. I went to Love's to try to recover some of the money which he owes me. But, alas, a single guinea was all I could get. He was just going to dinner, so I stayed and eat a bit, though I was angry at myself afterwards. I drank tea at Davies's in Russell Street, and about seven came in the great Mr. Samuel Johnson, whom I have so long wished to see. Mr. Davies introduced me to him. As I knew his mortal antipathy at the Scotch, I cried to Davies, "Don't tell where I come from." However, he said, "From Scotland." "Mr. Johnson," said I, "indeed I come from Scotland, but I cannot help it." "Sir," replied he, "that, I find, is what a very great many of your countrymen cannot help." Mr. Johnson is a man of a most dreadful appearance. He is a very big man, is troubled with sore eyes, the palsy, and the king's evil.[2] He is very slovenly in his dress and speaks with a most uncouth voice. Yet his great knowledge and strength of expression command vast respect and render him very excellent company. He has great humour and is a worthy man. But his dogmatical roughness of manners is disagreeable. I shall mark what I remember of his conversation.[3]

He said that people might be taken in once in imagining that an author is greater than other people in private life. "Uncommon parts require uncommon opportunities for their exertion.

<hr>

ple. At night see Pringle. Go to Piazza and take some negus ere you go; or go cool and take letter and bid him settle all, but not too fast. . . . "

[2] That is, bears the scars of scrofula. What Boswell here calls palsy was rather a number of convulsive tics. See above, p. 30.

[3] In the margin, with a reference to this place in the conversation, Boswell (probably as late as 1787) has written, "Mem. Garrick refusing an order to Mrs. Williams, &c." In *The Life of Johnson* he expands this hint as follows: "This stroke stunned me a good deal, and when we had sat down I felt myself not a little embarrassed and apprehensive of what might come next. He then addressed himself to Davies: 'What do you think of Garrick? He has refused me an order for the play for Miss Williams because he knows the house will be full and that an order would be worth three shillings.' Eager to take any opening to get into conversation with him, I ventured to say, 'O, Sir, I cannot think Mr. Garrick would grudge such a trifle to you.' 'Sir,' said he with a stern look, 'I have known David Garrick longer than you have done, and I know no right you have to talk to me on the subject.'"

[562] this morning with the illustrious Donaldson. In the evening I went to Temple's; he brought me ac=quainted with a Mr Claxton a very good sort of a young man tho' reserved at first. Mr Nicholols was there too. Our conversation was sensible & lively. I wish I could spend my time allways in such company.

Monday 16 May.
Temple & his Brother breakfas=ted with me. I went to Love's to try to recover some of the mo=ney which he owes me. But alas a single guinea was all I could get. He was just going to dinner, so I stayed & eat a bit, tho' I was angry at myself afterwards. I drank tea at Davies's in Russ=el Street and about seven came in the great Mr Samuel John=son, whom I have so long wished to see. Mr Davies introduced me to him. As I knew his mortal antipathy at the Scotch, I endea

Two pages of manuscript recording Boswell's
first meeting with Johnson.

to Davies; don't tell where I come
from. However he said From Scotland.
Mr Johnson said I indeed I come
from Scotland, but I cannot help
it. Sir replied he; That I find
is what a very great many of
your countrymen cannot help. —
Mr Johnson is a man of a most
dreadfull appearance. He is a
very big man is troubled with sore
eyes, the Palsy & the King's
evil. He is very slovenly in
his dress & speaks with a
most uncouth voice. Yet his
great knowledge, and strength
of expression command vast
respect and render him very
excellent company. He has
great humour and is a worthy
man. But his dogmatical rough-
:ness of manners is disagreable.

"In barbarous society superiority of parts is of real consequence. Great strength or wisdom is of value to an individual. But in more polished times you have people to do everything for money. And then there are a number of other superiorities, such as those of birth and fortune and rank, that dissipate men's attention and leave superiority of parts no extraordinary share of respect. And this is wisely ordered by Providence, to preserve a mediocrity.

"Lord Kames's *Elements* is a pretty essay and deserves to be held in some estimation, though it is chimerical.[4]

"Wilkes is safe in the eye of the law. But he is an abusive scoundrel; and instead of sending my Lord Chief Justice to him, I would send a parcel of footmen and have him well ducked.[5]

"The notion of liberty amuses the people of England and helps to keep off the *taedium vitae*. When a butcher says that he is in distress for his country, he has no uneasy feeling.

"Sheridan will not succeed at Bath, for ridicule has gone down before him, and I doubt Derrick is his enemy."[6]

I was sorry to leave him there at ten, when I had engaged to be at Dr. Pringle's, with whom I had a serious conversation much to my mind.

I stayed this night at Lord Eglinton's.

TUESDAY 17 MAY. I sauntered up and down all this forenoon, and dined with Lord Eglinton, where was Sir James, who said he wondered how I could complain of being miserable who had always such a flow of spirits. Melancholy cannot be clearly proved to

[4] A work on theory of criticism which enjoyed a great reputation for a long time. It had appeared the previous year.
[5] Wilkes's discharge from custody had not ended the determination of the Government to prosecute him for seditious libel. He had been served with a subpoena, but had refused to put in an appearance, holding that the subpoena was a violation of his privilege. Meantime the secretaries of state had foolishly allowed themselves to be drawn into a newspaper correspondence with him.
[6] "Mr. Sheridan was then reading lectures upon oratory at Bath, where Derrick was Master of the Ceremonies; or, as the phrase is, KING."—BOSWELL, in *The Life of Johnson*.

others, so it is better to be silent about it. I should have been at Lady Northumberland's rout tonight, but my barber fell sick; so I sallied to the streets, and just at the bottom of our own, I picked up a fresh, agreeable young girl called Alice Gibbs. We went down a lane to a snug place, and I took out my armour, but she begged that I might not put it on, as the sport was much pleasanter without it, and as she was quite safe. I was so rash as to trust her, and had a very agreeable congress.

WEDNESDAY 18 MAY. Much concern was I in from the apprehension of being again reduced to misery, and in so silly a way too. My benevolence indeed suggested to me to put confidence in the poor girl; but then said cool reason, "What abandoned, deceitful wretches are these girls, and even supposing her honest, how could she know with any certainty that she was well?"[7] Temple was much vexed and dreaded the worst.

I dined with him at Clifton's, and at five Erskine and I walked out to Dempster's, where we passed a very pleasant segment of a four-and-twenty. Erskine has now got into a way of going to taverns with one Fitzgerald and other riotous gentlemen, which I don't like.

THURSDAY 19 MAY. Mr. James Coutts told me that he and his brother and Mr. Cochrane were to dine with a Mr. Trotter, upholsterer, a particular friend, and that he never went thither without carrying somebody along with him; so he insisted that I should go. I accordingly went, and was introduced to Mr. Trotter, who is originally from Scotland, but has been here so long that he is become quite an Englishman. He is a bachelor, an honest, hearty, good-humored fellow. The company were all Scottish except an American lady, wife to Mr. Elliot, a son of Lord Minto's; Mr. Stewart, formerly the noted Provost of Edinburgh;[8] and some more

[7] ". . . Tell Temple your risk, and make him lay restrictions upon you never to have any connection without a permission from him, as you really may get into sad scrapes . . . " (Memorandum for this day).

[8] He was Provost in 1745, and opposed all plans for arming the city, so that the Highland army entered without opposition. After the collapse of the

of these kind of old half-English gentry. We had a good dinner and plenty of wine. I resolved to be merry while I could, and soon see whether the foul fiend of the genitals had again prevailed. We were plain and hearty and comfortable; much better than the people of high fashion. There was a Miss Rutherford there, a Scotch girl who had been long in America. She and I chatted very neatly.

We stayed and drank tea and coffee; and at seven, being in high glee, I called upon Miss Watts, whom I found by herself, neatly dressed and looking very well. I was free and easy with her, and begged that she would drink a glass of wine with me at the Shakespeare, which she complied with. I told her my name was Macdonald, and that I was a Scotch Highlander. She said she liked them much, as they had always spirit and generosity. We were shown into a handsome room and had a bottle of choice sherry. We sat near two hours and became very cheerful and agreeable to each other. I told her with a polite freedom, "Madam, I tell you honestly I have no money to give you, but if you allow me favours without it, I shall be much obliged to you." She smiled and said she would. Her maid then brought her a message that a particular friend from the country was waiting for her; so that I was obliged to give her up this night, as I determined to give her no money. She left me pleased, and said she hoped to have the pleasure of my company at tea when it was convenient. This I faithfully promised and took as a good sign of her willingness to establish a friendly communication with me.

I then sallied forth to the Piazzas in rich flow of animal spirits and burning with fierce desire. I met two very pretty little girls who asked me to take them with me. "My dear girls," said I, "I am a poor fellow. I can give you no money. But if you choose to have a glass of wine and my company and let us be gay and obliging to each other without money, I am your man." They agreed with

---

Rebellion, he was arrested and put in the Tower (he was M.P. for Edinburgh), and in 1747 was tried before the High Court of Justiciary for neglect of duty and misbehaviour in the execution of his office. The verdict (a popular one) was not guilty.

great good humour. So back to the Shakespeare I went. "Waiter," said I, "I have got here a couple of human beings; I don't know how they'll do." "I'll look, your Honour," cried he, and with inimitable effrontery stared them in the face and then cried, "They'll do very well." "What," said I, "are they good fellow-creatures? Bring them up, then." We were shown into a good room and had a bottle of sherry before us in a minute. I surveyed my seraglio and found them both good subjects for amorous play. I toyed with them and drank about and sung *Youth's the Season* and thought myself Captain Macheath;⁹ and then I solaced my existence with them, one after the other, according to their seniority. I was quite *raised*, as the phrase is: thought I was in a London tavern, the Shakespeare's Head, enjoying high debauchery after my sober winter.¹ I parted with my ladies politely and came home in a glow of spirits.

FRIDAY 20 MAY. My blood still thrilled with pleasure. I breakfasted with Macpherson, who read me some of the Highland poems in the original. I then went to Lord Eglinton's, who was highly entertained with my last night's exploits, and insisted that I should dine with him, after having walked in Hyde Park with Macpherson, who was railing against the human species, and in vast discontent.

After dinner my Lord and I went to Ranelagh in his chariot by ourselves, where he introduced me to a Mrs. Wattman, a young married lady, extremely pretty and agreeable. We drank tea and chatted well. I met Lady Margaret Hume, whom I had really used ill in not waiting upon her one Sunday evening, as I engaged to do. I apologized for myself by saying that I was an odd man. She seemed to understand my worth, and said it was a pity that I should just be lost in the common stream of people here. I went home and supped with Lord Eglinton.

⁹ "Youth's the season made for joys" is a song and chorus in *The Beggar's Opera*. Macheath is in a tavern near Newgate, surrounded by ladies of the town.

¹ "High debauchery" is debauchery with genteel ceremonial; "low debauchery" is debauchery without.

SATURDAY 21 MAY.[2] I dined in the City with my honest friend Cochrane, and in the afternoon drank tea and sat a long time with Temple, who was in fine frame and talked to me seriously of getting out of a course of dissipation and rattling and of acquiring regularity and reserve, in order to attain dignity of character and happiness. He had much weight with me, and I resolved to be in earnest to pursue the course which he admired.

SUNDAY 22 MAY. I went to St. Andrew's Church in Holborn, which is a very fine building. At one end of it is a window of very elegant painted glass. I was in an excellent frame and heard service with true devotion.

I dined at Douglas's very hearty. There is a dinner there every Sunday for Captain Blair, young Douglas of Douglas, young Steuart nephew to Douglas, and their own son (all Westminster scholars), and I believe I shall always too make one.

I passed the evening at Temple's very well. Temple has so much good sense, good temper, and steadiness that he makes the best friend in the world, a character truly great.

MONDAY 23 MAY. Temple and his brother and Captain Blair breakfasted with me. Then Temple and I called for Nicholls, with whom we went to see the Exhibition of the Artists[3] in Spring Garden, where we were well amused. We walked out to Kensington and strolled through the delightful Gardens. It is a glorious thing for the King to keep such walks so near the Metropolis, open to all his subjects. We were very calm and happy. Our conversation was mild and agreeable.

I dined with Dempster, having engaged to meet Dr. Blair and Macpherson at his house. The Sublime Savage (as I call Macpher-

[2] "For heaven's sake, think now that if you don't take care, you're gone for ever. Sit in all morning and bring up journal well, so as to have week clear with its warm transactions. At two call Temple, confess errors, and not only resolve but promise. So as to be under his power. In the mean time acquire dignity. Think of going abroad, and in short try all ways" (Memorandum for this day).

[3] That is, of the Society of Artists of Great Britain.

son) was very outrageous today, throwing out wild sallies against all established opinions. We were very merry. He and I and Blair walked into town together. I brought on the subject of reserve and dignity of behaviour. Macpherson cursed at it, and Blair said he did not like it. It was unnatural, and did not show the weakness of humanity. In my opinion, however, it is a noble quality. It is sure to beget respect and to keep impertinence at a distance. No doubt (as Blair affirmed) one must give up a good deal of social mirth. But this I think should not be too much indulged, except among particular friends. Blair and I went and sat a while by ourselves in Prince's Street Coffee-house and had a serious conversation.

TUESDAY 24 MAY. I received a very polite letter from Mr. Thornton, one of the authors of *The Connoisseur*, informing me that he had written the criticism on Erskine's and Boswell's *Letters* in *The Public Advertiser*, to which I had in return for their civility sent a little essay begging to know who had spoken so favourably of us. Mr. Thornton said he should be happy in our acquaintance. I wrote to him my thanks and said I would call upon him at eleven o'clock, which I did, and found him a well-bred, agreeable man, lively and odd. He had about £15,000 left him by his father, was bred to physic, but was fond of writing. So he employs himself in that way.

In a little, Mr. Wilkes came in, to whom I was introduced, as I also was to Mr. Churchill. Wilkes is a lively, facetious man, Churchill a rough, blunt fellow, very clever. Lloyd too was there, so that I was just got into the middle of the London Geniuses. They were high-spirited and boisterous, but were very civil to me, and Wilkes said he would be glad to see me in George Street.[4]

[4] To receive praise from Bonnell Thornton was peculiarly gratifying to Boswell, because he and Erskine had consciously patterned their literary partnership on that of Thornton and Colman (*The Connoisseur, The St. James's Chronicle*) and that of Colman and Lloyd (*Odes to Obscurity and Oblivion*). Indeed, the Soaping Club may have been an echo of the Nonsense Club of Thornton, Cowper, Colman, and Lloyd. If Boswell had not previously met Johnson, this meeting with the "Geniuses" might well have seemed to him the climax of his months in London.

From this chorus, which was rather too outrageous and profane, I went and waited upon Mr. Samuel Johnson, who received me very courteously. He has chambers in the Inner Temple, where he lives in literary state, very solemn and very slovenly. He had some people with him, and when they left him, I rose too. But he cried, "No, don't go away." "Sir," said I, "I am afraid that I intrude upon you. It is benevolent to allow me to sit and hear you." He was pleased with this compliment, which I sincerely paid him, and he said he was obliged to any man who visited him. I was proud to sit in such company.

He said that mankind had a great aversion at intellectual employment. But even supposing knowledge easily attained, most people were equally content to be ignorant.

"Moral good depends on the motive from which we act. If I fling half a crown at a beggar with intention to break his head, and he picks it up and buys victuals with it, the physical effect is good; but with respect to me, the action is very wrong. In the same way, religious services, if not performed with an intention to please GOD, avail us nothing. As our Saviour saith of people who perform them from other motives, 'Verily they have their reward.'

"The Christian religion has very strong evidences. No doubt it appears in some degree strange to reason. But in history we have many undoubted facts against which *a priori* in the way of ratiocination we have more arguments than we have for them; but then testimony has great weight, and casts the balance. I would recommend Grotius, Dr. Pearse on Miracles,[5] and Dr. Clarke."

I listened to this great oracle with much satisfaction; and as I feel myself uneasy by reason of scepticism, I had great comfort in hearing so able an advocate for Revelation; and I resolved to read

[5] "Dr. Pearse on Miracles" is changed in *The Life of Johnson* to "Dr. Pearson," who has been assumed to be Dr. John Pearson, 1613–1686, Bishop of Chester, one of the greatest of seventeenth-century divines. But perhaps at some stage in the revising or printing of the *Life* Boswell's "Pearse on" got misread as "Pearson," and "Dr. Pearson" is a ghost. Zachary Pearce (1690–1774), Bishop of Rochester, wrote *The Miracles of Jesus Defended* (1729), whereas Dr. John Pearson published no work with a title mentioning miracles.

the books he mentioned. He pressed me to stay a second time, which I did. He said he went out at four in the afternoon and did not come home, for most part, till two in the morning. I asked him if he did not think it wrong to live so and not make use of his talents. He said it was a bad habit.

He said Garrick was the first man in the world for sprightly conversation.

I begged that he would favour me with his company at my lodgings some evening. He promised he would. I then left him, and he shook me cordially by the hand. Upon my word, I am very fortunate. I shall cultivate this acquaintance.

Temple and I dined at Clifton's. Bob the Captain (his brother) is always with us. He is a fine spirited boy, much of a gentleman. He has taken a particular liking to me. We passed the evening with Nicholls. Claxton was there, and Morris, a young man of fortune and learning and worth, though uncouth manners. However, he is one of Temple's set. I am happy to be amongst them. The evening went well on.

WEDNESDAY 25 MAY.[6] Temple and his brother and I dined in their chambers, where we had dinner brought, thinking it a more genteel and agreeable way than in a chop-house. But we found it inconvenient, and so resolved to continue constant to Clifton's. I gave Bob a ticket to the play, and my worthy friend and I talked

[6] " . . . Go on with Geniuses moderately. Call Wilkes and leave card, with full directions. Cultivate acquaintance with wits to be *bel esprit*" (Memorandum for this day). One of the few disappointments of this journal is that it does not record Boswell's meetings with Wilkes. The reason was undoubtedly prudence. Wilkes was constantly watched by Government spies, and Boswell might well have believed that if he had been seen in Wilkes's company, his letters would be opened. And he planned to send this entire journal through the post. It is clear from various bits of evidence that he did call on Wilkes, and that he got on sufficiently easy terms with him to ask franks from him "to astonish a few North Britons." However, the almost complete lack of reference to Wilkes in the remainder of the London memoranda must mean that he was seeing little of him. The real intimacy with Wilkes was developed in Italy in 1765.

seriously. He advised me to force myself to be reserved and grave in a greater degree, otherwise I would just be Jamie Boswell, without any respect. And he said he imagined that my journal did me harm, as it made me hunt about for adventures to adorn it with, whereas I should endeavour to be calm and studious and regular in my conduct, in order to attain by habit a proper consistency of conduct. No doubt consistency of conduct is of the utmost importance. But I cannot find fault with this my journal, which is far from wishing for extravagant adventures, and is as willing to receive my silent and serious meditations as my loud and boisterous rhodomontades. Indeed, I do think the keeping of a journal a very excellent scheme if judiciously executed. To be sure, it may take up too much time from more serious concerns. But I shall endeavour to keep it with as much conciseness as possible.

THURSDAY 26 MAY. I breakfasted with Lord Eglinton and also dined with him. Honest Captain Blair was with us, who is a very worthy fellow; and yet he and I very seldom meet in this great city. I went quietly home at night.

FRIDAY 27 MAY. I breakfasted with Lady Frances Erskine. Mr. Erskine her husband is now in town. I sat a good while with him yesterday, but he was abroad today. I dined with Lord Eglinton and took as my guest a Mr. Gascoigne, a great catch-singer; and we were wond'rous merry, as the song goes. Yesterday I took as my guest the Earl of Kellie, and we had much laughing.[7]

SATURDAY 28 MAY. I breakfasted with Mr. Coutts, who is a sensible, mild, friendly man. His brother Mr. Thomas is a very good fellow and has a great deal of little humour and fun.

I then walked to Cochrane's and got an order on Sir Charles Asgill for my money. I am really angry with that fellow Love, who has put me off so long and never makes any apology or seems to be

---

[7] Thomas Alexander Erskine, sixth Earl of Kellie, one of the foremost musical composers of the day, was also a rake and a *bon vivant*. Samuel Foote said that his face would ripen cucumbers. He and Boswell were never intimate, in spite of the close association between Boswell and his brother Andrew.

concerned about the matter. I dined at Dolly's, where I met with George Home of Kames. I then came and sat a while with Temple, and then went home and wrote my letters. I continue to write to Sir David Dalrymple every Saturday.

SUNDAY 29 MAY. I breakfasted with Colonel Montgomerie.[8] At three o'clock I went to Westminster Abbey and the verger politely showed me into one of the prebend's stalls, where I sat in great state with a purple silk cushion before me. I heard service with much devotion in this magnificent and venerable temple. I recalled the ideas of it which I had from *The Spectator*.

I dined with Lord Eglinton. Lord Thanet, Lord Coventry and his brother, and Mr. Price, a Welsh member, were there. It was a day truly English and genteel. I was very comfortable, and spoke a little with a manly confidence. We drank coffee, and parted about eight at night.

MONDAY 30 MAY.[9] Young Bosville of the Guards breakfasted with me, and we walked in the Park together. I then sat at Lord Eglinton's to a miniature painter, at his Lordship's desire, but he proved to be a stupid, half-blind boy. So I engaged him to come this day sennight. He may come, but I shall not.[1] I dined at Clifton's with the Temples.

TUESDAY 31 MAY. Bob Temple, who is a handsome, spirited

[8] Eglinton's brother and successor in the title. He had served with distinction in America, especially in the expedition to Fort Duquesne in 1758, and in excursions against the Cherokees, 1760 and 1761.

[9] "Rise soon and run to Dash [Erskine's nickname] after dress and keep up *retenue* with him. 'Tis now time to carry it on. You're fairly begun. Engage him to breakfast with you on Wednesday. At ten, home, and Bosville, and be fine. At eleven, Eglinton's, and picture till twelve. Then call people till two, and then Piazza and Miss Temple, and behave nice and romantic and bold. Home at night. If you go to Edinburgh, you're ruined." (Memorandum for this day. Miss Temple is explained in the next day's entry in the journal.)

[1] His name appears to have been Low. Some of the later memoranda make it look as though Boswell repented and sat out the portrait. If he did, the miniature has dropped out of sight.

young dog, has introduced himself to a Miss Temple, an exceeding
pretty girl. She is kept by a man of £4000 a year. She is very amorous, and is kind to her favourites without any views of interest.
This is a very agreeable circumstance to little Robert, who is now
on half-pay, and it is no less so to me. With her permission he introduced me to her yesterday, under the name of Mr. Howard, a distant relation of the Duke of Norfolk's. I was quite charmed with
her. She told him today that she thought me very like a gentleman.
It is really generous in Bob to do this for me. But he is very fond of
me; more so than of anybody except his brother. I dined at Clifton's
today, and at night was at Temple's with Claxton. I stayed all
night, as Temple was anxious till Bob came in, who had been at
Vauxhall. I had Bob's bed, and slept fine.

WEDNESDAY 1 JUNE. This morning the *Critical Review* on
our *Letters* came out. Erskine breakfasted with me, and in great
form did we read it. They did not use us with candour, but they
were less abusive than we imagined they might be.[2] I introduced
the Captain to Mr. Thornton, with whom he was much pleased.

We then sauntered about an hour or two. I went and dined at
Lord Eglinton's without being invited. He made me very welcome,
but I felt myself mean somehow, and I resolved never to go in that
way again. This was quite an irregular day.

THURSDAY 2 JUNE. I am now getting into the habit of sitting
at home all the morning and reading, which composes my mind
and makes me happy all day. I dined at Clifton's, and at four called
on Miss Temple.[3] Her keeper was there; but she spoke to me in the
stair and said she would meet me in the Park. No, she bid me call,
as she was going to the Park. Bob and I called, but she was gone.

[2] "That the Honourable Mr. Erskine and Mr. Boswell are men of wit and
humour, in certain walks of both, cannot be denied; but we are afraid some
question will be made whether either of them is a genius." The poems contained in the letters are characterized as "the cheapest and most nauseous
drugs of this press-surfeited age and country."

[3] " . . . Then call Miss Temple, and if not up, fix time, and when with
her be honest and gross . . . " (Memorandum for this day).

We then walked in the Park with my friend Temple, who went home with me and drank a little negus. We were rather jaded and dull. Yet we made a shift to entertain ourselves.

FRIDAY 3 JUNE. Erskine and I walked out to Kensington and dined with Dempster. After getting into, or studying to get into, a proper well-behaved plan, with the assistance of my friend Temple, the Scotch tones and rough and roaring freedom of manners which I heard today disgusted me a good deal. I am always resolving to study propriety of conduct. But I never persist with any steadiness. I hope, however, to attain it. I shall perhaps go abroad a year or two, which may confirm me in proper habits. In the mean time let me strive to do my best.

SATURDAY 4 JUNE. Bob Temple breakfasted with me; and I carried him with me to Lord Eglinton's. I dined at Clifton's. The two Temples drank tea with me.

It was the King's birthnight, and I resolved to be a blackguard and to see all that was to be seen. I dressed myself in my second-mourning suit,[4] in which I had been powdered many months, dirty buckskin breeches and black stockings, a shirt of Lord Eglinton's which I had worn two days, and little round hat with tarnished silver lace belonging to a disbanded officer of the Royal Volunteers. I had in my hand an old oaken stick battered against the pavement. And was not I a complete blackguard? I went to the Park, picked up a low brimstone,[5] called myself a barber and agreed with her for sixpence, went to the bottom of the Park arm in arm, and dipped my machine in the Canal and performed most manfully. I then went as far as St. Paul's Church-yard, roaring along, and then came to Ashley's Punch-house and drank three threepenny bowls. In the Strand I picked up a little profligate wretch and gave her sixpence. She allowed me entrance. But the miscreant refused me performance. I was much stronger than her,

[4] A dark suit but less sombre than one worn for first or full mourning. This one happened to be Boswell's oldest or shabbiest suit, and as he had worn it while his hair was being powdered, it had grown more shabby.
[5] Virago, spit-fire.

and *volens nolens* pushed her up against the wall. She however gave a sudden spring from me; and screaming out, a parcel of more whores and soldiers came to her relief. "Brother soldiers," said I, "should not a half-pay officer r–g–r⁶ for sixpence? And here has she used me so and so." I got them on my side, and I abused her in blackguard style, and then left them. At Whitehall I picked up another girl to whom I called myself a highwayman and told her I had no money and begged she would trust me. But she would not. My vanity was somewhat gratified tonight that, notwithstanding of my dress, I was always taken for a gentleman in disguise. I came home about two o'clock, much fatigued.

SUNDAY 5 JUNE. The fatigues of last night rendered me very lazy and disposed to relish ease. I therefore caused the maid make tea for me, and I breakfasted in bed, which I think a piece of high luxury. I found myself calm and indolent and meditative, so I stretched my weary limbs at full length and lay till near three o'clock, when my friend Temple and his brother came in. They were diverted to see me solacing myself. I then got and dressed and went to Miss Temple's, whom I found at home by herself. She was in fine spirits; gave me strawberries and cream, and used every endearing amorous blandishment. But alas! my last night's rioting and this morning's indulgence, joined with my being really in love with her, had quite enervated me, and I had no tender inclinations. I made an apology very easily; and she was very good, and said it happened very commonly after drinking. However, I was much vexed. The Temples and I drank tea and coffee at the Piazza, and we were very comfortable.

MONDAY 6 JUNE. I must not omit to record in this my journal a most curious transaction. We have now in the house where I lodge a neat little maid called Nancy, newly imported from Cumberland. I had given her a frank of Lord Eglinton's, in which she had enclosed a letter to a companion in the country, but not having directed it fully, it was brought to my Lord, who opened it

⁶ Roger, a word of other meaning than it has acquired since the introduction of radio-telephony.

when I was with him. He gave it to me and put me upon the scheme of making her believe that I had the second sight. Accordingly, I picked out many circumstances from her letter about her friends and her journey to town and all her concerns, which I solemnly told her, and for two days she firmly believed that I had intelligence from the Devil. I then let her into the secret.

Nothing remarkable happened this day; and from henceforth I am determined to show more respect to this my journal. I shall never set down the mere common trifling occurrences of life, but say nothing at all, except when I have something worth while.

TUESDAY 7 JUNE. I just read, eat, drank, and walked.[7]

WEDNESDAY 8 JUNE. I breakfasted with Mr. Coutts, and I sauntered about idly all forenoon, which gave me pain. At night I received a very kind letter from my father, in which he told me that he would allow me to follow any profession that I pleased, but at the same time said that the Army was but a poor scheme, and that if I would pursue the law, though moderately, and be in the style of his eldest son, that he would give me all encouragement. It was a most sensible and indulgent letter. It made me think seriously, and I considered that I had now experienced how little I could depend on the favour of the great, which, when only founded on personal liking, is very slight. I considered too that I could have no prospect of rising in the Army. That my being in that way contrary to my parents' advice was uphill work, and that I could not long be fond of it. I considered that by getting into the plan of civil life, I should have all things smooth and easy, be on a respectful footing and of consequence in my own country, and please my worthy father, who, though somewhat narrow in his notions, is one of the best men in the world.[8]

[7] "Dress and breakfast, and learn to rise soon each morn to brace nerves. Then fall to journal, and resolve this day to bring it fairly up. Write till two. Then Bob comes, and be *moderately* cheerful with him; and get affairs settled for tonight. Write to Love strongly: 'Sir,' &c., and threaten him. Write Cairnie. Study *retenue*" (Memorandum for this day).

[8] Lord Auchinleck's letter is so important for the understanding of Boswell's

THURSDAY 9 JUNE. I communicated my designs to Temple, who approved much of my resolution. I however determined to insist on first going abroad, as I am resolved to maintain a grave and respectful character. Temple said that I might live like Sir David Dalrymple at Edinburgh; be at London three months in the year, and live more comfortably than if I pushed the scheme of the Guards. I dined with Lord Eglinton. At night I told Dr. Pringle my intentions.

---

life, and especially of that portion of his life covered by the present journal, that it has been printed entire, not cut to fit into the narrow space of a footnote. See Appendix II: below, p. 337.

Because of Boswell's reluctance to put his unfilial feelings on record, the journal has not been giving anything like a candid description of his relations with his father. Lord Auchinleck had written disparagingly of his keeping a journal and had cast aspersions on the loyalty and discretion of his confidants, Johnston and McQuhae; and when Johnston told him that on his going to get the copies of the letters to Erskine he had found that some one had already broken into the parcels, Boswell was furiously angry. "The unhappy fact which you have disclosed to me of my packets having been broke open shocked me a good deal. . . . It was doing what no parent has a right to do in the case of a son who is a man and therefore an independent individual. It is equally unjust to steal his secrets as his money. . . Happily, they could not possibly know the hands of some of the letters written to me. . . From many circumstances you must see, my friend, how very terrible a situation I should be in were I to live as young laird in my father's family. . . . As to my commission, I find the Duke of Queensberry will do nothing. He has certainly had instructions. Lady Northumberland I am doubtful of. Lord Eglinton, with all his dissipation, is yet my best friend. [He then mentions the appeal to Bute and the half-pay scheme: above, p. 223.] It is a matter of some consequence once to fix myself fairly out of my father's reach, as he still imagines he is to have me under his eye, as you may judge from a letter of my mother's, which I send you. . . You will see mention made of taking away my allowance, in order, I suppose, to force me back, but you know by a transaction last summer with my father, I have a settlement of £100 a year lying by me in form; so I am really my own master. He little thinks of my stealing this half-pay march" (To John Johnston, dated 22 April 1763 but probably written on 22 March). He wrote in high terms to his father, whereupon Lord Auchinleck broke off correspondence. Various people sent him warnings that his father was talking of

FRIDAY 10 JUNE. Crookshanks breakfasted with me. He is a fine, lively, extravagant fellow. I shall give a specimen of him. "Mr. Boswell, you could not deceive my Lord Auchinleck. Such a sensible man, by the Lord, can pick the truth from falsehood as easily as one picks the strawberries from among the leaves.

"Poh! Poh! What is it to me that Lord Bute is a Scotsman? If he had dropped from the brains of a woodcock in his passage from the moon, I should have thought him equally my countryman."[9]

At night, I went to Chelsea and saw Johnson ride, standing upon one and then two horses at full gallop, with all his feats of agility. I was highly diverted. It was a true English entertainment. The horses moved about to the tune of *Shilinagarie;*[1] for music,

selling the estate, and that he really meant to do it. By the 16th of May, Boswell had repented and was planning to ask Pringle "to settle all, but not too fast" (above, p. 259 *n.* 1), and on 21 May he begged Sir David Dalrymple to intercede: "I wish from my soul, Sir David, that you would use your good offices between us. It is not from the fear of being disinherited (which he threatens) that I am anxious. I am thoughtless enough not to mind that. But my affection for him makes me very unhappy at the thoughts of offending him. I beg you may talk with him and try to make matters easy. It will be a most humane office. Tell him to have patience with me for a year or two, and I may be what he pleases" (*Letters,* ed. C. B. Tinker, i.11). Dalrymple returned a manly and sensible answer, saying that he would gladly use his best endeavours with Lord Auchinleck on Boswell's assurance that he was ready to settle down to "any course of life, be it what it will," but on the same day that Dalrymple wrote, and apparently without urging from Dalrymple, Lord Auchinleck broke his silence.

It is probable that Boswell's deeper nature was set all along to comply with his father's plans. If he had been successful in the Guards scheme, he would have found some way to get out of it.

[9] Bute was Scots in blood but English by education (Eton); he had married an Englishwoman (daughter of Lady Mary Wortley Montagu), and had lived in England for the last sixteen years.

[1] Boswell could have saved his readers momentary confusion if he had introduced the Johnson of this paragraph as "Johnson the famous equestrian." *Shilinagarie* was an Irish Jacobite song by Timothy O'Sullivan: in modern Irish spelling it is Síle ni Gadra, in English Sheila O'Gara. Sheila O'Gara, like Cathleen ni Houlihan, is a personification of Ireland.

such as it is, makes always a part of John Bull's public amusement.

While I stood gazing about, whom did I suddenly perceive but —Miss Sally Forrester, my first Lady of Venus's Bedchamber, whom I have sought for eagerly but could never find? I approached her with something like the air of a tragedy hero. She immediately knew me. I felt really a fine romantic sensation at meeting her. Miss Simson, who lodged in the house with her and was very civil to me, was with her tonight. We went into the Star and Garter, and I treated them with tea. We resumed[2] our former adventures. I cannot express the curious feelings which I had when I looked back three years; called up my ideas then, and all that has happened to me since. Alas! my ideas have not now that giddy fervour which they had when I was first in London. However, I now walk on surer ground. She said she was married to Captain Peter Grant, a Scotch officer, and she would not allow me to renew my joy. But she promised to meet me at her companion's house, who also said she was married, and[3] called herself Mrs. Tredwell. We walked into town together. The evening was delicious, and I glowed with pleasing imagination. I felt a great degree of satisfaction at thinking that my father would now be happy, and all things go well, and that I might indulge whim with a higher relish. I parted from them at Spring Gardens, and promised to see my dear Sally. They surely joked about their marriages.

I then called on Miss Temple. She pretended that she had waited two hours at home for me; said she was busy and could not admit me. I was piqued, and resolved never again to go near her, except she let me know that I should be exceedingly welcome. I passed the evening very pleasantly with my friend Temple.

SATURDAY 11 JUNE. Bob Temple breakfasted with me. I dined at Mr. Cochrane's.

SUNDAY 12 JUNE.[4] Captain Blair and I breakfasted at Tem-

---

[2] Related, recapitulated.   [3] The manuscript reads *as.*

[4] " . . . Dine Pringle and be fine, and at six Eglinton's and settle affairs with him about Lord Bute . . . " (Memorandum for this day). The journal does

ple's, after which I went to St. Sepulchre's Church upon Snow Hill.
I dined at Dr. Pringle's, where was the celebrated Monsieur de la
Condamine. He was very old, and so deaf that he could hear only
by the assistance of a horn.[5] He said he knew Madam Maintenon.
But that she was a very discontented woman. He said that Helvétius *De l'esprit* was a dangerous book for women and young people
whose principles were unfixed. Pringle said, "If I thought Deism
the true religion, I would not say so to my wife."

MONDAY 13 JUNE.[6] Temple and I came up by water from
the Temple Stairs to Whitehall. This is the first time this season
that I have been upon the silver Thames. It is very pleasant to sail
upon it; and I shall do it oftener.[7] We drank tea cordially at my
lodgings, and my friend gave me much good advice.

At night, Lord Eglinton and Bob Temple called in my Lord's
coach and carried us to Vauxhall, which was quite delicious.[8]
There was a quarrel between a gentleman and a waiter. A great
crowd gathered round and roared out, *"A ring—a ring,"* which is
the signal for making room for the parties to box it out. My spirits
rose, and I was exerting myself with much vehemence. At last
the constable came to quell the riot. I seized his baton in a good-
humoured way which made him laugh, and I rapped upon the
people's heads, bawling out, "Who will resist the Peace? A ring, a
ring." However, all would not do. My Lord brought us home in
his coach, and the Temples supped with me on a slight repast.

TUESDAY 14 JUNE. I should have mentioned yesterday that
I waited on Mr. Johnson, who was very civil to me. He said that

not show when Bute's offer of an ensigncy was declined, but it must have
been about this time.

[5] Charles Marie de la Condamine (he was in fact only sixty-two) was a
famous French traveller and mathematical geographer who in 1735 had
gone to Peru to measure a meridional arc at the equator, and had explored
the Amazon.

[6] Boswell has written in the margin. "This day was with Johnson. See the
opposite page"—that is, the entry for 14 June.   [7] See above, p. 26.

[8] For Vauxhall, see the passage of the Introduction referred to in the note
immediately preceding this.

such a man as Johnson the rider should be encouraged, as his performances showed the extent of the human powers in one instance
and so tended to raise our opinion of the nature of man; and that
he showed the great effects of industry and application. "So that
every man might hope that by giving as much application, although perhaps he might never ride three horses at a time, or
dance upon the wire, yet he might be equally expert in whatever
profession he chose to pursue." Such is[9] the views that Mr. Johnson has of the most trivial matters. I never am with this great
man without feeling myself bettered and rendered happier.

He shook me by the hand at parting, and asked me why I did
not call oftener. I said I was afraid of being troublesome. He said
I was not; and he was very glad to see me. Can I help being vain of
this? Nothing happened today.

WEDNESDAY 15 JUNE. I breakfasted with Lord Eglinton.
We then walked in the Green Park. He said I was the only man
he ever knew who had a vast deal of vanity and yet was not in the
least degree offensive. I dined with him today. He had some Newmarket people with him. We sung some catches and were very
jolly, as the saying is.

THURSDAY 16 JUNE. Erskine and I went out to Dempster's
and passed the whole day very merrily. They were glad to hear
that I was upon good terms with my father.[1]

[9] Scots grammar. In Scots the verb in the present tense takes a form in *–s*
for all persons, singular and plural, unless the personal pronoun immediately
precedes: "They are" but "The views is" and "Such is the views."

[1] "And now, my friend, I am to inform you that I have laid aside all thoughts
of going into the Army. I am disgusted with the neglect and hollowness of
these Great People from whom I expected great cordiality. Besides, I have
lately had a most affectionate letter from my father. He is truly a worthy
man. I assure you he is. All his little mistakes are owing to a confined and
narrow education. He has set before me both schemes, and he seems so very
anxious to have me in a civil capacity, as his eldest son, and in a creditable
way in my own country; and he promises to give me all encouragement and
mentions my getting into Parliament as a noble incitement. . . . However,
I have begged first to go abroad, which I hope will be allowed, as I could not

FRIDAY 17 JUNE. I breakfasted at Mr. James Erskine's. The day was trifled away.

SATURDAY 18 JUNE. I breakfasted with Colonel Montgomerie, then strolled about with young Graham of Gartmore. I dined with Mr. James Erskine, and I was very vivacious, yet kept myself in moderate bounds. I am happy every Saturday in writing to Sir David Dalrymple. It always puts me in a good frame. At night I took a streetwalker into Privy Garden[2] and indulged sensuality. The wretch picked my pocket of my handkerchief, and then swore that she had not. When I got home, I was shocked to think that I had been intimately united with a low, abandoned, perjured, pilfering creature. I determined to do so no more; but if the Cyprian fury should seize me, to participate my amorous flame with a genteel girl.

SUNDAY 19 JUNE.[3] I sat a good part of the forenoon at Erskine's with Macpherson and Scott, who writes *An Evening's Walk near the Royal Palace of Linlithgow*.[4] At two I breakfasted at the Somerset, and at three went to St. Paul's. Mr. Cooper, one of the gentlemen of the Chapel Royal, who belongs to the choir of this cathedral and whom I have seen at Lord Eglinton's, gave me a good seat by himself; and after service, which elevated my mind, I drank tea with him; then walked in the Park. Then supped at Temple's.

---

well come down immediately. I may after travelling come back a decent, grave man . . . " (To John Johnston, 16 June 1763).

[2] The area behind Whitehall, now called Whitehall Gardens. It was called Privy Garden because it was originally the private garden of the King's Palace at Whitehall.

[3] " . . . Take Temple privately by himself and own your depravity, and how vexed you are, and promise never more to indulge low venery. This last *thief* and *monster* may cure you completely. Attain self-government and please father . . . " (Memorandum of this day).

[4] A poem which Boswell probably admired greatly, for his own first poem to be published was *An Evening Walk in the Abbey Church of Holyroodhouse*. Apart from his publications, nothing is known of Scott except that his first name was Robert and that he appears to have been an officer in the Army. *Writes* meaning *is the author of* is a Scotticism.

MONDAY 20 JUNE. Temple and I breakfasted with Captain Blair, after which we went and saw Reynolds's portraits, which pleased us much.[5] I then went with Erskine and had some games at billiards, not for money. It is a pretty game. I scarcely ever play at it, as I would grow too fond of it. At night I went to the opening of Mr. Foote's Little Theatre in the Haymarket for this season, with *The Minor*, in which I saw Wilkinson for the first time, a most admirable mimic. *The Mayor of Garratt*, a new piece, was also played. I laughed much at it.[6] I sat by Churchill just at the spikes.[7] I was vain to be seen talking with that great bard. After the play I carried Bob Temple home to a repast.

TUESDAY 21 JUNE. I went to Love's in the evening and received £10 of his debt to me. I supped with him. He was free and ill bred.

WEDNESDAY 22 JUNE. Dr. Boswell is now in town.[8] I breakfasted with him today. He was very happy to see me. We walked about all the forenoon. It was a curious thing to see the Doctor in London. At night Temple and Bob and Claxton supped with me. We were moderately cheerful.

THURSDAY 23 JUNE. Dempster and Erskine breakfasted with me. I then strolled about with them up and down the City, and then we went out to Dempster's and dined. In the evening we walked in Kensington Gardens, and talked of being abroad, and what was to

[5] At the fourth Exhibition of the Society of Artists of Great Britain: see above, 23 May. Reynolds's pictures in the exhibition were (1) "Two Ladies" (the Ladies Elizabeth and Henrietta Montagu); (2) "A Nobleman, half length" (Lord Rothes); (3) "A Gentleman, three-quarters"; (4) "A Portrait, half length" (Nelly O'Brien).

[6] Both plays were by Foote. In *The Minor* Wilkinson was, as it were, playing himself, for Foote had written the part of Shift as a caricature of Wilkinson. Foote's license permitted him to give evening performances only in the summer. It will be noted that the performance which Boswell saw at the Little Theatre on 9 May (above, p. 255) was given in the afternoon.

[7] See above, p. 25.

[8] Boswell's uncle, Lord Auchinleck's brother. He and Boswell were much alike in temperament and were very fond of each other.

be acquired. I said I wanted to get rid of folly and to acquire sensible habits. They laughed.

FRIDAY 24 JUNE. The Doctor breakfasted with me. I dined at Lord Eglinton's with Lord Lichfield, Chancellor of the University of Oxford, a most humane, agreeable man, and Dr. Jardine, minister at Edinburgh, a hard-headed, jolly dog. We were very well.

SATURDAY 25 JUNE. Mr. Johnson dined at Clifton's in the same room with me. He and an Irishman got into a dispute about the reason of some part of mankind being black. "Three ways have been taken to account for it: either that they are the posterity of Ham, who was cursed; or that GOD at first created two kinds of men, one black and another white; or that by the heat of the sun the skin is scorched, and so gets the sooty hue. This matter has been much canvassed among naturalists, but has never been brought to any certain issue." The Irishman grew very hot, and Johnson just rose up and quietly walked off. The Teague said he had a most ungainly figure and an affectation of pomposity unworthy of a man of genius.

At nine in the evening Mr. Johnson and I went to the Mitre Tavern in Fleet Street. He was vastly obliging to favour me with his company. I was quite proud to think on whom I was with.

He said Colly Cibber was by no means a blockhead; but by arrogating to himself too much, he was in danger of losing what he really had. He said his friends gave out that he intended his Birthday Odes should be bad, but that was not the case. "For a few years before he died, he showed me," said Johnson "one of them with the greatest care, and I made some corrections. Sir, he had them many months by him. Indeed Cibber's familiar style was better than that which Whitehead has taken. That grand nonsense is terrible. Whitehead is but a little man, to write verses inscribed to players."

I shall mark Johnson's conversation without any order or without marking my questions; only now and then, I shall take up the form of dialogue.

"Sir, I do not think Mr. Gray a superior sort of poet. He has not a bold imagination, nor much command of words. The obscurity in which he has involved himself will not make us think him sublime. His *Elegy in a Churchyard* has a happy selection of images, but I don't like his great things. His ode which begins

> Ruin seize thee, ruthless King.
> Perdition on thy banners wait!

has been celebrated for its abrupt breaking off and plunging into the subject all at once. But such arts as these have no merit but in being original. The first time is the only time that we admire them; and that abruptness is nothing new. We have had it often before. Nay, we have it in the song of Johnny Armstrong:

> There is never a man in the North Country
> To compare with Johnny Armstrong.

There, now, you plunge into the subject. You have no previous narration."[9]

I then told my history to Mr. Johnson, which he listened to with attention. I told him how I was a very strict Christian, and was turned from that to infidelity. But that now I had got back to a very agreeable way of thinking. That I believed the Christian religion; though I might not be clear in many particulars. He was much pleased with my ingenuous open way, and he cried, "Give me your hand. I have taken a liking to you." He then confirmed me in my belief, by showing the force of testimony, and how little we could know of final causes; so that the objections of why was it so? or why was it not so? can avail little; and that for his part he thought all Christians, whether Papists or Protestants, agreed in the essential articles, and that their differences were trivial, or were rather political than religious.

[9] Boswell adds a note in the margin with a reference to this place: "The next lines I think very [pretty *above line*] good: 'Tho' fanned.'" In *The Life of Johnson* this is expanded to: "The two next lines in that ode are, I think, very good:

> Though fann'd by conquest's crimson wing,
> They mock the air with idle state."

He talked of belief in ghosts; and he said that he made a distinction between what a man might find out by the strength of his imagination, and what could not possibly be found out so. "Thus, suppose I should think that I saw a form and heard a voice cry, 'Johnson! you are a very wicked fellow, and unless you repent you will certainly be punished.' This is a thought which is so deeply impressed upon my mind that I might imagine I saw and heard so and so; and therefore I would not credit this, at least would not insist on your believing it. But if a form appeared, and a voice told me such a man is dead at such a place and such an hour; if this proves true upon inquiry, I should certainly think I had supernatural intelligence given me." He said that he himself was once a talker against religion; for he did not think against it, but had an absence of thought.

I told him all my story. "Sir," said he, "your father has been wanting to make the man of you at twenty which you will be at thirty. Sir, let me tell you that to be a Scotch landlord, where you have a number of families dependent upon and attached to you, is perhaps as high a situation as humanity can arrive at. A merchant upon 'Change with a hundred thousand pounds is nothing. The Duke of Bedford with all his immense fortune is but a little man in reality. He has no tenants who consider themselves as under his patriarchal care.

"Sir, a father and a son should part at a certain time of life. I never believed what my father said. I always thought that he spoke *ex officio*, as a priest does.

"Sir, I am a friend to subordination. It is most conducive to the happiness of society. There is a reciprocal pleasure in governing and being governed.

"Sir, I think your breaking off idle connections by going abroad is a matter of importance. I would go where there are courts and learned men."

I then complained to him how little I knew, and mentioned study. "Sir," said he, " don't talk of study just now. I will put you upon a plan. It will require some time to talk of that." I put out my hand. "Will you really take a charge of me? It is very good in you, Mr. Johnson, to allow me to sit with you thus. Had I but thought some years ago that I should pass an evening with the Author of *The Rambler!*" These expressions were all from the heart, and he perceived that they were; and he was very complacent and said, "Sir, I am glad we have met. I hope we shall pass many evenings and mornings too together."

He said, "Dr. Goldsmith is one of the first men we have as an author at present, and a very worthy man too. He has been loose in his principles, but he is coming right.

"Sir," said he, "there is a good deal of Spain that has not been perambulated; and a man of inferior parts to you might give us useful observations on that country." This pleased me. We sat till between one and two and finished a couple of bottles of port. I went home in high exultation.

SUNDAY 26 JUNE. I should have mentioned that Mr. Johnson said he thought I had a lucky escape from the Guards (*of* the Guards I mean),[1] as I was past those puerilities. I breakfasted with Douglas and dined with my landlord, which brought back the ideas of the beginning of winter. I then walked out to Islington and went to Canonbury House, a curious old monastic building, now let out in lodgings, where Dr. Goldsmith stays. I drank tea with him, and found him very chatty. He lamented however that the praise due to literary merit is already occupied by the first writers, who will keep it and get the better even of the superior merit which the moderns may possess. He said David Hume was one of those, who, seeing the first place occupied on the right side, rather than take a second, wants to have a first in what is wrong. I supped with Lord Eglinton.

This forenoon Mr. Cooper took me to the Chapel Royal, where I had a good seat and saw the King.

[1] Boswell (or Johnson) seems to be making a distinction between "escape" in the sense "effecting one's flight from" and the same word meaning "to succeed in avoiding." Since he had not been *in* the Guards, he could not escape *from* them.

MONDAY 27 JUNE. The Doctor breakfasted with me. At night Temple, Claxton, Bob, and I went to Vauxhall by water. Somehow or another, I was very low-spirited and melancholy, and could not relish that gay entertainment, and was very discontent. I left my company, and mounting on the back of a hackney-coach, rattled away to town in the attitude of a footman. The whimsical oddity of this, the jolting of the machine, and the soft breeze of the evening made me very well again.

TUESDAY 28 JUNE. Temple and I drank coffee at *Will's*, so often mentioned in *The Spectator*.

WEDNESDAY 29 JUNE. The Doctor and I dined at Dr. Pringle's. They dulled me by telling how I was to study at Utrecht for the winter.[2] The Doctor was weakly passionate with me for insisting on a gayer place. In the evening my friend Erskine and I walked a while in the Park. But I did not now set the same value on our *outré* flights, being really bent on pursuing a grave, prudent course.

THURSDAY 30 JUNE. My friend Temple, who is my great comfort in all difficulties, kept up my spirits by saying that I might go to Utrecht, and if I turned gloomy, might move to some more agreeable place.

FRIDAY 1 JULY.[3] Mr. Johnson, Dr. Goldsmith, and I supped

[2] Lord Auchinleck had promised that if Boswell would study civil (Roman) law for a winter at a Dutch university, and would promise to become an advocate on his return to Scotland, he might visit Paris and some of the German courts. Scots law, which is a quite different system from the English, makes a great deal of Roman law, and as the Dutch were the great masters of the subject, it was traditional for young men preparing for the Scots bar to study in Holland. Boswell's father and grandfather had both gone to Leyden. Utrecht had been selected for Boswell on the advice of Sir David Dalrymple, who had studied there.

[3] " . . . Dress neat and have Erskine at breakfast; and *Review* after calling on him. Read it with relish as your last. Be sensible yet free with Erskine . . . " (Memorandum for this day). The *Monthly Review* for June did contain a kindly review of the Erskine-Boswell *Letters*, written by the editor, Ralph Griffiths.

together at the Mitre. I had curious ideas when I considered that I was sitting with London authors by profession. Goldsmith wanted too much to show away. He tried to maintain that knowledge was not always desirable on its own account, as it was often attended with inconveniences. Johnson allowed that it might have disadvantages, but affirmed that knowledge *per se* was certainly an object which every man would wish to attain, although perhaps he might not choose to take the trouble necessary for attaining it.

He said that Campbell who wrote the *Lives of the Admirals* is a man of much knowledge and a very good share of imagination; and he told us a diverting enough anecdote, that his wife was a printer's devil (as the cant word is), and when she used to bring him the proof-sheets, he fell in love with her and married her.

He began to lash Churchill. I said he was not a fair judge, as Churchill was a sort of enemy of his.[4] "Sir," said he, "I am a very fair judge; because he turned my enemy when he found that I did not like his poetry. And, indeed, I have a better opinion of him now than I had at first, as he has shown more fertility than I expected. To be sure, he is a tree that cannot produce true fruit. He only bears crabs. But, Sir, a tree that produces a great many crabs is better than one which produces only a few crabs."

He said that Campbell's *Hermippus Redivivus* is very entertaining as an account of the Rosicrucian Philosophy, and furnishing some history of the human mind. If it were merely imaginary, it would be nothing at all.

He was repeating some of Thornton's burlesque ode, which he said had humour. He said *The Connoisseur* wanted matter.[5]

[4] Churchill had mentioned Johnson not unfavorably in *The Rosciad* (1761), but had attacked him bitterly and at length as Pomposo in the Second Book of *The Ghost* (1762).

[5] "Bonnell Thornton had just published a burlesque 'Ode on St. Cecilia's Day, adapted to the ancient British music, viz. the salt-box, the jew's-harp, the marrow-bones and cleaver, the hum-strum or hurdy-gurdy.' "—BOSWELL, in *The Life of Johnson. The Connoisseur* was a periodical by Colman and Thornton.

Before Johnson came in, Goldsmith repeated me some poetry of his own, which I liked, and I advised him to publish a volume. He said I had a method of making people speak. "Sir," said I, "that is next best to speaking myself." "Nay," said he, "but you do both." I must say indeed that if I excel in anything, it is in address and making myself easily agreeable. This evening passed very well. I was very quiet and attentive.

SATURDAY 2 JULY. I should have mentioned yesterday that Erskine and I passed a very good morning at Dempster's, where we met with Dr. Robertson[6] and Mr. Fordyce. I was in an excellent moderate lively humour, so that Robertson observed afterwards that I was "a pleasant man." Although our conversation that morning was admirable, yet I was hurt with a mixture of the Edinburgh familiarity and raillery. The Doctor breakfasted with me, and I brought him acquainted with my friend Douglas in Pall Mall. I met Lord Eglinton today, whom I have not seen for near a week. "Jamie," said he, "I hear you are giving up all your bad company. But I beg I may not be included in the number."

SUNDAY 3 JULY. I was too late of rising to go to church. I called upon Cochrane, who is just come from Utrecht; and he gave me a dreary account of it. However, I considered that after I am abroad, I can proceed as I please. I then passed all the day with Temple, who advised me by all means to acquire habits of study and self-command, and then I will be happy in myself and respected by others. At night we walked in the Park.

Lord Eglinton advised me much against going to a dull place. He said it would revolt me against improvement; as it would make study appear gloomy, and that I would grow very bad. I said application depended upon habit. "Yes," said he, "as a blacksmith's arm grows stronger by use. But except he have natural vigour, he may make his bread, but will never excel; and so it is with the mind, which if it has not natural strength, will never do a great deal." The Earl is very happy in his allusions; and this, I believe, may be pretty just. However, the mind may be covered up so many ways

[6] The well-known historian, Principal of the University of Edinburgh.

that its natural powers may be hid; so that by application alone we can judge how far a man is able to go in any branch of improvement. The Temples and I supped at Claxton's in our usual light, elegant way. It is very agreeable to me to have good English acquaintances in the Inns of Court.

MONDAY 4 JULY. I should have mentioned some days ago that Ogilvie the poet[7] is come to town, and breakfasted with me, and chatted away finely, and showed me much respect.

I breakfasted with Temple, and the Doctor and I drank tea with him. This afternoon I went and saw Mrs. Salmon's famous wax-work in Fleet Street.[8] It is excellent in its kind, and amused me very well for a quarter of an hour.

TUESDAY 5 JULY. I waited upon Mr. Johnson. He said he had looked at Ogilvie's poems, but he could find no thinking in them. "And what might be called imagination in them was, to be sure, imagination once; but it is no more imagination in him than the echo is sound. And his expression too is not his own. We have long ago seen white-robed innocence and flower-bespangled meads." In short, I found that Mr. Johnson had a poor opinion of my Aberdeenshire poetical friend. I cannot help, however, thinking that he has more merit than this great censor will allow. There is some thought prettily expressed in his poetry, with some elegance of imagination. And for his want of novelty, I fancy that can scarcely be had. Johnson indeed might answer that it *is* scarcely to be had, because true genius is very scarce.

At night Temple and his brother sat with me at my lodgings over some negus, and as they were in a frolicsome humour, and were tickling me and jumping about, we made a good deal of noise. Mr. Terrie, my landlord, whose character I have formerly delineated pretty strongly in this my journal, now showed himself in full force of low rudeness and passionate ill manners. He took it into his head that we had the maid with us, and came and rapped

[7] A Scots clergyman.

[8] "Mrs. Salmon was the Madame Tussaud of the last half of the 18th century" (Wheatley and Cunningham, *London Past and Present*).

furiously at the parlour door, calling my name. I went out and asked him what he meant. He bawled out that he would be in, and would turn us every one out. He then called the watch, desired him at his peril to bring more of his brethren, and said he charged us with a riot, and would send us to the roundhouse. However, when the watch returned, he began to dread the consequence of false imprisonment, and desisted. But he still behaved very impertinently. Unluckily, I had taken the parlour only for the mornings, and my being there at night was a matter of courtesy; for if it had been my own lodging, I could have got him severely soused. I luckily kept my temper and behaved with the greatest calmness. I determined, however, to quit his house, as Temple was of the same opinion.

WEDNESDAY 6 JULY. Those who would endeavour to extirpate evil from the world know little of human nature. As well might punch be palatable without souring as existence agreeable without care. I got up this morning before seven, finely agitated, and away I went to Mr. Cochrane, my merchant, with whom I breakfasted; and after telling my story, got him to advance me my next allowance, and carried him with me to the Plantation Office, where we found Terrie, with whom I talked over the affair. The dog denied he was drunk, and continued as obstinate as ever. When he had told Mr. Cochrane his story, Mr. Cochrane said, "I was afraid, Sir, that my friend had perhaps been in the wrong, but from your own account of the matter, I find that you have behaved very rudely; and, Sir, no gentleman can put up with such usage." I then demanded how much I owed him. He said, with a hard-faced impudence, "We go by English laws." "I wish, Sir," said I, "that you had English manners." He looked at me with a Northland sulkiness. As he would not then say how much was due, I left him.

By the advice of Mr. Coutts, I went to Sir John Fielding's, that great seat of Westminster justice. A more curious scene I never beheld: it brought fresh into my mind the ideas of London roguery and wickedness which I conceived in my younger days by reading *The Lives of the Convicts*, and other such books. There were whores and chairmen and greasy blackguards of all denominations assembled together. The blind Justice had his court in a back hall. His clerk, who officiates as a sort of chamber counsel, hears all the causes, and gives his opinion. As I had no formal complaint to make, he did not carry me in to the Justice, but told me that as my landlord had used me rudely, although I had taken my lodging by the year, I was only obliged to pay him for the time that I had lived in his house.

A great difficulty still remained. I had engaged Mr. Johnson and some more company to sup at my lodgings, and as my having the parlour of an evening was a favour from my landlord, I would by no means think of it. I went to Mr. Johnson and told him my distress. He laughed and bid me consider how little a distress it would appear a twelvemonth hence. He said that if my landlord insisted that the bargain should stand and the lodgings be mine for a year, that I could certainly use them as I pleased. "So, Sir," said he, "you may quarter two Life Guard men upon him; or you may get the greatest scoundrel you can find and send into his house; or you may say that you want to make some experiments in natural philosophy and may burn a large quantity of asafoetida in his house." Such ludicrous fertility can this great man throw out!

What amazing universality of genius has Mr. Johnson, who has written *The English Dictionary*, a work of infinite labour and knowledge; *The Rambler*, which contains a rich store of morality and knowledge of human life, embellished with great imagination; *Rasselas*, where we find a humane preceptor delighting the fancy and mending the heart; *The Life of Savage*, which is distinguished for perspicuity of narration, and abounds with excellent reflection; *The Translations of the Third and Tenth Satires of Juvenal*, and *The Prologue spoken at Mr. Garrick's Opening Drury-Lane Theatre*, which display strong poetical genius, strength of sentiment, keenness of satire, vivaciousness of wit and humour, and manly power of versification. His conversation, too, is as great as his writing. He throws out all his powers with force of expression; and he mixes inimitable strokes of vivacity with solid good-sense and knowledge, so that he is highly instructive and highly entertaining.

I made myself easy as to my company by letting them know that they were to consider the Mitre Tavern as my lodgings for that night. Accordingly, I ordered supper there, and I had as my guests Mr. Samuel Johnson, Dr. Goldsmith, Mr. Ogilvie, Mr. Davies, bookseller, and Mr. Eccles, an Irish gentleman of fortune, a good ingenious sort of man.[9] I was well dressed and in excellent spirits, neither muddy nor flashy. I sat with much secret pride, thinking of my having such a company with me. I behaved with ease and propriety, and did not attempt at all to show away; but gently assisted conversation by those little arts which serve to make people throw out their sentiments with ease and freedom.

Ogilvie was rapt in admiration of the Stupendous Johnson. Goldsmith was in his usual style, too eager to be bright, and held a keen dispute with Johnson against that maxim in the British Constitution, "The King can do no wrong"; affirming that what was morally false could not be politically true. And as the King might command and cause the doing of what was wrong, he certainly could do wrong. Johnson showed that in our Constitution the King is the head, and that there is no power by which he can be tried; and therefore it is that redress is always to be had against oppression by punishing the immediate agents. "The King cannot force a judge to condemn a man wrongfully; therefore it is the judge that we pursue. Political institutions are formed upon the consideration of what will most frequently tend to the good of the whole, although now and then exceptions may occur. Thus it is better in general that a nation should have a supreme legislative power, although it may at times be abused. But, then, there is this consideration: that if the abuse be enormous, Nature will rise up, and claiming her original rights, overturn a corrupted political system."

[9] Eccles, who appears nowhere else in the journal or the memoranda, was an acquaintance of Davies.

We talked of the geniuses in England in Queen Anne's reign. Mr. Johnson said he thought Dr. Arbuthnot the first man among them; as he was the most universal genius, being an excellent physician, a man of deep learning, and also great humour. "Mr. Addison was, to be sure, a great man. His learning was not very deep, but his morality, his humour, and his elegance of writing set him very high."

In recollecting Mr. Johnson's conversation, I labour under much difficulty. It requires more parts than I am master of even[1] to retain that strength of sentiment and perspicuity of expression for which he is remarkable. I shall just do my best and relate as much as I can.

He said that great parts were not requisite for a historian, as in that kind of composition all the greatest powers of the human mind are quiescent. "He has facts ready to his hand, so he has no exercise of invention. Imagination is not required in any high degree; only about as much as is used in the lower parts of poetry. Some penetration, accuracy, and colouring will fit a man for such a task, who can give the application which is necessary."

He said Bayle's *Dictionary* was a very useful work to consult for those who love the biographical part of literature; which he said he loved most.

We talked of Scotland. Ogilvie, who is a rank Scot, defended his native land with all the powers that he could muster up. I was diverted to see how great a man a London wit is in comparison of one of your country swans who sing ever so *bonnily*. Ogilvie said there was very rich country round Edinburgh. "No, no," said

[1] Probably "than even I am master of"—a humorous bit of vanity. In *The Life of Johnson* (1 July 1763), where he presents a parallel apology, he says, "In the early part of my acquaintance with him, I was so rapt in admiration of his extraordinary colloquial talents and so little accustomed to his peculiar mode of expression that I found it extremely difficult to recollect and record his conversation with its genuine vigour and vivacity. In progress of time, when my mind was, as it were, *strongly impregnated with the Johnsonian ether*, I could with much more facility and exactness carry in my memory and commit to paper the exuberant variety of his wisdom and wit."

Goldsmith, with a sneering laugh; "it is not rich country."[2] Ogilvie then said that Scotland had a great many noble wild prospects. "Sir," said Johnson, "I believe you have a great many noble wild prospects. Norway too has some noble wild prospects; and Lapland is remarkable for prodigious noble wild prospects. But, Sir, I believe the noblest prospect that a Scotsman ever sees is the road which leads him to England!"

We gave a roar of applause to this most excellent sally of strong humour. At the same time, I could not help thinking that Mr. Johnson showed a want of taste in laughing at the wild grandeur of nature, which to a mind undebauched by art conveys the most pleasing awful, sublime ideas. Have not I experienced the full force of this when gazing at thee, O Arthur Seat, thou venerable mountain! whether in the severity of winter thy brow has been covered with snow or wrapped in mist; or in the gentle mildness of summer the evening sun has shone upon thy verdant sides diversified with rugged moss-clad rocks and rendered religious by the ancient Chapel of St. Anthony. Beloved hill, the admiration of my youth! Thy noble image shall ever fill my mind! Let me travel over the whole earth, I shall still remember thee; and when I return to my native country, while I live I will visit thee with affection and reverence!

Mr. Johnson was exceeding good company all this evening. We parted at one. I was very happy. I am now reaping the fruits of my economy during the winter; and I have got rid of the narrowness and love of money which my frugality made me contract. I am afraid I have a disposition to be a miser. But I will combat this by my benevolence, which I have much of. I find I can cure narrowness by practicing free liberality. I have certainly had more enjoyment of my money this evening than if I had spent it in one of your splendid Court-end taverns[3] among a parcel of peo-

[2] Goldsmith had studied medicine at the University of Edinburgh, as Boswell points out in the *Life*.

[3] Fashionable taverns; taverns in the west end of London, where the Court was.

ple that I did not care a farthing for, and could receive no benefit from. This evening I have had much pleasure. That is being truly rich. And riches are only a good because men have a pleasure in spending them, or in hoarding them up. I have received this night both instruction and pleasure.

THURSDAY 7 JULY. Yesterday afternoon, before I went to the Mitre, I went to my lodgings in Downing Street, got Chetwynd, who has been a sort of prime minister to me, and packed up all my things. Then called up Mrs. Terrie and discharged what little debts I owed her. Poor woman! she seemed much affected and hoped I would not mention Mr. Terrie's behaviour. I told her that I should always speak well of her, but that I would most certainly represent her husband as a very rude unmannerly fellow, in whose house no gentleman could be safe to stay. And I advised her to make him give over letting lodgings, as he was very unfit for it. So curious a composition is the mind of man that I felt a degree of sorrow at leaving the room in which I had passed the winter, where I had been confined five weeks, and where this my journal and all my other little lucubrations have been written.

I then put my baggage into a hackney-coach, got into it myself, and drove to the Temple. My friend Temple was to go to Cambridge this morning, and kindly insisted that I should live in his chambers, which he has taken by the year. This morning he and I got up at five and breakfasted, after which I accompanied him to Bishopsgate Street, where the Cambridge machine inns. Nobody had taken a place besides himself, so I got in also, and rode till we were fairly out of London. The pleasing melancholy which possesses the mind when about to separate from a friend in the highest sense of the word had full power over us both. We recollected the many happy days which we have passed together, the long intimacy which has subsisted between us, and which continues as strong as ever. We expressed in the warmest manner our mutual cordiality and affection. We regretted that we were now to part for some years. (Good GOD! that is a very serious thought!) We promised to correspond as frequently as we could, and as fully. My friend advised me with much earnestness to study propriety of behaviour, and to acquire a habit of study, so that I might be independently happy and keep up the dignity of my character. He advised me to go to Utrecht, as my father wished me to do so. He said I might find it favourable to study and to getting rid of dissipation, so as to prepare me for travelling into the other parts of Europe with advantage. He said I might diversify the scene by trips to The Hague and other places; and if I found Holland very disagreeable, I might move away to some other place, such as Berlin or any other gayer capital. He said he hoped that I would return to England much improved, and that we might live much together with pleasure and comfort. He also advised me to follow virtue, which, upon the whole, would yield me most satisfaction. We then took leave of each other. My friend pursued his journey, and I walked calmly back to London.

This morning has left a very good impression upon my mind. I hope it will be pleasing and useful to me while I am abroad. True friendship is a noble virtue. None but finer souls can possess it. I am very happy in that respect.

And here I must relate an interview which I had with Captain Erskine. Two days before he left London, I went and sat a while with him. "I believe, Boswell," said he, "you don't consider me as a friend. You don't consider Dempster and me as you do Temple and Johnston. You would not tell us your deep secrets." I replied that I liked Dempster and him much, but that I considered them more as literary partners and as companions than as friends. That I had known Temple and Johnston very long and very intimately, and therefore could have the greatest confidence in them. That if I were to fall into misfortune and become void of mirth and lively conversation, that Dempster and Erskine would probably have their jokes and say, "Poor brute, he is turned an arrant idiot now," but that Temple and Johnston would then regard me as much as ever. I showed him the difference between a companion and a friend. A companion loves some agreeable qualities which a man may possess, but a friend loves the man himself. I was very happy to find that honest Erskine understood perfectly what I meant, and yet was very well pleased.

I joked and said that if I was going to be married, Temple and Johnston would be the men whom I would have in my room, with the door locked, a piece of cheese, two moulded candles, and a bottle of claret upon the mahogany table, round which we would sit in quiet attention consulting and examining the settlements. But that when the wedding was over and festivity was going on, then I would send for Dempster and Erskine, and we would be jolly and hearty and laugh and talk and make sport. Erskine said we ought to write now and then to each other a letter of good amusing facts, which I agreed to. We were both in excellent humour; so I took leave of him then, so as to carry off a good impression. "Farewell," said he, "may you be the best of travellers, and may you *perambulate Spain.*"

And now I was left in my chambers in the Temple, with little Captain Bob, who waited in town till he should receive some money, and then he was to go to Cambridge. This day passed pretty well.

FRIDAY 8 JULY. I dined with Lord Eglinton. M. de Léry, a Canadian, was there. I made a sort of shift to speak a little French with him. At night I met at the Queen's Head in Holborn with Chandler my printer and Flexney my bookseller. We had a bit of supper, and every man drank his bottle of Rhenish with sugar. Flexney is a fine, smart, obliging, merry little man, and Chandler an honest, well-behaved, good-humoured, laughing fellow. I thought an evening of this kind very proper after our *Letters* were fairly published. They admired me much, and I gave them all encouragement. We were very good friends, and very lively and chatty. They saw me half way home. They parted from me at the *Rolls*[4] in Chancery Lane, and Flexney said he hoped I would have

[4] The Rolls House, where the records of the Court of Chancery were kept, so called because the early records were literally rolls of parchment or vellum.

one for breakfast next morning; for Flexney is a punster of his kind. The connection between authors, printers, and booksellers must be kept up.

SATURDAY 9 JULY.[5] Master Robert and I agree pretty well. But as he is very young and has not read much, he can be a companion to me in no other way than in laughing and talking harmless lively nonsense, and this will not last long. I have unluckily let myself too much down by my extreme jocularity before him, so that when I want to assume any superiority over him, the little dog immediately rebels and cries, "Come, come, James, you are wanting to be the Great Man. But it won't do." Being *the Great Man* has been quite our cant word for some time. Bob is however so sprightly a boy that any little quarrels between us never last long. I wish I had kept him all along at a due distance, for too much familiarity, especially with those much younger than ourselves, is always attended with disagreeable circumstances. I really find this is what I am most apt to fall into; and as it often makes me look little and so gives me pain, I must guard against it.

I dined this day at Lord Eglinton's. Lord March, Dr. Robertson, Dr. Jardine, and Dempster were there. Before dinner my Lord was roasting me about my publications. "Gentlemen," said I, "I let my Lord go on a while. But only think of a man's criticizing books who can scarcely read his own name." This was so home to his Lordship, who reads so little, that it made him look very foolish for the space of a minute. He can bear no manner of licking, although he is much disposed to use the lash to others. But I am determined always to return him as much as he gives. The same genius and temper that qualifies a man to cut others make him sensible of being cut himself. Indeed, I think the less cutting which is used in a society, so much the happier will it be. Lord March acquitted himself very well today. He was polite, sensible and acute and even lively. The two lords went to Vauxhall, and I and the rest of the company went to the Green Park. But we gathered many more

[5] Boswell has made a marginal notation: "Was with Johnson, but remember nothing. See p. 659" (that is, the entry for Tuesday 12 July).

Scotsmen, and the conversation grew familiar to a detestable degree. I therefore left them; happy to be rid of their rude want of distinction, and to retreat to my calm retirement in the Temple.

SUNDAY 10 JULY. I went to Bow Church, the true centrical temple for the bluff citizens. I had many comfortable ideas. And here I must mention that some days ago I went to the old printing-office in Bow Church-yard kept by Dicey, whose family have kept it fourscore years. There are ushered into the world of literature *Jack and the Giants*, *The Seven Wise Men of Gotham*, and other story-books which in my dawning years amused me as much as *Rasselas* does now. I saw the whole scheme with a kind of pleasing romantic feeling to find myself really where all my old darlings were printed. I bought two dozen of the story-books and had them bound up with this title, *Curious Productions*.[6] I thought myself like old Lord Somerville or some other man of whim, and wished my whims might be all as quiet.

MONDAY 11 JULY. Claxton passed the evening with us. We were very well. Being in such company is improving, at any rate, whether much be said or not, as it accustoms me to decent and polite behaviour.

TUESDAY 12 JULY. I neglected last Saturday to mention that I called for Mr. Johnson. But there were several people with him, and I remember nothing that passed.[7] This night I supped

[6] This volume (with two other similar volumes which Boswell added later) is now in the Child Memorial Collection of chap books in the Harvard College Library. It bears the following inscription: "James Boswell, Inner Temple, 1763. Having, when a boy, been much entertained with *Jack the Giant-Killer* and such little story-books, I have always retained a kind of affection for them, as they recall my early days. I went to the printing-office in Bow Church-yard and bought this collection, and had it bound up with the title of *Curious Productions*. I shall certainly some time or other write a little story-book in the style of these. It will not be a very easy task for me; it will require much nature and simplicity and a great acquaintance with the humours and traditions of the English common people. I shall be happy to succeed, for he who pleases children will be remembered with pleasure by men."

[7] "I have been patrolling the City this forenoon. I have been upon the top of St. Paul's. And I have been buying a travelling-trunk from the famous trunk-

tête à tête with Sir William Maxwell at Howell's in Half Moon Street. I was in sound cheerful frame. I found myself much more prudent and less extravagant that when I last saw him in Annandale. We talked like cousins and friends, as the word goes. We sat till near two, and I went home and slept at his lodgings; a thing which disconcerted me.

WEDNESDAY 13 JULY. I took leave of Sir William, who was to set out next day for Paris. I walked round Grosvenor Square with Mr. Fordyce of Edinburgh, who gave me his opinion with regard to the steps proper for my brother Davy.[8] Fordyce is a sensible, clever, good-humoured man. But I must find one fault with all the *Poker Club*, as they are called; that is to say, with all that set who associate with David Hume and Robertson. They are doing all that they can to destroy politeness. They would abolish all respect due to rank and external circumstances, and they would live like a kind of literary barbarians. For my own share, I own I would rather want their instructive conversation than be hurt by their rudeness. However, they don't always show this. Therefore I like their company best when it is qualified by the presence of a stranger. This afternoon I had some low debauchery with girls who patrol the courts in the Temple.

THURSDAY 14 JULY.[9] Mr. Johnson and I met at the Mitre

---

maker at the corner of St. Paul's Church-yard. Sir William Maxwell of Springkell is in town. He is just going abroad, but will not stay long. He and I are to pass the evening quietly by ourselves. He is a genteel man. He is an Annandale knight. He will recall to me many pleasing ideas of his worthy mother, the English Border, diet loaf [a kind of cake], and nonjurant clergymen" (To John Johnston, 12 July 1763). Sir William's mother was Boswell's first cousin of the half-blood; that is, they had the same grandfather but different grandmothers.   [8] David was already planning to be a banker.

[9] "When you rise, speak grave to Bob, and try to make him ride. Write to Temple today to take him down by all means. As you had low profligacy last night and could not fulfill your purpose, think either to have one in Park tonight or to let it alone altogether. But, to be sure, you have time before nine, when you are to be with Johnson, to go and have one in Park . . . " (Memorandum for this day, most of it written in shorthand cipher).

by ourselves. He was in most excellent humour, though the night was very rainy. I said it was good for the vegetable part of the creation. "Ay, Sir," said he, "and for the animals who eat those vegetables, and for the animals who eat those animals." We had a good supper, which made us very comfortable.

I said, "You and I, Sir, are very good companions, but my father and I are not so. Now what can occasion this? For you are as old a man as my father, and you are certainly as learned and as knowing." "Sir," said he, "I am a man of the world. I live in the world, and I take in some measure the colour of the world as it moves along. But your father is a judge in a remote part of the country, and all his notions are taken from the old world. Besides, there must always be a struggle between a father and son, while the one aims at power and the other at independency." I told him that I was afraid of my father's forcing me to be a lawyer. "Why, Sir," said he, "you need not be afraid of his forcing you to be a laborious practising lawyer. That is not in his power. For, as the proverb says, 'One man may lead a horse to the water, but twenty cannot make him drink.' He may be displeased, but it will not go far. If he only insists on your having as much law as is necessary for a man of property, and endeavours to get you into Parliament, he is quite in the right."

We talked of denying Christianity. He said it was easy to be on the negative side. "If a man were now to deny that there is salt upon the table, you could not reduce him to an absurdity. I deny that Canada is taken, and I can support my assertion with pretty good arguments. The French are a much more numerous people than we; and it is not likely that they would allow us to take it.— 'But the Ministry tell us so.'—True. But the Ministry have put us to an enormous expense, and it is their interest to persuade us that we have got something for our money.—'But we are told so by thousands of men who were at the taking of it.'—Ay, but these men have still more interest in deceiving us. They don't want you should think they have gone a fool's errand; and they don't want you should think that the French have beat them, but that they have beat the French. Now suppose you should go over and see if it is so, that would only satisfy yourself; for when you come home, we will not believe you. We will say you have been bribed.—Yet, for all these plausible objections, we believe that Canada is really ours. Such is the weight of common testimony."

He said he would not advise a plan of study, for he had never pursued one two days. "And a man ought just to read as inclination leads him, for what he reads as a task will do him little good. Idleness is a disease which must be combated. A young man should read five hours every day, and so may acquire a great deal of knowledge."

He advised me when abroad to be as much as possible with men of learning; especially the professors in the universities, and the clergy. Indeed, I imagine myself that the clergy, especially the Jesuits, will be my most instructive companions. I hope to learn from them, and to settle by degrees into a composed and a knowing man.

I told Mr. Johnson what a strange mortal Macpherson was, or affected to be; and how he railed at all established systems. "So would he tumble in a hog-sty," said Johnson, "as long as you look at him and cry to him to come out. But let him alone, never mind him, and he'll soon give it over."

Mr. Johnson and I had formerly drank the health of Sir David Dalrymple, whom he gave as his toast. I this night read part of a letter from Sir David, since my informing him of it, in which he bid me assure him of the veneration which he entertained for the author of *The Rambler* and of *Rasselas*. He paid Mr. Johnson some very pretty compliments, which pleased him much.

Mr. Johnson considered reading what you have an inclination for as eating what you have an appetite for. But then I consider that a stomach which has fasted very long will have no desire for any kind of food. The longer it wants food, it will be the worse; and therefore we must not wait till an appetite returns, but immediately throw in some wholesome sustenance. The stomach may then recover its tone, and its natural taste may spring up and grow vigorous, and then let it be indulged. So it is with the mind, when by a long course of dissipation it is quite relaxed. We must recover it gradually, and then we can better judge what course of study to pursue. This must now be my endeavour. And when I go to Utrecht, I hope to make proficiency in useful literature.

When we went into the Mitre tonight, Mr. Johnson said, "We will not drink two bottles of port." When one was drank, he called for another pint; and when we had got to the bottom of that, and I was distributing it equally, "Come," said he, "you need not measure it so exactly." "Sir," said I "it is done." "Well, Sir," said he, "are you satisfied? or would you choose another?" "Would you, Sir?" said I. "Yes," said he, "I think I would. I think two bottles would seem to be the quantity for us." Accordingly we made them out.

I take pleasure in recording every little circumstance about so great a man as Mr. Johnson. This little specimen of social pleasantry will serve me to tell as an agreeable story to literary people. He took me cordially by the hand and said, "My dear Boswell! I do love you very much."—I *will* be vain, there's enough.

FRIDAY 15 JULY. A bottle of thick English port is a very heavy and a very inflammatory dose. I felt it last time that I drank it for several days, and this morning it was boiling in my veins.[1] Dempster came and saw me, and said I had better be palsied at eighteen than not keep company with such a man as Johnson. I sailed with Dempster up to the Navy Office, and then sailed back to his house in Manchester Buildings (for he has now got a house in town). It was a prodigious bad day. We got into a covered boat. But it was very horrid, as it rained and thundered all the time that we were going up the river. I dined with Dempster and his sister. We talked

---

[1] Since in the general estimation the character of drunkard is so firmly fixed on Boswell, it is well to remember that at this period of his life and for some years afterwards he drank very little; in fact, would have been regarded as abstemious by most of his acquaintances.

lively enough. But conversation without a subject and constantly mixed up with ludicrous witticisms appears very trifling after being with Mr. Johnson.[2]

SATURDAY 16 JULY. I carried Bob Temple with me to breakfast at Dempster's and introduced him to Dempster and his sister, where he was very well received. Since my being honoured with the friendship of Mr. Johnson, I have more seriously considered the duties of morality and religion and the dignity of human nature. I have considered that promiscuous concubinage is certainly wrong. It is contributing one's share towards bringing confusion and misery into society; and it is a transgression of the laws of the Almighty Creator, who has ordained marriage for the mutual comfort of the sexes and the procreation and right educating of children. Sure it is that if all the men and women in Britain were merely to consult animal gratification, society would be a most shocking scene. Nay, it would soon cease altogether. Notwithstanding of these reflections, I have stooped to mean profligacy even yesterday. However, I am now resolved to guard against it.[3]

At my last meeting with Mr. Johnson, he said that when he came first to London and was upon his shifts, he was told by a very

[2] "I have had a long letter from my father, full of affection and good counsel. Honest man! he is now very happy. It is amazing to think how much he has at heart my pursuing the road of civil life. He is anxious for fear I should fall off from my prudent system and return to my dissipated unsettled way of thinking; and in order to make him easy, he insists on having my solemn promise that I will persist in the scheme on which he is so earnestly bent. He knows my fidelity, and he concludes that my promise will fix me. Indeed, he is much in the right. The only question is how much I am to promise. I think I may promise this much: that I shall from this time study propriety of conduct, and to be a man of knowledge and prudence as far as I can. That I shall make as much improvement as possible while I am abroad, and when I return shall put on the gown as a member of the Faculty of Advocates and be upon the footing of a gentleman of business, with a view to my getting into Parliament" (To W. J. Temple, 15 July 1763: *Letters,* ed. C. B. Tinker, i. 21).

[3] The memoranda are not quite so firm: [" . . . Swear to have no more rogering before you leave England] except Mrs. ———— in chambers. . . . " (The bracketed words are in cipher.)

clever man who understood perfectly the common affairs of life
that £30 a year was enough to make a man live without being contemptible; that is to say, you might be always clean. He allowed
£10 for clothes and linen. He said you might live in a garret at
eighteen-pence a week, as few people would inquire where you
lodge; and if they do, it is easy to say, "Sir, I am to be found at such
a place." For spending threepence in a coffee-house, you may be
for hours in very good company. You may dine for sixpence, you
may breakfast on bread and milk, and you may want supper.

He advised me to keep a journal of my life, fair and undisguised. He said it would be a very good exercise, and would yield
me infinite satisfaction when the ideas were faded from my remembrance. I told him that I had done so ever since I left Scotland.
He said he was very happy that I pursued so good a plan. And now,
O my journal! art thou not highly dignified? Shalt thou not
flourish tenfold? No former solicitations or censures[4] could tempt
me to lay thee aside; and now is there any argument which can
outweigh the sanction of Mr. Samuel Johnson? He said indeed that
I should keep it private, and that I might surely have a friend who
would burn it in case of my death. For my own part, I have at
present such an affection for this my journal that it shocks me to
think of burning it. I rather encourage the idea of having it carefully laid up among the archives of Auchinleck. However, I cannot
judge fairly of it now. Some years hence I may. I told Mr. Johnson
that I put down all sorts of little incidents in it. "Sir," said he,
"there is nothing too little for so little a creature as man. It is by
studying little things that we attain the great knowledge of having
as little misery and as much happiness as possible."

[4] Especially from his father and Temple. In a letter to Johnston dated 8
February 1763 but probably written on 8 March, he says, "I received this day
a letter from my father, which I enclose for your perusal and beg you may
immediately return to me. It is in answer to my letter to him which you saw
and praised so much. You will observe how severe he is upon me, how he
treats my scheme of keeping a journal and sending it down, and in what a
light he considers you." See also Lord Auchinleck's letter of 30 May 1763,
below, p. 337. For Temple's deprecatory remarks, see above, p. 269.

He told me that he intended to give us some more imitations of Juvenal. When I some time ago mentioned the universality of Mr. Johnson's abilities and mentioned his Works, I am surprised how I omitted *The Idler*, which is a more easy and lively paper than *The Rambler*, but is distinguished for the same good sense and strong humour; and his tragedy of *Irene*, which is far from deserving the indiscriminate censure of frigidity which Dempster gave it in the beginning of winter, as may be seen in a former page of this my journal.[5] *Irene* is upon the whole, perhaps, no great play, but it abounds with sentiment and with poetry. I had not read it when I marked Dempster's criticism, and I have read it now; though, to be sure, I have read it with some partiality to the work of my valuable friend. It is surprising to think how much the judgment even of the greatest men may be biased in this way.

SUNDAY 17 JULY. The method of living in the Inner Temple, is, in my opinion, the most agreeable in the world for a single man. We have genteel agreeable chambers in that calm retreat, of which I have given a pretty full picture in a former part of my journal. When a Templar goes out, he shuts his door, which locks of itself, and takes his key in his pocket, so that he can come in and go out at all hours without giving disturbance to any mortal. If he has a servant, it is a piece of luxury, and he is somewhat easier. But he may do very well without one.

At present we have an old woman called Mrs. Legge for a laundress, who has breakfast set every morning, washes our linen, cleans the chambers, wipes our shoes, and, in short, does everything in the world that we can require of an old woman. She is perhaps as curious an animal as has appeared in human shape. She presents a strong idea of one of the frightful witches in *Macbeth*; and yet the beldame boasts that she was once as handsome a girl as you could clap your eyes upon, and withal exceedingly virtuous; in so much that she refused £500 from the late Lord Hervey. She was servant in many great families, and then she married for love a tall strapping fellow who died. She then owns that she married Mr.

[5] Above, p. 69.

Legge for money. He is a little queer round creature; and claiming kindred with Baron Legge, he generally goes by the name of *The Baron*, and fine fun we have with him. He serves as porter when we have any message to send at a distance.

To give a specimen of Mrs. Legge, who is a prodigious prater. She said to Bob this morning, "Ay, ay, Master Robert, you may talk. But we knows what you young men are. Just cock-sparrows. You can't stand it out. But the Baron! O Lord! the Baron is a staunch man. Ay, ay, did you never hear that GOD never made a little man but he made it up to him in something else? Yes, yes, the Baron is a good man, an able man. He laid a married woman upon the floor while he sent the maid out for a pint of porter. But he was discovered, and so I come to know of it." In this way will she run ye on as long as you please to hear her; and longer too, for rather than be silent, she'll talk to herself till any moderate tongue would be as dry as a crust of brown bread.

Bob this day was obliged to go down to Salisbury to attend the Assizes, where an appeal from a court martial of which he was one was to be tried. I took a seat in his chaise to Hounslow, and returned in it to town. I took in Lord Shelburne's steward, a sensible, well-behaved man, who has travelled a great deal. We got to town about one. I dined and went to the Temple Church. The afternoon turned very wet. I went to Dempster's to pass away the time. But time surely never passed on with so woeful a visage. A rainy Sunday in Scotland is but a type of the misery which we endured. Dempster and his sister were both low-spirited. I thought him a poor contemptible fool and her an ugly disagreeable wretch and myself the silliest and most dreary of mankind. I stayed till twelve at night. But there was nothing but the most gloomy wretchedness.

MONDAY 18 JULY. I called at Dempster's a minute to take off last night's gloom. He and Miss Dempster were very well today. At the head of St. James's Street I observed three Turks staring about in a strange manner. I spoke a little of English, French, and Latin to them, neither of which they understood a word of. They showed me a pass from a captain of a ship declaring that they were

Algerines who had been taken by the Spaniards and made slaves. That they made their escape, got to Lisbon, and from thence were brought to England. I carried them with me to a French house, where I got a man who spoke a little Spanish to one of them, and learnt that they wanted to see the Ambassador from Tripoli, who though not from the same division of territory, is yet under the Grand Signior, as they are. I accordingly went with him to the Ambassador's house, where I found a Turk who could speak English and interpret what they said; and he told me that they had landed that morning and had already been with the Ambassador begging that he would get liberty for them to go in an English ship to their own country; that he was to get them liberty from the Lords of the Admiralty; and that he had ordered them victuals. I gave them half a crown. They were very thankful, and my Turkish friend who spoke English said, "God reward you. The same God make the Turk that make the Christian. But the English have the tender heart. The Turk have not the tender heart."

I was anxious to have my poor strangers taken care of, and I begged that they might sleep in the house with the Ambassador. The landlady, a hard-hearted shrew, opposed this vehemently. "Indeed," said she, "I would not suffer one of 'em to lie in my beds. Who knows what vermin and nastiness they may have brought with them? To be sure I may allow them to sleep upon the floor, as they do in their own country; but for my beds, Sir, *as I'm a Christian*, I could not let them sleep in a bed of mine." Her Christian argument was truly conclusive. Abandoned wretch! to make the religion of the Prince of Peace, the religion which so warmly inculcates universal charity, a cloak for thy unfeeling barbarity! However, I was glad to have it fixed that they should sleep under a roof; and I begged my friend to take care that they lay comfortably.

I then went to Lord Eglinton's. He was in a serious humour. I said nothing but power or riches could engage the mind of man when he comes to a certain age, for that all other pursuits were frivolous and vain. "No, Jamie," said the Earl, "I cannot agree with you. My Lord Bute is a strong instance that power is not a great enjoyment, for you see he gave it up very soon."[6] "Beg your pardon, my Lord," said I, "my Lord Bute is no instance at all. He was not fit for power, and so he could not keep it. His complaining of power is just as if a very unskilful rider should be thrown off and then cry, 'This riding is a damned bad exercise.' Now it is not a bad exercise, but he is a bad rider. Now my Lord Bute, instead of getting upon one of his own Highland *shelties* and then upon a Galloway and so training himself by degrees, he must mount the great state-horse all at once, and take Sir Harry Erskine before him and John Home behind him, while you and Lord March and the rest of you were running like so many ostlers to hold his Lordship's stirrup, till he should mount, and every man getting half a crown for his pains: 'My Lord, you shall be a Lord of the Bedchamber'; and Lord Talbot being the servant out of livery, he must have a crown—be made Lord Steward. And so, my Lord, away goes this equipage prancing along till Wilkes, a Colonel of Militia, came by, beating his drum to the tune of *Britons*, *Strike Home*, and Churchill, a parson, with great zeal blowing the trumpet in Zion. The horse, frightened at this noise, fell to plunging and capering; when Sir Harry, with the perpendicular dignity of a prologue-maker, flew off at the ears, while Johnny Home came tragically off at the tail. And then his Bootship[7] came souse into the mire, crying out, 'My Lord Shelburne, I told you a year ago that I was to *take* this fall.' "

His Lordship did not seem over fond of this, and fell a whistling and turned absent, but I waked him out of his reverie, with a "My Lord! how do you like my nag?" I supped with him tonight for the last time this many a day, and bid him recollect our old days in his

[6] Bute had resigned and retired from public life in April, having been Prime Minister less than a year.

[7] "Bute" was presumably not pronounced "boot" in standard English, but in Cockney and Scots "Bute" and "boot" were pronounced exactly alike. Consequently a jack-boot (Bute's Christian name was John) was commonly used as a derisive emblem of the Premier; and the mob indicated his supposed intimacy with the Princess of Wales by parading a jack-boot and a petticoat through the town.

house when I was first in town. We took leave and agreed to correspond. Our parting had a mixture of sorrow in it.

TUESDAY 19 JULY. I breakfasted with Dr. Boswell, who said the longer he knew me the better he liked me. However, I found the honest Doctor had not the refined notions of friendship which I have. He said he would trust his journal to no man, from which I saw that he had no idea of people being so connected that they were but as one person. He talked, too, something about Jesus Christ's being his friend. I was quite provoked at this. "My dear Doctor," said I, "you would bring your religion into everything. I believe you will make it mend your breeches and sole your shoes by and by."[8] This was ludicrous. But I could not help it.

At eleven I went to St. Paul's Church;[9] walked up to the whispering gallery, which is a most curious thing. I had here the mortification to observe that the noble paintings in the ceiling of the Cupola are a good deal damaged by the moisture of winter. I then went up to the roof of the Cupola, and went out upon the leads, and walked around it. I went up to the highest storey of roof. Here I had the immense prospect of London and its environs. London gave me no great idea. I just saw a prodigious group of tiled roofs and narrow lanes opening here and there, for the streets and beauty of the buildings cannot be observed on account of the distance. The Thames and the country around, the beautiful hills of Hampstead and of Highgate looked very fine. And yet I did not feel the same enthusiasm that I have felt some time ago at viewing these rich prospects.

I called upon Mr. Johnson. Sir Thomas Robinson was with him. He said the King of Prussia[1] valued himself upon three things: upon being a hero, a musician, and an author. "Pretty well," said Mr.

[8] Dr. Boswell had left the Kirk and had joined the independent presbyterian sect of Glassites or Sandemanians. The Glassites followed various "primitive" practices, such as the kiss of peace and the love-feast or common meal.
[9] This really happened on the previous Tuesday: see the note on 12 July. His memorandum for this day shows that he had fallen far behind in posting his journal.   [1] Frederick the Great.

Johnson, "for one man. But as to his being an author, I have not looked at his poetry, but his prose is cursed stuff. He just writes as you would suppose Voltaire's footboy to do. He has such a share of parts as the valet might have, and about as much of the colouring of his master's style as might be got by transcribing his works." I could not help observing, "How much less parts is required to make a king than to make an author. For the King of Prussia is confessedly the greatest king now upon earth, and yet he makes but a very poor figure as an author."

Mr. Johnson has a curious-looking little man called Levett who stays with him. I asked Goldsmith what this man was. "Sir," said he, "he is poor and honest, which is enough to Johnson."[2] Levett went up with me to Mr. Johnson's library, which is four pair of stairs up,[3] in two garrets where Lintot (son to the famous Lintot) had his printing-house. I was much pleased to be in the library of this great man, where I saw a number of good books, but very dusty and confusedly placed. I saw too an apparatus for chemical experiments, of which it seems Mr. Johnson was fond. And I saw manuscript leaves scattered up and down which I looked upon with a degree of veneration, as they perhaps might be pieces of *The Rambler*, or of *Rasselas*. Mr. Johnson goes up to his library when he wants to study, as he will not allow his servant to say he is not at home when he is. I don't know but I may have mentioned before in my journal that he thinks that a servant's notions of truth would be hurt by such a practice. A philosopher may know that it is a mere form of denial, but few servants are such nice distinguishers. No place can be more favourable for meditation than such a retirement as this garret. I could not help indulging a scheme of taking it for myself many years hence, when its present great possessor will in all probability be gone to a more exalted situation.

[2] In *The Life of Johnson* Boswell describes Levett as "an obscure practiser in physic amongst the lower people, his fees being sometimes very small sums, sometimes whatever provisions his patients could afford him." On his death in 1782, Johnson wrote the most moving of all his poems.

[3] Over Johnson's chambers.

This was in a strong sense "building my castle in the air." I sat in all the afternoon at French and writing letters. Claxton came and passed the evening with me.

WEDNESDAY 20 JULY. Mr. Johnson, Dr. Boswell, and Mr. Dempster supped with me at my chambers. Johnson said pity was not a natural passion, for children are always cruel, and savages are always cruel. "Pity is acquired and improved by the cultivation of reason. We have no doubt uneasy sensations from seeing a creature in distress, without pity; for it is not pity unless you wish to relieve them." The Doctor was much shocked at this, who is exceedingly fond of his children and imagines them possessed of all human virtues as soon as they are born.

Mr. Johnson then abused Donaldson as a rogue who took advantage of the law to cheat his brethren. "For, notwithstanding of the statute, which allows only fourteen years, it has always been understood by *the trade* that he who buys a book from the author obtains a perpetual property; and upon that belief numberless bargains are made to transfer property after the expiration of the legal term. Now, Donaldson takes advantage here of people who have really an equitable right from usage; and if we consider how few books which they buy the property of succeed so well as to bring profit, we should be of opinion that fourteen years is too short a term. It should be sixty years."[4] "But," said Dempster, "Mr. Donaldson is anxious for the encouragement of literature. He brings books so cheap[5] that poor students may buy them." "Well," said Johnson, "allowing that to be his motive, he is no better than

[4] Down to 1710, there was no copyright law in England, but the publishers assumed a right in perpetuity. In that year a statute was passed fixing the period of copyright at fourteen years, with a power of renewal for another fourteen if the author were still alive at the expiration of the first term. The English book-sellers, however, continued to assert a power of copyright in perpetuity at common law, and, as Johnson says, continued to sell and exchange copyrights beyond the statutory limit. Donaldson challenged them by printing and selling books which were not covered by the statute. He was finally vindicated by a judgment of the House of Lords.

[5] Causes books to be so cheap.

Robin Hood, who robbed the rich in order to give it to the poor."
"Come," said the Doctor, "here is a health to bold Robin Hood."

Mr. Johnson said that the structure of David Hume's sentences
was quite French. "Now, that structure and the English structure
may in the nature of things be equally good. But if you allow
that the English language is established, he is wrong. My name
might have been Nicholson originally as well as Johnson; but if
you were to call me Nicholson now, you would call me very
absurdly."

Dempster argued on Rousseau's plan, that the goods of fortune and advantages of rank were nothing to a wise man, who
ought only to value internal merit. Replied Johnson: "If man
were a savage, living in the woods by himself, this might be true.
But in civilized society we all depend upon each other, and our
happiness is very much owing to the good opinion of others. Now,
Sir, in civilized society, external advantages make us more respected by individuals. A man who has a good coat upon his back
meets with a better reception than he who has a bad one. Sir, you
may analyze this, and say what is there in it? But that is not fair.
Pound St. Paul's Church into atoms, and consider every single
atom. It is, to be sure, good for nothing. But put all these atoms
together, and you have St. Paul's Church. So it is with human
felicity, which is made up of many ingredients, each of which may
be shown to be very insignificant. In civilized society internal goodness will not serve you so much as money will. Sir, you may make
the experiment. Go to the street and give one man a lecture of
morality and another a shilling, and see who will respect you most.
Sir, I was once a great arguer for the advantages of poverty, but I
was at the same time very discontented. Sir, the great deal of arguing which we hear to represent poverty as no evil shows it to be
evidently a great one. You never knew people labouring to convince you that you might live very happily upon a plentiful fortune. In the same way, you hear people talking how miserable a
king must be. And yet every one of them would wish to have his
place."

Dempster suggested that kings must be unhappy because they are deprived of the greatest of all satisfactions, free and agreeable society. Replied Johnson: "That is an ill-founded idea. Being a king does not exclude a man from society. Great kings have always been social. The King of Prussia, the only great king at present, is very social. Charles the Second, the last King of England who was a man of parts, was social; and our Henrys and Edwards were all social."

Dempster then argued that internal merit *ought* to make the only distinction amongst mankind. Replied Johnson: "Mankind have found from experience that this could not be. How shall we determine the proportion of internal merit? Had we no other distinction but that, we should soon fall a fighting about the degrees of it. Were all distinctions abolished, the strongest would not permit it long. And why not let people be distinguished by their bodily strength? But, Sir, as subordination is absolutely necessary for society, and contentions for it very dangerous, mankind (that is to say, all civilized nations) have settled it upon a plain invariable footing. A man is born to hereditary rank, or his obtaining particular offices gives him a certain rank. Subordination tends greatly to the happiness of men. There is a reciprocation of pleasure in commanding and in obeying. Were we all upon an equality, none of us would be happy, any more than single animals who enjoyed mere animal pleasure.

"Sir, if you want merely to support nature [for now I recollect some more about poverty and riches that must not be omitted], Sir William Petty[6] fixes your allowance at three pounds a year. But as times are much altered, we shall call it six. This will fill your belly, shelter you from the weather, and even get you a strong lasting coat, supposing it made of good bull's hide. Now, Sir, all beyond this is artificial taste, and is desired in order to obtain a greater degree of respect from our fellow-creatures. And, Sir, if six hundred a year procure a man more consequence and of course more happiness than six, the same proportion will hold good as to six thousand,

[6] A famous English political economist of the seventeenth century.

and so on as far as opulence can be carried. Perhaps he who has a large fortune may not be so happy as he who has a small one; but that must proceed from other causes than from his having the great fortune. For *caeteris paribus* he who is rich in a civilized society must be happier than he who is poor; as riches, if properly used (which it is a man's own fault if they are not), must be productive of the highest advantages. Money, to be sure, of itself is of no use, for its only use is to part with it. Rousseau and all these people who deal in paradoxes are led away by a childish desire of novelty. When I was a boy, I used always to choose the wrong side of a debate, because most ingenious things (that is to say, most new things) could be advanced upon it. Sir, there is nothing that you may not muster up some plausible arguments for. Why there, now, is stealing; why should it be considered as a crime? When we consider by what unjust methods property has been often acquired, and that what was unjustly got it must be unjust to keep, I see no harm in one man's taking the property of another from him. Besides, when we consider the bad use that many people make of their property and how much better use the thief would make of it, I think it is a very allowable practice. And yet, Sir, the experience of mankind has discovered stealing to be so very bad a thing that they make no scruple to hang a man for it."

I said that in civilized society I considered distinction of rank of so much importance that if I were asked to dine with the Duke of Norfolk or with the first man for genius and instructive and agreeable conversation, I should hesitate which to prefer. Dempster looked odd at this. But Johnson said, "To be sure, Sir, if you were to dine only once, and if it were never to be known where you dined, you would choose to dine with the first genius. But in order to gain most respect, you would dine with the Duke of Norfolk. For nine people in ten that you meet with would have a higher opinion of you because you had dined with the Duke; and the great genius himself would receive you better in some degree because you had been with the great Duke."

Thus did Mr. Johnson show upon solid principles the necessity

and the advantages of subordination, which gave much satisfaction to me, who have always had strong monarchical inclinations
but could never give strong reasons in their justification. The republican Dempster was fully silenced; but being obstinately fond
of his shallow views, he would not own his conviction.

I shall now mark some scattered fragments of Mr. Johnson's
conversation. He said that no man who lived by literature had lived
more independent than he had done. He said that through idleness
he had taken longer time to compose his Dictionary than was necessary. (The honest Doctor drank to him, returning him many thanks
for his noble Dictionary.) He said the Academy *della Crusca* at
Florence would not believe that his Dictionary had been done by
one man.

The Doctor left us at eleven; and when I accompanied him to
the door, he looked very serious and said, "There are few people in
Edinburgh who would keep company with this man"—meaning
Mr. Johnson, who had been somewhat of the bashaw to the Doctor.
Well may I reverse the Doctor's saying; for sure I am there are very
few people in Edinburgh with whom Mr. Johnson would keep
company.

I behaved extremely well tonight. I was attentive and cheerful
and manly. After Johnson went away, I took up the argument for
subordination against Dempster, and indeed after his hearty drub-
bing from the hard-tongued Johnson, he was but a feeble antagonist. He appeared to me a very weak man; and I exulted at the
triumph of sound principles over sophistry.

THURSDAY 21 JULY. I remember nothing that happened
worth relating this day. How many such days does mortal man
pass!

FRIDAY 22 JULY. Bob Temple returned last night. In his absence I had an opportunity of knowing how very comfortable and
independent chambers in the Temple are. Although Robert is a
good-humoured little fellow, yet he is a good deal selfish. He insists
upon having the best things to himself. He persisted, notwithstanding of my most serious remonstrances, in taking up his brother's

bed, which is in the bedchamber, while I was obliged to sleep in the study, where I was disturbed by the light breaking in upon me at the earliest dawn, as the windows have only half-blinds. Such things as these (trifling as they are) disturb human life; and really it is a bad thing in Robert to discover such dispositions.

I called upon Mr. Johnson. He said he did not like Dempster. He said he had not met with any man of a long time who had given him such general displeasure. That he was totally unfixed in his principles, and wanted to puzzle other people. I told him that Dempster's principles were poisoned by David Hume, but that he was a good, benevolent sort of man. "Sir," said Mr. Johnson, "I can lay but little stress upon that instinctive, that constitutional, goodness that is not founded upon principle. I grant you that such a man may be a very good member of society. I can conceive him placed in such a situation that he is not much tempted to deviate from what is right; and so, as goodness is most eligible when there is not some strong enticement to transgress its precepts, I can conceive him doing no harm. But if such a man stood in need of money, I should not like to trust him. And even now, I should not trust Mr. Dempster with young ladies, for there is always a temptation." Mr. Johnson was rather hard upon Dempster, but his reasoning is very just. Indeed, it is of the utmost consequence to be well established in good principles, without which there is no living in comfort.

Mr. Johnson said that Mr. Hume and all other sceptical innovators were vain men; and finding mankind already in possession of truth, they could not gratify their vanity by supporting her; and so they have taken to error. "Sir," said he, "Truth is a cow which will yield such people no more milk, and so they are gone to milk the bull." He said that all the things which David Hume has advanced against Christianity had passed through his own mind long before Hume wrote. He bid me always remember this, that after a system is well settled upon positive evidence, a few objections ought not to shake it. "The human mind is so limited that it cannot take in all parts of a subject; so that there may be objections raised against anything. There are objections against a *plenum*, and objections against a *vacuum*.[7] Yet one of them must certainly be true."

I told him that I was somewhat staggered with David Hume's argument against miracles: "That to believe a miracle, we must have such powerful testimony that it would be more improbable that the witnesses should be asserting a falsehood than that the miracle should be true; and that as yet we have no such testimony for miracles." Mr. Johnson said that the great difficulty of proving miracles should make us very cautious in believing them. He said that although God has made Nature operate by certain fixed laws, yet it is not unreasonable to think that he may suspend these laws in order to confer credit on a system highly beneficial to mankind. "Now, the Christian religion is a most beneficial system, as it gives us light and certainty, when before we were in darkness and doubt. The miracles which prove it are attested by men who had no interest in deceiving us, but who on the contrary were told that they should suffer tribulation, and did actually lay down their lives in confirmation of what they taught. And indeed for some centuries the heathens did not pretend to deny the miracles, but they said they were performed by the aid of evil spirits. This is a strong argument for them. Then when we consider the prior proofs by prophecies which have been so exactly fulfilled, we have very strong evidence. Supposing a miracle possible, we have as strong evidence for the miracles in support of Christianity as can be."

At night Mr. Johnson and I had a room at the Turk's Head Coffee-house, which he encouraged because the mistress of the house is a good civil woman and wants business. And indeed we found better entertainment here than at the Mitre, and as reasonable. I said that our reason for going to the Mitre was its being an orthodox tavern. Perhaps I may have mentioned this before.

Mr. Johnson said he loved the acquaintance of young people.

[7] That is, against either the theory that all space is full of matter or that parts of it are empty of matter.

"Because," said he, "in the first place, I don't like to think myself
turning old. In the next place, young acquaintances must last
longest, if they do last; and in the next place, young men have
more virtue than old men. They have more generous sentiments
in every respect. I love the young dogs of this age: they have more
wit and humour and knowledge of life than we had. But then the
dogs are not so good scholars. Sir, in my early years I read very
hard. It is a hard enough reflection, but a true one, that I knew almost as much at eighteen as I do now. My judgment, to be sure,
was not so good, but I had all the facts. I remember very well when
I was about five and twenty an old gentleman at Oxford said to
me, 'Young man, ply your book diligently now and acquire a
stock of knowledge; for when years come upon you, you will find
that poring upon books will be but an irksome task.' "

I complained to Mr. Johnson that I was much afflicted with
melancholy, which was hereditary in our family. He said that he
himself had been greatly distressed with it, and for that reason had
been obliged to fly from study and meditation to the dissipating
variety of life. He advised me to have constant occupation of mind,
to take a great deal of exercise, and to live moderately; especially
to shun drinking at night. "Melancholy people," said he, "are apt
to fly to intemperance, which gives a momentary relief but sinks
the soul much lower in misery." He observed that labouring men
who work much and live sparingly are seldom or never troubled
with low spirits. It gave me great relief to talk of my disorder with
Mr. Johnson; and when I discovered that he himself was subject
to it, I felt that strange satisfaction which human nature feels
at the idea of participating distress with others; and the greater
person our fellow sufferer is, so much the more good does it do
us.[8]

[8] The charge that Boswell's "melancholy" was an affectation assumed in
imitation of Johnson has been refuted so many times that it is hardly worth
calling attention to evidence against it. But it may be of some interest to
underline the point, not explicitly made in *The Life of Johnson,* that Boswell
first heard of Johnson's melancholy after telling Johnson of his own.

Mr. Johnson said that he had been writing and sauntering about for these many years and that no man had ever lived more independent who lived by literature.

After this, I shall just mark Mr. Johnson's *Memorabilia* as they rise up in my memory, observing, however, as much as convenient the times at which they were said.

He insisted again on subordination of rank. "Sir," said he, "I would no more deprive a nobleman of his respect than of his money. I consider myself as acting a part in the great system, and do to others as I would have them do to me. Sir, I would behave to a nobleman as I would expect he should behave to me were I a nobleman and he Sam. Johnson. Sir, there is one Mrs. Macaulay in this town, a great republican.[9] I came to her one day and said I was quite a convert to her republican system, and thought mankind all upon a footing; and I begged that her footman might be allowed to dine with us. She has never liked me since. Sir, your levellers count down only the length of themselves. They would all have some people below them; why not, then, have people above them? Suppose a shoemaker should claim an equality with Dr. Robertson, as he does with a lord. How would the Doctor stare. 'But, Sir,' says the shoemaker, 'I do great service to society. 'Tis true, I am paid for doing it. But so are you, Sir; and I am sorry to say it, better paid than me for doing something not so necessary, for mankind could do better without your history than without my shoes.' And so it would go on, were there no fixed, invariable external rules of distinction of rank, which create no jealousy, as they are allowed to be accidental."

He said Joseph Warton was a very pretty man and his *Essay on Pope* very agreeable.

He said Thomas Warton had also good parts, but being originally poor, had got a turn for mean company and low jocularity,

[9] Mrs. Catharine Macaulay published in this year the first volume of her *History of England from the Accession of James I to that of the Brunswick Line*. She visited Paris more than once with great honour, and in 1785 spent ten days with Washington at Mt. Vernon.

a very bad thing. "You ought no more to think it enough if you laugh than you think it enough if you speak. You may laugh in as many ways as you speak; and surely every way of speaking that is practised cannot be admired." This was a very good lesson for me, who am addicted to low jocularity. I am determined to get rid of it.

I told him that Sir James Macdonald had never seen him, but that he had a great respect, though at the same time a great terror, for him. "Sir," said he, "if he were to see me, it might lessen both."

He said he wished to visit the Western Isles of Scotland, and would go thither with me when I returned from abroad, unless some very good companion should offer when I was absent, which he did not think probable.

He said, "There are few people whom I take so much to as you"; and when I talked of leaving England, he said (with an affection that almost made me cry), "My dear Boswell! I should be very unhappy at parting, did I think we were not to meet again."

He maintained that a boy at school was the happiest being. I maintained that a man was more so. He said a boy's having his backside flogged was not so severe as a man's having the hiss of the world against him. He talked of the anxiety which men have for fame; and how the greater it is, the more afraid are they of losing it. I considered how wonderful it must be if even the great Mr. Johnson did not think himself secure. But indeed, I have seen people who even attempted to rail at him as a writer.

He drank a bumper to Sir David Dalrymple, whom he considers as a very worthy man, a scholar, and a man of wit. He never heard of him but from me. But he bid me let Sir David know his opinion, as he did not show himself much in the world, and so should have the praise of the few who hear of him.

SATURDAY 23 JULY. I wrote letters almost all day.

SUNDAY 24 JULY. I was at a church by Lombard Street, but I do not remember the name.[1] I dined at Douglas's. Captain Blair was there. He is a good worthy lad. But he has not enough of imagi-

[1] St. Mary Woolnoth, Allhallows, or St. Edmund.

nation, and mixes too much in the common rough intercourse of society for me. So we are very seldom together.

MONDAY 25 JULY. I went to the Robin Hood Society,[2] and took a great inclination to speak. An impudent blockhead who is a great orator there said that the prejudice against excise was a giant which he would combat; and he said he was for an excise upon principle. I rose up. "Mr. President! We have had the prejudice against excise represented to us as an enormous giant; and this gentleman, like the valiant Jack the Giant-killer, has stood forth to combat this giant. But, Sir, I wish he had been an abler antagonist, for although he has put himself a good deal in a heat and a good deal out of breath, the giant seems to me to be as strong and in as good health as when he began with him. Sir, the gentleman says he is a friend to excise upon principle. I don't know, indeed, how the gentleman's principles may be founded. A great many philosophers have considered self-interest as a very strong principle. I can see how a number of my countrymen may be friends to excise upon that principle, when there are so many excisemen's posts to be given away. Far be it from me to suspect that the honourable gentleman is actuated by any such views." I then gave them the commonplace arguments against excise, and when I sat down they gave me a thunder of applause. Yet I was so bashful and so distrustful that I thought I did but poorly. Whether or not I shall ever make a tolerable public speaker it is impossible to say. I should like it much. But when one does not succeed, it must be very galling. However, I shall not determine now, but wait some years.

TUESDAY 26 JULY. I called upon Mr. Johnson. It was a very wet day, and I complained that it made me gloomy. He said it was

[2] A debating society frequented by artisans and tradesmen. The subjects for debate were chosen a week in advance, there was no restriction on membership except the payment of sixpence at each meeting attended, and any man present could speak for five minutes with complete freedom of utterance. The Society got its name from the tavern in Butcher Row at which it held its meetings.

all imagination, which physicians encouraged. "For man lives in air as a fish does in water; so that if the atmosphere press heavy from above, there is an equal resistance from below." However, Mr. Johnson is a strong man, and not easily affected. I am sure the weather affects me. He said, to be sure, bad weather was hard upon those who were obliged to be abroad, and they could not labour so much as in good weather. But he said a smith or a tailor, whose work is within doors, would surely do as much in rainy weather as in fair. He owned that delicate frames might be affected, but not the common run of constitutions.

We talked of the education of children and what was best to teach them first. "Sir," said he, "there is no matter what you teach them first, any more than what leg you shall put into your breeches first. Sir, you may stand disputing which is best to put in first, but in the mean time your backside is bare. Sir, while you are considering which of two things you should teach your child first, another boy has learnt 'em both."

I should have mentioned last Sunday that I met the worthy Doctor[3] in St. Paul's Church-yard. We went into the King's Arms and had some white wine (though it was the forenoon) and drank most cordially to each other's health, as he was to sail for Leith next day, and we were parting for a long time, probably some years. Honest man! there is a great affection between us.[4]

[3] Dr. Boswell.

[4] "Were your indolent personage in my place just now, you would scarcely sit down to write a letter even to your most intimate friend. I shall briefly tell you the circumstances. I sat up all last night writing epistles of an uncommon kind—for me: that is to say, to my Lord President, my Lord Advocate, Mr. Fergusson of Pitfour, all about my important self; and indeed, Johnston, since I have taken it into my head to prefer the rational plan, I may, without joking, turn out a man of some importance. But only think of a man who has written these epistles, besides several more to Lord Kames, Commissioner Cochrane, and my mother; and who has been wandering all day up and down the cities of London and Westminster in quest of French servants and English poets—can such a man with any colour of reason be called upon to write a fresh letter, not altogether stupid, at seven o'clock in the evening?" (To John

WEDNESDAY 27 JULY. Captain Maxwell of Dalswinton and his brother Captain George and I dined together at Clifton's and were very merry. This was a cheap method both as to time and money of meeting with my cousins.

THURSDAY 28 JULY. I sat up all last night writing letters and bringing up my lagging journal, which, like a stone to be rolled up a hill, must be kept constantly going. I sat up some nights ago, I believe on Monday.[5] I was not a bit the worse for it this morning. Poor Bob was to leave me and go down to his brother at Cambridge. I accompanied him to Gray's Inn Lane and saw him into the fly. When I took leave of the little dog, not to meet, perhaps, for many years, it affected me. I dined with Mr. Cochrane.

I should have mentioned that Mr. Love breakfasted with me. I should also have mentioned some time ago that Peggy Doig, the mother of my little boy, is in town. I have seen her and advised her not to fall into such a scrape again. I really don't know how to talk on such a subject, when I consider that I led her into the scrape. However, it was not the first time, and she has been well taken care of.[6]

Johnston, 26 July 1763. "English poets" probably refers not to Dr. Johnson but to a copy of Gray's *Poems* which Temple had requested as a parting gift. See also below, 29 July 1763, *n.* 8.

[5] Boswell's inability to remember with certainty what happened only three days before will seem odd till one remembers that he was posting the journal several days later than this date, and probably without notes to guide him. His letter to John Johnston quoted in the preceding note shows that on 26 July he had brought the journal up only as far as 18 July.

[6] Boswell received word that he was a father in late November, 1762, soon after his arrival in London; and it would have been better from our point of view if he had seen fit to divulge the fact at once in his journal. The situation was of course different at the time the journal was being written. The one person who was reading it then (Johnston) was in on the secret; in fact, was Boswell's principal source of information about the child. But if Boswell had chosen to enter in the journal even a part of what he was putting into his letters to Johnston on the subject, it would have made his characterization of himself much more attractive than it now is.

Boswell records Peggy Doig's full name nowhere outside this entry. In

'At night, Mr. Johnson and I had a room at the Turk's Head. He said Swift had a higher reputation than he deserved; that his excellency was in strong sense, for his humour was (though very well) not remarkably great. He doubted if the *Tale of a Tub* was

---

his diary fragments for 1762 she figures merely as "P.," and that in cipher. She was probably a servant. He met her in Edinburgh in January, 1762 ("Adventure with P., the most curious young little pretty, but though all out— Good now! no opportunity for a long time"), and "made it out" on 3 March. By July he was conferring with Dr. Cairnie and the "Kirk Treasurer of the Canongate" about his responsibilities towards his expected child. He left Scotland shortly before the child was born, but his letters to Johnston are filled with queries and instructions. He has left £10 with Cairnie for the girl's use. When the child is born, Johnston is to stand godfather, and Grant (an Anglican clergyman) is to baptize it. By 14 December he has had a report from Johnston of the child's baptism, and is highly pleased. "I am really fond of the character of a father. I feel myself more dignified somehow. . . . GOD bless him." The boy is named Charles after the Royal Martyr, and turned over to a foster-mother. "By all means let the nurse give my child the surname of Boswell immediately. I am not ashamed of him. And I am not afraid of its being known. Besides, the Kirk Treasurer of the Canongate noised it about." Davy (Boswell's fourteen-year-old brother) is to see him. Finally, just before leaving England Boswell wrote to Johnston as follows: "You can scarcely believe what pleasure I received from the description of your Sunday's visit at the residence of Charles. The circumstances delight my romantic imagination. Fancy herself could not form finer ideas of the scene, the time, the persons, the situation. And then your taking my boy in your arms and feeling your heart warm to him is an exquisite stroke. Poor little creature! I wish from my heart that I had seen him before I left England. His resembling me is a most agreeable thing. I am positive that he is my own. He shall always find me an affectionate father, and I must indulge many fond—perhaps foolish—ideas of his making a figure in life. I am determined that nothing shall be wanting to accomplish him for whatever his genius leads him to. . . . I suppose he may remain where he is for a year or two longer, as his nurse is a good creature and loves him. After that time I shall send him to some school at a pleasant village in England, where his parentage shall not be known, as the scoffing of his companions might break his spirit."

Boswell never saw Charles, for he died in late February, 1764, while Boswell was in Utrecht. The memoranda of that period show Boswell to have been greatly distressed.

Swift's, as he never owned it, and as it is much above his usual manner. He said that Addison was a great man. (This I now remember was illustrated in a former conversation.)

We then talked of Me. He said that I was very forward in knowledge for my age; that a man had no reason to complain who held a middle place and had many below him; and that perhaps I had not six above me. Perhaps not one. He did not know one. This was very high. I asked him, if he was my father, and if I did well at the law, if he would be pleased with me. "Sir," said he, "I should be pleased with you whatever way of life you followed, since you are now in so good a way. Time will do all that is wanting. Indeed, when you was in the irreligious way, I should not have been pleased with you." I returned him many thanks for having established my principles.

He said that human experience, which was constantly contradicting theory, was the great test of truth. He said that the experience built upon the discoveries of a great many minds was always of greater weight than the mere workings of one mind, which can do little of itself. "There is not so poor a book in the world but would be a prodigious work were it wrought out entirely by a single mind without the aid of prior investigators. The French are so superficial because they are not scholars, and so proceed upon the mere power of their own minds; and we see how very little power they have.

"As to the Christian religion, Sir, we have a balance in its favour from the number of great men who have been convinced of its truth after a serious consideration of it. Grotius[7] was an acute man, a lawyer, a man accustomed to examine evidence, and he was convinced; and he was no recluse man, but a man of the world, who surely had no bias towards it. Sir Isaac Newton set out as an infidel, but came to be a very firm believer."

[7] Hugo Grotius (van Groot), 1583–1645, the great Dutch jurist. Johnson had already (24 May 1763) recommended his treatise on the Christian evidences.

Mr. Johnson persisted in advising me to go to Spain. I said it would divert him to get a letter from me dated at Salamanca. "I love the University of Salamanca," said he, "for when the Span-iards were in doubt if they should conquer the West Indies, the University of Salamanca gave it as their opinion that they should not."

We talked how wretched a writer Derrick was. "To be sure, Sir," said he. "But it was his being a literary man that got him made King of Bath. Sir, he has nothing to say for himself but that he is a writer. Had Derrick not been a writer, he must have been sweeping the crosses in the streets and asking halfpence from everybody that passed."

I begged Mr. Johnson's advice as to my method of study at Utrecht. "Come," said he, "let us make a day of it. Let us go down to Greenwich and dine." Accordingly Saturday was fixed for that jaunt, if a sail on the river may be so expressed. It must be some-thing curious for the people in the Turk's Head Coffee-house to see this great man and poor Me so often together by ourselves. My vanity is much flattered.

As we walked along the Strand tonight, arm in arm, a woman of the town came enticingly near us. "No," said Mr. Johnson, "no, my girl, it won't do." We then talked of the unhappy situation of these wretches, and how much more misery than happiness, upon the whole, is produced by irregular love. He parted from me at the Temple Gate, as he always does.

And here I must record perhaps the most curious singularity that ever a man had. When Mr. Johnson's wife was alive, she brought into the house as a companion Miss Williams, an amiable, ingenious woman who had attained a remarkable knowledge of the modern languages. This lady's eyes were tender. The disorder increased and ended at last in a gutta serena, so that she became stone-blind. Mrs. Johnson died, and while Mr. Johnson continued to keep house, Miss Williams remained with him. When he took to chambers in the Temple, Miss Williams then went to a lodging of her own. But Mr. Johnson is never a night without seeing her. Let him be never so late in company, Miss Williams sits up till he comes and drinks tea with her. I believe Miss Williams is supported chiefly by Mr. Johnson's generosity, and I believe nobody has ever had the folly or the malice to suspect anything criminal between them. He has promised to introduce me there soon.

FRIDAY 29 JULY. Sound was the sleep which I enjoyed last night. As I am now determined to humour my father as much as I can, and may in time, perhaps, apply to the law in Scotland, I have written to Lord President, to whom I said that experience had now taught me that my father is as wise as myself, and that I am to follow his plan of life. I thank his Lordship for his former good offices while I was an idler, and hope he will not withhold them from me when I endeavour to be a man of business. To Pitfour I say that his prophecy that I would return to the law will be fulfilled; and I say that if a saint nowadays obtained the gift of prophecy, none can have a better chance for it than Pitfour. I bid him tell his son to hasten on at the bar lest he be overtaken by a younger man. To Lord Advocate I talk in the easy style of a companion, as he and I were always easy, and mention with satisfaction my having more rational views. Such is the substance of these letters, which I expressed very neatly. I am sure they will do good, as they will be shown, or at least quoted, to my father. I have touched every man on the proper key, and yet have used no deceit.[8]

SATURDAY 30 JULY. Mr. Johnson and I took a boat and sailed down the silver Thames. I asked him if a knowledge of the Greek

[8] See above, 26 July 1763, *n.* 4. The suggestion for this prudent course of action had come from Lord Auchinleck himself: "I should have mentioned to you that it will be proper for you to write to my Lord Advocate a letter of compliment and to let him know your schemes. A letter too to my Lord President will be well taken" (to Boswell, 18 June 1763; repeated in letter of 23 July 1763). "My Lord President" (Robert Dundas of Arniston, Lord President of the Court of Session) presided over the bench of fifteen judges of which Boswell's father was one. The American equivalent would be something like Chief Justice of the Supreme Court.

and Roman languages was necessary. He said, "By all means; for they who know them have a very great advantage over those who do not. Nay, it is surprising what a difference it makes upon people in the intercourse of life which does not appear to be much connected with it." "And yet," said I, "people will go through the world very well and do their business very well without them." "Why," said he, "that may be true where they could not possibly be of any use; for instance, this boy rows us as well without literature as if he could sing the song which Orpheus sung to the Argonauts, who were the first sailors in the world." He then said to the boy, "What would you give, Sir, to know about the Argonauts?" "Sir," said he, "I would give what I have." The reply pleased Mr. Johnson much, and we gave him a double fare. "Sir," said Mr. Johnson, "a desire of knowledge is the natural feeling of mankind; and every man who is not debauched would give all that he has to get knowledge."

We landed at the Old Swan and walked to Billingsgate, where we took oars and moved smoothly along the river. We were entertained with the immense number and variety of ships that were lying at anchor. It was a pleasant day, and when we got clear out into the country, we were charmed with the beautiful fields on each side of the river.

We talked of preaching, and of the great success that the Methodists have. He said that was owing to their preaching in a plain, vulgar manner, which was the only way to do good to common people, and which men of learning and genius ought to do, as their duty; and for which they would be praised by men of sense. He said that talking of drunkenness as a crime, because it debases reason, the noblest faculty of man, would do no service to the vulgar. But to tell them that they might have died in their drunkenness, and show how dreadful that would be, would affect them much. He said when the Scotch clergy give up their homely style, that religion must decay.

When we got to Greenwich, I felt great pleasure in being at the place which Mr. Johnson celebrates in his *London: a Poem.* I had the poem in my pocket, and read the passage on the banks of the Thames, and literally "kissed the consecrated earth."[9]

Mr. Johnson said that the building at Greenwich[1] was too magnificent for a place of charity, and too much detached to make one great whole.

He said Buchanan was a very fine poet. That he first gave the different perfections of the goddesses to a lady; but that Johnston improved upon it, by making her also free from their defects.[2]

He said he had country lodgings at Greenwich, and used to compose in the Park; particularly, his *Irene*.

We walked about and then had a good dinner (which he likes very well), after which he run over the grand scale of human knowledge, advised me to select some particular branch to excel in, but to have a little of every kind. We then came up by water. I was a little discomposed even by this small excursion, and felt warm comfort at being again in London.[3]

[9]   On Thames's banks in silent thought we stood,
             Where Greenwich smiles upon the silver flood;
             Struck with the seat which gave Eliza birth,
             We kneel, and kiss the consecrated earth.

As Professor Tinker points out (*Letters of Boswell*, i. 39) a letter to Sir David Dalrymple, written this morning while Boswell was waiting for word that Johnson was ready to start, shows him preparing himself for this scene.

[1] Greenwich Hospital, begun by Charles II as a royal palace, completed by Queen Mary as a hospital for disabled sailors. Sir Christopher Wren was the architect. In 1873 it was assigned to the Royal Naval College for the higher education of naval officers.

[2] George Buchanan and Arthur Johnston were both Scotsmen and both wrote Latin verse.

[3] The manuscript bears the following marginal note: "Park not equal to Fleet Street—An elegant man of fashion, smell of flambeau more agreeable than breath of May—Shivering on water," which in *The Life of Johnson* is expanded into four brilliant paragraphs. This note is of extraordinary interest, for the "elegant man of fashion" who preferred the smell of a flambeau at a playhouse to the fragrance of a May evening in the country is identified by Boswell in the *Life* as Sir Michael Le Fleming, whom he appears not to have met until 1787. We therefore see Boswell, at a distance of upwards of twenty-

We supped at the Turk's Head. Mr. Johnson said, "I must see thee go; I will go down with you to Harwich." This prodigious mark of his affection filled me with gratitude and vanity. I gave him an account of the family of Auchinleck, and of the Place. He said, "I must be there, and we will live in the Old Castle;[4] and if there is no room remaining, we will build one." This was the most pleasing idea that I could possibly have: to think of seeing this great man at the venerable seat of my ancestors. I had been up all last night yet was not sleepy.

SUNDAY 31 JULY. In the forenoon I was at a Quakers' meeting in Lombard Street, and in the afternoon at St. Paul's, where I was very devout and very happy. After service, I stood in the center and took leave of the church, bowing to every quarter. I cannot help having a reverence for it. Mr. Johnson says the same. Mr. Johnson said today that a woman's preaching was like a dog's walking on his hinder legs. It was not done well, but you were surprised to find it done at all.

MONDAY 1 AUGUST. I have nothing more to record but that Dempster and I went upon the Thames and saw the watermen row for Doggett's Badge and other prizes.[5] We saw most excellent sport.

---

five years, *remembering* details which he had failed to record when he posted the journal. The paragraph which expands "Shivering on water" ought to be quoted here: "We stayed so long at Greenwich that our sail up the river in our return to London was by no means so pleasant as in the morning, for the night air was so cold that it made me shiver. I was the more sensible of it from having sat up all the night before recollecting and writing in my journal what I thought worthy of preservation; an exertion which, during the first part of my acquaintance with Johnson, I frequently made. I remember having sat up four nights in one week without being much incommoded in the day-time."

[4] "The Place" means Auchinleck House and its surroundings. There were three mansions at Auchinleck: the "Old Castle," a ruin; the "Old House," a sixteenth-century building, until 1762 the family dwelling; and Lord Auchinleck's new Adam-style house, recently opened.

[5] Thomas Doggett, actor, on 1 August 1716, in celebration of the accession of the Hanoverian line to the throne, gave an orange-coloured livery and a badge representing Liberty "to be rowed for by six watermen that are out of

TUESDAY 2 AUGUST. I should have mentioned yesterday that I dined with Coutts, where we were very merry. Friday the fifth of this month was now fixed as the day of my departure. I had taken leave of Dr. Pringle, and had all my letters of recommendation and other things prepared. Mr. Johnson did me the honour to come and see me at my chambers this forenoon. Dempster too came in.

Johnson said that he always felt an inclination to do nothing. I said it was strange to think that the most indolent man in Britain had written the most laborious work, *The English Dictionary*. He said he took ten years to do it; but that if he had applied properly, he might have done it in three.

In the afternoon he carried me to drink tea with Miss Williams, who has a snug lodging in Bolt Court,[6] Fleet Street. I found her a facetious, agreeable woman, though stone-blind. I was cheerful, and well received. He then carried me to what he called his walk, which is a paved long court overshadowed by some trees in a neighbouring garden. There he advised me when fixed in a place abroad to read with a keenness after knowledge, and to read every day an hour at Greek. And when I was moving about, to read diligently the great book of mankind. We supped at the Turk's Head. I was somewhat melancholy, but it went off. Mr. Johnson filled my mind with so many noble and just sentiments that the Demon of Despondency was driven away.

WEDNESDAY 3 AUGUST. I should have mentioned that on Monday night, coming up the Strand, I was tapped on the shoulder by a fine fresh lass. I went home with her. She was an officer's

---

their time within the year past. They are to row from London Bridge to Chelsea. It will be continued annually on the same day for ever." The Badge is, in fact, still rowed for, the management of Doggett's fund being entrusted to the Fishmongers' Company. See the charming fantasy by Dr. W. S. Lewis in *The Virginia Quarterly Review*, 25 (1949): 66–73, where it is suggested that the prize may have been won by the boy whom Johnson had quizzed about the Argonauts two days before.

[6] Where Johnson himself later lived.

daughter, and born at Gibraltar. I could not resist indulging my-self with the enjoyment of her. Surely, in such a situation, when the woman is already abandoned, the crime must be alleviated, though in strict morality, illicit love is always wrong.

I last night sat up again, but I shall do so no more, for I was very stupid today and had a kind of feverish headache. At night Mr. Johnson and I supped at the Turk's Head. He talked much for restoring the Convocation of the Church of England to its full pow-ers, and said that religion was much assisted and impressed on the mind by external pomp. My want of sleep sat heavy upon me, and made me like to nod, even in Mr. Johnson's company. Such must be the case while we are united with flesh and blood.

THURSDAY 4 AUGUST. This is now my last day in London before I set out upon my travels, and makes a very important pe-riod in my journal. Let me recollect my life since this journal began. Has it not passed like a dream? Yes, but I have been attain-ing a knowledge of the world. I came to town to go into the Guards. How different is my scheme now! I am now upon a less pleasur-able but a more rational and lasting plan. Let me pursue it with steadiness and I may be a man of dignity. My mind is strangely agitated. I am happy to think of going upon my travels and seeing the diversity of foreign parts; and yet my feeble mind shrinks somewhat at the idea of leaving Britain in so very short a time from the moment in which I now make this remark. How strange must I feel myself in foreign parts. My mind too is gloomy and dejected at the thoughts of leaving London, where I am so com-fortably situated and where I have enjoyed most happiness. How-ever, I shall be the happier for being abroad, as long as I live. Let me be manly. Let me commit myself to the care of my merciful Creator.

THE END OF MY JOURNAL BEFORE MY TRAVELS.

APPENDIX I

Scheme of Living Written at the
White Lion Inn, Water Lane, Fleet Street, the Morning
After My Arrival in London, 1762.[1]

My allowance from my father is £25 every six weeks; in all £200 a year. To support the rank of a gentleman with this is difficult. Yet I hope to do it in the following manner.

A genteel lodging in a good part of the town is absolutely necessary. These are very dear. None proper for me can be had under two guineas or a guinea and a half. But if I take it for a year, I think I may have it for £50.

As a man who is known to be at large upon the town and to have no home where he can dine, is exposed to the solicitations of expensive company, I would by all means have a regular place to dine at. If the house in which I lodge is convenient for that, so much the better. If not, I must go somewhere else. I would choose to make a bargain with a good decent family who have every day a tolerable dinner and who should make no difference on my account, that I might dine there when I had no other place, and for each time that I dined, pay them 1s. 6d.; or if they would not choose that, I would pay them just 1s. a day. I should endeavour to make myself as little troublesome and as agreeable as possible. The whole charge of this article may be £18. I would choose to breakfast in my own room. I would have a tea-chest in which I would lock up my tea and sugar. The maid would bring me in so much bread every morning and so much butter a week. I would have seldom anybody to breakfast with me, and when they came it

[1] This heading was written later than the document itself; probably a good deal later, for the name of the inn was actually the Black Lion. Indeed, the Scheme was probably not written at the inn at all, but at the home of Douglas the surgeon (see above, p. 45).

335

should be by invitation. And I would sometimes breakfast abroad. I reckon breakfast may be £9.

I would only have a fire in my dining-room and that for seven months a year, which may be 20s. a month. In all the year, £7.

I would burn wax candles. They have a finer light, and I can lock them up without offence, having those for immediate use always in a stand in my room. I reckon this may be £6.

I would have a suit of clean linens every day, which may be 4d. a day. I shall call it for the year £7.

I would have my hair dressed every day, or pretty often, which may come to £6.

I must have my shoes wiped at least once a day and sometimes oftener. I reckon this for the year £1.

To be well dressed is another essential article, as it is open to everybody to observe that. I allow for clothes £50.

Stockings and shoes I reckon for the year £10.

The whole of my necessary expense is as follows:

Lodging	£50
Dinner	18
Breakfast	9
Candles	6
Coals	7
Washing	6
Shoe-cleaning	1
Clothes	50
Stockings and shoes	10
In all,	£157[2]

£200
157
———
43

[2] Really £164, for in making his summary he has run Washing and Hair-dressing together, entering the heading for one opposite the sum budgeted for the other. Boswell's arithmetic remained shaky throughout his life.

By this calculation, I have just £43 left for coach-hire, diversion, and the tavern, which I will find a very slight allowance. However, I hope to conform my method of living to my circumstances. They may grow better in time.

If I get a commission in the Guards, I shall then have about £90 a year more, which will make me pretty easy.

There is one circumstance a little hard upon me, which is that I have encroached upon this quarter's allowance by my journey to town, the expense of which comes to £11. I must endeavour to get my father to pay this. I hope Dr. Pringle, his great friend, will think it reasonable and will assist me. If I cannot get that, I must live private for the first six weeks and endeavour to save it. In short, I will find myself hard put to it to live as I could wish without exceeding my allowance. But I am determined not to contract a shilling of debt; and as my father has now made me my own master, I shall be upon honour to do well.

APPENDIX II[1]

Auchinleck, 30 May 1763

JAMES:

My last letter, which was wrote in February, let you know how much I was displeased with some particulars of your conduct which had come to my knowledge. The answer you wrote me was telling me in pretty plain language you contemned what I could say or do. When I thereafter came to the country, I found that what I represented would probably be the consequence of your strange journals actually had happened. Mr. Reid came here, informed us he had seen them, and, having a good memory, repeated many

[1] See above, 8 June 1763 and *n.* 8 on that entry.

things from them.[2] He made these reflections, that he was surprised a lad of sense and come to age should be so childish as keep a register of his follies and communicate it to others as if proud of them. He added that if the thing were known, no man would choose to keep company with you, for who would incline to have his character traduced in so strange a manner, and this frequently after your receiving the greatest civilities and marks of friendship? When I went on my Circuit to Jedburgh, I received a fresh mortification. The news[3] were brought to me, and therein was contained an account of the publishing some letters of yours; and one of them was insert as a specimen. I read it, and found that though it might pass between two intimate young lads in the same way that people over a bottle will be vastly entertained with one another's rant, it was extremely odd to send such a piece to the press to be perused by all and sundry. The gentlemen at Jedburgh imagined and endeavoured to persuade me that it had been somebody who put in that article in the news by way of jest, for they could not suspect the letter to be genuine. At the same time they said it was a cruel jest, as it was exposing you. From Jedburgh I came to Dumfries, where I found that while you were in that country you had given yourself up to mimicry, and had at different times and places taken off (as you called it) Lord Dumfries, Sir George Preston, and Logan.[4] This, too, you may believe behoved to give me vast pain. To make a mock of others is not praiseworthy; besides, such things are seldom concealed. You create enemies to yourself and even to your

---

[2] Boswell had sent his journal of his Harvest Jaunt, 1762, to Mr. McQuhae, as he later sent the London journal to Johnston. McQuhae, who was living at the time with the Reverend George Reid, Minister of Ochiltree, had injudiciously allowed Mr. Reid to get a sight of it.   [3] Newspaper.

[4] This occurred at Springkell, the seat of Sir William Maxwell, on 12 October 1762, and was pretty public: "After dinner we sung as before, and in the evening we had a dance. I discovered that Miss Gilpin was an excellent mimic. So I made a fair exchange with her, and gave her Logan and Lord Dundonald and Sir George Preston and Lord Dumfries for as many of her acquaintances. I contrived to make our personages talk together, which was a most ludicrous scene" (Boswell's "Journal of My Jaunt, Harvest, 1762").

friends, it being the way of the world to resent such impertinences against all who show any countenance to the person guilty of them. To all which I may add that mimicry has been justly considered as the lowest and meanest kind of wit.

After mentioning these particulars, if you'll at all reflect, you must be sensible what I suffer by your means. Is it not hard that after all the tenderness I have shown you and the expense and labour I have bestowed upon you, you should not only neglect your own reputation, but do what you can to bring me to shame on your account? The offices I hold entitle me to some respect, and I get it beyond my merit from all that know me except from you, who by the laws of God, nature, gratitude, and interest are bound to do what you can to make me happy, in place of striving, as it were, to find out the things will be most galling to me and making these your pursuit. What I have said will account for my not having wrote you these three months. Indeed, finding that I could be of no use to you, I had determined to abandon you, to free myself as much as possible from sharing your ignominy, and to take the strongest and most public steps for declaring to the world that I was come to this resolution. But I have been so much importuned by your excellent mother, the partaker of my distresses and shame on your account, again to write to you, and your last letter, which I received at Ayr when on the Circuit, is wrote in a strain that is becoming and speaks out that you are satisfied of some of your errors; therefore it is that you receive this from me in answer to those you sent me since the Session rose.

As in yours you desire me to give you my advice with freedom, you cannot be dissatisfied with the introduction to this letter. Every wise man would rather be informed for what things he is censured, that he may correct them, than be flattered when he don't deserve it; and he alone is a true friend who informs us of our faults. It is true such a friend is rarely to be met with, but you have had such friend in me.

You are under a mistake in your last when you write I have been struggling for authority over you. I have a right to it, indeed,

but it is a thing I never wished or desired. And every step in my conduct has shown that to be the case. I always used you with lenity
and tenderness; and though you were behaving in a way highly
disrespectful to me, settled an annuity upon you for life and so put
you in a state of independency. You say that you was struggling
for independency. What you mean by becoming independent I am
at a loss to conceive, for it would seem to be something very different from what anybody else would aim at. Your notion of independency seems to consist in contemning your relations and your
native country, where and from whom you have a natural right to
receive regard and friendship, and to live in dependence upon
strangers in another country, where you have no title to notice, and
from whom you have nothing to expect but fair words. They have
their relations to provide, their political connections to keep up,
and must look on one who comes from Scotland as an idle person
to have no right to share of their bounty; in the same way that we
here would never think of bestowing anything upon a vaguing[5]
Englishman except a dinner or a supper. When you left this, I told
you that you would find this to be true on trial.[6] You would not then
believe it, but now you candidly own you have found the thing turn
out according as I said it would do.

You desire my advice as to your after schemes in life. As to this,
I have already told you I have no authority; and the mention I
have made of sundry things in your conduct that vex and distress
me and every friend and acquaintance of yours who has common
sense, is not from authority but from friendship. I am bound by the
ties of nature to love you; and though it is disagreeable still to be

[5] Wandering, foot-loose.

[6] "If you improve yourself at London, the honour as well as the benefit will
redound to yourself, for my aversion to your going there you know well.
Before you left this, I told you that it was in vain for you to expect a commis-
sion in the Guards, nor do I think you should be sorry at the disappointment.
A man of your age to enter into the Guards on a peace and to live all his days
and die an ensign, is a poor prospect, which no man would be sorry to lose.
The entry is shabby and the exit the same" (Lord Auchinleck to Boswell, 27
November 1762).

finding fault, I should be wanting in my duty not to tell you my mind. If you'll call to remembrance sundry of your past schemes which I advised you against and were happily disappointed, you must be sensible how dangerous it is for a young man to propose to give himself up to be governed by whims. You have escaped from a variety of ruinous snares that you were quite bent upon, and now are convinced were such as behoved to have brought you to misery. This should make you cautious in time coming. The poet says, "Felix quem faciunt aliena pericula cautum,"[7] but he must be unhappy indeed who won't learn from his own past dangers. To come more close to the point in your letter wherein you ask my advice as to what scheme of life you should follow, I shall convince you that I do not insist on authority, for though you tell me you will return to Scotland if I tell you your absence from it makes me unhappy, I will not insist either on one thing or another, but fairly and candidly lay matters before you. All that ever I insisted upon was that you should behave as the young gentlemen of your station do and act with prudence and discretion. If you set up in the character of my eldest son, you may expect regard and respect, but in the style of a vagrant must meet with the reverse. Be assured of this; for even I, who am your father and who, while you trod the paths of virtue and discretion was bound up in you and carried on all my projects with a view to you in whom I flattered myself to find a representative worthy of this respectable family—I say, even I by your strange conduct had come to the resolution of selling all off, from the principle that it is better to snuff a candle out than leave it to stink in a socket. And this purpose, though interrupted at present by your last letters being wrote in a strain that gives hopes of amendment, upon my being disappointed in that hope, I should certainly carry into execution.

As for your manner of life, I never declared positively against any kind of life except that of dissipation and vice, and as a consequence against your going into the Guards. But I told you if you

[7] "He's a lucky man who learns caution from other people's dangers" (a proverbial saying of unknown authorship).

chose to be a soldier and make that your business in good earnest, though I did not like the business, I should procure you a commission in a marching regiment, and had one pressed upon me by my good friend General Sinclair, now no more. But you signified your unwillingness to serve in a marching regiment, so that scheme went over and you fell to the study of the law; and I can say with truth, showed as much genius for it when you applied as any ever I knew. Be assured that your following the study of the law, whether as a lawyer or as a gentleman, to fit you to be useful in the world, is what to me is most agreeable and what I verily think is the only thing will make you go through life agreeably; for as you well observe, without some pursuit that is rational, one of your turn can never be happy. In the plan I propose you have for your objects being respected, being useful with your advice, getting into Parliament, and having the power of conferring places, instead of going about begging one. And to these I may add, you have the satisfaction of making your parents happy and adding more lustre to the family you have the honour to be come of. And if you were truly fixed on this plan, I would make no difficulty, when you were a little settled from your reelings, to let you go abroad for a while. But if you are bent on the Army, as you say you have the offer of an ensigncy in a marching regiment, though I am far from liking the thing, if better cannot be, take it, and hold by that as your business for life. But be more on your guard for the future against mimicry, journals, and publications, still acting with prudence and discretion, which is as necessary for a soldier as for a man of any other employment. I would further recommend to you to endeavour to find out some person of worth who may be a friend, not one who will say as you say when with you and when he is away will make a jest of you as much as of any other.

Your mother is in her ordinary, so is Johnny. Both remember you with affection.

Farewell. It is in your power to make us all happy and yourself too. May God dispose you to the best.[8]

[8] The letter ends without a signature.

INDEX

This is for the greater part an index of proper names, but general headings are provided in three articles: GREAT BRITAIN, JOHNSON, SAMUEL, Part II (*Character, Sayings, Opinions*), and LONDON. Observations on persons and places are generally entered under the person or place in question; for example, Johnson's remarks on Wilkes should be looked for under Wilkes, not under Johnson. Churches, inns, streets, parks, mountains, etc., are not grouped under larger territorial designations, such as Scotland or London, but are given separate articles in the main alphabet. When a city, town, or county is given without further specification, it may be assumed that it is in Great Britain; streets, churches, inns, etc., listed with no name of city following are in London. The key after London names (A1, B2, etc.) indicates their approximate location on the map printed on the endpapers of this volume. If the key is in italic, the name is not actually printed on the map. Peers and peeresses, Lords of Session and their wives are indexed under titles rather than family names, the titles chosen being usually those proper to 1763; but this rule has been broken when a person is decidedly better known by a later title or a family name. The following abbreviations are employed: D. (Duke), E. (Earl), M. (Marquess), V. (Viscount), JB (James Boswell), SJ (Samuel Johnson).

clothes, 115; Louisa sets next day (Sunday) for making him happy, 116; JB at assignation is at first feeble, then is interrupted, 117; Louisa agrees to spend the night with him somewhere, 118; JB gets back money due him from Roman Catholic bookseller, 118–119; gives charity to a poor old man, 119, 123, 127–128; engages room for Louisa and himself at Black Lion, 119; low-spirited, 120–121; Louisa postpones his felicity again, 126, fixes Wednesday as the happy night, 130; Craufurd of Auchenames promises to help him get a commission, 130; JB has long conversation with Lady Northumberland about his commission, 131–134; receives his allowance, 135; takes Louisa to Black Lion and spends the night with her, 137–140; renews his acquaintance with Garrick, 140; plans intrigue with Lady Mirabel, 142–143; low-spirited, 144; Louisa permits him the rites of love, he feels his passion abated, 145; JB joins the Kellie ladies in professing love for Royal Family of Stuart, 146–147; calls on Lady Mirabel, 149; feels an alarm of unexpected evil, 149, 153; enjoys Louisa, 149; Sheridan rejects his prologue for Mrs. Sheridan's comedy, JB is mortified and angry, 150–152; walks from one end of London to the other with Erskine and Dempster, and attends opening of Mallet's *Elvira*, 152–155; joins with Erskine and Dempster in composing strictures on *Elvira*, 155; finds that he certainly has got an infection, 155–157, melancholy ruminations thereat, 155–156; has another brush with D. of Queensberry, 158; taxes Louisa with perfidy, 158–160; breakfasts with Garrick, 161–163; with Erskine and Dempster corrects *Critical Strictures* and takes copy to printer, 162; he and Dempster get copy back and revise it, 163–164; goes into seclusion in his lodgings for five weeks for medical treatment, 164–204; peevish, considers the Guards an improper scene of life, thinks he will be an advocate,

165; has long dialogue with Eglinton about their differences, 166–171; ill from too much medicine, 172; *Critical Strictures* published, 172; reads Hume's *History*, 173, 197; writes harsh letter to Louisa, 175; leaves his seclusion to attend opening of Mrs. Sheridan's comedy, 175–178; illness worse, 178; his day's schedule, 183–184; calculates how he can save £70 from his allowance, 184–185; gives up one of his rooms to save money, 185; Louisa sends back his two guineas, 187; low-spirited, 189; writes several fanciful little essays, 189; angry at Dempster and Erskine for trick they have played on him, 190–192; low-spirited, 192, 194–195; writes to Lady Northumberland, 195; reads the Bible, 196; thinks he will follow the law, 200–201; changes his mind, 201–203; quits his confinement, 205; convinced that he should remain firm in Guards scheme, 205–206; has evidence Lady Northumberland is avoiding him, 209–210, 213; Eglinton promises to intercede with Bute, 212; deeply depressed, 213–214; scared by ghost story, 214; exults over Kellie ladies on their leaving London, 216; he and Eglinton concert about letter to Lord Bute, 217–220; Bute says commission in Guards cannot be had, but promises commission in another regiment, 223–224, 229 *n*.2; JB puts out his candle accidentally, gets a light from watchman, 224; casual fruition, 227, 231, 237, 255, 262, 272, 280, 300, 304, 332; low-spirited, 228–229; meets Temple and renews friendship, 231–233; Lady Northumberland appears to be trying to shift doing anything, 238; *Letters between the Hon. Andrew Erskine and James Boswell, Esq.* published, 238–239; adventure with a monstrous big whore, 240–241; Lady Northumberland sends polite letter showing she does not mean to do anything, 243; JB makes jaunt to Oxford, is very unhappy, 244–248; low-spirited, 249; visits Newgate, 251–252; sees an execution, terribly shocked,

This edition of "Boswell's London Journal"
was set in Waverley type and printed by the
Maple Press Company of York, Pennsylvania
Bound by the J. C. Valentine Company of New York
Designed by Alvin Eisenman